# American Perspectives on Learning Communities and Opportunities in the Maker Movement

Bradley S. Barker
*University of Nebraska - Lincoln, USA*

A volume in the Advances in Educational Technologies and Instructional Design (AETID) Book Series

IGI Global
DISSEMINATOR OF KNOWLEDGE

Published in the United States of America by
IGI Global
Information Science Reference (an imprint of IGI Global)
701 E. Chocolate Avenue
Hershey PA, USA 17033
Tel: 717-533-8845
Fax: 717-533-8661
E-mail: cust@igi-global.com
Web site: http://www.igi-global.com



Library of Congress Cataloging-in-Publication Data

Names: Barker, Bradley S., author.
Title: American perspectives on learning communities and opportunities in the maker movement / by Bradley S. Barker.
Description: Hershey, PA : Information Science Reference, 2019. | Includes bibliographical references.
Identifiers: LCCN 2018050682| ISBN 9781522583103 (hardcover) | ISBN 9781522583110 (ebook)
Subjects: LCSH: Maker movement in education--United States--Case studies. | Makerspaces--United States--Case studies.
Classification: LCC LB1029.M35 B367 2019 | DDC 371.390973--dc23 LC record available at https://lccn.loc.gov/2018050682

This book is published in the IGI Global book series Advances in Educational Technologies and Instructional Design (AETID) (ISSN: 2326-8905; eISSN: 2326-8913)

British Cataloguing in Publication Data
A Cataloguing in Publication record for this book is available from the British Library.



For electronic access to this publication, please contact: eresources@igi-global.com.

# Advances in Educational Technologies and Instructional Design (AETID) Book Series

ISSN:2326-8905
EISSN:2326-8913

Editor-in-Chief: Lawrence A. Tomei, Robert Morris University, USA

### MISSION

Education has undergone, and continues to undergo, immense changes in the way it is enacted and distributed to both child and adult learners. In modern education, the traditional classroom learning experience has evolved to include technological resources and to provide online classroom opportunities to students of all ages regardless of their geographical locations. From distance education, Massive-Open-Online-Courses (MOOCs), and electronic tablets in the classroom, technology is now an integral part of learning and is also affecting the way educators communicate information to students.

The **Advances in Educational Technologies & Instructional Design (AETID) Book Series** explores new research and theories for facilitating learning and improving educational performance utilizing technological processes and resources. The series examines technologies that can be integrated into K-12 classrooms to improve skills and learning abilities in all subjects including STEM education and language learning. Additionally, it studies the emergence of fully online classrooms for young and adult learners alike, and the communication and accountability challenges that can arise. Trending topics that are covered include adaptive learning, game-based learning, virtual school environments, and social media effects. School administrators, educators, academicians, researchers, and students will find this series to be an excellent resource for the effective design and implementation of learning technologies in their classes.

### COVERAGE

- Game-Based Learning
- Web 2.0 and Education
- Adaptive Learning
- Hybrid Learning
- Online Media in Classrooms
- Curriculum Development
- Social Media Effects on Education
- Higher Education Technologies
- Educational Telecommunications
- K-12 Educational Technologies

IGI Global is currently accepting manuscripts for publication within this series. To submit a proposal for a volume in this series, please contact our Acquisition Editors at Acquisitions@igi-global.com or visit: http://www.igi-global.com/publish/.

The Advances in Educational Technologies and Instructional Design (AETID) Book Series (ISSN 2326-8905) is published by IGI Global, 701 E. Chocolate Avenue, Hershey, PA 17033-1240, USA, www.igi-global.com. This series is composed of titles available for purchase individually; each title is edited to be contextually exclusive from any other title within the series. For pricing and ordering information please visit http://www.igi-global.com/book-series/advances-educational-technologies-instructional-design/73678. Postmaster: Send all address changes to above address. 

## Titles in this Series

*For a list of additional titles in this series, please visit:*
*https://www.igi-global.com/book-series/advances-educational-technologies-instructional-design/73678*

***Handbook of Research on Assessment Literacy and Teacher-Made Testing in the ...***
Eddy White (University of Arizona, USA) and Thomas Delaney (University of Oregon, USA)
Information Science Reference • ©2019 • 410pp • H/C (ISBN: 9781522569862) • US $255.00

***Interdisciplinary and International Perspectives on 3D Printing in Education***
Ieda M. Santos (Emirates College for Advanced Education, UAE) Nagla Ali (Emirates College for Advanced Education, UAE) and Shaljan Areepattamannil (Emirates College for Advanced Education, UAE)
Information Science Reference • ©2019 • 346pp • H/C (ISBN: 9781522570189) • US $195.00

***Bayesian Networks for Managing Learner Models in Adaptive Hypermedia Systems ...***
Mouenis Anouar Tadlaoui (Abdelmalek Essaadi University, Morocco) Mohamed Khaldi (Abdelmalek Essaadi University, Morocco) and Rommel Novaes Carvalho (University of Brasília, Brazil)
Information Science Reference • ©2019 • 199pp • H/C (ISBN: 9781522574132) • US $165.00

***Handbook of Research on TPACK in the Digital Age***
Margaret L. Niess (Oregon State University, USA) Henry Gillow-Wiles (Southern Oregon University, USA) and Charoula Angeli (University of Cyprus, Cyprus)
Information Science Reference • ©2019 • 490pp • H/C (ISBN: 9781522570011) • US $255.00

***Educational and Social Dimensions of Digital Transformation in Organizations***
Paula Peres (Polytechnic of Porto, Portugal) Fernando Moreira (Universidade Portucalense, Portugal & Universidade de Aveiro, Portugal) and Anabela Mesquita (Polytechnic of Porto, Portugal)
Information Science Reference • ©2019 • 372pp • H/C (ISBN: 9781522562610) • US $185.00

***Handbook of Research on Curriculum Reform Initiatives in English Education***
Christopher Denman (Sultan Qaboos University, Oman) and Rahma Al-Mahrooqi (Sultan Qaboos University, Oman)
Information Science Reference • ©2019 • 372pp • H/C (ISBN: 9781522558460) • US $225.00

*For an entire list of titles in this series, please visit:*
*https://www.igi-global.com/book-series/advances-educational-technologies-instructional-design/73678*

IGI Global
DISSEMINATOR OF KNOWLEDGE

701 East Chocolate Avenue, Hershey, PA 17033, USA
Tel: 717-533-8845 x100 • Fax: 717-533-8661
E-Mail: cust@igi-global.com • www.igi-global.com

# Table of Contents

# Foreword

I grew up in my parent's hardware store in a central Nebraska town of 1,300 people. It was a 40-mile drive through cow pastures and cornfields to get to a chain store or a movie theater. I spent a lot of my youth selling nuts and bolts to farmers who largely had to solve problems for themselves. It was a culture of making, of creativity, of innovation, and of independence.

Early in my college career I was back at home for a weekend and spending a Saturday with my parents at the store (because there, or church, is where they spent their time). I crusty old farmer walked in and I popped up to ask how I could help. He explained he needed a "woodruff key." I confidently led him to the front of the store and asked if it was a key to his house, his car, or maybe a padlock? He paused and looked at me with a pained and amused face. He asked "What are they teaching you in that fancy engineering school?" It was a fair question. Luckily, my father was close and came over and bailed me out. He helped the farmer find the semi-circular key that would re-attach the driveshaft to the flywheel on his piece of farm equipment.

This was an interaction I haven't forgotten. Not because of the embarrassment of not knowing what kind of key he was describing (should a 19-year-old know what a woodruff key is?), but because this crusty old farmer did know a lot about this mechanical fastener and it's uses. This gentleman, who I knew over many years, wasn't what we'd consider "smart" in today's terms. He never went to college and didn't know calculus. However, he had other talents. He could build and fix many things. He was a problem solver and could think through complex challenges. He really did know many things that I wouldn't learn in a "fancy engineering school" although we did eventually get to lectures involving woodruff keys. The idea that intelligence and talent comes in many forms was highlighted for me.

There is a growing recognition that intelligence is diverse and that students learn in different ways. This is why makerspaces are so important. I have known people who panic at the sight of a math problem, but their blood pressure drops when they pick up a cordless drill. People are different and everyone has important skills.

I have come to believe there is a second major disconnect between my "fancy engineering school" and the daily work I now do in my career. Every day I am constantly interacting with people to accomplish my engineering goals. *Everything* I do involves other people. I need their help. I need to convince them to do things differently, or to change our shared goals, or to stop going down this path. Engineering, for me, is about people. Entrepreneurship is about people. Art is about people. And, as you will read in this book, makerspaces are about people.

This is why this book is so important. I have shared an anecdote here, and some of my opinions. But in this book, Dr. Barker takes a quantitative and analytical approach to makerspaces and the maker movement. He has investigated over 25 different spaces by visiting them and documenting how they operate.

Now the word 'makerspace' and 'maker' can mean many things to different people. I generally embrace the larger definition of making including fine art, craft, poetry, and music. With my favorite, woodworking, wedged in the middle. Likewise, makerspaces can run a large spectrum. At one end, makerspaces can be as simple as a few people gathering in a church basement to make quilts to the other end that can be elaborate university-based innovation centers. Makerspaces can be categorized in many ways. Some example parameters are given in Figure 1.

Some makerspaces allow very dirty work and some require the work to be quiet and clean. Some makerspaces have employee's that supervise all activity and some are completely organized by members. Some makerspaces focus on one specific activity and others try to provide equipment for a variety of disciplines. Some makerspaces are open to all and some operate for profit and require membership fees. Now, it is important to note that all of these types of makerspace can be good communities. There is not "good" and "bad" associated with these parameters. They are just different.

Consider makerspaces in libraries. These spaces are generally clean spaces with a fairly structured management system (i.e. librarians supervise activities). Library spaces are generally open to all without membership fees. A different example would be a community-based woodworking makerspace that might only focus on woodworking. It may require a membership fee but

*Figure 1.*

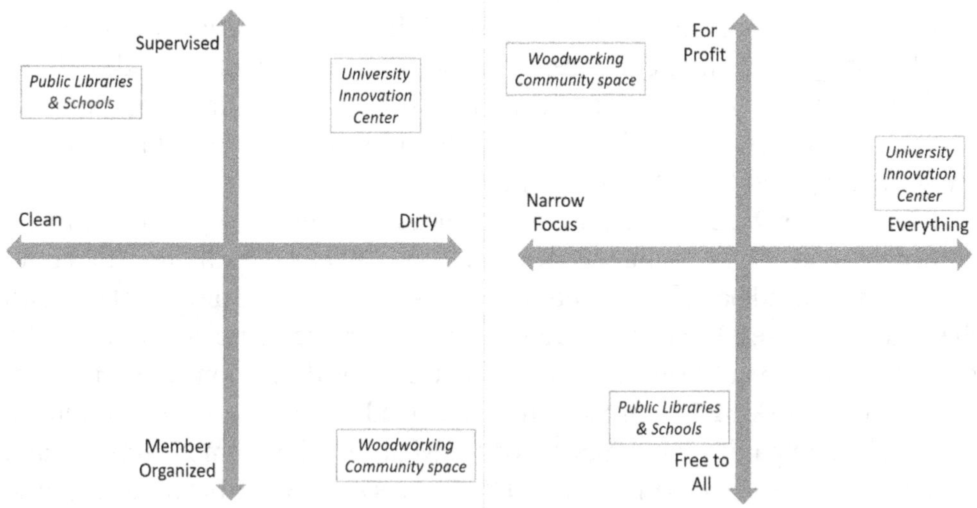


it may also be entirely member organized. As a third example, a university-based innovation center may have many types of equipment (e.g. a fab lab) but it may only be open to students and may be structured to support specific classes. There are many types of makerspaces. This is another important thing Dr. Barker does in this book. He gives real-world example of different types of makerspaces and how they function.

The book also talks about learning communities and how people learn different skills and learn in a different way when they learn as part of a community. Dr. Barker helps to quantify the methods and procedures in makerspaces that can either encourage or choke learning communities.

Some people see the maker movement as a movement backward to pre-industrial revolution manufacturing. They see it as craft. They think it is cute but ultimately not innovative or productive. Making can be craft, but it can also be much more. I often view making as a method of thinking. It is a way to think about a problem when you can't even fully define the problem. It is an equally valid method of solving a problem as numerical analysis, or simulation. It is often the best approach. I think of my engineering heroes such as the Wright brothers who built several gliders before making a functional airplane. I think of Henry Ford who built his first automobile prototype around 1896 when no one in the world knew what a car should look like. He built many versions and even had a couple failed companies before he sold 15 million Model T's (note T is the 20th letter in the alphabet). Maybe Thomas Edison is the master of making as a way of thinking. Edison has famously quipped "I have not failed. I've just found 10,000 ways that won't work." The list of experimental entrepreneurs and innovators goes on and on but I don't want to limit this to engineering invention. I think making-as-thinking is important in art and music and many pursuits. The important lesson is to try something and learn from that attempt.

It's my strong belief that we need more people making more things. Attorneys, hedge fund managers, financial consultants, are all important but I think we would all benefit if our educational system created more makers with the maker mindset. We need more people who create value rather than who provide professional services for a fee. Making is by definition value creation. I like to view making in a broad sense. We need people who make products, who make companies, who make stories. Making takes some resources and modifies these resources in a way that the sum is more valuable than the parts.

This is why this book is so important. It is because education is so important. It is because making is so important.

Enjoy this book. I certainly did.

*Shane Farritor*
*Maker, USA*

# Preface

## INTRODUCTION

*In learning communities, social relations and knowledge-creation meet. Knowledge (both individual and shared) is seen to be the product of social processes. (C. Watkins, 2005)*

These books (*American Perspectives on Learning Communities and Opportunities in the Maker Movement* and *European Perspectives on Learning Communities and Opportunities in the Maker Movement)* are a two-part series of case studies capturing, for a brief moment in time (February to May 2017), how a number of diverse makerspaces supported learning communities in the United States and Europe. In this volume, *American Perspectives on Learning Communities and Opportunities in the Maker Movement,* 14 individual case studies from the United States are presented and in a sister volume, eight case studies are presented from European sites. *Note: Four sites are included in the survey data but not included in the individual case studies.* The author set about investigating the different models of learning various makerspaces adhered to and what brought about those models. Sites documented in this book were located on the US East Coast, beginning in Maryland, Pittsburgh, and Virginia; to the Midwest states of Nebraska, Kansas, Iowa, and Missouri; and finally, west to California. In Europe, the author traveled east to Bucharest, Romania and Heidelberg, Germany in Central Europe. Other sites visited were the Barcelona area of Spain and then west to cities in the United Kingdom and the Republic of Ireland.

Figures 1 and 2 indicate sites visited by the author.

A multiple case study research design was used to describe how various maker sites designed their learning methodology and supported learning communities. According to Stake (2006), a quintain "is an object or phenomenon or condition to be studied." The word is used in multiple case studies because

*Figure 1. US sites*

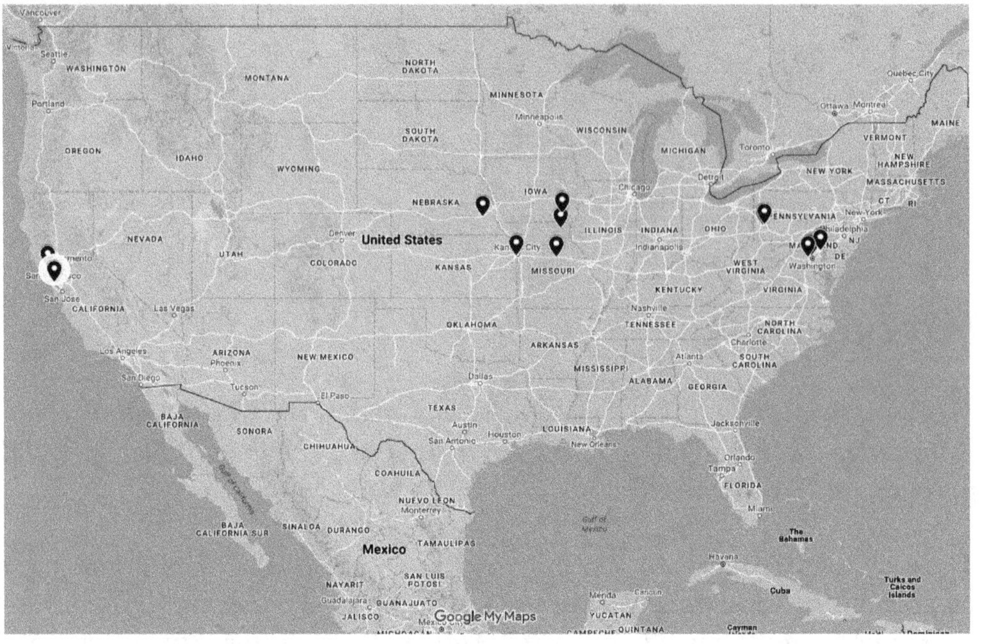


he notes that words like program or phenomenon don't adequately describe the scope of a multiple case study. For the present study, the quintain being examined is the maker movement in general and, specifically, learning communities within the makerspace. This empirical inquiry was combined with an online survey for each site specifically asking about equipment, space considerations, and size, as well as demographics and usage patterns of users. This book is intended for readers with an interest in the maker movement, especially as it pertains to site characteristics and learning models. Others, including policy makers, librarians, museums, out-of-school-time learning organizations, and educational institutions, will also be interested in the case studies as they come to understand how learning communities in making can be supported in a number of different environments.

At the outset, a multiple case study (Yin, 2014), supported by a survey, was identified as an appropriate research methodology to understand the role of collaborative learning communities that support the making environment and how those spaces arrived at that model. A case method is heuristic and employs analysis to help draw conclusions about a phenomenon under consideration (Ellet, 2007). Case study research, according to Yin (2014), investigates the case as it occurs in the real world. For this study, each "case"

*Figure 2. European sites*

is in fact a physical makerspace that the author personally visited, conducting an interview with one or more stakeholders at the site. Sites were selected based on convenience, looking at clusters of sites in a geographic area and their willingness to participate in the face-to-face interview and complete the online survey. Because of limited funds and availability only sites in the US and Europe were selected for inclusion in the books. In addition, sites received no remuneration for participation in the study. The cases selected described their space as practicing some form of making (hacking, tinkering, print studio, tool library) and generally can be described as makerspaces. Once completed, each case was presented to the site for review and corroboration of the evidence collected and the analysis by the author. Note: not all sites provided a review of their site. The multiple case study methodology used was to find theoretical replications, of both makerspace models and the models to support learning communities. The case study design used in this study utilized an embedded design whereby a secondary unit of analysis, in this case an online survey, was included in the data collection. A multiple case study provides a number of replicable designs showing how different spaces support learning communities. Watkins (2005) described learning communities as the intersection of social relations and knowledge creation. He stated that "Knowledge (both individual and shared) is seen to be the product of social processes" (Watkins, 2005, p. 48).

Each case describes the specific audience it serves and the reasoning behind the supportive practices in the space. In general, case conclusions were not compared with other cases since each case had its own unique reason for its learning models and decisions. However, a cross-case summary concerning learning communities is presented in this chapter. In addition, combined data from the survey is included in the analysis portion of this chapter in an effort to provide a holistic view of the cases under study. Survey data is further broken down between US and European sites to provide additional understanding of the case studies presented in each book.

## REVIEW OF THE LITERATURE

The research literature provides a number of competing terms and keywords to describe the maker movement, makerspaces, makers, and making. As an overview, the *maker movement*, the recent documented increase in the number of makers interested in sharing with other communities their designs and building efforts, will be described. Next, a working definition of what constitutes a *makerspace* will be explored as well as the making process and the participants engaging in makerspaces.

### The Maker Movement

The maker movement probably began around 1998 when Dr. Neil Gershenfeld from the Massachusetts Institute of Technology (MIT) for the first time taught a class at MIT called *How to Make (Almost) Anything*, which later sparked his idea for the creation of FabLabs (Dunn, 2005). The movement grew in 2001 as the MIT FabLabs began appearing and with the publication of the Make Magazine followed by the first Maker Faire in 2006 (Clapp, Ross, Ryan, & Tishman, 2017). Halverson & Sheridan (2014) noted that the maker movement in general "refers broadly to the growing number of people who are engaged in the creative production of artifacts in their daily lives and who find physical and digital forums to share their processes and products with others." A catalyst for the maker movement is the cultural resurgence of DIY attitudes, that is, the building and making of things as opposed to just consuming goods (Resnick & Rosenbaum, 2013; Brahms & Werner, 2013). The internet has been another important driver in the rise of the maker movement as communications and designs can be readily shared amongst makers (Dougherty, 2013). Rosa, Guimaraes Pereira, & Ferretti (2018) explained that the concept of the open-source paradigm where makers share design and development of their projects to the entire community is an important characteristic and catalyst in the maker movement. While making can be a mix of old and new technologies, it may be argued that the availability of relatively low-cost digital fabrication equipment has democratized innovation and making (Halverson & Sheridan, 2014). The access to tools has also sparked a renewed interest in small-scale production and prototyping, anti-consumerism, and innovation and entrepreneurialism (Clapp, Ross, Ryan, & Tishman, 2016; Peppler, Halverson, & Kafai, 2016).

The maker movement is not confined to the US and has a massive global presence (Graves, Graves, & Rendina, 2017). Growth within the maker movement has been impressive and continually increasing in size and participation (Dougherty, 2013; Peppler & Bender, 2013). For example, in 2017, there were 1,092 FabLabs in 116 countries and 1,336 hackspaces in 43 countries (Smith, 2017).

## Making and Makerspaces

Makerspaces, FabLabs, Hackspaces, and Tool Libraries are all inclusive of the maker movement as each promotes active participation, collaboration, and open exploration (Rosa, Guimaraes Pereira, et al., 2018). Graves, Graves, and Rendina (2017) note that a makerspace is a "concept" more than a specific room or place but a "gathering place for tools, projects, mentors, and expertise" (p.1). The physical space can be just about any size, possess an unlimited variety of equipment and tools, and focus on any number of creative endeavors from textiles and computing, to art and music. Brahms and Werner (2013) defined a makerspace as a facility where "groups of individuals of diverse ages, genders, and backgrounds come together to make: to mess around at the crossroads and fringes of disciplines …" (p.71). Overall, a makerspace is the location either physical or online where makers come together and create, innovate, learn, and teach. As noted, defining making and a makerspace is not a trivial task as many people have come to use the terms to serve a number of different situations. Therefore, the author will put forward a definition based on the literature and the results of this multiple case study research. Martin (2015) defines the components of a makerspace using three elements: a) *tools,* including computers, Computer Numerical Control (CNC), analog and human powered machines; b) *community infrastructure* that includes the physical makerspace and online and in-person resources and events; and c) the *"maker mindset"* or the growth mindset of the individuals that includes the use of common design standards and rapid prototyping (Martin, 2015; Halverson & Sheridan, 2014).

The *tools,* including the CNC and rapid prototyping equipment, are important aspects of the maker movement and indeed have come down in price and availability has increased. These digital or CNC devices provide users with abilities for rapid prototyping and design intricacies that were unimaginable just a decade ago. However, a makerspace is more than just the inclusion of digital tools, it also consists of hand and power tools, science and biology equipment, as well as tools for music, art, and printing. To be sure, the means for rapid prototyping is included in many makerspaces but they do not require specific equipment. All makerspaces in the present study had a number of tools in their arsenal in a combination of hand and power tools, all needed to make and create. Not every makerspace has a 3D printer or a laser cutter, and they are not a prerequisite for a makerspace if the other two components (community infrastructure and maker mindset) are present.

The second component needed for a makerspace is a physical space, which includes the infrastructure required to operate. A physical space does not have to be permanent; for example, a number of mobile makerspaces go out into communities temporarily. Most makerspaces consist of a physical meetup area because the physical shared experience and development of learning communities is an important aspect of learning. The connected learning theory (Ito et al., 2013) purports that there are ways of supporting learning communities online. In addition, Rafalow (2016) reported the development of online supports for makers, providing them with the skills necessary to create in the physical and digital worlds. The infrastructure in a makerspace provides the means for a space to operate, instruct, and notify members/users or visitors. The infrastructure takes many forms, from printed manuals to online repositories of information about machines and equipment. Events and courses are often part of the infrastructure as well for many sites.

The final component of a makerspace is the maker mindset. The maker mindset was defined by Dougherty (2012) as a growth orientation with the belief that skills and knowledge for participants in making can be "developed, improved, and expanded." Fittingly, the maker mindset rewards makers who take risks to innovate and can tolerate degrees of failure as a process of learning and iteration (Dougherty, 2012).

Like the movement itself, makerspaces and making are the result of a resurgent culture around do-it-yourself (DIY) epitomized by problem-solving, creativity, open exploration, intrinsic interest, innovation through the use of new digital fabrication tools (laser cutters, 3D printers, etc.) and traditional hands-on tools (Peppler et al., 2016).

While making can be a mix of old and new technologies, it may be argued that the availability of relatively low-cost digital fabrication equipment has democratized innovation and making (Halverson & Sheridan, 2014). Martin (21015) defined making as "designing, building, modifying, and/or repurposing material objects, for playful or useful ends, oriented toward making a 'product' of some sort that can be used, interacted with, or demonstrated" (p.31). Making can be a mixture of new and old tools and processes combined in new and unexpected ways and achieving unexpected results. For example, Ilana Halperin in Dundee, Scotland submerged laser cut wood art in an Icelandic hot spring where the art became encrusted in silica. Dissemination avenues from the popular Make Magazine to online sources like Instructables and Etsy, and large-scale social events like maker fairs and hackathons have popularized the movement. The maker culture is not age bound, allowing for participation at any age. Likewise, makers are not required to possess any specific knowledge as skill sharing and learning from others is a trademark of the movement.

Making and the access to tools has also sparked a renewed interest in small-scale production and prototyping, anti-consumerism, and innovation and entrepreneurialism (Clapp et al., 2016; Peppler et al., 2016). Smith (2017) noted that a typical makerspace is equipped with small-scale versions of highly versatile, digitally-enabled design and fabrication tools developed originally for rapid prototyping in industry, as well as more traditional hand tools associated with various crafts. Smith (2017) stated: "So, for example, your local makerspace in Madrid, Medellín, or Manilla might be equipped with 3D printers, a large router, a laser cutter, milling machines, drills, lathes, microelectronics stations, sewing machines, traditional hand tools, and even, in some cases, a bio-hacking lab." Participants in these spaces learn by doing and swap skills with one another. Some makerspaces also run training courses for members and the wider public.

As previously mentioned, makerspaces can also encompass other entities like fablabs, hackspaces, and tool libraries as they promote active participation, collaboration, and open exploration. The term "FabLab" is short for *fabrication laboratory*, which is a makerspace that adheres to the Fab Charter. The Fab Charter simply outlines the seven principles of FabLabs (Fab Foundation, n.d.). Furthermore, FabLabs share a prescribed set of hardware and software, making it possible for projects to be developed across sites (Rosa, Guimaraes Pereira, et al., 2018). The Green FabLab, part of the FabLabs in Barcelona and part of the IAAC (Institute for Advanced Architecture of Catalonia), is an example of a FabLab that adheres to the charter yet at the same time has a special charter to be self-sufficient, sustainable, and use locally sourced material.

Hackspaces, derived from hacking, are community-based spaces originally focused on programming. Now they are generally broader in scope and share much of the same interests as a traditional makerspace such as prototyping and digital fabrication. Digital fabrication according to Diez (2012) is the practice of using information technology combined with computer-controlled machines to "run codes specifying coordinates and instructions like subtract, add, or deform materials in different physical states." The stated objective of the TOG Dublin Hackerspace in Dublin, Ireland is to advance science, technology, modern culture, and the creative arts in the Dublin area, which is similar to any makerspace included in this book.

Tool Lending Libraries began in the mid-1970s with sites in Columbus, Ohio and Berkeley, California as a way to provide local communities with access to tools and create a sense of community around the use of the tools. Station North Tool Library (SNTL) or "Station North" in Baltimore, Maryland has the goal of empowering and serving the local community through access to tools and low-cost training and membership. While access to tools is its main emphasis of operation, Station North also acts as a makerspace by having classes and open times for its workshops.

Makerspaces can be organized in a number of different environments from shared community-based spaces, museums, and secondary schools, to university-run makerspaces. Makerspaces can have a semi-permanent home in a physical space or as previously mentioned may be more mobile, meaning they travel to a certain location and set up for a short or longer-term set of activities. Community-based makerspaces are usually more member-driven spaces with a shared governing body usually more focused on an adult community of learners. Community-based makerspaces frequently take on the identity of their members. A space with makers interested in woodworking, like the Tool Station North Tool Lending Library in Baltimore, Maryland, will have a plethora of lathes and rasps to shape and create personally relevant artifacts, which may be displayed throughout the space. In another example, the NOD makerspace in Bucharest, Romania is focused on digital fabrication and entrepreneurship, which is reflected in the space with a number of laser cutters, CNC mills, 3D printers and the like as well as prototypes from members that are displayed as they work to bring their ideas to market. Once such prototype is a large model airplane prominently displayed in the space, clearly meant as a conversation piece that conveys the development process for entrepreneurs. NOD also provides opportunities for its members to consult on projects brought into the space. NOD is a clean space containing a number of desks and even offices for members while Tool Station North has no desks or offices and has dedicated the space to hands-on making in a loud and dusty environment.

## The Maker Movement and Industry

The maker movement challenges traditional manufacturing models with a shift to local producers from large corporations. This shift is possibly due to the availability of digital fabrication tools, and the collective and open source of projects and ideas available over networks of information (Rosa, Guimaraes Pereira, et al., 2018). This in turn may have an impact on the global supply chains and use of fossil fuels as transportation networks for goods and supplies are reconfigured (Diez, 2012). As an example, the Green FabLab in Barcelona, Spain is working towards a FabCity model of DIDO (data-in data-out) where data comes in and data goes out, and materials for production stay in one place. This is the opposite of the traditional PITO (product-in trash-out) model where products come in and trash goes out. Key to this emerging model are micro-factories where individual citizens produce goods with raw materials from local sources of recycled materials to create specific and personalized products based on open-source design and open-source software principles (Rosa, Pereira, & Ferretti, 2018). Micro-factories and the new cities capable of DIDO will rely on the knowledge society, where knowledge is not centralized but is shared through interconnected networks. The maker movement is highly dependent on collaboration and open source design principles (Clapp et al., 2016; Diez, 2012; Rosa, Guimaraes Pereira, et al., 2018; Sheridan et al., 2014; Smith, 2017). Open source design, where designs and processes are open or shared with others, is an important characteristic of the maker movement and believed to lead to innovation (Martin, 2015; Rosa,

Pereira, et al., 2018). Open source hardware and software is developed in a decentralized, participatory manner and provides means for experimentation, communication, collaboration, sharing, and learning based on constructionism (Kostakis, Niaros, & Giotitsas, 2014; Pearce, 2012).

## Maker and Education

In addition, the maker movement has found purchase in educational environments as a way to improve learning while at the same time breaking down barriers to STEM content knowledge and attainment (Calabrese Barton & Tan, 2018; Martin, 2015). These educational environments may be formal as in the case of the Lighthouse Community Public School in Oakland, California where making is found in every classroom, or informal environments like museums, after-school programs, and libraries. According to Clapp et al. (2016), making in education has been espoused to improve economic conditions and manufacturing practices within a community and also to improve STEM content knowledge and attitudes for students. In another example, Anderson (2012) argued that through the maker movement students are on the ground floor of a manufacturing revolution whereby small batches of customized items can be produced for mass customization. Kalil (2013) stated that the maker movement "improves STEM education by getting kids excited about science and technology" (p.14) as well as promoting values such as "creativity, problem-solving, collaboration, and self-expression" (Kalil, 2013). Others have linked making with active engagement, problem-based learning as a mechanism to support content knowledge and skills attainment as well as self-guided inquiry skills that may lead to improved school attendance and graduation rates (Bennett & Monahan, 2013; Zipkes, 2013). In a similar approach the Lighthouse Community Public School prescribed to the Expeditionary Learning (EL) Outward Bound model that includes a learner-centered focus, an emphasis on knowledge authentic to the learners, assessment that is formative and continual, and a focus on learning that is community-centered (Ikpeze, 2013). Overall, the maker movement has roots in the constructivism theory of learning whereby learners construct their own understanding and knowledge of the world (Piaget, 1972). The constructionist extension by Papert (1993) argues that learning is most effective when it is part of a learning activity and involves constructing a meaningful product (Papert, 1993). These theories purport that learners' new knowledge is actively constructed from the world around them through experiential practice and by independent/guided research to integrate new knowledge and to arrive at a deeper understanding (Barker, Melander, Grandgenett, & Nugent, 2015). This knowledge is translated into a tangible product, with technologies acting as context, so learners can (re)make knowledge in concrete ways (Papert, 1980). The product becomes a representation of the learner's thinking and knowledge. In addition, these physical creations can bring experienced and novice learners together (Lave & Wenger, 1991; Vygotsky, Embong, & Muslim, 1978).

Within educational environments, the making moniker is misused periodically by giving the attainment of equipment priority over the learning taking place. Chu et al. (2015) provided a definition of making as it compares with other hands-on learning activities, especially in the formal classroom. They defined making as "the use of technological resources to build something of interest." Making activities are infused with technology and students are engaged in an ongoing exploratory activity that includes an end product as well as the design process, whereas typical school-based activities focus on a specific product that emphasizes task completion (Chu et al., 2015). Activities that use technology yet continue the tradition of a specific product focused on tasks may fall somewhere between the two learning paradigms. Blickstein and Worsley (2016) refer to this as the *key chain syndrome*, where a short activity based on one piece of digital technology is used in short introductory workshops and learners never build additional skills. Likewise, Hatch (2018) noted that without proper training of educators, he worries that makerspaces in education will become "maker lab time" as opposed to a true integration of making into the classroom experience. Daniel Goldstein, a maker/academic/ artist from Columbia Gadget Works in Columbia, Missouri aptly noted that the movement has enjoyed a great deal of momentum and popularity; that many activities have subscribed to the name and yet they really don't fit the makerspace model. He was incredulous that schools, especially the university, would have a makerspace. He stated:

*Schools have a makerspace. The university has a makerspace. It's like, you're a university, what do you mean you have a makerspace? This is a place where people can come in and learn. It's like, you're a university. The whole damn thing is supposed to be a place where people can come in and learn. If it uses a certain technology, they call it makerspace; 3D printers are a makerspace.*

In an effort to more closely examine maker learning, Clapp et al. (2016) used a symptoms-based approach defining symptoms frequently found in a maker learning environment that they defined as a maker-centered learning environment. Symptoms, then, of a maker-centered learning environment include community process and environment (Clapp et al., 2016). Similar to Martin (2015), Clapp et al. (2016) view community as an important characteristic found in maker-centered learning. Process characteristics are ways learners approach problems in making and include the ideas of experimental learning and rapid prototyping, which are similar to the maker mindset set forth by Dougherty (2013). Finally, the physical environment is another characteristic of maker-centered learning and includes open, accessible spaces with the necessary tools and media (Clapp et al., 2016).

The maker-centered learning framework along with Martin's (2015) components provides a lens to determine if activities are more or less making in nature. Because making is such a nebulous activity, measuring gains in STEM content knowledge in a quantifiable way is often difficult. Within informal learning environments and even in the classroom, specific content may be of secondary importance to the broader outcomes. Therefore, researchers have looked into maker-centered learning beyond just content knowledge and skills and found that developing agency and building character as the primary outcome of maker-centered learning (Clapp et al., 2016). Clapp et al. (2016, p.19.) define agency as:

"Having a sense of agency means feeling empowered to make choices about how to act in the world." While a maker-centered learning environment encourages agency and a growth mindset it will not necessarily lead to significant gains in STEM tests scores. Making in educational environments is not necessarily going to create the next generation of scientists and engineers but it does promise to bring about excitement and passion around learning. Lianna Kali, Program Leader for the Tinkering Studio located San Francisco, California noted that they are not concerned with development of STEM skills. She noted the primary mission of the studio as:

*I would say more specifically we care about people loving learning. I don't care if people come to the Tinkering Studio and then walk out and want to be an engineer. That's less important to me than the experience they had and how they felt about approaching learning through making something.*

When youth leave the Tinkering Studio there is an expectation that they will continue to be excited about learning. Not just STEM-based learning but a passion for open-ended learning. Kali noted:

*I think if they go home and they want to keep trying things in their kitchen, that internal motivation and excitement about this approach to learning is what I'd be looking for. But I think in terms of saying, "This will lead to a career in XYZ" is kind of a hard claim to make, first of all, but also just that I think people choosing to have this experience and then say, "I want to be an artist," or have this experience and say, "Now I want to be a teacher and I'm going to remember that feeling I had, and I want my students to have that same feeling." I think people can do these activities and take them in infinite directions that aren't just STEM fields.*

As digital technologies transform the world of work, formal higher educational attainment may not necessarily guarantee work in the future (Ford, 2016). In addition, as many new jobs replace old jobs, new types of work are created that will drive retraining and learning. As the makerspaces instill in their members agency and an excitement of learning these unpredictable changes in the job market may be met with learners eager and nimble enough to move into new career pathways (Rosa, Guimaraes Pereira, et al., 2018).

## Not a Panacea

While there is little doubt that the maker movement has many fine and important attributes, there are some who find fault with the movement. In the most extreme, a FabLab in Grenoble, France was set on fire as a protest to the greed of the start-ups and because the space was established in a trendy neighborhood (Braybrooke & Smith, 2018). The arsonists stated: "While the telegenic fablab manager is acting up pathetically in the media, we are publishing our statement as an inseparable echo of our fiery act against this institution that is notoriously toxic for spreading digital culture. ... City managers cater to start-ups greedy for money and the fashionably geek masses by opening fablabs in trendy neighborhoods" (Rédaction, n.d.). Other critics have been skeptical of the sharing economy as large well-financed companies take profits and value from transactions while at the same time move away from being fair and participatory (Rosa, Pereira, et al., 2018; Schor, 2014). Some feel that micro-factories will not change the current models of production and globalization because they will not be able to compete on price. Others have argued the maker movement is about manufacturing ideas and not products.

Moreover, equity in the making movement is a concern. According to Calabrese Barton & Tan (2018), most makers are males, affluent, of the dominant culture with ample leisure time to make. This trend was echoed in the author's visit to US and European sites with 10 out of the 26 visited describing their members as 80-100% white and 6 sites being between 60 and 100% male. No sites reported a member base of 80-100% female. Females, youth and minority populations may feel that making does not belong to them. In Heidelberg, Germany, for example, the makerspace membership worked with refugees from the Syrian civil war to invite them into the space to work on an art exhibit called "Weltliga," which focused on the soccer World Cup. In another project, the makerspace members built 3D printers with refugees from Gambia expecting that the experience would help them learn new skills and join the Heidelberg and maker community. These outreach events brought in minority community members to the makerspace but none of these visits led to membership in the space. While culture and distance may have played a part in the lack of refugee membership, one can assume that the lack of diversity of the membership also played a role. Makerspaces also lack female representation, which may lead to the silencing of the female voice and expression. Brett Kennedy from the Innovation Studio in Lincoln, Nebraska explained the idea of mansplaining as when something is explained while assuming ignorance of the other party. Rebecca Solnit in her collection of essays *Men Explain Things to Me,* as noted by Lewis, 2014, describes a situation where she, an author who had just written a book on a particular subject, had the subject explained to her by a man. Mansplaining in effect dismissed a woman's expertise because of gender. As Will Blevins from Made Makerspace in Barcelona, Spain noted, in an overwhelmingly male-dominated space females may not feel welcomed because the men don't see making as a female pursuit. Unequal power distribution within the makerspace whereby peers and mentors/teachers are given more power in interactions calls into question the democratizing effects of making (Calabrese Barton & Tan, 2018).

Access is another important consideration for the maker movement and oftentimes makerspaces are located in large metropolitan areas with few found in rural areas. Sustaining rural community-based makerspaces can be a difficult proposition due to lack of expertise, funding, and community dynamics. In a poignant example, the Deep Green Machines makerspace in Rutledge, Missouri, population 77, was shuttered because of the lack of expertise, the lack of assimilation into the local community, the inability to recruit passionate people to the space, and a transient population. The Fairfield MakerSpace located in Fairfield, Iowa, population 10,000, runs a makerspace through the Sustainable Living Department at the Maharishi School of Management. The Fairfield MakerSpace, a relatively new space started in 2017, reported that they struggled to recruit members outside of the university because of trust dynamics within the community. Even sites near large urban areas find themselves struggling to attract members. For example, TechCreate, founded in Clane, Ireland, population of about 20,000, which is just 45 minutes from Dublin, has found it difficult to recruit adult members. They believe the distance from the city center and the demographics of the commuters in the area in which TechCreate operates have detracted from their original vision as a makerspace for the area.

## Communities

Individuals in concert to form communities are vital to a healthy makerspace. Workshops and laboratories with equipment have been around for a long time but when there is no sense of community, they are not, by definition, makerspaces in the truest form. Community is an important construct in the maker movement, as Pepler, Halverson and Kafai (2016) defined the movement as a network of learning communities that mixes a "can-do attitude" with the willingness to collaborate and inspire other learners. For this study, the conceptual idea of a learning community is borrowed from Gabelnick (1990) and further refined by Brower and Dettinger (1998), stating that a learning community must "integrate academic subject matter and social interactions while providing the physical space or facility for an intellectually stimulating environment to emerge." Furthermore, learning communities must be designed to develop a triad of responsibilities within learners' professional, ethical, and civic domains. Other characteristics of a learning community include the notion that they have boundaries because of their unique identities and members can join and leave the community, so they should be large enough to allow new members, and the roles within the community could evolve over time (Brower & Dettinger, 1998).

Learning communities in this instance should not be confused with professional learning communities (communities of practice) for teachers, meant as ways to reduce the isolation of teachers by connecting them through theories of learning (Hodges, 2003). Learning communities share similar characteristics to the community of practice framework, which also supports learning in a shared community based on shared knowledge and experiences (Lave & Wenger, 1991; Wenger, 1997; Sheridan et al., 2014). As Sheridan et al. (2014) explained, researching makerspace communities (learning/community of practice) provides an insight on how the space is used for instruction as well as how the tools and materials within a makerspace are used.

This multiple case study design specifically provides insight into what the impetus is—whether it is members, visitors, staff members, or the arrangement of the environment that enables the formation or lack thereof of learning communities in a makerspace. Specifically, the three main components needed for learning communities are 1) an academic or shared domain of interest, 2) learning in a social context, and 3) a physical place for the community to meet (Brower and Dettinger, 1998). While the last component may be supplemented by online communities, as specified in the connected learning framework (Rafalow, 2016), online platforms provide a space for community members to contribute knowledge and sharing. Many sites use these online repositories, like the popular website Instructables, to help build community through the contributions of members. However, all sites in this study had a physical space where members met and utilized the online community building tools to supplement their learning communities.

## METHODS

A multiple case study embedded with survey data was used in the present study (Yin, 2014). The research goals were to understand how learning communities were established and supported in the various models of makerspaces that currently exist. A comparison case approach was not suitable for this study since each site under examination had variability in critical aspects, like its audience, funding, goals and objectives, equipment, and staffing. Due to the variations, it was predicted that each site would have contrasting results. It should be noted, however, that in this chapter themes around learning communities were pulled together for use in a literal translation, where the case studies were used to corroborate theories around the creation and support of learning communities.

Each site included in the study also completed a survey developed in Google Forms, hosted online as shown in Appendix A. The survey was modeled on an earlier survey developed by the National Endowment for Science, Technology and the Arts (Nesta), a UK charity (Nesta, n.d.). The survey was released through a Creative Commons Attribution license. The author did not receive specific permission from the organization but has used it under the Creative Commons License. The survey was used to create a dataset of makerspaces across the UK and was completed by 92 spaces. Nesta released a report of findings in 2015 titled 'Top Findings from the Open Dataset of UK Makerspaces' (Nesta, n.d.). In addition, Nesta made available the dataset so that end users can run their own reports. The author modified the survey, adding questions about race and ethnicity as well as altering some of the language to clarify certain questions. The survey consisted of two sections. The first section contained three questions, beginning with name, email, and the respondent's role or relationship with the space. The second section of the survey examined the types of tools and equipment, and the purpose of visits for members. Additional questions explored demographic information about the members of the space, including gender and ethnicity. The response rate was 100%, with 26 sites completing the survey.

## SITE SELECTION

A maximum variation/heterogeneous purposive sample was used to find a diverse range of makerspace models and resultant learning communities (Palinkas et al., 2015). The sites included described themselves as makerspaces, hackspaces, FabLabs, print studios, and tinkering studios. Geographic clustering of sites, in many cases, was used to optimize travel costs, although in some situations the author traveled to distant single sites. Once sites were identified, the author requested site visits to conduct face-to-face, structured interviews with stakeholders; questions were not provided ahead of the interview. In addition, each site was sent a link to the survey. Follow-up emails were sent prior to the visits and approximately three weeks after the site visits. If sites did not complete the survey request, a final email was sent approximately six weeks after the initial visit. Not all sites that completed the online survey were included in the multiple case study. If sites were not included, it was mainly due to space considerations in the book and the author's decision that the site did not contribute to the overall study. In one case, the Baltimore Underground Science Space in-person interview had to be cancelled and was conducted over the phone, and therefore was not included in the multiple case study. Included sites can be generally classified into one of five types of makerspaces, based on the audience served and facilities (museum, for-profit, educational, library, community-based). Table 1 provides a list of all sites, whether or not they were included in the multiple case study, and type of site.

*Table 1. List of sites and types*

| US/EU | Location | Site Name | Type |
|---|---|---|---|
| US | Baltimore, Maryland | Open Works | Community |
| US | Baltimore, Maryland | Tool Library Station North | Community |
| US | Bethesda, Maryland | KID Museum | Museum |
| US | Baltimore, Maryland | Digital Harbor Foundation | Educational |
| US | Pittsburgh, Pennsylvania | MAKESHOP | Museum |
| US | Pittsburgh, Pennsylvania | Assemble | Educational |
| US | Herndon, Virginia | Nova Labs | Community |
| US | Bethesda, Maryland | Baltimore Underground Science Space | Community * |
| US | Rutledge, Missouri | Deep Green Machines, Inc. | Community |
| US | Kansas City, Kansas | Johnson County Library Makerspace | Library |
| US | Columbia, Missouri | Columbia Gadget Works | Community |
| US | Fairfield, Iowa | Fairfield MakerSpace | Educational |
| US | Lincoln, Nebraska | Nebraska Innovation Studio | Educational |
| US | Sonoma, California | Sonoma County Office of Education | Educational * |
| US | Oakland, California | Lighthouse Creativity Lab | Educational |
| US | San Francisco, California | Tinkering Studio at the Exploratorium | Museum |
| EU | Barcelona, Spain | Green Fab Lab | Educational |
| EU | Heidelberg, Germany | Heidelberg Makerspace | Community |
| EU | Barcelona, Spain | Made Makerspace Barcelona | Community |
| EU | Barcelona, Spain | (UPC) Camins Makers | Educational * |
| EU | Bucharest, Romania | Nod Makerspace | Community |
| EU | Dublin, Ireland | Lexicon Lab | Library |
| EU | Dublin, Ireland | TOG Hackerspace | Community |
| EU | Clane, Ireland | TechCreate | For-profit |
| EU | Dundee, Scotland | Dundee Contemporary Arts Print Studio | Educational |
| EU | London, England | South London Makerspace | Community* |

* Indicates that site was not included as a case study.

## Data Collection

The author collected data through structured interviews, online surveys, and secondary data collection methods online, and at the sites from January 2017 to May 2017. Nearly 70 hours of interviews were recorded and transcribed. Final transcriptions were imported into MAXQDA 12 and coded by the author. Data was coded and sub-coded, based initially on the structured interview questions included in Appendix B. Following Saldana's (2015) codes-to-theory model for qualitative inquiry, initial data was coded, then categorized, and later organized into themes based on the structured interview questions. Interviews were conducted face-to-face and recorded for transcription at a later date. Structured interviews lasted, on average, two hours and the interview questions follow:

1. How did the space build trust with the wider community?
2. How do learning communities support participation of youth and support successful making experiences?
   a. Describe in detail how learning communities are established in the makerspace. How do members collaborate on projects and other learning activities? What is the process for new members to join? Are members able to move in and out of learning communities/activities?
   b. What is the role of experts in the space? How are they identified and recruited? How do you encourage healthy youth-adult relationships? Do learning community members meet outside of the makerspace?
   c. What role do families typically play in the makerspace?
   d. How do making activities benefit females?
   e. Describe how youth participate in the space.
3. What does learning look like in the makerspace?
   a. Describe the typical learning pathways (classes, online lessons, workshops). What are the areas of instruction offered in the space? Describe what prior knowledge members need to possess, and if they have a deficiency what is done to alleviate this deficiency? What is a typical project or artifact?
   b. How do you develop the maker mindset? How are members prepared for failure?
   c. What is the impact of the makerspace on the community? (What have you observed as direct benefits of having the space in the community?)

   d. What is the impact of the makerspace on individuals (learning, attitudes, interest, careers)? How do you gather this data, if applicable?
4. How would you define a makerspace and what are some of the components of a makerspace?
5. Review of artifacts
   a. Please share some artifacts that were created through the makerspace. Describe the process of design and creation of the artifact. What role did the learning community play? What factors led to the creation of this particular artifact? How did they arrive at creating this particular artifact?
   b. Are there other learning environments/situations that would have allowed the youth to create a similar artifact?
6. What did I not ask that I should have?

While at each site, the author toured the space with the assistance of a stakeholder and was allowed to capture photographic images of the space and machines, but avoided, when possible, capturing images of members working in the space. Photographs were used to provide a visual context for the equipment and organization of the space. In addition, secondary printed materials were collected while at the spaces, such as informational and marketing pamphlets and course handouts/syllabuses. Additional information was collected from the online presences (web, Wiki, Facebook). Finally, each site was sent a link to the online survey. Only one individual from the site was asked to complete the survey. Stakeholders from the sites verified each case and data was triangulated by collecting various sources of information (Sheridan et al., 2014).

## Data Analysis

Survey data for the 26 sites was downloaded from Google Forms and imported into Microsoft Excel, then imported into Stata 14 for the Macintosh. Overall survey data will be provided for all sites and then further displayed for US and EU sites.

# RESULTS

## Physical Space

For all sites, the location types for the makerspaces visited were as follows: 57.69% community, 19.23% school-based, 11.54% library, 7.69% museum, and 3.85% for-profit. The average size of the makerspaces visited as shown in Table 2 was 4,988 $sq^2$ (n=24, SD 7,377), with a minimum of 400 $sq^2$ and a maximum size of 34,600 $sq^2$. The first site opened in 1999 at Dundee Contemporary Arts and the latest to open was the Fairfield MakerSpace in 2017. The number of visits per month reported by the spaces started at 0 to 10, all the way up to over 5,000+ visits per month.

Location types for the 16 US sites were: 62.50% community, 18.75% school-based, 6.25% library, 12.5% museum, and 0 for-profit. The average size of the makerspaces visited was 6,148 $sq^2$ (n=15, SD=2,298), with a minimum of 900 $sq^2$ and a maximum size of 34,600 $sq^2$.

Location types for the 10 European sites were 50% community, 20% school-based, 20% library, 0 museum, and 10% for-profit. The average size of the makerspaces visited was 6,148 $sq^2$ (n=9, SD=1,106), with a minimum of 400 $sq^2$ and a maximum size of 10,750 $sq^2$.

Figure 3 shows the frequency of average monthly visits for all sites (US and Europe) in 2016. Most spaces had between 250 to 1,000 visitors per month followed by a much smaller 10 to 50 visits per month. Total reported membership or user base for the sites ranged from four to 2,223 members. Two sites reported a membership level of over 1,000, while five reported membership between 200 and 250, and another eight sites had membership levels under 100.

At US sites, 50% reported visitors of 250-1,000 on average as shown in Figure 4.

European sites reported average monthly visits as 40%, 10 to 50 visits per month, followed by 50 to 100 (30%) and 100 to 250 (30%) visits per month as shown in Figure 5.

As shown in Figure 6, of the 26 sites most (73%) had bookable event space, followed by a library (46%) and a social area for meetings (46%). Less than 20% of sites had offices or incubator spaces for startups.

US and European sites had similar amenities available as shown in Figures 7 and 8.

*Table 2. Sites, date opened, floor space, and visits per month*

| Site Name | Date Opened | Floor Space $ft^2/m^2$ | Membership |
|---|---|---|---|
| Open Works | September 28, 2016 | 34,000/3,158 | 225 |
| Tool Library Station North | April 26, 2013 | 2,000/186 | 2,311 |
| KID Museum | October 28, 2014 | 7,500/697 | 200 |
| Digital Harbor Foundation | January 14, 2013 | 5,000/465 | |
| MAKESHOP | April 1, 2007 | 3,000/279 | |
| Assemble | April 1, 2011 | 1,200/111 | |
| Nova Labs | January 1, 2011 | 10,500/975 | 78 |
| Baltimore Underground Science Space | August 1, 2012 | | 22 |
| Deep Green Machines, Inc. | May 29, 2013 | 1,375/128 | |
| Johnson County Library Makerspace | March 15, 2013 | 1,700/158 | |
| Columbia Gadget Works | April 1, 2009 | 3,650/339 | 18 |
| Fairfield MakerSpace | January 1, 2017 | 1,900/177 | |
| Nebraska Innovation Studio | October 1, 2015 | 17,000/1,579 | 223 |
| Sonoma County of Education | June 25, 2015 | 900/84 | 60 |
| Lighthouse Creativity Lab | August 5, 2013 | 1,500/139 | 1500 |
| Tinkering Studio at the Exploratorium | April 17, 2013 | 1,000/93 | |
| Green FabLab | December 14, 2014 | 3,000/279 | |
| Heidelberg Makerspace | April 25, 2015 | 1,600/149 | 43 |
| Made Makerspace Barcelona | June 18, 2013 | 2,000/186 | 35 |
| (UPC) Camins Makers | November 1, 2014 | 1,070/99 | |
| Nod Makerspace | May 1, 2015 | 10,750/999 | |
| Lexicon Lab | August 1, 2014 | 1,075/1000 | |
| TOG Hackerspace | January 26, 2010 | 6,000/557 | 7 |
| TechCreate | January 14, 2016 | 400/37 | |
| Dundee Contemporary Arts Print Studio | January 1, 1999 | | 190 |
| South London Makerspace | October 1, 2014 | 1,600/149 | 248 |

*Figure 3. All sites frequency of reported visits per month*

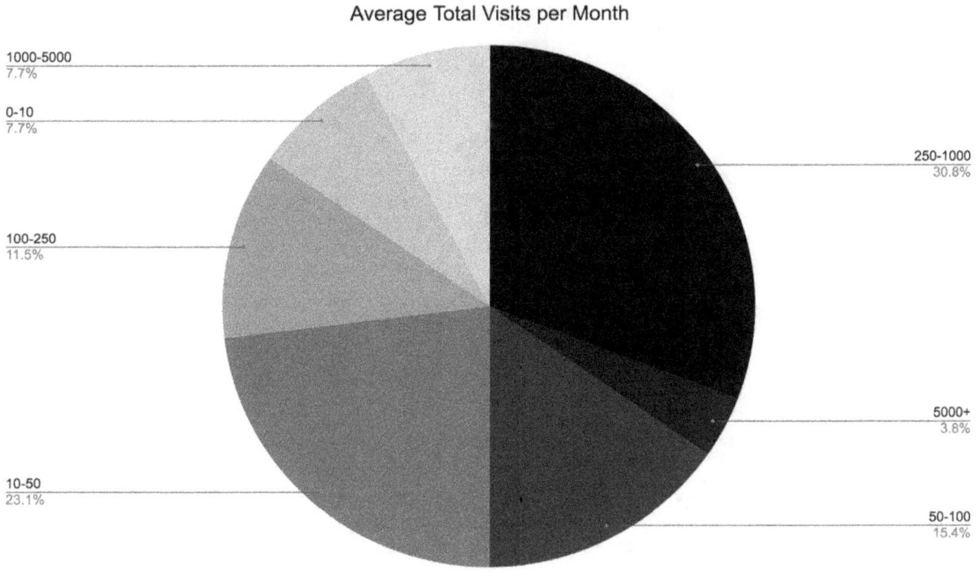


*Figure 4. US sites frequency of reported visits per month*

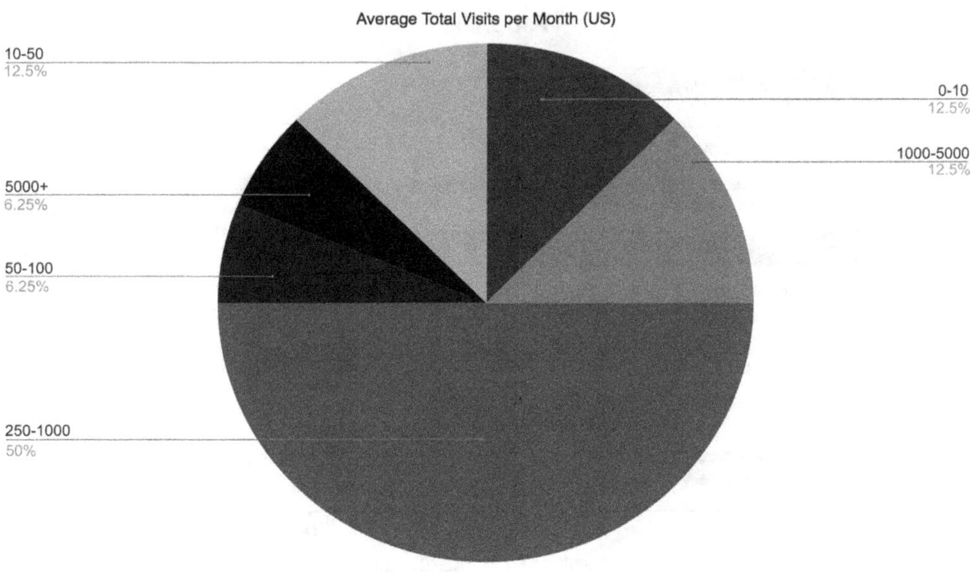

*Figure 5. European sites frequency of reported visits per month*

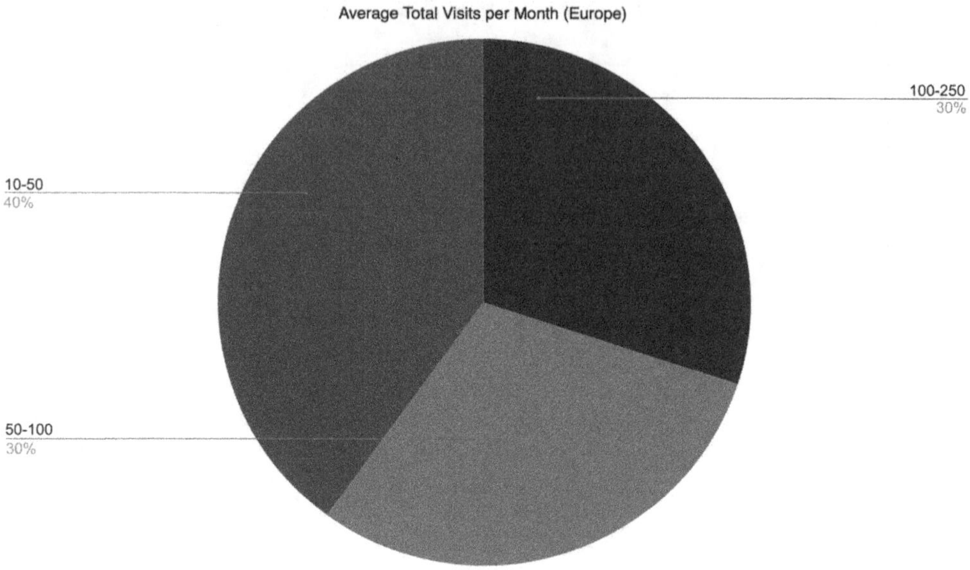


*Figure 6. All sites amenities*

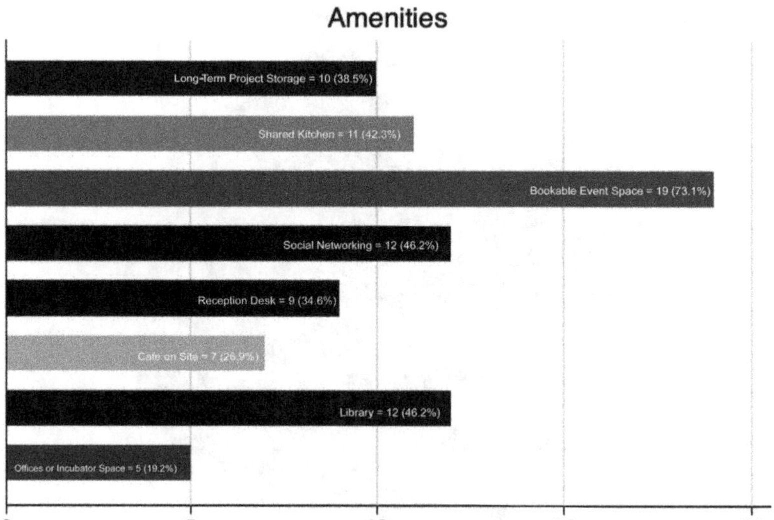

*Figure 7. US site amenities*

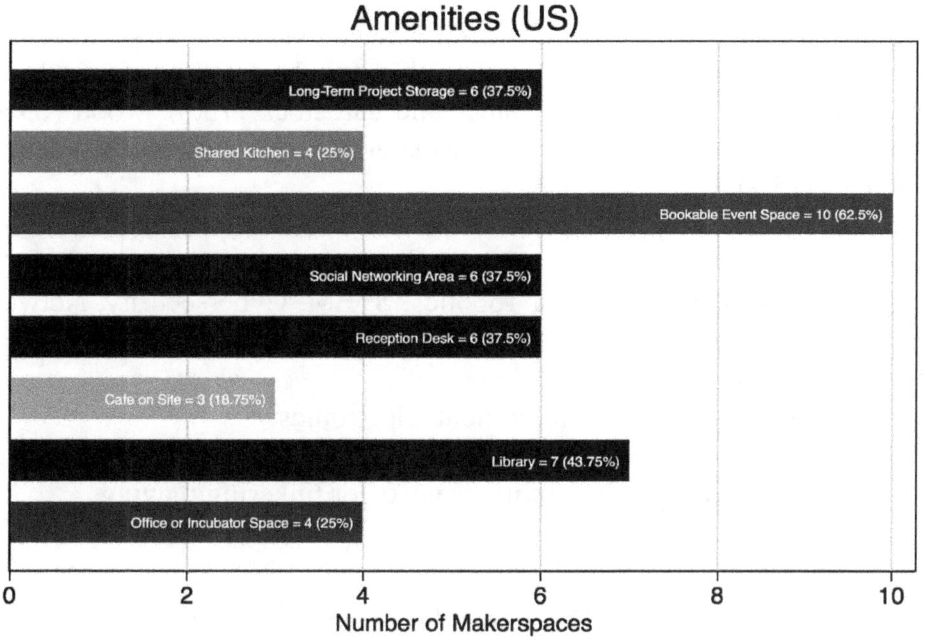


*Figure 8. Europe site amenities*

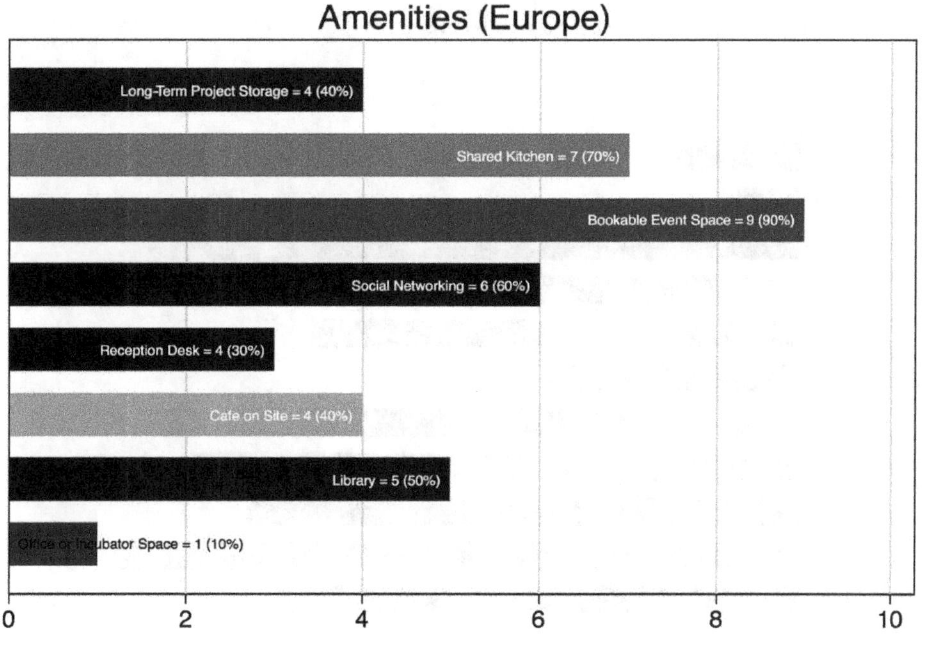

## Tools and Equipment

As shown in Figure 9, 80% of all sites indicated materials like plastics used in vinyl cutting projects were popular. Other popular materials found in the spaces were electronics (76%), paper and cardstock (73%), wood (69%), and textiles (65%), while least popular materials were biologics (15%) and chemicals (15%).

In addition, sites reported a number of other areas supported, including:

- HAM Radio, Youth FIRST robotics, STEM, Cybersecurity, Network engineering, Cosplay
- Microcontrollers
- Fabrication, software development, electronics
- Science communication, science outreach, science education, and hands-on learning, community projects for tinkering/playing
- Agriculture
- Photography
- Theatrical art and scenography, IOT, educational practices
- Skateboard making

*Figure 9. Frequency of materials used by all sites*

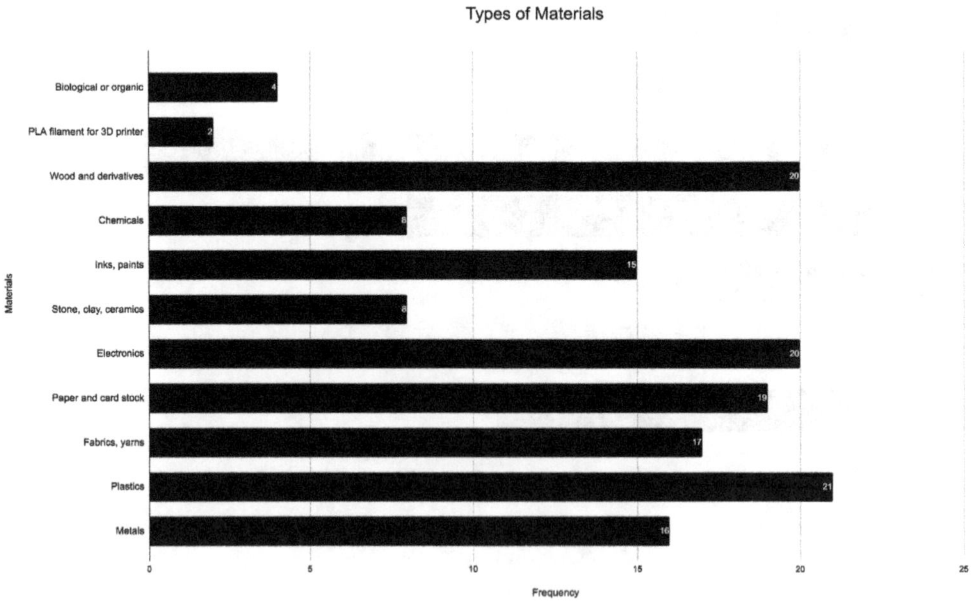

- Small animal husbandry (rabbits/chickens), gardening methodologies: straw bale gardening, permaculture, aquaponics, hugelkultur (raised garden beds made with decaying wood), small plot intensive gardening, mushroom cultivation
- Graphic design, illustration
- Low-tech: cardboard, paper craft, etc.
- Hands-on activities for STEAM education
- Resin casting
- Cardboard prototyping, LEGO prototyping, K'nex.

Twenty-one of the 26 sites (76.9%) indicated that some or all of the tools/ machines in the space required training or an orientation.

Figures 10 and 11 display reported frequencies of materials used by US and European sites.

## People in the Space

Makerspaces refer to those who frequent their spaces as members, visitors, or users, and in the following section, the word "member" will encompass all three possibilities. Each site has a policy for access to the space, whether it is to provide 24-hour access or if access is restricted to times during open hours, as shown in Figure 12. In many community-based sites, members can become key holders and access the site at any time. In other instances, members are restricted to open hours or times when other key-holding members are present. Public sites, like libraries and museums, have open hours each day for the public or for courses and workshops. Figures 13 and 14 show the breakdown for US and European sites, respectively.

Other access rules include:

- Middle/high school youth complete a 14-week intro course. Elementary youth: depends on course.
- Access to lab only occurs for members with our safety training. Otherwise, classes and workshops are open to public with lab manager on site.
- You can't use the [3D printer/laser cutter/CNC] until you have been trained by a member who knows how to use it.
- Depending on the tools and equipment used, some members are required to go through a training session.
- Anyone with an agreed-upon ongoing maker project.

*Figure 10. Frequency of materials used by US sites*

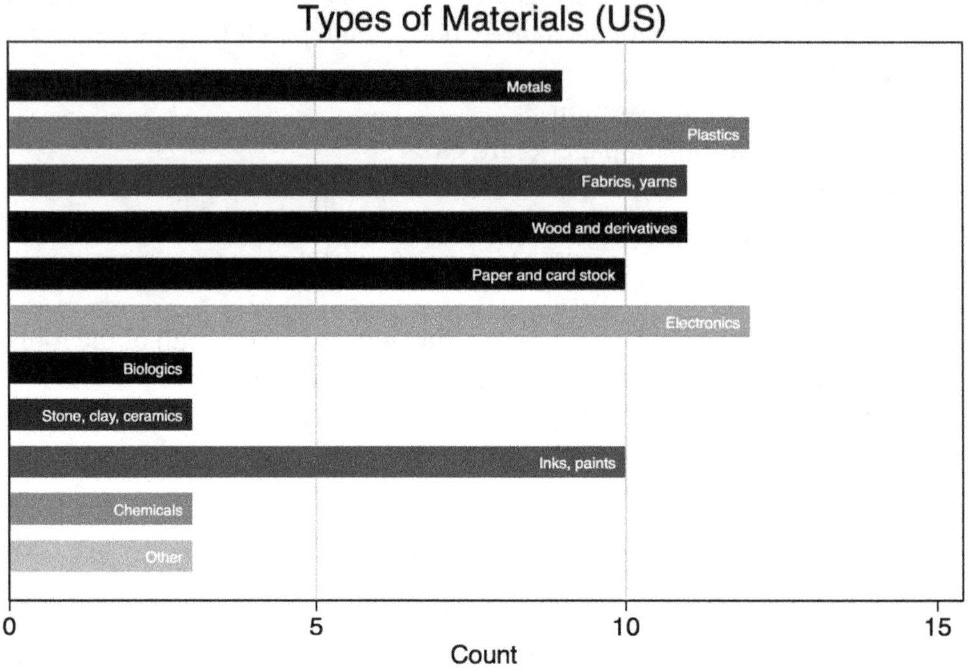


- Safety trainings for our shop, machine specific.
- Training required for use of machines.
- We are currently limited to training events.
- Safe Work practices training; equipment specific training.
- Three-month probation period.
- Must be member for one full month before unrestricted access is permitted.
- Yes, need to have completed induction training.
- Occasionally age restricted.
- All users must have basic safety and proper-use training of tools they want to use.
- Training required for CNC tools and anything that can cut a finger off.
- Safety classes are required in five out of seven workshops.
- Teachers attend orientation classes before having access to machinery.
- Members need to be vouched for by two established members before they can have full "key holder" status and unlock the space; before then they can only use the space if a key holder member is there already.

*Figure 11. Frequency of materials used by European sites*

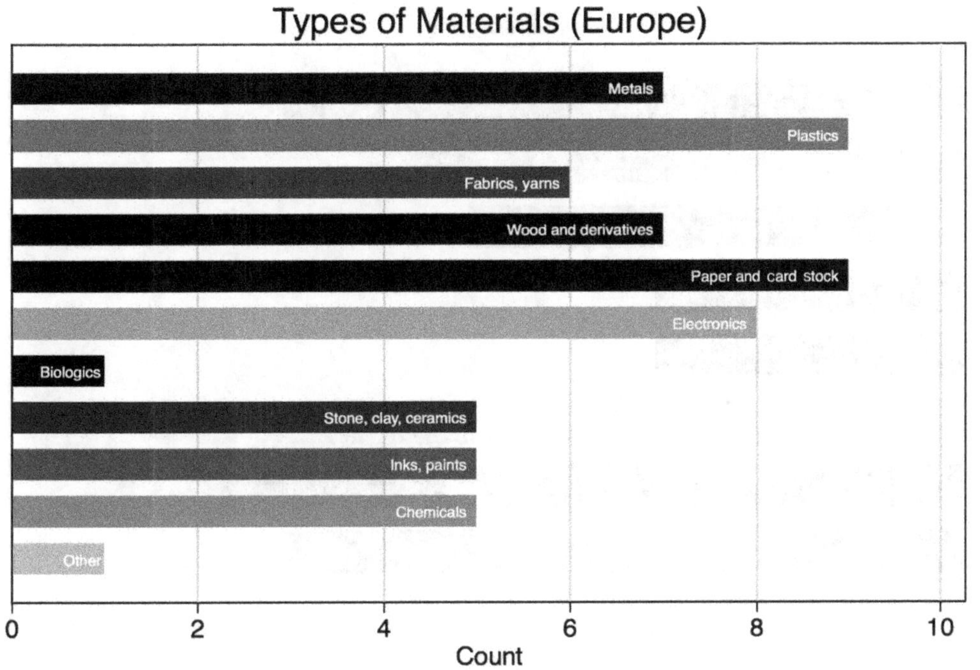


- Teachers usually can provide access for students and can train them. If a teacher isn't trained, we work with them to provide support.

For all sites, approximately 11% of the makerspaces indicated that youth under the age of 13 were not allowed under any conditions, while one site noted youth were allowed for field trips only, as shown in Figure 15. Most spaces allowed youth as long as they had been trained or were under supervision, while 30.8% of sites permitted youth with no restrictions.

Sites in the US reported that only about 6% did not allow youth under the age of 13 in their space as shown in Figure 16. European sites reported that around 30% of sites are not open to youth under the age of 13 as shown in Figure 17.

The minimum age for all sites that allow youth to use equipment at the space was sporadic, with the youngest being 5 years of age. Three sites indicated that the minimum age was 8, while another three noted the minimum age was 16. The oldest minimum age reported was 20.

Overall, makerspaces most frequently (16 out of 23) reported that females constituted around 20 to 59% of the members while males were reported (17

*Figure 12. Access to the space*

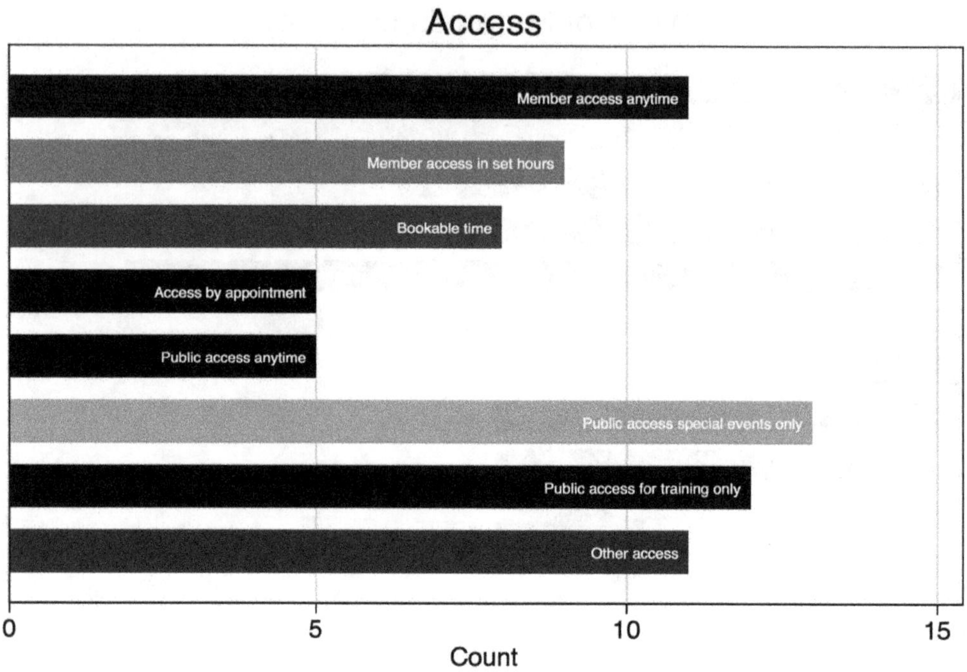


out of 23) at 40 to 79% of members, as shown in Figure 18. Three makerspaces reported male membership in the range of 80 to 100%. Four spaces reported more female than male members, estimating between 60 to 79% of members as females.

US sites reported that females comprised 40-59% of members at six sites. European sites reported most often that females made up 20-39% of members as shown in Figure 19.

In the US male members were reported most frequently as 40-59% of the membership base, followed by 60-79%. In European sites male members had the highest frequency of membership at 60-79%, followed by 80-100% and 40-59% as shown in Figure 20.

In addition to gender, sites also reported the range of ethnic groups of members (Figure 21).

Table 3 provides a look at the reported ethnicities split by continent.

Users in the spaces had a number of different reasons for visiting. Most sites reported that under 20% of users were just visiting or observing, as shown in Figure 22. Seven sites estimated that 40 to 100% of members in the site were hobbyists. Eight sites reported that less than 20% of their members

*Figure 13. US access to makerspace sites*

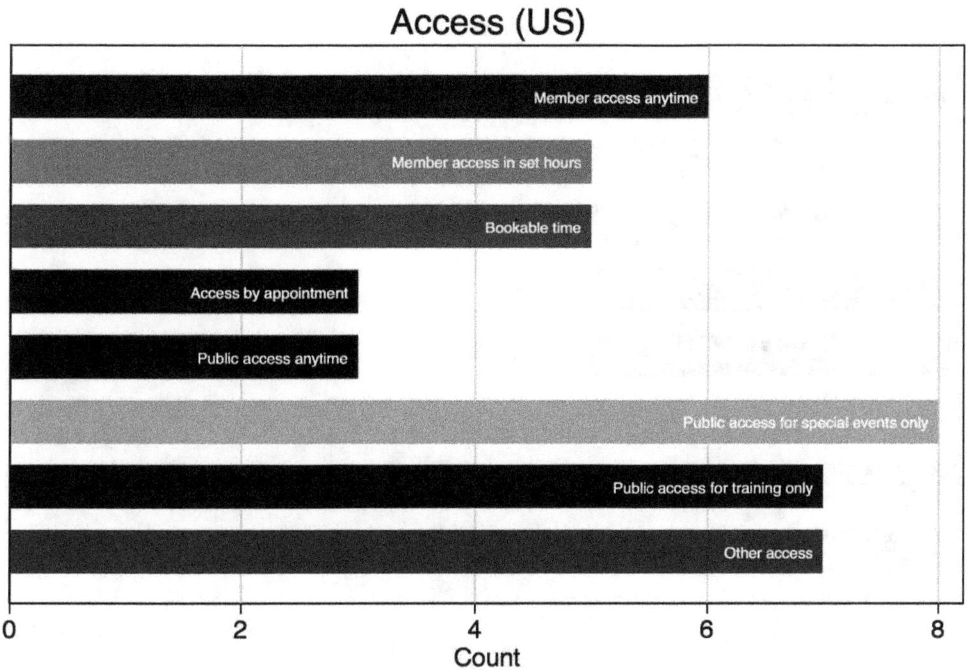


were there as start-ups. Four sites reported that youth under the age of 13 were 60 to 100% of their user types and youth 13 to 18 were 20 to 79% of user types for eight sites. College-age students (18 to 24 years of age) as a user type were prevalent in nine sites. Teachers were also reported in six sites as being 20 to 79% of the user types.

Table 4 displays the frequency of reported user types from the US and Europe.

In addition to user types, sites were also asked to report the purpose of visits on average per month, as shown in Figure 21. Six sites reported that 60 to 79% of visitors received training. Nine sites reported that 20 to 39% of users visited the space to receive an introduction to making in general, 14 sites reported that users were there to make something specific. Other purposes were for small batch production, to network, and to socialize in the space.

Table 5 provides an overview of the types of visits split by US and European makerspaces.

Other reported visit purposes were:

- Science outreach/communication, 20%.

*Figure 14. European access to makerspace sites*

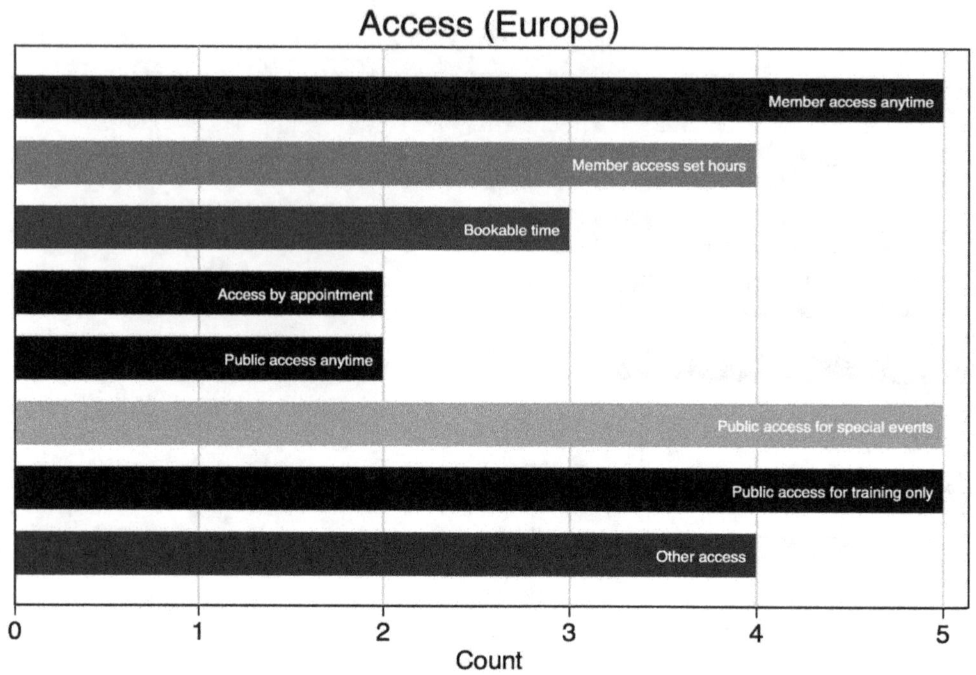


*Figure 15. Youth under the age of 13 allowed in all spaces*

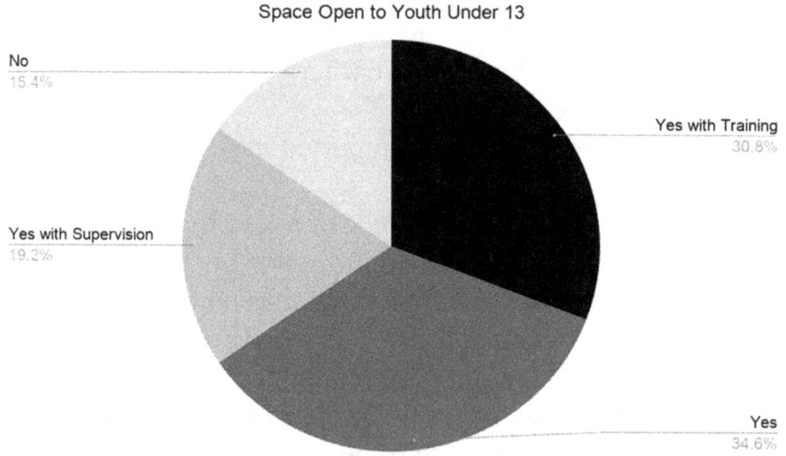

*Figure 16. Youth under the age of 13 allowed in US*

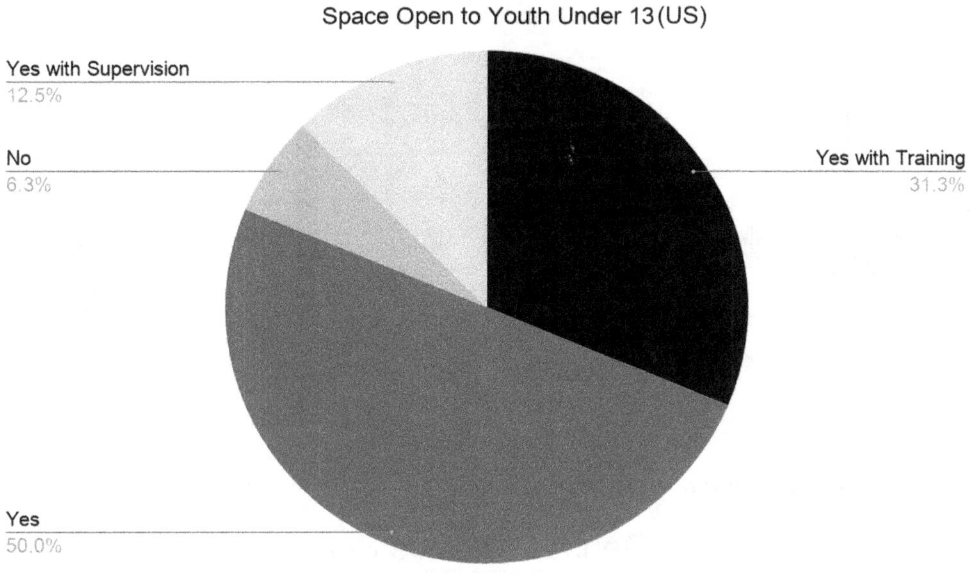


*Figure 17. Youth under the age of 13 allowed in Europe*

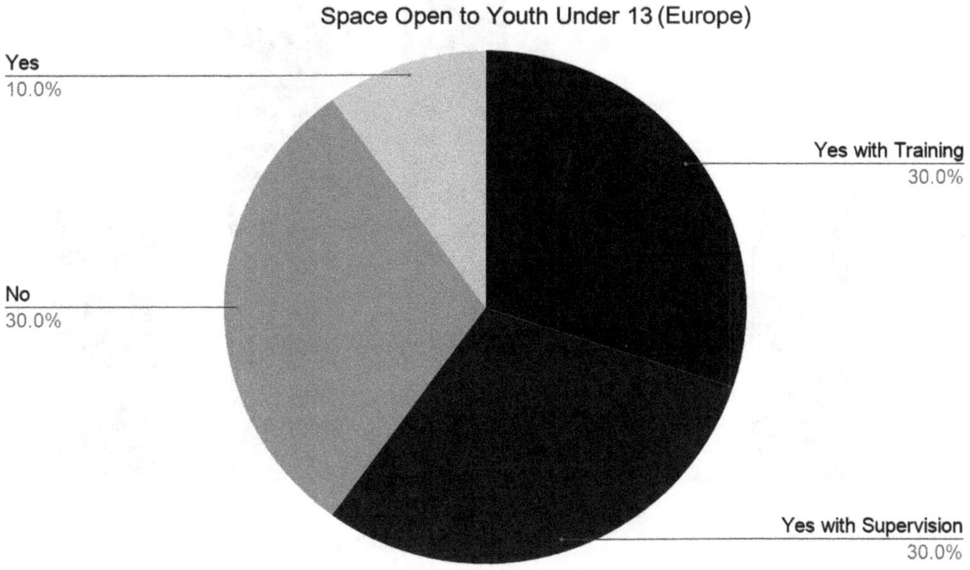

*Figure 18. Gender balance of members*

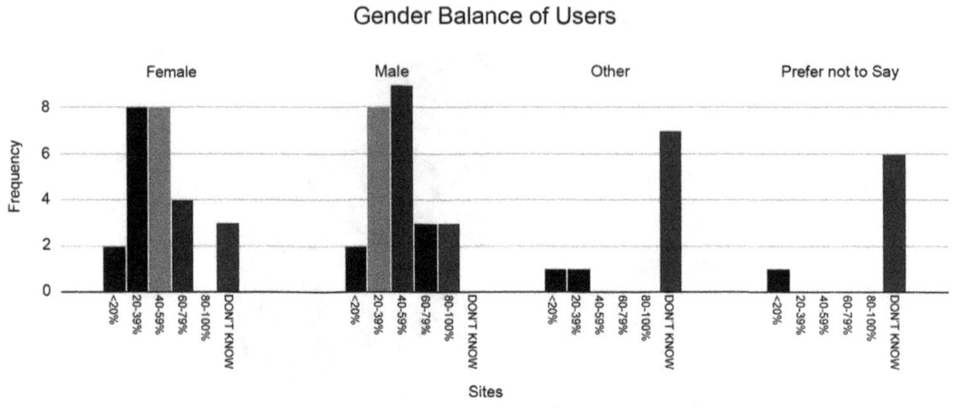


*Figure 19. Gender balance of female members*

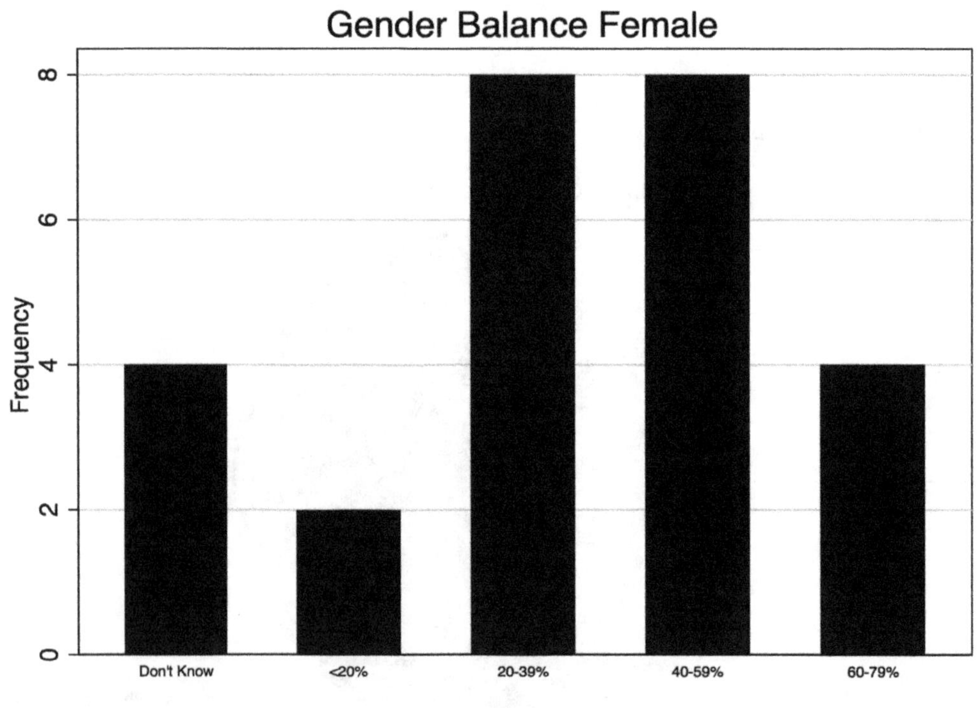

*Figure 20. Gender balance of male members*

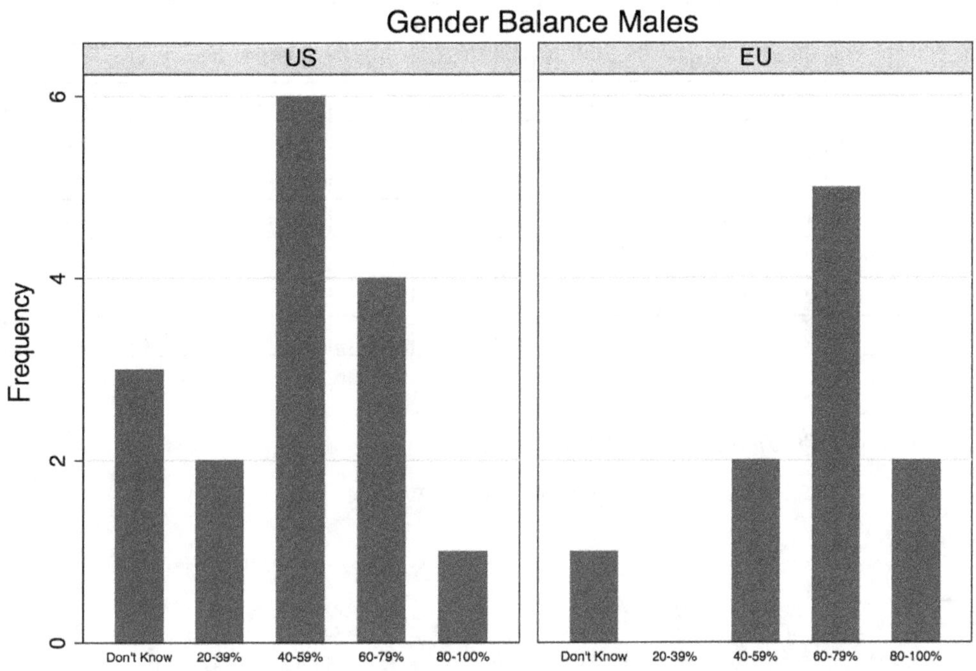


*Figure 21. Ethnicity of members*

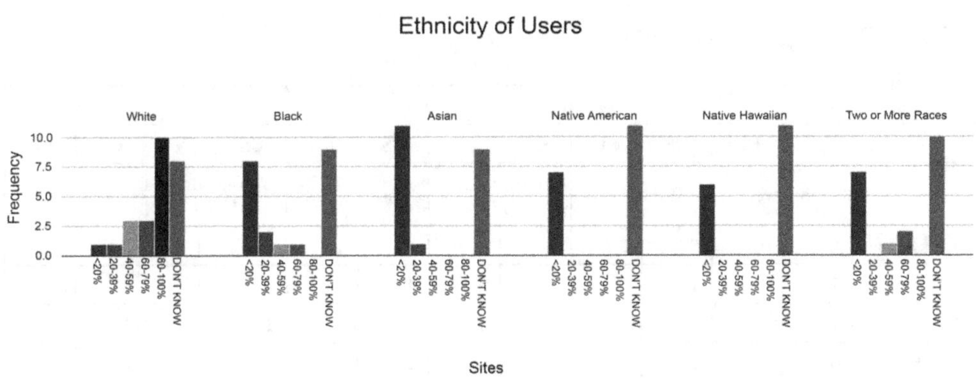


- Student research and master's projects.
- To check out tools for home repair and off-site projects.

Sites were also asked how members were recruited to their makerspace. In an open-ended question, "How do you recruit new members?" the makerspace responses included:

*Table 3. Reported frequency of ethnic groups by continent*

| | Reported Ethnicity | | | | | | | | | |
|---|---|---|---|---|---|---|---|---|---|---|
| | US | EU | US | EU | US | EU | US | EU | US | EU |
| | White | | Black | | Asian | | Native Am | | Two races | |
| Don't Know | 4 | 4 | 4 | 5 | 4 | 5 | 5 | 6 | 4 | 6 |
| < 20% | 1 | 0 | 6 | 2 | 9 | 2 | 6 | 1 | 6 | 1 |
| 20-39% | 1 | 0 | 2 | 0 | 1 | 0 | 0 | 0 | 0 | 1 |
| 40-59% | 2 | 1 | 1 | 0 | 0 | 0 | 0 | 0 | 0 | 0 |
| 60-79% | 2 | 1 | 1 | 0 | 0 | 0 | 0 | 0 | 2 | 0 |
| 80-100% | 6 | 4 | 0 | 0 | 0 | 0 | 0 | 0 | 0 | 0 |

*Figure 22. User types from all sites*

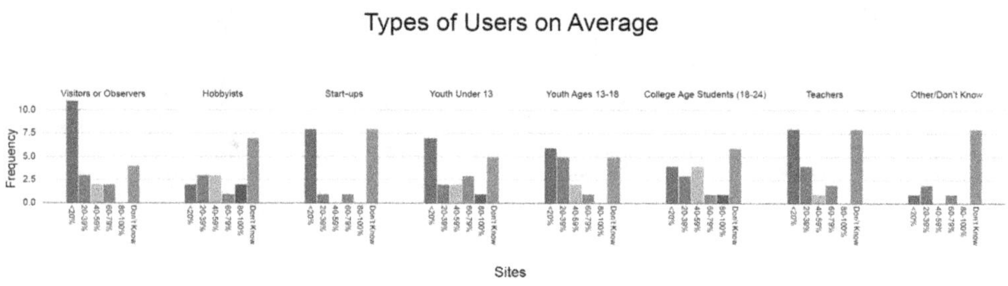


*Table 4. Reported frequency of user types*

| | Reported user types | | | | | | | | | | | |
|---|---|---|---|---|---|---|---|---|---|---|---|---|
| | US | EU | US | EU | US | EU | US | EU | US | EU | US | EU |
| | Observers | | Hobbyists | | Youth under 13 | | Youth 13-18 | | Young adults 18-24 | | Teachers | |
| Don't Know | 4 | 0 | 5 | 2 | 4 | 1 | 4 | 1 | 5 | 1 | 5 | 3 |
| < 20% | 7 | 4 | 1 | 1 | 4 | 3 | 4 | 2 | 3 | 1 | 5 | 3 |
| 20-39% | 1 | 2 | 1 | 2 | 1 | 1 | 3 | 2 | 1 | 2 | 2 | 2 |
| 40-59% | 0 | 2 | 1 | 2 | 2 | 0 | 2 | 0 | 3 | 1 | 1 | 0 |
| 60-79% | 2 | 0 | 1 | 0 | 2 | 1 | 1 | 0 | 0 | 1 | 2 | 0 |
| 80-100% | 0 | 0 | 2 | 0 | 1 | 0 | 0 | 0 | 1 | 0 | 0 | 0 |

*Figure 23. Purpose of visits*

*Table 5. Reported frequency of types of visits*

| | Reported Frequency | | | | | | | | | | | | | |
|---|---|---|---|---|---|---|---|---|---|---|---|---|---|---|
| | **US** | **EU** | **US** | **EU** | **US** | **EU** | **US** | **EU** | **US** | **EU** | **US** | **EU** | **US** | **EU** |
| | **Training** | | **Intro to making** | | **Make something specific** | | **Make one off** | | **Small batch production** | | **Network with others** | | **Socialize** | |
| Don't Know | 5 | 1 | 4 | 1 | 4 | 1 | 6 | 6 | 6 | 2 | 5 | 2 | 4 | 3 |
| < 20% | 3 | 1 | 2 | 3 | 2 | 2 | 2 | 3 | 4 | 1 | 5 | 2 | 3 | 2 |
| 20-39% | 2 | 3 | 5 | 4 | 1 | 3 | 2 | 2 | 1 | 4 | 1 | 2 | 3 | 2 |
| 40-59% | 0 | 2 | 2 | 0 | 4 | 3 | 2 | 0 | 0 | 1 | 0 | 0 | 1 | 0 |
| 60-79% | 4 | 2 | 1 | 0 | 3 | 1 | 1 | 1 | 0 | 0 | 0 | 0 | 1 | 1 |
| 80-100% | 1 | 0 | 1 | 0 | 0 | 0 | 0 | 0 | 0 | 0 | 0 | 0 | 0 | 0 |

- Open events/programs, Maker Faire, DC-TOM
- Word-of-mouth, marketing materials, publications, special events
- School outreach
- Social media, word-of-mouth, community projects, science fairs, and public engagements
- They find us, publicity
- Get them hooked during public hours
- Word-of-mouth, flyers, Facebook ad campaign
- Online, social media, events, etc.
- School activities

- Snake oil, healthy community, offer next to free access to a library of tools, and offer sweet classes
- No memberships
- Social media
- Press releases, Facebook, word-of-mouth
- Marketing, programs, outreach
- We don't have a plan. We do lots of events to show off our projects and we just hope people like what we do and join
- Word-of-mouth, random encounters
- Online marketing, word-of-mouth, shows
- Usually through friends. We are developing new member incentive strategies.
- Almost all through word-of-mouth, or community events
- Dundee Contemporary Arts Marketing
- Social media, general ad campaigns, tabling at events, word-of-mouth, community outreach, classes
- Workshops, word-of-mouth
- Word-of-mouth: via social media and weekly open evenings
- School community.

A number of different staffing models were identified in the spaces, with 42.3% reporting at least one full-time staff member, 34.6% reporting part-time staff, 7.7% reported no paid staff at all, 53.9% had volunteers who were on staff in the space, 19.2% had informal user groups, 7.7% had a business support group, and 26.9% reported other staff in the space. Other staff included teachers, students, interns, and Vista volunteers working as staff members.

## Programs in the Makerspaces

Sites were asked to report what types of training they offer in the makerspace. Overall, 25 sites responded to the survey question. A large number of sites, 93.0%, reported providing members with informal help, 84.0% of sites offered formal classes, 72.0% of sites offered specific training on tools and equipment, while 48% offered technical help. Only 8.0% of sites offered online training and 13.0% offered online user groups. Table 6 provides an overview of training offered split by US and European makerspaces.

A majority, 96.2%, of sites held public events, while 88.5% of spaces held free events, 69.2% held member-only events, while 57.7% of sites held family-based events. Corporate and business events were held in 46.2% of

*Table 6. Reported frequency of types of training offered in the space*

| | Reported Frequency | | | | | | | | | | | | | | | |
|---|---|---|---|---|---|---|---|---|---|---|---|---|---|---|---|---|
| | US | EU | US | EU | US | EU | US | EU | US | EU | US | EU | US | EU | US | EU |
| | Formal classes | | Technical support | | Informal help | | Specific training on machines | | No training offered | | Online training | | Online user groups | | Other | |
| No | 3 | 2 | 8 | 6 | 2 | 1 | 5 | 3 | 16 | 10 | 15 | 9 | 15 | 9 | 11 | 8 |
| Yes | 13 | 8 | 8 | 4 | 14 | 9 | 11 | 7 | 0 | 0 | 1 | 1 | 1 | 1 | 5 | 2 |

the spaces. Other programs offered in the spaces included youth camps or classes, 65.2%, school programs, 60.9%, after-school programs, 43.5%, home school classes, 30.4%, and commercial services, 26.1%. Table 7 breaks down reported frequency of events by continent.

## Discussion: Makerspaces and Learning Communities

Based on the sites visited in the research project, a number of different organizational models based on location, funding, and membership emerged as shown in Table 3. While there are exceptions to the models, for the most part the stratification works. For example, a museum-based space is usually located in a public building and has a top-down management structure that does not include a member base that is able to make decisions in the space. Typically, the museum spaces don't have a high number of repeat visitors and yet spend the most time researching the interaction between the maker environment and visitors. This is mainly because museums are interested in how they can extend the learning interaction during the brief time that museum visitors spend at a particular exhibit.

*Table 7. Reported frequency of events types*

| | Reported Frequency | | | | | | | | | | | |
|---|---|---|---|---|---|---|---|---|---|---|---|---|
| | US | EU | US | EU | US | EU | US | EU | US | EU | US | EU |
| | Public events | | Free events | | Member events | | Family events | | Corporate events | | Other events | |
| No | 1 | 0 | 3 | 0 | 6 | 2 | 5 | 6 | 10 | 5 | 13 | 9 |
| Yes | 15 | 10 | 13 | 10 | 10 | 8 | 11 | 4 | 6 | 5 | 3 | 1 |

Similar to museums, library-based makerspaces have a top-down hierarchy management model that serves library patrons in the space. Libraries typically are "clean" makerspaces, catering to areas that are relatively quiet and don't create large amounts of dust, fumes, or waste. Library patrons have the opportunity to visit the space multiple times and take advantage of training opportunities and to connect with other learners in the space. However, libraries provide limited access to patrons, based on their hours and availability of staff to oversee the space. While volunteers are utilized in some libraries, they are normally under the direct supervision of a staff member. Both museums and libraries are part of the public infrastructure and are paid for via public funds and subsidized by minimum user fees.

Makerspaces in educational environments take several different forms. In one instance, the makerspace is integrated into the school day and run by teachers at the school. In another case, the makerspace is part of an after-school program taught by staff employed by a nonprofit entity. In each case, activities are focused on student learning and engagement and are taught by full- or part-time staff. Funding for schools is a mix of public and private funds, and the buildings are part of the school or public infrastructure. In higher education, makerspaces can be located on or off campus, and have several funding mechanisms, from public funds to student registration fees, and if they are open to the public, they may have a membership model. The spaces tied to a university were run by faculty and staff and were available only when a staff member was present.

For-profit makerspaces were rare and run like a business, using private funds and income from courses and manufacturing contracts. Unlike many of the other makerspaces, the for-profit space was at a distinct disadvantage due to the overhead costs of facilities.

Finally, the nonprofit community-based spaces were the most common model found in the study. Typically, in this model the organizational structure is flat, with an elected board of volunteers that carry out the day-to-day logistical operations of the space. In larger, well-established spaces, there were instances of paid staff, but more often community spaces were run by volunteers. Decision-making in the community spaces was done by a committee, with members voting on issues within the space and conveying their wishes to the board of directors. Funding, for the most part, in the community spaces was private, relying mostly on membership fees for operational budgets. Often, equipment in the community space, as well as other spaces, was donated either through members of the space or via a public donation. Many community spaces were founded in spaces with low or no rental costs and did much of the build-out of the space through the talent of members.

## Creating and Supporting Learning Communities

As previously stated, three main components are needed for the formation of learning communities: 1) an academic or shared domain of interest, 2) learning in a social context, and 3) a physical place for the community to meet (Brower and Dettinger, 1998). The creation of learning communities in the makerspaces is quite diverse and somewhat dependent on the structure of the space, but in all cases, the three learning community components were present, to various degrees. The first component (domain of interest) easily falls under the idea that members of a space are interested in one or more aspects of making, whether it is electronics, woodworking, prototyping, or textiles, etc. Interests are varied and diverse, and makers are free to pursue these interests. Interests and project ideas can be fostered at the individual level, but at the same time, it would be a real challenge to walk into a makerspace with a room full of wood lathes, for example, and not find common interests

*Table 8. Makerspace models*

| | Building ownership | Funding | Management | Membership Model | Staff |
|---|---|---|---|---|---|
| Museums | Public | Public/private | Traditional hierarchy | Visitors | Full- and part-time staff, volunteers |
| Libraries | Public | Public/private | Traditional hierarchy | Patrons | Full- and part-time staff, some volunteers |
| Formal education Primary/secondary | Public/school | Public/private | Educators | Students | Educators |
| Higher education | Public or private | Public/private | Hierarchy | Transitory student memberships, community memberships | Faculty, full- and part-time staff |
| For-profit/business | Private | Private | Traditional hierarchy/Flat | Membership | Full- and part-time staff |
| Community-based spaces | Private | Private | Nonprofit boards, flat structure | Membership | Volunteers, few paid staff |

amongst members in the space. Interests can also be channeled into group projects, whereby members work as a team on a common goal.

The second component, learning in a social context, was present but the approach was different for each space. Often, it was up to the individual member to initiate social interactions in the space. For example, many community-based spaces had experts that frequented the space but were not assigned as mentors to new members with shared interest in the space. Experts, in most cases, were willing to share knowledge while in the space but the social interaction had to be initiated by the neophyte. Conversely, some sites engineered the physical environment to promote learning in a social context. Strategies included situating learners so that interactions were more likely to occur while working in a shared interest area. Another common strategy was to have small group courses for new members, encouraging interactions and communication between course participants. Many sites relied on staff to make initial social interactions by simply connecting learners based on their interests. For example, a new member interested in electronics would be introduced to other members working in the same domain. Other sites had show-and-share meetings to encourage members to showcase their work and interests. In addition, online tools were also used as a way to connect learners in the physical space.

The final component, a physical space, again varied widely from site to site. At the time of the visit, each site had a physical location. Prior to having a true, dedicated physical space, some sites existed as clubs that met at members' houses like Columbia Gadget Works. Another site existed as an organization that ran maker events but did not have a space. The largest spaces have coffee shops and meeting rooms as ways to facilitate social interactions, while other smaller spaces exist without walls, which also encourages social interaction as making becomes a very social event. Emergent themes of learning community formation from the structured interviews included:

Libraries and museums typically don't have deep engagement of repeat members and therefore don't see the formation of community like those in community-based or school-based makerspaces. For example, the Tinkering Studio at the Exploratorium does not expect visitors to visit the space more than once. Learning communities, if they form, will be transitory. Moreover, these communities will be based on the learning environment presented to the visitors in the floor space where the exhibit is located. Typically, the space will use the exhibits to draw visitors together to tinker and make, under the tutelage of a staff member or trained volunteer. These spaces typically have a high level of staff/volunteer interaction with visitors.

*Table 9.*

| | | |
|---|---|---|
| • Communities to support a single tool or piece of equipment | • Membership meetings to showcase and discuss projects | • Members share a common identity as a maker |
| • Shared goals of members for the space | • Use of the environment/physical space to foster learning communities | • Facilitators and staff create welcoming environments |
| • Create experts in the space that can help others/develop a learning pathway | • Spaces that aren't hierarchical, all members are learners | • Members are present and engaged in the space |
| • Members noticing each other's work, learning from each other in different ways | • Students are asked to share what they are thinking | • Allowing members to make what they want (agency) |
| • Formal workshop and courses where learners connect | • Developing a sense of respect in the space | • Creation of formalized subcommunities in and around various topics and interests led by volunteers |
| • Multigenerational bridges | • Learn by doing | • Tours of the space/membership orientation |
| • A willingness of community members to share knowledge | • Working on community projects | • Physically locating makers near each other |
| • Staff connect members by interests and project area | • All members are friendly and welcoming to new members and their interests | • Deferred judgment on projects |
| • Ensuring an inclusive environment | • Emphasis is on the process of learning and making, and not focused on the final product | • Shared access and shared information |
| • Peer/near-peer teaching | • Small class size, allowing learners to be more comfortable and establish trust | • Ask probing questions |

Libraries, on the other hand, may have more established learning communities based on the equipment in the space, but not to the degree of a community-based site. Libraries broadly rely on classes or training to provide basic skills to patrons, either allowing them time to tinker or directing them to alternative opportunities that will support their making aspirations. Libraries, unlike community-based makerspaces, are not run by their maker community members. Therefore, many don't have a membership model and makers usually drop in only during open hours. Of course, visitors can and do connect and form communities based on tools and interests, but it's less prevalent than in a community-based makerspace. Typically, libraries are clean spaces meant to provide an introduction to patrons. Often there are specialized spaces in the community where patrons can graduate and join to advance the skills first acquired at the library. Finally, in libraries staff play an important role in providing instruction, but to a lesser degree are charged with connecting members to create learning communities.

Somewhat of an enigma are for-profit makerspaces, with the desire to establish maker-based learning communities and serve the community as a whole, while at the same time creating revenue streams to support their business. This type of model has the distinct advantage of being nimble and can adapt to changing economic opportunities, but at the same time at a disadvantage because of the lack of public funds and the costs of space and equipment. Equipment is unlikely to be donated to the for-profit spaces because it may be used to generate income for the space and owners. Communities of learning in for-profit spaces are engineered by staff through teaching in teams and group-based projects for youth. Adult makers in these spaces will typically be interested more in product development and may or may not share their expertise with others in the space. Staff presence is very high, and volunteers are not usually utilized in these types of spaces.

Primary and secondary student-based educational makerspaces obviously have a high degree of faculty and staff interaction as certified teachers or after-school educators oversee the learning in the spaces. Again, many use the environment to encourage the development of learning communities. For example, placement of chairs in a specific arrangement encourages interactions between youth. Group projects for public events like Maker Faires and other showcase events also encourage youth to share knowledge and understanding. Educators will use questioning techniques to prompt learning and to reinforce communities of learning in the classroom and ask students to share their understanding. Educators also carefully craft a sense of respect between learners and ensure a safe environment where students are free to express themselves. Schools that support making provide context through curriculum for learners and unit exploration that combines several content areas. These types of exploration units integrate a variety of mathematics and science standards as well as maker activities such as modeling (2D and 3D) and digital fabrication to create physical objects representative of the phenomenon under study. Typically, students don't have a great deal of agency over their learning in these types of environments due to the specific learning standards that need to be addressed.

University-based makerspaces contain some of the same classroom contextual-based activities found in school-based spaces. For example, at Innovation Studio in Lincoln, Nebraska, a graduate class met in the space to design and build an exhibit for a local children's museum. Formal for-credit courses may be offered in university spaces, spanning areas like engineering, electronics, architecture, museum studies, and art. These courses provide typical strategies for learning community formation, like small group learning and shared goals. In addition to these courses, many university spaces are open to the public and provide learning opportunities in the form of workshops and noncredit courses. These spaces are part school-based and part community-based maker models. Paid staff in the space provide courses and learning pathways and yet are also very engaged in creating a sense of community through connections with members around shared interests and goals. Staff work to create a safe and welcoming environment and provide continuous support to learners in the space. Learning communities may form around equipment or interests, usually supported through the logistical help of paid staff in the space. These spaces have membership options for students and the general public, usually charging the public more for access to the space. These types of spaces are generally funded (in part) through the schools, public or grant funds, and user fees.

Finally, community-based makerspaces were the most common type of site visited in the present study. Most formed as a result of interest from a group of like-minded individuals who pooled resources and equipment in an effort to further build their interests and capabilities. Many of the community spaces went through a growth process whereby they became an official space with some sort of governance and management strategy, to a fledgling site interested in growth and creating community within the space, to a mature site offering learning pathways for members.

In general, community spaces rely heavily on expert volunteer members within the space. Typically, a volunteer will specialize in a certain area, such as electronics, woodworking, etc., and lead a community of learners in these areas for what may be called subcommunities. The subcommunities can be formal, like a wood turners group that regularly meets, or more transitory, whereby members meet for a special project or one-time learning opportunity and then disperse. Most makerspaces encourage their members to become experts, or at least very competent novices, and give back to the space through their time and talents. It's the sense of giving back to the community that perpetuates a strong and healthy makerspace. Community makerspaces are very purposeful in educating their members on the ethos of the space, which usually can be boiled down to "respect, give more than you take from the community, and be a risk-taker."

To build learning communities, sites have a number of strategies. In particular, community-based makerspaces are adept at creating learning communities through the initial tours and orientation where they cover the initial ethos and expectations of potential members. Mature spaces have strict policies of how members behave in the space. For example, the idea of mansplaining, that is, explaining to a person as though she is a child, is a violation in many spaces, and members can be reprimanded and expelled for repeat violations of this behavior. When the spaces foster an expectation of graciousness and respect amongst members, it becomes a building block of trust, allowing them to build strong learning communities.

Additional strategies to build community include instruction around a machine or technique in the form of one-to-one instruction, workshops, meetups, and even formal courses. A challenge for the community makerspace and others as well is to inform members of current projects and interests within the space so that learning communities can form. Efforts to share this type of information take the form of monthly show-and-share meetings and special interest group meetups. Many spaces use online tools like Trello or Slack to inform the membership of projects or potential projects. These meetings help establish and connect members. A final strategy to create learning communities is to devise a group project for members. These projects can be anything, from building a drone to track rhinos to a floating cardboard boat. Projects ideally bring members together from many different interest areas and allow them to work as a team to reach an agreed-upon goal. These types of projects have been successful in bringing about teams in the space but are ephemeral and will disband once the goals of the project have been met.

## CONCLUSION

This multiple case study examined how makerspaces of various models (school-based, museums, libraries, community, for-profit) established and supported learning communities. It was revealed that sites used a variety of strategies to support learning communities. Some of the strategies have evolved from experience, while other sites have used very systematic approaches based on research to determine effective ways to support learning and community. The very nature of the maker movement calls for the establishment of learning communities, and it can be argued that a makerspace without community is a laboratory or production facility churning out widgets to be consumed. The beauty of making is that it's not so much a means to create a widget but a means to understand the underlying processes in concepts needed to build the widget. Hatch (2018) noted that access to knowledge has fueled the maker movement. Learning communities, along with other outlets like online learning and certification courses, have reduced the barriers to knowledge. Results from this study provide evidence that the makerspace movement is deeply situated in a social context and provides the three components (shared interest, learning in a social context, a physical space) needed to foster learning communities. A number of practices to encourage the formation of learning communities emerged from the study and may be of use to many stakeholders interested in furthering the learning in makerspaces. However, it has a number of limitations. Primarily this study was conducted by one researcher with a particular set of biases. Moreover, the data was collected and interpreted by the author without the luxury of a research team. Any and all misinterpretations of the data and interview questions are the sole responsibility of the author. In addition, the results of this study can't be generalized to all makerspaces.

Hatch (2018) calls the current trend in making a *revolution;* riding a wave of technological innovation that has far-reaching societal impacts. These include impacts around economics, innovation, creativity, and education. To fully understand these impacts, more research is needed. In particular, questions about how effective and efficient learning can take place in the spaces is a critical question. Although makerspaces are open to almost everyone, there are still barriers that need to be better understood and addressed. While financial barriers are low-hanging fruit, other issues such as gender inequality and cultural practices als o need close attention and study. Additionally, those ideas around the maker mindset referenced by Dougherty (2012) should be further researched. The mindset is an important area in need of additional understanding as it can lead to immense increases in the building capacity of individuals to contribute to the making of the revolution.

## REFERENCES

Anderson, C. (2012). *Makers: The new industrial revolution.* New York: Crown.

Barker, B., Melander, J., Grandgenett, N., & Nugent, G. (2015). Utilizing wearable technologies as a pathway to STEM. In D. Rutledge & D. Slykhuis (Eds.), *Proceedings of Society for Information Technology & Teacher Education International Conference 2015* (pp. 1770-1776). Chesapeake, VA: Association for the Advancement of Computing in Education (AACE).

Bennett, D., & Monahan, P. (2013). Nysci design lab: No bored kids! In Design, Make, Play: Growing the Next Generation of STEM Innovators. Academic Press. doi:10.4324/9780203108352

Blikstein, P., & Worsley, M. (2016). Children are not hackers: Building a culture of powerful ideas, deep learning, and equity in the maker movement. *Makeology, 1*, 1–14.

Brahms, L., & Werner, J. (2013). Designing makerspaces for family learning in museums and science centers. In Design, Make, Play: Growing the Next Generation of STEM Innovators (pp. 71–94). Academic Press. doi:10.4324/9780203108352

Braybrooke, K., & Smith, A. (2018). Liberatory technologies for whom? Exploring a new generation of makerspaces defined by institutional encounters. *Journal of Peer Production*, (12).

Brower, A. M., & Dettinger, K. M. (1998). What "Is" a learning community? Toward a comprehensive model. *About Campus: Enriching the Student Learning Experience*, *3*(5), 15–22. doi:10.1177/108648229800300504

Calabrese Barton, A., & Tan, E. (2018). *STEM-Rich maker learning designing for equity with youth of color*. Teachers College Press Columbia University.

Chu, S. L., Quek, F., Bhangaonkar, S., Ging, A. B., & Sridharamurthy, K. (2015). Making the maker: A means-to-an-Ends approach to nurturing the maker mindset in elementary-aged children. *International Journal of Child-Computer Interaction*, *5*, 11–19. doi:10.1016/j.ijcci.2015.08.002

Clapp, R., Ross, J., Ryan, J., & Tishman, S. (2017). *Maker-centered learning: Empowering young people to shape their worlds*. San Francisco, CA: Wiley.

Diez, T. (2012). Personal fabrication: Fab labs as platforms for citizen-based innovation, from microcontrollers to cities. *Nexus Network Journal*, *14*(3), 457–468. doi:10.100700004-012-0131-7

Dougherty, D. (2012). The Maker movement. *Innovations: Technology, Governance, Globalization*, *7*(3), 11–14. doi:10.1162/INOV_a_00135

Dougherty, D. (2013). The maker mindset. In Design, Make, Play: Growing the Next Generation of STEM Innovators. Academic Press. doi:10.4324/9780203108352

Dunn, K. (2005). How to make (almost) anything. *The Boston Globe*. Retrieved from http://archive.boston.com/news/globe/ideas/articles/2005/01/30/how_to_make_almost_anything/

Ellet, W. (2007). *The case study handbook, how to read, discuss, and write persuasively about cases.* Harvard Business Press. doi:10.1017/CBO9781107415324.004

Fab Foundation. (n.d.). Retrieved from http://www.fabfoundation.org/index.php/the-fab-charter/index.html

Gabelnick, F. G. (1990). Learning communities: Creating connections among students, faculty, and disciplines. *New Directions for Teaching and Learning, 41.*

Graves, C., Graves, A., & Rendina, D. (2017). *Challenge-based learning in the school library makerspace.* ABC CLIO.

Halverson, E. R., & Sheridan, K. (2014). The Maker movement in education. *Harvard Educational Review, 84*(4), 495–504. doi:10.17763/haer.84.4.34j1g68140382063

Hatch, M. (2018). *The Maker Revolution.* Hoboken, NJ: John Wiley & Sons. Inc.

Hodges, C. (2003). Professional learning communities at work: Best practices for enhancing student achievement. *Childhood Education, 80*(1), 42. Retrieved from https://search.proquest.com/docview/210385424?accountid=10673%0Ahttp://openurl.ac.uk/redirect/athens:edu/?url_ver=Z39.88-2004&rft_val_fmt=info:ofi/fmt:kev:mtx:journal&genre=unknown&sid=ProQ:ProQ%253Aeducation&atitle=Professional+Learning+Communities+at+Work%253

Ikpeze, C. (2013). Increasing urban students' engagement with school: Toward the expeditionary learning model. *Journal of Urban Learning, Teaching, and Research.*

Ito, M., Gutiérrez, K., Livingstone, S., Penuel, B., Rhodes, J., & Salor, K. (2013). *Connected learning: An agenda for research and design.* Watkins, SC: Connected Learning.

Kalil, T. (2013). Have fun—learn something, do something, make something. In Design, Make, Play: Growing the Next Generation of STEM Innovators. Academic Press. doi:10.4324/9780203108352

Kostakis, V., Niaros, V., & Giotitsas, C. (2014). Open source 3D printing as a means of learning: An educational experiment in two high schools in Greece. *Telematics and Informatics.* doi:10.1016/j.tele.2014.05.001

Lave, J., & Wenger, E. (1991). Situated learning: Legitimate peripheral participation. *Learning in Doing*, *95*, 138. doi:10.2307/2804509

Lewis, H. (2016, April 22). The Essay That Launched the Term 'Mansplaining.' *New Republic*.

Martin, L. (2015). The Promise of the maker movement for education. *Journal of Pre-College Engineering Education Research, 5*(1). doi:10.7771/2157-9288.1099

NESTA. (n.d.). *Makerspace website brief*. Retrieved from https://www.nesta.org.uk/makerspaces-website-brief

Palinkas, L. A., Horwitz, S. M., Green, C. A., Wisdom, J. P., Duan, N., & Hoagwood, K. (2015). Purposeful sampling for qualitative data collection and analysis in mixed method implementation research. *Administration and Policy in Mental Health*, *42*(5), 533–544. doi:10.100710488-013-0528-y PMID:24193818

Papert, S. (1980). *Mindstorms: Computers, children, and powerful ideas*. Basic Books. Retrieved from http://dl.acm.org/citation.cfm?id=1095592

Papert, S. (1993). *The children's machine*. New York: Basic Books.

Peppler, K., & Bender, S. (2013). Maker Movement Spreads Innovation One Project at a Time. *Phi Delta Kappan*, *95*(3), 22–27. doi:10.1177/003172171309500306

Peppler, K., Halverson, E., & Kafai, Y. (2016). Introduction to this volume. In K. Peppler, E. Halverson, & Y. Kafai (Eds.), *Makeology: Makerspaces as learning environments* (Vol. 1, pp. 64–69). New York, NY: Routledge.

Piaget, J. (1972). Intellectual evolution from adolescence to adulthood. *Human Development*, *15*(1), 1–12. doi:10.1159/000271225

Rafalow, M. (2016). Tinkering online: Digital supports for making and sharing. In K. Peppler, E. Halverson, & Y. Kafai (Eds.), *Makeology: Makerspaces as learning environments* (Vol. 1, pp. 64–69). New York, NY: Routhledge.

Rédaction, L. (n.d.). *A fablab burned down in France by anarchists*. Academic Press.

Resnick, M., & Rosenbaum, E. (2013). Designing for tinkerability. In Design, Make, Play: Growing the Next Generation of STEM Innovators (pp. 163–181). Academic Press. doi:10.4324/9780203108352

Rosa, P., Guimaraes Pereira, A., & Ferretti, F. (2018). *Futures of Work: Perspectives from the Maker Movement.* Academic Press.

Saldana, J. (2015). The coding manual for qualitative researchers. *Sage (Atlanta, Ga.).* doi:10.1109/TEST.2002.1041893

Schor, J. (2014). *Debating the sharing economy. Great Transition Initiative.* Tellus Institute. doi:10.7903/cmr.11116

Sheridan, K., Halverson, E. R., Litts, B., Brahms, L., Jacobs-Priebe, L., & Owens, T. (2014). Learning in the making: A comparative case study of three makerspaces. *Harvard Educational Review*, *84*(4), 505–531. doi:10.17763/haer.84.4.brr34733723j648u

Smith, A. (2017). *Social innovation, democracy and makerspaces*. Academic Press. doi:10.2139srn.2986245

Stake, R. E. (2006). *Multiple case study analysis.* Guilford Press.

Vygotskie, L. S., Embong, A. R., & Muslim, N. (1978). *Mind in society: The development of higher psychological processes info*. Cambridge, MA: Harvard University Press.

Watkins, C. (2005). Classrooms as learning communities: A review of research. *London Review of Education*, *3*(1), 47–64. doi:10.1080/14748460500036276

Wenger, E. (1997). Practice, learning, meaning, identity. *Training (New York, N.Y.)*, *34*(2), 38–39. doi:10.2277/0521663636

Yin, R. (2014). *Case study research: Design and methods*. Thousand Oaks, CA: SAGE.

Zipkes, S. (2013). Manor New Technology High School. In Design, Make, Play: Growing the next generation of STEM innovators. Academic Press. doi:10.1093/rheumatology/kew468

# Acknowledgment

I'd would like to first and foremost thank my wife and children Katie and Camden for their unfailing support of my travels and the time I spent on this endeavor. I would also like to Drs. Lodl, Hibberd and all the administration at the University of Nebraska-Lincoln for granting me the privilege and opportunity to travel and learn.

Thanks to my brother Greg, my mother Trudy and everyone else I asked to review chapters. Thanks to Linda Ulrich for the quick reviews on the final introductory chapters. I would also like to acknowledge Dagen Valentine for inspiring me to travel, for looking at the early drafts of the interview questions and keeping me grounded. Thanks to Andy Burnett for introducing me to many great people in the US and Europe and getting the ball rolling. A big thank you to Dr. Bob Russell from the National Science Foundation who was also a valuable resource in connecting me with makers around the country. Finally, I'd like to thank my research and creativity team Neal, Gwen, and Jenny for keeping me inspired.

I'm indebted to all the people that freely gave of their time to talk with me, tour their space, and review chapters.

*Bradley S. Barker*
*University of Nebraska – Lincoln, USA*

# Section 1

# Informal Learning Communities in Museums

# Chapter 1
# KID Museum

## ABSTRACT

*Once a museum without walls, the KID museum is a place where everything is meant to be touched. KID offers unique, maker experiences for elementary and middle school-aged children that integrate hands-on science, technology, engineering, art, and mathematics (STEAM) learning with an exploration of world cultures and global citizenship. The museum has four focus areas or studios including woodworking, textiles, electronics, and a fabrication lab. KID Museum's current site at Davis Library in Bethesda, Maryland provides schools and the wider community with programs and workshops during the school day, on weekends, after-school, and in the summer. It is a first step toward the museum's vision of a larger, permanent home in Montgomery County, focused on empowering the next generation to invent the future with creativity and compassion. Programming in the space is designed, developed, and facilitated by KID Museum's educators. KID Museum's educational approach blends formal and informal learning by intersecting STEAM principles with hands-on learning. It also supports public and private school educators in their endeavors to lead quality maker learning experiences in the classroom. KID Museum has developed unique partnerships, including with Montgomery County Public Schools, the 18th largest system in the US, to meet the needs of underrepresented populations. With an eye to the future, KID Museum expects to leave the Davis Library and will open a new, larger, 50,000 to 60,000 square foot museum that will serve 250,000 visitors per year. However, situated in a well-to-do Bethesda, Maryland neighborhood, the museum is challenged with meeting the needs of underrepresented populations due to location and costs associated with running the space. This chapter explores KID Museum.*

DOI: 10.4018/978-1-5225-8310-3.ch001

## ORGANIZATION BACKGROUND

*At its core, maker learning equips kids with the skills to create something of their own design, challenging them to figure out what's necessary to bring their ideas to life. It feeds the sense of agency that is missing in many of our traditional school settings. - Cara Lesser, KID Museum Founder*

*... and see that genuine respect being elevated between parent and child or parent towards child ... sometimes parents come in and they feel like, "Well, I'm not an expert in this. How can I show my kid how to do that?" But then when they understand that they can learn from their child too, that changes the dynamic of the relationship. - Claire Cocciole*

Settled in a well-to-do neighborhood of Bethesda, in Montgomery County, Maryland, is KID Museum, a youth and family focused educational makerspace. The museum occupies 7,500 square feet in the lower floor of Montgomery County's Davis Library and was officially opened in October 2014. The museum has 13 full-time employees and a part-time staff of 20, whose hours total over 7 FTEs. Prior to moving into the Davis Library, it was a museum without walls with a small and committed volunteer staff, organizing events such as Maker Faire Silver Spring and the World of Montgomery Festival.

The current space that the museum occupies is in the lower level of the Davis Library, which historically was underused as a library space, mostly for storage and special collection for the library system. Once the Montgomery County found a permanent space for their special collections the lower level of Davis sat mostly unused. At the same time as the space was going unused, the Montgomery County Council Executive wanted to bring a STEM and making program to the county and was very supportive of what the KID Museum was doing, even before they had a physical location. Cocciole, Director of Maker and Community Partnerships, stated that their very first Maker Faire (2013) in the county brought in roughly 10,000 participants, almost double what they had expected and introduced the DC metropolitan region to the energy and excitement of the "maker movement." With this early success and apparent demand, it was clear the museum had inroads to establishing a space in the community. By building on the excitement of Maker Faire, and with the County's support, KID Museum has been able to expand the reach of their programs. Getting established was not always easy as Cocciole recalled:

*They didn't know the word 'making' when we introduced it, and so now they know what making is, and they know what it gives them, and so we had that track record going when we came into the space. We still had to make a lot of connections for community, "What are you going to do? Are you going to solder?" So, there was some of that, and we tried to be respectful of our neighbors. We tried to invite local communities who we worked with. There's an elementary school just a block away. We tried to work with the PTA, "Hey, we're coming," and we wanted to work with the children and families, and, you know, we're open. So, we did a lot of that. The library was a little bit, you know, it's their space, and they were concerned like, "You're there, you're not paying. What are you going to do?" But they've been great to work with. We've been really lucky to have them as a partner.*

Cocciole also recalls community members questioning the need for another museum in the DC area. The KID Museum had to convince the community and stakeholders that what they were doing was much different to what happens in typical museums. What they proposed was a museum where visitors are expected to touch and interact with everything. The museum is a place for STEM education through explicit tactile learning experiences, using tools and equipment. It was important in the beginning for the space to get that point across. Another factor in founding the museum is their location near the National Institute of Health (NIH) and the National Institute of Standards and Technology (NIST). NIH, a part of the U.S. Department of Health and Human Services, is the leading medical research agency in the U.S. and is charged with improving health and saving lives (NIH, n.d.). Founded in 1901, NIST is one of the oldest physical science laboratories in the U.S. and supports the development of many technological innovations (NIST, n.d.). In addition, NASA Goddard and many other federal agencies, helped KID cultivate relationships with STEM expert volunteers who work closely with the museum's educators to help the organization achieve its goal of family STEAM engagement.

Inside the KID Museum the first thing that jumps out is the number of different brightly colored items in the space. During the visit, there were a number of kites hanging from the ceiling colored in bright and vivid colors, shaped in circles and squares, with runners hanging down, as seen in Figure 1. Cocciole explained:

*It's Japan day. Another focus of ours is cultural programs. Every month, we'll celebrate the culture of a different country, and we work with our cultural partners on that. We highlight those activities which merge culture and making. So, for example, we'll have workshops where you're making some sort of artifact that comes from this cultural tradition. Our first year we focused on kite-making, and we had kite traditions from around the world, and you could make your own kites. Then recently on Brazil Day visitors were invited to make a Brazilian instrument, and later in the day, use that same instrument to play along with a Samba band performing on our stage.*

In addition to the kite installation there are a number of other built-in activity stations, including a pneumatic tube transport activity. In this activity visitors are able to build the system using plastic tubes, running them from one side of the library to the other. The air is compressed with fans on buckets on one end and the idea is that visitors working together—children of all ages as well as adults—can build a transport system that then moves objects from one side of the museum to the other side, shown in Figure 2.

*Figure 1. Kites in KID museum*

*Figure 2. The KID museum pneumatic transport system*

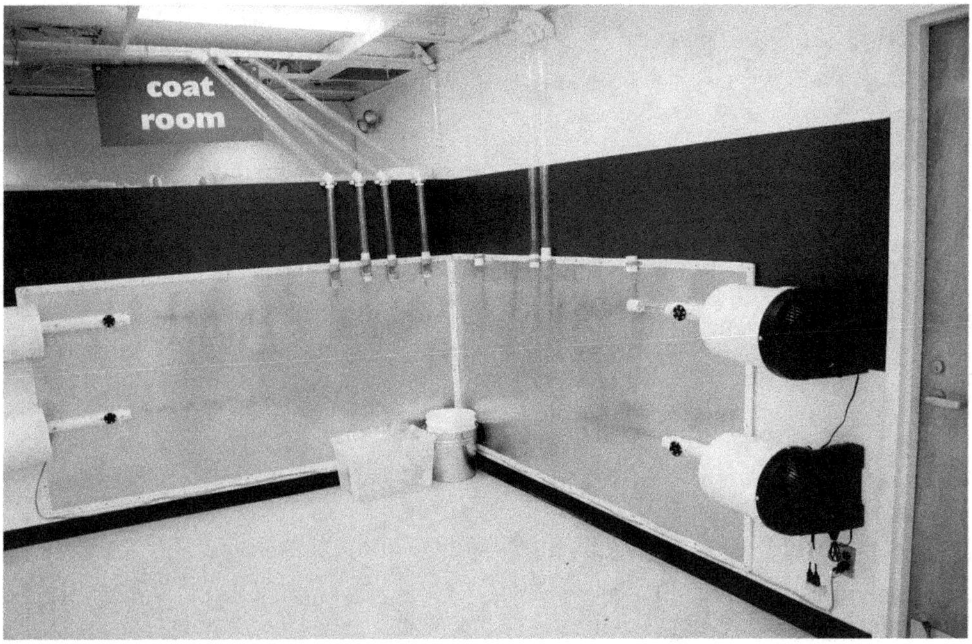


While the larger portion of the space is open, with wide windows extending the east and west perimeter, there are also four separate studios: woodshop, fab lab, textile and electronics. Workshops that focus skills related to these areas are held for small groups. Additionally, a Maker Studio program with three distinct levels for tools and processes in each of the four studios was created to help students to demonstrate competency and achieve recognition for their accomplishments. For example, in the woodshop level one tools are mostly hand tools and include items such as hand saws, coping saws, clamps, screwdrivers, sandpaper and hammers. Level 2 tools introduce youth to electric drills, drill bits, miter boxes and miter saws, electric sanders and various sized pliers. Level three tools include a hammer drill, jigsaw and similar tools. Each set of tools hangs on a sheet of plywood, with individual tools outlined where they hang. Each tool rack clearly states the tool level at the top, as shown in Figure 3.

The museum also offers a textiles, electronics and fab lab areas. Each of the areas also has three levels of certification on tools or processes. The textiles studio contains equipment for machine and hand sewing, fabrics, and ways to make sewing patterns. The electronics studio contains nine soldering stations, breadboards, microcontrollers and materials to create circuits.

*Figure 3. Tool racks in the woodshop*

Finally, the fabrication lab studio contains three 3D printers and computers with TinkerCad software for design. The studio also contains a laser cutter and vacuum-former. Each weekend youth that have earned certifications in the studios are eligible to make their own project during the *Open Build* studio times.

## SETTING THE STAGE

The KID Museum is located in a library but is not actually a part of the Montgomery County Library system. The museum's main focus is on educational making for youth and they have different avenues to reach children. All programming in the space is delivered by KID Museum's Maker Educators, a team of instructors skilled in a wide-range of areas, and each committed to the museum's mission to inspire the next generation of curious, creative and compassionate leaders. What sets KID Museum apart from other spaces devoted to making is the important role that social emotional development plays alongside skill-building and exploration. For these maker educators, teaching youth to become self-motivated is a life skill. The maker educators ensure that students understand failure is part of the creative process and celebrate the courage that comes along with making.

During the weekends, the museum operates like many museums with public hours from 10:00 a.m. to 5:00 p.m. It is an open time for children and families. General admission to the space is $12 per child, with free admission to 2 adults. Children under 9 years of age must be accompanied by an adult on the floor space, while children under 12 must have an adult at the museum. During the weekends eight to ten interactive learning stations are set up for the museum visitors, in what is called the *Open Explore* program. Visitors are able to flow from one station to another and spend as much time at the stations as they choose. Some example stations are the *Draw Bots*, where participants build simple machines that can scribble using motors and circuits; *Creative Coding and Game Design*, where participants use drag and drop coding to design a game; and *a wall of moveable gears.*

The types of users that visit the space are shown in Figure 4. Most visitors (80 to 100%) are youth under the age of 13, followed by youth 13 to 18 (60 to 79%), and many users (20 to 39%) are teachers.

As shown in Figure 5, nearly all users visit the space for skills building, followed by making something specific (60 to 79%), and an introduction to making (20 to 39%).

*Figure 4. Types of visitors per month*

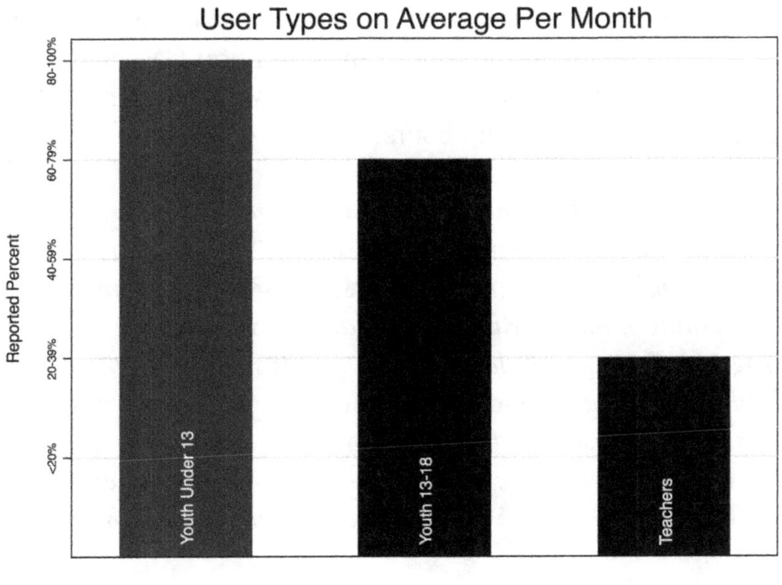

*Figure 5. Purpose of visits per month*

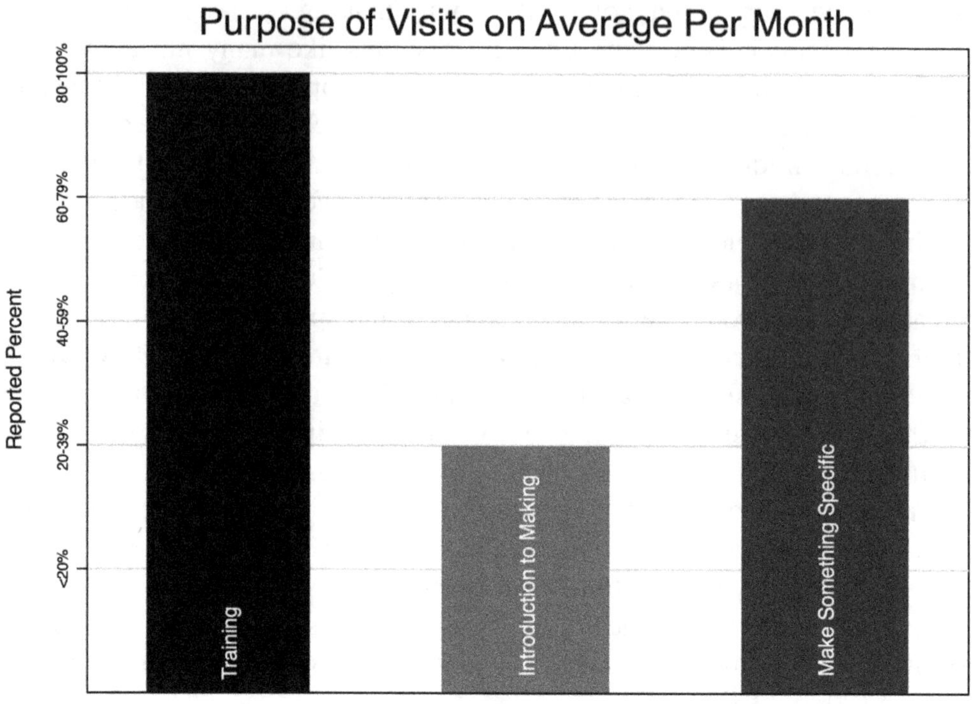


There are also planned workshops on the weekends that are broken down into two types: Maker Studio, which cover using processes and tools, "one-off" workshops that explore different aspects of the studio programs. Additionally, KID Museum introduced the Invention Basecamp workshops for middle school students working on the Invent the Future Challenge. Cocciole described the weekend courses in this way:

*We have the four students in the Fab Lab, wood shop, textile, and electronics. So, we rotate two different types of workshops. We have sort of the one-off, like, "Hey, let's build LED-lighted flowers, or use the vacuum-mold machine to make chocolate molds." But then we also have what we call our Maker Studio program. So, you would have sort of a lesson in, say, it's Wood Shop Maker Studio. We have a lesson in what we call our Level 1 Tools, and once we obviously go over safety and then how to use those tools, and once the instructor says, "Okay, you're certified in Level 1 Tools," then you can come back for a different session, which we call Open Build, where you're able to use those tools in your level to make whatever you want. And you have access to all of those tools. There's an instructor nearby, but it's not a lesson.*

Examples of one-off workshops include: Spy Plants (working with sensors), KIBO Robotics, 3-D print jewelry making, electronic flowers, Peek-a-Boo pouches in textiles, and monster trucks. To attend the weekend programs visitors can sign-up online. Costs start at $5 for the workshop, plus admission to the museum.

The 90-minute Maker Studio courses provide learners with instruction on safety and how to use the tools in each of the four studios (fab lab, textiles, woodshop and electronics). The classes are offered on a rotating basis during the weekends, with each studio offering three levels of certifications. Each certification level consists of different tools or processes that increase in complexity for each level. For example, woodworking levels cover increasingly more complex tools, the Fab Lab levels increase in software design tool and 3D printed output. In the electronics studio, students learn to heat shrink wires in level one and solder in level two, and in textiles they move from hand sewing to machines.

Participants receive certification once they have mastered the tools and processes in that level, which can take one or more lessons. Once certified on a tool and level, youth can come back and participate in the Open Build times for the studios using the tools for which they have certification. Typically, during the weekends, each studio will have Open Build times for youth with the proper certification usually lasting for two hours. An instructor is present in the studio during Open Build times to help if they get stuck, but these instructors do not provide direct teaching instruction during this time.

During the week, KID Museum hosts a number of middle and elementary schools that utilize the space for field trips and external learning activities. Home school, elementary-age and occasionally pre-school students may experience one-off activities where up to 60 students will rotate through the different stations depending on the requests from teachers. The museum and the schools and groups collaborate on the choice of activities for each visit.

In 2017, through a mix of public and private funding, 65% of the middle school students KID Museum served were from middle schools with at least 50% Free and Reduced Meals (FARMS) status. A large majority of these students were African-American or Hispanic. For elementary school visits, approximately 25% of the group visits were from Title 1 equivalent schools.

Montgomery County Public Schools and KID Museum partner together in a number of ways. At the middle school level, students from several schools participate in the museum's Invention Studio Program that exposes kids to STEM fields, including woodworking, analog circuits, engineering and microcontrollers, over the course of multiple sessions.

In 2017, the two partners rolled out "Invent the Future Challenge" a STEM competition for middle school students. The challenge calls on students to develop, design and build a prototype of an innovative solution to a sustainability issue. Students worked collaboratively in teams and use technical skills, creative problem solving and STEAM concepts to come up with a solution. This first challenge, which will span the academic year, will conclude with a final summit and judging competition of the projects.

The museum also runs after-school programs later in the day (after 4:00 pm) and has day-long programs when there is no school. Federal holidays are typically very busy in the space because a lot of families will come in and engage together at the museum. On these days families can drop in and float from activity stations that are set up in the space.

For the pre-school set, there is the Mini-Makers program, which promotes exploration in the maker environment. Led by museum educators, the sessions last for three weeks for 1.5 hours per session and cover topics like KIBO robotics, rocketry and engineering.

KID Museum facilitates non-residential summer programs in full-day camp configurations for youth ages 7 through 15, and facilitated by museum educators. The summer camp offerings are divided by grade bands ($2^{nd}$–$4^{th}$, $5^{th}$–$7^{th}$, and $6^{th}$–$9^{th}$) and last for five days. Example camp offerings are shown in Table 1. by grade band.

Instructionally, KID Museum works with their young visitors on Maker Mindset practices like persistence and learning by failure. The museum understands that during the school days students all too often are not allowed the opportunity to try something and fail and persist in the task until it is done. The museum provides youth those opportunities to fail and learn about the importance of persistence. Educators work with makers to turn those challenges into teachable moments. Cocciole provided the following example from a summer camp:

*We're strong proponents of learning by failure. Just to give you an example, we had the summer camps last year which were really great, but there were some difficult things in it. We had a few of the kids, you know, crying. You never want to have a kid crying in your space apart from like hot-glue gun*

*Table 1. KID museum summer offerings (2018)*

| Grade Band | Camp Title Description | Description |
|---|---|---|
| 2nd–4th | Fun in the Sun | Building rockets, balloon launches, motorized fans |
| 2nd–4th | Around the World | Explore cultures and making traditional artifacts from the cultures (kites, wooden sandals, etc) |
| 2nd–4th | Harry Potter | Create artifacts from the movie (code a wand, create sound effects) |
| 2nd–4th | Inventioneering | Solve engineering challenges |
| 2nd–4th | KID Arcade | Make versions of classic arcade games |
| 2nd–4th | Music Makers | Create your own instruments and make music with your camp ensemble |
| 5th–7th | Toy Hackers | Open toys up, harvest parts, hack controllers, and bend circuits |
| 5th–7th | Design-It | Learn maker skills such as programming Arduino boards, creating analog circuits, and wielding power tools |
| 5th–7th | Wearable Gadgets | Create "smart" electronic-embedded clothing that you can interact with and control |
| 5th–7th | Strategy Board Games: Fab Lab Edition | Explore board game strategy and design, and then using 3D printing, laser cutting, CNC routing and digital graphic design, create custom versions of these games. |
| 5th–7th | Video Game Design | Learn the high-level coding that goes into your favorite video games. |
| 5th–7th | Pinball Wizard | Make your own working pinball machine and along the way, learn to use power tools, try 3D design and printing, and power things up with circuits. |

*burn or something like that, but they were crying, and we said, "Okay, this is a good point to just sort of come off to the side for a minute. Let's think about the project." They came over, sort of cooled down, rested for a few minutes, and then went back, and had a deeper experience and eventually got their project to work.*

Along with its middle school programming, KID Museum has developed the "Mind of a Maker" framework, a set of six high-level skills and corresponding habits of mind. Making (engineering, design, tinkering) is an ideal vehicle to ground these high-level skills for middle schoolers so they can see specific instances of themselves practicing these skills. These six characteristics are further reinforced in reflection journals that students of multi-session programs maintain.

- EXPLORATION
- CONFIDENCE
- GRIT

- TECHNICAL SKILLS
- COLLABORATION
- AGENCY

The museum's motto is "Every Kid a Maker" and all forms of making are open to everyone. Girls with power tools and boys seated at sewing machines fail to be noticed as anything other than students engaged in making. In the museum, they also have a mandate to promote female making, and also work with underserved communities within the space because they believe it will lead towards getting those higher-paying STEM jobs. The mandate is carried out by their hiring practices, with only two males on staff, and through their work with Title One elementary schools. While they have occasionally run female-only events like a Girls-Got-Game video design class and Happy Hour of Code for Girls they limit running female-only programs as it does not change perceptions of girls in STEM for the broader population. Cocciole commented:

*We have had some girls-only events, and we all sort of struggle with that, because if you have girls-only video game design class, then the boys aren't seeing that the girls can do it. We have offered them, but we don't do that a lot. Every time we have, they've been tremendously popular. We've had Happy Hour of Coding for Girls Only. I mean, it filled up within minutes I think. It was just very, very popular, but again, we want to make sure that everybody knows that girls can do that, not just the girls. When you see, that's one of the things I'm really proud about with this program, with the coding program, is the way that they're working together, that you'll see girls and boys working together, and that's a really hard mix, that sixth and seventh grade, to get them to work together but then be respectful towards each other and they are, I mean that's just where they're all at the same starting point on this.*

An example of a project or artifact made in the space is from a summer program called Toy Hack as shown in Figure 6. In the Toy Hack camp youth integrated various up-cycled materials like wood, plastic, electronics, broken toy pieces, and combined them using solder and glue to make new creations.

To start Toy Hack, youth had to re-imagine the purpose and function of materials as Cocciole described it:

*Figure 6. Toy hack project*

*This item is no longer a broken glue gun. Cables can turn into arms or legs. Students look at those bins of miscellaneous materials and find a new purpose for them. That is the first step. Then thinking about wood, cutting wood, and measuring, and thinking about how to combine the elements in a way that would be structurally sound, or electronically charged. This type of activity also allows us to talk about issues related to sustainability.*

Youth had three sessions for actually building their Toy Hack models during the summer camp. Journals were used to encourage the youth to write and sketch their ideas. Youth in the camp experienced a modified engineering design ideation type process. In the project youth learned about wind power and experimented with different propeller pitches for efficiency, as well as circuitry and electronics.

Community members have different options when it comes to joining the KID Museum. They can pay an admission price for the day and visit the Open Explore stations, attend a scheduled weekend course by paying a course fee, purchase summer camps, or purchase an annual membership, which provides discounts to workshops, summer programs, and unlimited admission to the museum.

In KID Museum, events often have fees for either instruction or materials, including the Open Build activities which, for the electronics studio, start at $6 for members and $19 ($7 + $12 admission fee) for non-members. Mini-Maker sessions (3 visits) cost $65 for members and $72 for non-members. Weekly full-day camps are $375 for members and $415 for non-members. An individual membership starts at $80, and family memberships are $160, and can be used by any combination of immediate family members and includes up to two adults and unlimited children.

## LEARNING COMMUNITIES

The KID Museum is a place for youth to learn and experience making through mostly formalized courses and some open making times. Establishing learning communities is difficult since many times they have students for such a short duration. Moreover, establishing the composition of the learning community for each school visit is at the discretion of the schools themselves. However, multiple funding sources have supported students from underserved communities and schools. For many of these schools there is often a high correlation of African-American or Hispanic students particularly from highly diverse Montgomery County schools.

A pilot initiative by Montgomery County introduced a grant called Maker Fund that with the support of modest funds, schools were able to achieve maker learning goals. Some schools applied for grants to cover the cost for 25 students to visit KID Museum and the Invention Studio Program. The funds targeted certain schools that had identified needs, and it was up to the schools to select the students that participated in the program. KID Museum was not a part of the selection process for the students, but the grant review process was committed to adhering to the target demographic.

Once at the museum, students were able to create community by working in small groups. Cocciole recalled:

*They're working, on a visit like this, they're working in small groups. The bigger groups, so it's like 12 or 13 kids in each half of the content, and then they'll pair up or maybe three people would come together. And then during the open explore, which is the elementary school visits, where they sort of rotate through three stations, the bigger groups are grouped into manageable sizes, like maybe eight or ten kids in one group, and they're working together in that group on an activity.*

KID Museum has a large staff with a wide variety of backgrounds in areas such as early childhood education, museum education, technology, 3D and industrial design, filmmaking, communications, carpentry, etc. in the museum. In addition to the professional staff, the museum works with high school-aged students in the apprenticeship program. Each year students can apply for the apprenticeship program by completing an application found on the KID Museum website. Students that are selected for the program work with youth ages 5 through 12 and families on weekends and during summer camps.

Apprentices receive professional development training prior to leading activities and can attend specialized courses on equipment or software if they choose. Apprentices are expected to work 12 hours per month in one semester and during the school year they are expected to work weekends. Many form bonds with the kids who come in and develop older-younger student mentor relationships.

These are experiences that are helping shape future career paths, wherever these students are headed. Cocciole explained:

*High school students apply for our apprenticeship program, and we've gotten these amazing candidates, so we've been able to be selective about who we take. And they go through training, and they work for our Outreach Coordinator like here. She helps us on new talent. So. they're used primarily at the weekends. They man the stations, but they're also used for our summer camp programs. They come in the summer and help out.*

Cocciole also talked about the role of the apprentices in creating learning communities:

*... you see our apprentices working, and they've formed bonds with these kids who've come in, and then the kids are coming back to see that particular apprentice whose work for them was, you know. So we get that sort of younger, older kid relationship dynamic, and we have this incredible fan club of our male maker educators, you also see that sense of that mentoring that they're doing outside of the skill building that they're doing, that young boys are looking to male role models, and they're developing those bonds as well.*

## FAMILIES IN THE SPACE

KID Museum is a museum dedicated to cultivating creativity and curiosity in children and families through hands-on experiences. Families occupy the space most weekends, compared to the weekdays and after-school programs. Occasionally, families are able to establish informal learning communities as they come together at the museum. Families are also a significant portion of the membership base for the museum. Families enjoy the economic incentives of membership but also join to be a part of making and the KID Museum community.

In some instances, on the weekends, parents may need to be reminded that the space is not meant to be a place to drop off their kids, but it's meant as a place to engage and learn as a family. Museum educators will assist parents when they are not sufficiently engaged by redirecting them to the learning taking place with their child(ren). Simple redirects like:

*Hey, did you see what your kid just did over here? He just put this together. Have you seen that? I think that's really cool." Helping parents remember, "This is not a drop-off and leave place. We want you to build together."*

The weekends are where families engage in Open Explore interactive activities. Moreover, youth and families are able to take advantage of the open studio times to create and make interest-driven projects. The Open Explore activities, combined with educator facilitation from the museum educators, allows families to engage in deep and meaningful learning activities. Cocciole was encouraged by the level of engagement early on:

*We hear things from parents like, "Wow, I was so impressed with my kid. I never knew that they'd be able to do that." And see that genuine respect being elevated between parent and child or parent towards child. So parents don't feel like, "Well, I'm not an expert in this. How can I show my kid how to do that?" But then when they understand that they can learn from their child too, that changes the dynamic of their interaction.*

## IMPACT ON THE COMMUNITY

KID Museum is having an impact on youth engagement, which is expected in a space that is dedicated to youth and families and a community that has over 150,000 students. The other impact has been on teachers in the area and how they are making the connection to making and learning. Educators are very interested in bringing back the making experience to their classrooms. The museum is working toward building capacity to train and prepare teachers to facilitate making experiences either in their classrooms or in a dedicated maker space.

One avenue has been their work as part of the *Making Spaces program*, a nationwide program supported by Google, the Maker Education Initiative (Maker Ed) and the Children's Museum of Pittsburgh (CMP). The idea behind the Making Spaces program is that KID Museum is a hub for local schools, providing professional development and guidance as the schools develop their own makerspaces. The Making Spaces program uses crowdfunding campaigns to raise money and community support to build out a makerspace or making experiences in the schools. In the first year, KID Museum was one of 10 hubs across the country working with local schools to help them firstly come up with a vision of what their makerspace is, and what they want it to do, and then guide them on developing a campaign to fund the space that the schools will then run. In year 2, five more hubs were added to the national network.

When asked if standing up all these makerspaces in schools would hurt attendance at the KID Museum Cocciole noted that it is something they talk about but right now the museum does not have the capacity to meet the demands of educators in the area and not every school has the resources to come to the museum. Moreover, they believe that having school-based maker programs will still drive interest to visit the museum.

Another peril of school-based maker programs is what is referred to as the "keychain syndrome", where the maker space is institutionalized, and the educational encounter is reduced to all the students making the same keychain. To counter that, KID Museum has established an informal Maker Learning Collaborative, where local educators involved in making come together, in a Community of Practice, to talk about their experiences, share ideas and find ways to harness the learning outcomes with an approach that meets the needs and interests of each school.

## DEFINING A MAKERSPACE

When asked to define a makerspace and the core components of a makerspace Cocciole responded:

*Often the wider world defines it with high-end tools or specific technology and the precise construction of something. But I really like the idea of a makerspace as being a place where you shift perspectives. Taking a known item, material, tool, etc. and turning it into something unique and purposeful for the maker. Or learning something entirely new and along the way, learning more about yourself. They are often spaces that invite collaboration, but also self-direction. It's a space that can provide options for people to look at themselves and their place in the world differently.*

## CURRENT CHALLENGES

The Kid Museum has a lot of momentum and a large, diverse staff. In addition, they offer a vast array of youth-based courses and learning opportunities during the school day, after-school and on the weekends and summer camps. However, one challenge is tied to sustainability and the target audience of the Museum. Cocciole explained that they very much want to serve underrepresented audiences but being located in a relatively wealthy area makes it a challenge to reach those communities.

Even with county and foundation grants, user fees are an important part of sustaining the museum. Location and the fee structure may be obstacles for underrepresented populations from being able to visit the space outside of funded school visits. Membership costs for a family of four is $160, which may be a barrier to participation for lower-income families, through an Access Fund attempts to help some families defray these costs. Moreover, the location of the space may also be a barrier for those coming a long distance without a vehicle. Public transportation is possible via the DC Metro system to buses in Montgomery County. Bus stops are a few blocks away from the physical space. There are additional costs and time considerations for visitors trying to take classes or visit the space.

KID Museum, in its current configuration, is in a temporary space and is planning for a larger (60,000 square foot) space in an arguably better location to serve Washington DC and outlining areas. The vision includes the capacity to serve 250,000 visitors per year and serve as a hub for children, families and educators in the area.

Another challenge for the KID Museum is working with adults. The space is designed for children and families but does not have programs for adults (non-educators) to come into the space when they are without children. They have led Family workshops where the whole family learns together, but there have not been adult-only workshops. They hope to eventually have a permanent home that has a large enough space to hold adult community workshops. Cocciole described the challenge like this:

*Well, we don't work with adults without kids. So, we really don't know how adults want to interact in a makerspace. We hope to eventually have a permanent home that has a large enough space that we could have an adult community, but right now, adults for us are only as they are connected to children, either bringing children in, or experts who are coming in and sharing their knowledge with children. But we don't see adults as their own individual identity. So, I'd like to know more about that, and how we can, one day, help adult's perspective as well.*

Cocciole noted that under an Institute of Museums and Library Services (IMLS) funded research study with George Mason University, KID Museum educators have led Family STEM workshops at off-site locations by partnering with both the Montgomery County Library system and local STEM experts. This research work has been informative and will guide future programs which bring children and parents together in a STEM learning environment, for workshops both at their home base and at other locations.

## REFERENCES

National Institute of Heal (NIH). (n.d.). *Who we are*. Retrieved January 28, 2018, from https://www.nih.gov/about-nih/who-we-are

National Institute of Standards and Technology (NIST). (n.d.). *About NIST.* Retrieved April 12, 2018, from https://www.nist.gov/about-nist

## KEY TERMS AND DEFINITIONS

**Bethesda, Maryland:** A neighborhood located in southern Montgomery County, Maryland.

**KID Museum:** Makerspace located in Bethesda, Maryland.

**Institute of Museums and Library Services (IMLS):** A US federal agency that provides library grants, museum grants, policy development, and research.

**Maker Education Initiative (Maker Ed):** A us non-profit organization to support maker education.

**Maker Educators:** Educators at the KID Museum trained in many different disciplines.

**Maker Studio Program:** A program at KID Museum with three distinct levels for tools and processes in each of the four studios.

**Mini-Makers Program:** A program at KID Museum for younger makers.

**Montgomery County's Davis Library:** Public library located in Montgomery County, Maryland.

**National Institute of Health (NIH):** Is the leading medical research agency in the U.S. and is charged with improving health and saving lives.

**National Institute of Standards and Technology (NIST):** Is one of the oldest physical science laboratories in the U.S. and supports the development of many technological innovations.

**Open Build:** A program at KID Museum that allows youth to choose projects to make.

**Open Explore Program:** A Kim Museum program on the weekends consisting of 8-10 interactive learning stations.

**STEAM:** Science, technology, engineering, arts, and mathematics.

**Title I:** A US Department of Education program to provide financial assistance to local educational agencies and public schools with high numbers or percentages of poor children.

# Chapter 2
# MAKESHOP


## ABSTRACT

*MAKESHOP is striving to improve what is known about making and learning by carefully examining and documenting what practices create the best experiences for learners in a makerspace. At the forefront is the belief in using real materials and real tools to foster learning. Located in the Pittsburgh Children's Museum, MAKESHOP is an exhibit that occupies approximately 3,000 square feet. Approaching the MAKESHOP, visitors see three rings of activities. Very simple tinkering activities are in the outermost ring. More complicated electronics and circuitry-based activities that are somewhat facilitated are in the second ring. The middle ring is the core of the makerspace with the typical makerspace fabrication equipment. Nationally known for its research on informal learning using making technology, MAKESHOP helps other makerspaces get started. Through its work with Google, MAKESHOP will soon help launch nearly 100 makerspaces across the United States. Like many makerspaces, MAKESHOP has challenges in reaching underserved populations. This chapter explores MAKESHOP.*


DOI: 10.4018/978-1-5225-8310-3.ch002

*The space itself is just one part of the story. It's not about the stuff that you put in the space as much as it is about people that they connect with. — Chip Lindsey*

## ORGANIZATION BACKGROUND

Situated in the heart of Pittsburgh, Pennsylvania's North Side neighborhood, sits the Children's Museum of Pittsburgh. Opened in 1983 in the basement of the old post office, the museum has become a cultural and educational treasure for the neighborhood, the city, and the country. Around 2004, the museum was expanded and the post office was connected to the former Buhl Planetarium to create 80,000 square feet of space that has more than 250,000 visitors per year.

Within the museum is the relatively new MAKESHOP, which was established in 2007 and consists of 3,000 square feet of space dedicated to DIY making by using new and old technologies with youth and families. The MAKESHOP is a special application of the ethos of the Children's Museum, which has developed over the years through local foundations and citizen groups to foster the learning of skills for children and families using real tools and materials. Understanding this ethos and the community focus of the museum is important to understanding the underpinnings of the MAKESHOP. Chip Lindsey, Director of Education for the Children's Museum, described the museum's philosophy:

*See the motto of this joint, which is here at MAKESHOP: use your tools and raw materials, play with real stuff, create real things and learn the real skills. You won't see Play-Doh in here, you see ceramic clay. You won't see tempura paint silk screen, you see real silk screens and ink. You see real artists working with real crafts in here. Fundamentally, a very important part of the spirit of this place, is that there's great respect for kids and what kids can get if you give them a chance.*

In addition to using real materials and the processes to teach real skills, the museum is also dedicated to responding to the needs of children and families in a sustainable manner, preserving the buildings where the museum is located, using the potential of technology, and improving access to the North Side neighborhood.

Real materials and processes include renowned artists that work and teach in the space. These artists come from many different backgrounds, such as graphic novelists and ceramicists. A Tough Art exhibition features artists who have created exhibitions — some interactive — that are tough enough to withstand children. There are also artists like Ned Kahn, who has created exhibitions across the country and created an amazing cascading exhibit in the studio area for the Children's Museum. Kahn provides a study in material and how it cascades, as shown in Figure 1.

Lindsey noted that unlike many other museums, the Children's Museum of Pittsburgh invests in its partners:

*The other thing that's really fundamentally a very important part of what makes the Children's Museum, the Children's Museum, is that we invest in working with partners ... What I have seen in my career is that a lot of times, children's museums and science centers will want to engage an artist, and they'll go, "Can you just do that thing you do and we can't pay you anything." Here at our Children's Museum, we really honor the artists and respect what they do, so some of the art pieces have labels so that people can read about what they do.*

*Figure 1. Cascades by Ned Kahn*

Unique to the museum is the practice of turning outward to enhance the neighborhood and its residents as part of its mission to increase access and to serve youth and families. In one such project the museum led an effort to revitalize a rundown public area owned by the city near the museum. The museum took what Lindsey describes as an "old, derelict, sunken, trash collector park" and renovated it into a community center. In addition, Ned Kahn was commissioned to build a public art piece called *Cloud Arbor* that emits mist every two minutes and forms a cloud that moves across the park in the summer months. The museum then gave the park and public art piece back to the city with the belief that what is good for the community is good for the museum.

Architecturally, the museum occupies the historic post office and a building that was once the Buhl planetarium. The structures have been mostly preserved, and the science center built an adjoining structure to connect the space. On entering the museum, the MAKESHOP is just behind the lobby on the first floor. Other areas on the first floor include the attic, garage, and a rotating exhibit space, which at the time of the author's visit was hosting an exhibit called Tough Art.

On the second floor is the nursery and the third floor hosts the Waterplay area. The studio, café, and outdoor areas are on the ground floor. The basement includes two classrooms, a group lunchroom, a theater, and a radio station space. In addition to the MAKESHOP, the museum has a number of different exhibits. The attic explores how children perceive the environment around them. It has a number of optical illusion experiences and allows children to experiment with puppets and animateering. Three Andy Warhol works are on display in the attic. Throughout the space are also original materials from the Fred Roger's company, due to the long history of the museum working with Mr. Rogers and his wife.

Another area is the garage where children and families experience hands-on learning with things that *drive, fly, and roll.* The nursery is a place for infants and toddlers, the youngest of the young, to play and explore using lights and colors and other hands-on activities. Book readings and activities throughout the day are also conducted in the space.

The Waterplay space consists of activities that allow visitors to experiment with water. Here they may create a dam, build a fountain, and use a hand pump to move water. The art studio space is a dedicated multimedia studio for children and families where they paint and create with paint, clay, and other mediums.

Visitors also have the opportunity to work with and learn from the artists in residence. In the space, a resident artist, who is a graphic novelist, was inspiring visitors by teaching ink and cartooning techniques, as shown in Figure 2.

The studio space caters to school groups and drop-in visitors. For large school groups, a set of guides meets with the group and leads them through the experience. The museum also helps visitors make the most out of their exhibit area visit by providing tips for before and after the visit. These tips are written for children to maximize their experience in each of the exhibit areas. They also guide visitors on how to interact with the activities and which pieces to reflect on their experience, after the visit.

For guests that have been to the exhibit before, there are ideas for connecting to the space in new and different ways. The art studio tips include the following (Makeshop, n.d.):

- **Tips for Before and After Your Visit to the Studio.** Get dirty. Don't hesitate to become fully involved in your art. We have smocks to protect your clothes and plenty of soap and water to wash up when you are done.

*Figure 2. Children's ink drawings*

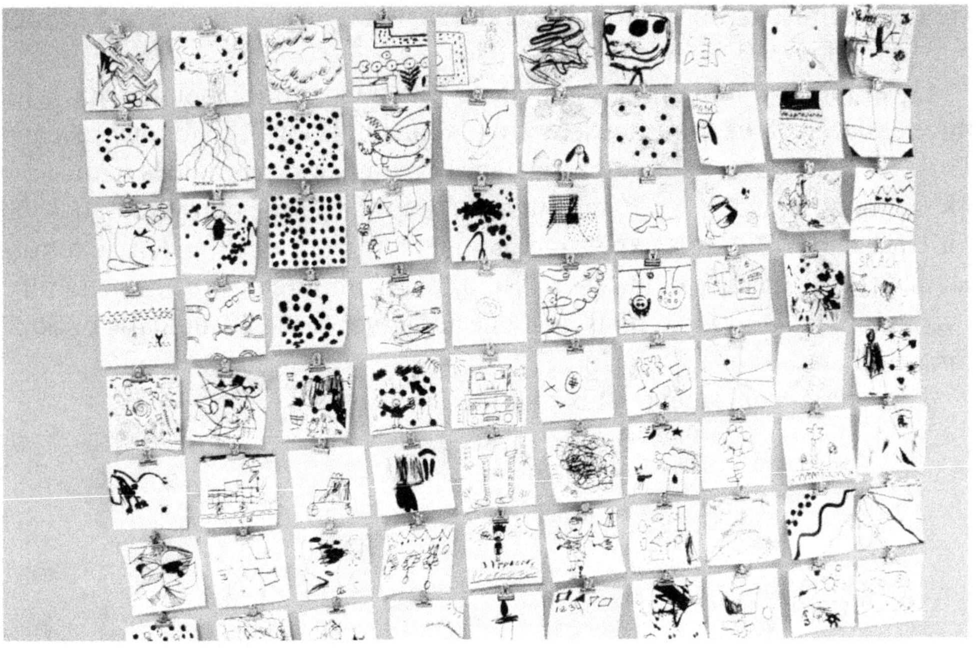

- Focus on the process not the final product. The learning and fun is in the effort that goes into making the art, not necessarily what it looks like when you are done. What tools did you use? How could you use them differently? Art is another language. What are you trying to say?
- Try new things. If you have visited us before, think of new ways to approach old favorites:
- Try color mixing at the easels, what colors can you create?
- Silkscreen both the positive and negative image of your design. How are the images the same and how are they different? Which image do you prefer and why?

The Children's Museum of Pittsburgh is open from 10:00 to 5:00 daily. However, the Studio and MAKESHOP close at 4:30. Admission runs $16 (U.S.) for an adult, and $14 for children ages two to 18 and seniors age 60 and older. Children under age two receive free admission and member guests can visit for $13. Becoming a member of the museum allows unlimited visits to the museum, discount parking, and a reduced price for guests amongst other benefits.

A number of different membership options with one- and two-year membership choices are offered. Examples of types of memberships include a single parent family membership for $115 a year, which provides admission for three children (2 to 18) and one adult. A family membership, which includes admission for up to three children and two adults, runs at $135 for one year and $250 for two years.

Other membership options include an extended family membership with three children of the same household and four adults for $185 for one year and $250 for two years. A grandparent family membership provides admission for up to six grandchildren and two adults for $185 for one year and $350 for two years. The most expensive membership option is the deluxe family membership, which provides admission for six children of the same family, two parents, four grandparents, and one caregiver for $320 annually or $620 for two years.

The overall equipment list is provided in Table 1.

*Table 1. MAKESHOP equipment*

| **General workshop equipment** | **Workbenches**<br>**Sink** | **Vices**<br>**Clamps** |
|---|---|---|
| **General Hand tools (powered)** | Bandsaw<br>Soldering irons<br>Hot glue guns | Hand saws<br>Files |
| **Fabrics** | Looms<br>Needles | Sewing machine |
| **Computing** | Computer microprocessors | WiFi |
| **Digital fabrication** | 3D printer | Laser cutter |
| **Electronics** | Soldering irons | |

*Figure 3. Tinkering areas with bolts*

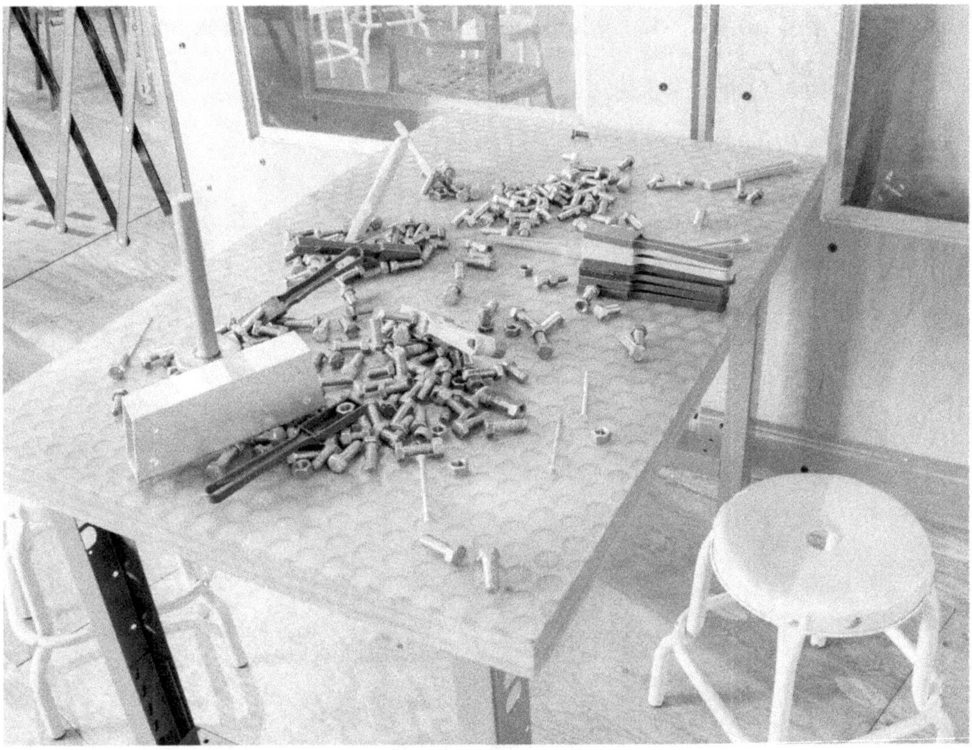

## SETTING THE STAGE

The MAKESHOP started as a prototype in the Attic Space area of the museum for six months prior to being housed in its current space. Visitors to the space experience a gentle approach, beginning with a hands-on introduction to tinkering and making without the need for facilitation. The outermost ring of the space is a carpeted area with different activity stations, including building with bolts as shown in Figure 3.

The second tier of activities is a little more involved and requires some facilitation. Stations include creating circuits from individual components and power supplies with alligator clips or generating electricity with a bike tire as shown in Figure 4. Visitors decide whether they are going to invest more time to move from the carpeted tinkering area to the second tier.

The workshop area of MAKESHOP is the inner sanctum and is an in-depth area that is facilitated by staff. The space can be closed off with a set of doors to promote a focused, deep dive into the activities and materials.

*Figure 4. Bike tire used to generate electricity*

*Figure 5. MAKESPACE workshop area*

The workshop has a laser cutter, band saw, soldering iron, and other tools that require facilitation and instruction prior to use. Figure 5 shows the workshop, looking in from the carpeted tinkering space. The space is used for children and also for teacher professional development.

The MAKESPACE is an area that encompasses and teaches with all technology, old and new, according to Lindsey. An interesting observation he noted from other spaces is the lack of utility around 3D printers. Lindsey stated:

*The other thing that's true about this joint, which was based on results of a survey of all the makerspaces in the country, is that of 60 some odd different makerspaces, 95% of them had a 3D printer and 95% of the printers had an inch of dust on them. It's the first thing that they buy and then they never use it. There's a lot of reasons for that. Laser cutters tend to work better because you can actually do something quickly and get it turned around fast. 3D printers take longer and need a lot of babysitting. They're more in depth and it takes a while ... The other thing is that this place is epitomized by, is that it's not high tech, it's not low tech, it's all tech. Knowing that technology, like old technologies, such as using a loom, is still a really great experience because when you use it and you think about what it is that you're doing, you end up thinking differently about the world. Sometimes technologies are new because they're not good enough to be old so we look at old technologies as being worthy of taking a look at and really examining them as much as the new stuff.*

Facilitators in the studio are either called teaching artists or specialists. Lindsey commented that many of the facilitators have a strong art background, and art is well represented in the space. In a survey done by the museum, respondents felt that the MAKESHOP was representing, equally, art and science, which affirms the goals of the space. Teacher professional development is another common focus for the studio, and many times teachers work in the main area of the studio or in the classrooms, focusing on maker education. An exchange program exists for artists in residence and teachers, whereby staff members are swapped for a year. On the day of my visit, the teacher resident and artist in residence had collaborated and were delivering a teacher professional development workshop on literacy and making. The close collaboration supports new approaches to what the teachers are already covering in their classrooms.

Lindsey also pointed out that the MAKESHOP does not provide curriculum for teachers. He noted:

*That's another peculiarity, I guess, of this place is that, again, very thoughtfully, we don't have curriculum for teachers. Actually, when you start talking to a teacher group and say, "We're here for the museum, and we have no curriculum for you, you see the teachers go, Oh, thank God." They get hit by a lot of groups that say, "We've got the solution to the problem. Here's the curriculum packet." They don't have enough time to do their own curriculum, much less having some do-gooder group come in and foist another set of curricula on them, so we let teachers know they're the professionals in the classroom. They know their curriculum. As a result, we have some things that we find are very compelling for kids.*

Also, unique to the museum makerspace is the idea that it is an exhibit and the success of exhibits for museums is measured in stay times. On the shorter end of the bell curve, visits will last 15 minutes and 45 minutes is probably an average stay time, while the top end will see visits of two hours or longer. According to Lindsey, these stay times are very good compared with the national average of galleries, which is around seven minutes. He describes the national finding as:

*ASTC, the Association of Science-Technology Centers, did a national survey of exhibit galleries. In a 5,000-square-foot exhibit gallery, the average stay time is seven minutes. You could spend $3 million on a 5,000 square foot exhibit and have the average stay time be seven minutes. You can hardly walk through 5,000 square feet in seven minutes, so that means you've got people screaming through ... Who knows what the impact is, but the amount of stay time is pretty short. The interesting thing is that what happens here and certainly in the tinkering studio, the Exploratorium, is extremely long stay times. Something here is working. There are some really important things that are going on. We're trying to impact that.*

Making in museums is a red-hot topic right now, and according to Lindsey, there was a similar interest around 1969 when the Exploratorium in San Francisco, the New York Hall of Science, and the Ontario Science Center opened and grounded their exhibits on phenomena-based experiences, where visitors built their understanding of the everyday experiences by interacting with phenomena (Allen, 2004). These learning models promoted direct experience with natural, physical, and technological phenomena that allowed learners to study and reflect on the problem. These museums, according to Lindsey, experience large increases in attendance and longer stay times very similar to what museums are witnessing with maker exhibits now. In the mid-70s there was a backlash because, according to Lindsey, the instruction was no longer top down, it became constructivist based, and there was an argument that young people were not learning. The constructivist theory of learning (Piaget, 1972) and the constructionist extension by Papert purport that learning is most effective when part of a learning activity involves constructing a meaningful product (Papert, 1993). These theories reason that students' new knowledge is actively constructed from the world around them through experiential practice and by independent/guided research to integrate new knowledge and to arrive at a deeper understanding.

As noted by Lindsey, there were also exhibitions that may not have followed the tenants of constructivism:

*Additionally, you had exhibit design firms who were going, "Whoa, lot of interest here. We could make some money." They started designing museum exhibits that were interactive because that's the difference. It's interactivity. That's the difference that it is making. There's a parallel there. You saw a lot of exhibit designers who created exhibits that were not based on constructivism but were based on B.F. Skinner, positive reinforcement, negative reinforcement, so push the button. That's wrong, bing, got it right. Read the label, push the button. That's not the same focus. As a matter of fact, it's about as far away from that philosophy as you can get. They produced a lot of museum exhibits, and then the curators were right. They're just running around punching buttons. In fact, yes.*

An important asset of the space and the museum in general, is the significance staff have placed on pedagogy and the unpacking of learning that happens in MAKESPACE. Research and practitioners work together to test and refine learning experiences that take place. Many of the studies are led by two research scientists: Lisa Brahms, Ph.D., Director of Learning and Research, and Peter Wardrip, Ph.D., Learning Scientist, both on staff at the museum. Most recently, the two published a chapter titled 'Taking Making to School' (2016) in the chapter book *Makeology: Makerspaces as Learning Environments*, Volume 1 (2016). Lindsey commented about the importance of the research that happens in the space:

*Research asks the really important questions. When you change those materials, when you were working with that kid, what were you looking at? I noticed that the kid was doing this, so I wanted to go deeper. Let's talk about that. Researchers that are unpacking the thing that practitioners do instinctively, reflecting that back, asking good questions and then the practitioners are going, "Oh, that's what it's called." Then they become very articulate in talking about the learning that happens. We don't do that here. Why don't we do it? Because we believe these things. These are the behaviors, these are the activities that we want to reinforce, and that's not one of them.*

*All the sudden, you have this clarity of vision. It's a very articulate way of thinking about the kind of learning of the makerspace that ultimately will help the field go, "It's not about getting the 3D printer and a couple of work tables, and then we're done."*

The role of the practitioner is very important to unpacking the learning, as practitioners provide deep learning experiences for young people as they engage with real tools and materials. As Lindsey points out, other newer spaces may not have had the chance to consider the role of the facilitator in the space and may have more of an equipment focus, i.e. making sure every student makes a keychain on the 3D printer. These types of spaces may be looking for one outcome from all students, whereas in the MAKESHOP they expect highly divergent outcomes based on student choice. It's not a make-and-take environment but one where young people choose what and how they make with the materials at hand. Lindsey stated:

*There will never be a make-and-take activity in MAKESHOP, because by its very nature, you end up with, "I want my thing" and you put the stamp on it, off they go, and you can't tell one thing from another. There's no creativity. There's nothing that comes out of the learning to make that special.*

Free choice learning is another important concept and is taken very seriously in the space. In the museum if an exhibit is not compelling, visitors will "vote with their feet" and walk away. Since it is an informal learning environment, it's not possible to force people to participate or commit to the learning unless they see the benefit of participation. In the museum environment, materials and activities are set out and visitors will choose to participate or walk away. Assessment, according to Lindsey, is how fast they run away from the exhibit. That is how free choice learning happens in the museum, and it is "feral learning, learning in the wild." Even larger school groups do not experience make-and-take activities, but they participate in activities that again are using real materials and tools.

In some instances, the space does perform direct teaching out of necessity. For example, when using soldering irons, it is imperative that youth learn how to properly and safely use them. To begin using the soldering iron is to allow them to see what happens when the soldering iron is in use and to hear from the teaching artist to understand what they are trying to do with the tool. The conversation will go something like this:

*They'll start by allowing them to see what happens and then hear from the facilitator, "This is what I'm trying to do, this is what you look for," letting youth hold the soldering iron, and this is the hot bit, if you touch that your finger will fall off. But if you follow the rules, you can do whatever you want." So, then you open up the landscape in front of them. They know that they've got the thing that can damage stuff. "Don't leave it on the table or you'll burn a hole in it or start a little fire." ... Then you can see that learners are treating it with respect and then for themselves and the people around them, then you step back and they're doing it.*

It's always a challenge to figure out what experience and background knowledge a learner brings to the space. Lindsey talks about how to gauge where learners are at:

*You have to sort of watch for people who are coming in and not sure whether they want to invest, and then you can sort of welcome them in and say, "Hey, this is what we're doing. We're soldering wires to make, whatever. Have you ever soldered before?" "No." That's good. Sometimes they say, "Yes, I haven't."*

*"Have you ever used a sewing machine?" "Yes!" And so there's that negotiation and that's what's so fascinating because me being from a traditional museum environment and a traditional classroom environment, I'm always nervous like, whoa, these people just entered, somebody should be like intercepting them, and the teaching artists here know that it's okay if people just wander in and watch what's going on because there's this natural way that people get closer and their body language changes and then they'll sit down and then you can say, "Hey, we're sewing today, have you ever sewn before? Do you want to use a needle and thread?" And you can gauge very quickly what level that person's comfortable at and then look for them to level up.*

*For some reason, the sewing machine is the thing that people go when asked "Have you used a sewing machine before?" "Yes." And the facilitator goes, "Really, where did you use it?" ... a lot of times kids will say, "Yeah I've used it before," and they haven't. I don't know if it's they've watched their grandmother and so they sort of have this sense that they know how it works but the teaching artists don't just go on what the kids say. They say, "So tell me about that. What does it look like and what did you sew?" And when they find out that the kids haven't used a sewing machine before, they really start at ground zero. It's never an assumption that what the kids say is true. That's like, tell me about it.*

On average, MAKESHOP will see 5000+ visits per month. Visitors are evenly split between male and female visitors.

*Figure 6. Ethnicity of membership*

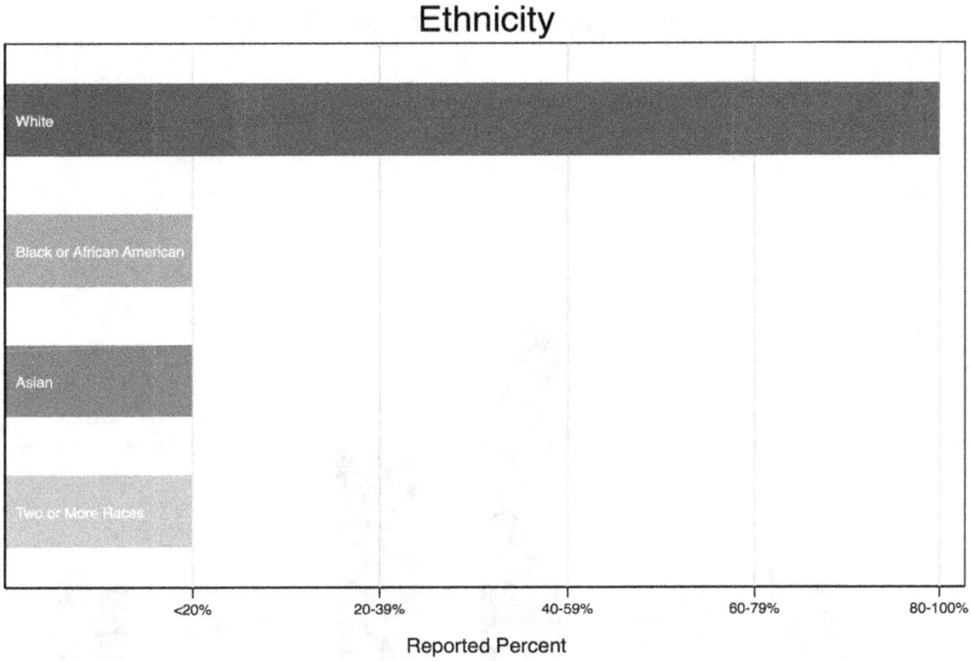


The ethnicity of visitors is shown in Figure 6. About 80 to 100% are white, less than 20% are black or African-American, Asian, and two or more races that may be included in the other ethnicities.

The types of users that visited the space are shown in Figure 7. Less than 20% of users are visitors, teachers and college age students while 20 to 39% are hobbyists, 40 to 59% are youth under the age of 13, and 20 to 39% are youth ages 13 to 18.

The purpose of visits to MAKESHOP are shown in Figure 8. Around 20 to 39% of visitors were there for an introduction to learning, 40 to 59% to socialize and less than 20% were there to receive training, instruction, or learn a skill and make something specific.

## LEARNING COMMUNITIES

Pittsburgh has a vibrant making community, with an estimated 120 groups in the city; supported by local university connections from Carnegie Mellon University, the University of Pittsburgh, Duquesne University, and Robert

*Figure 7. Types of visitors per month*

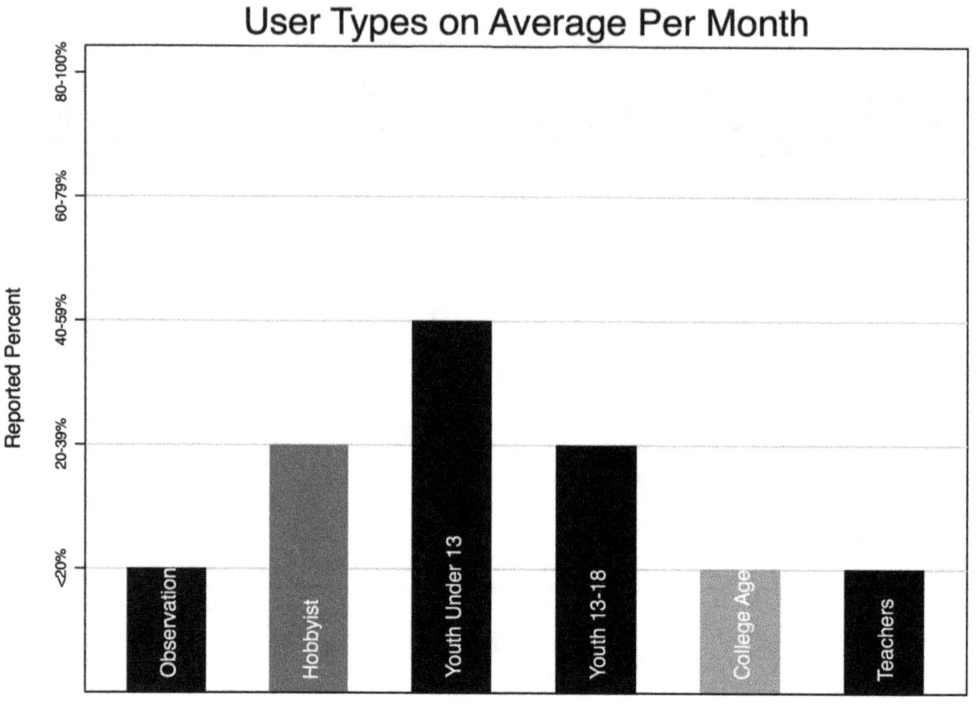


Morris University. In particular, the University of Pittsburgh's Center for Learning in Out-of-School Environments (UPCLOSE) worked closely with the museum to develop the framework for MAKESHOP.

MAKESHOP has spent a lot of time and effort to try and understand learning through making, and to that end they have developed principles of practice to facilitate maker-based learning experiences. Lindsey explained a card game titled *MAKING CONNECTIONS: Facilitating Learning Through Making* that they use with facilitators to help them understand the principles of practice. The game is for groups of two to six players. It is meant to be a way to introduce the three factors (learners, learning objectives, and strategies) that are related to the facilitation of a maker experience.

The practices originated in a published report by Lisa Brahms and Peter Wardrip, titled *The Learning practices of making: An evolving framework for Design,* published in 2014 for the Children's Museum of Pittsburgh. In the report Brahms and Wardrip situate practice-based learning and making in the social and cultural theories of learning (Brahms & Wardrip, 2014). Using the definition from Spillane (2012) they define practices as coordinated,

*Figure 8. Purpose of visits per month*

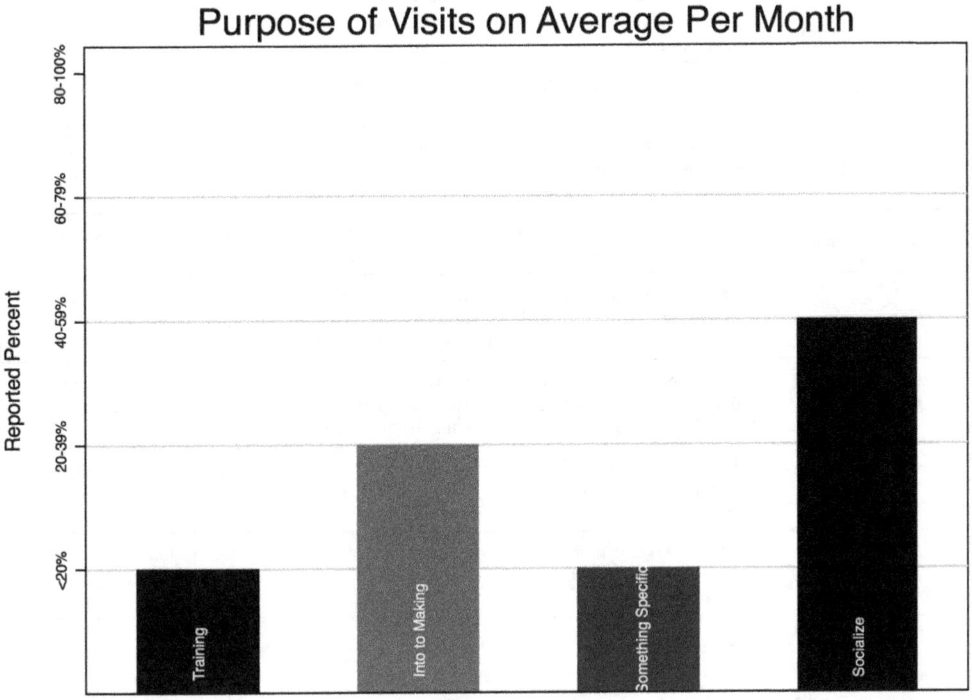


*Table 2. Facilitation strategies*

| | | | | |
|---|---|---|---|---|
| Congratulate Curiosity | Be Impressed by Everything | Have Them Describe the Project to You | Create a Real-Life Comparison | Take Away the Finish Line |
| Show Off Other's Work | Ask Them to Ask Another | Ask them to Teach You | Be the Devil's Advocate | Be a Quiet Sounding Board |
| Level the Playing Field | Expose Your Own Thinking | Ask Them to Teach Another | Work in Parallel on Something Else | Celebrate Small Victories |
| Think Out Loud | Feign Ignorance | Tell Them What to Expect Before They Arrive | Abandon Them Once They Are Safe | Ask Them Why Twenty Times |
| Step Off the Podium | Let Them Sound Smart | Simplify | Suggest a Starting Point | Grant Permission to be Silly |
| Show Them Their Progress | Be Patient | Suggest a Sketch | Inquire About Their Process | Think About Thinking |
| Make Them the Model | Reassure Them of Their Progress | Give Real- World Examples | Make Them Feel Dangerous | Provide a Reference |
| Dare Them | Introduce a New Variable | Scale Up | Encourage Planning | Provide a Soundtrack |
| Tell Them Why You Love It | Expect Greatness | | | |

*Table 3. Learner types*

| | |
|---|---|
| **The Template-Bound** | The Template-Bound learner is engaged and motived to try new things, but prefers to have direction, clear goals, and expectations set in advance. |
| **The Lone Wolf** | A Lone Wolf is confident in their ability, values trying new things, and enjoys the unexpected of the making process, but prefers to work independently |
| **The Hesitator** | The Hesitator is interested in the making process but might be uncomfortable with the possibility of failing, shy away from experiences that seem difficult, and may need reassurance along the way. |
| **The Window Shopper** | The Window Shopper loves to try new things and is drawn to activities that have a fast result but may not have the patience to engage deeply over time. |
| **The Novice** | The Novice learner has never been to a makerspace or engaged with the materials, tools, and processes of making before, may approach the learning experience with assumptions, or not know what to expect or how to proceed. |
| **The Lifeguard** | Lifeguard learners are eager to take part in the experience, but their anxiety of failure and fixed notions of how to engage with certain materials, tools, and processes can make it difficult for them to fully embrace the making process. |
| **The Scout** | The Scout is open, fully engaged and comfortable in the making process; they enjoy messing around with materials, trying new things and sharing their exploration with others. |
| **The Observer** | The Observer is more comfortable sitting back and watching what is going on around them, and thinking through the process on their own, before engaging in the process directly. |

patterned, and meaningful interactions. Furthermore, these practices in the making environment define the learning communities and can be observed and/or recorded as evidence of learning engagement in making.

Facilitators involved in the Principles of Practice card game have five simple rules to follow. First, five to ten facilitation strategy cards are distributed to each player. There are 42 facilitation strategies in the game listed in Table 2.

The *Facilitation Strategies* are ways to help and encourage learners as they work through the making experience. However, these strategies will work better with some learners than others, and that brings about the second step of the game. In this step, one 'Learner Type' card and one 'Learning Practice' card are placed face up on the table, or whatever playing surface the facilitators are working from. There are eight Learner Types that have been identified, which are listed in Table 3.

Lindsey provided detailed descriptions of the Lone Wolf, Window Shopper, and Template Bound learners:

*Lone wolf, window shopper, you see this a lot with human beings and with kids in particular ... on a field trip you see it all the time because the teacher will say, "Okay we're going to be in this gallery for a little while," and then the kids just, "Pffff," and then the teacher's like, "I don't know, they're just running around," and then I can saddle up and say, "You know what, we call that window shopping." So the kids will go through the whole exhibit and try things out, which takes them about 20 minutes for 5,000 square feet. Then they'll come back to you, and some of them, usually the gifted and talented, will say "Okay, I'm done," and then you have to say, "No, we're going to spend another 15 minutes in here, so go find something you really like and become an expert at it." Template Bound is also a gifted and talented trait. "Give me the instructions and I'll just do it," then they do it, and they say, "I'm done, move on the next thing."*

Part two of this step of the game is to turn over a Learning Practice card from the deck. There are seven learning practice cards, as shown in Table 4, each representing elements of design and ways in which learners engaged in

*Table 4. Learning practices*

| | |
|---|---|
| **Inquire** | Learners' openness and curious approach to the possibilities of the context through exploration and questioning of its material properties. |
| **Develop Fluency** | Learners' development of comfort and competence with diverse tools, materials, and processes; developing craft. |
| **Tinker** | Learners' purposeful play, testing, risk-taking, and evaluation of the properties of materials, tools, and processes. |
| **Express Intention** | Learners' discovery, evolution, and refinement of personal identity and interest areas through determination of short- and long-term goals; includes learners' responsive choice, negotiations, and pursuit of goals alone and with others. |
| **Seek and Share Resources** | Learners' identification, pursuit, and sharing of expertise with others; includes recognition of one's own not knowing and desire to learn. |
| **Simplify to Complexify** | Learners' demonstration of understanding of materials and processes of materials and processes by connecting and combining component elements to make new meaning. |
| **Hack and Repurpose** | Learners' harnessing and salvaging materials, tools, and processes to modify, enhance, or create a new product or process, includes disassociating object property from familiar use. |

maker activities (Brahms & Wardrip, 2014). Learning practices also provide a common language for making as a learning process.

Step three of the game is to have each player choose one Facilitation Strategy from their hand that they feel could be used to best facilitate the selected learner engagement in the selected learning practice. The players are then instructed to place the facilitation strategy card next to the other two cards. For example, if a player drew the Hack and Repurpose learning practice card, and the Hesitator learning type the player must then think about which strategies would be appropriate. From the list in Table 3 a few strategies that might be appropriate for the Hesitator are: Congratulate Curiosity, Celebrate Small Victories, and Suggest a Starting Point. In the fourth step of the game, players discuss as a group their answers and reasoning for the approach. The final step of the game is to draw different combinations of learner types and learning practices.

Lindsey described playing the game with facilitators:

*So, you can play the game by saying, "Okay, we got a novice and maybe we want to get him to seek and share resources, how do we do it?" and then they can pick one of these. And the staff have found that this creates great stories like, I had this little girl who was… because educators do that, they always speak in stories right? They speak in case studies. I had this kid who ... and then you have to listen for a long time, and ask, "Is there a pattern here?"*

*This is a way of exposing some of those patterns and looking deeper at archetypes and then learning outcomes that we really want to get at, and here are some techniques, not all of them, but some techniques that our folks have found to be useful. It also helps to open up the conversation with our educators to say, "Oh, I always just dare them, it's always a challenge." Well, sometimes you're leaving big chunks of archetypes, where people are away from things that you might want them to be at. It doesn't work for everything so expand your arrows and your quiver so that you can really study and be a good student of the learner and then figure out the ways to make those connections.*

The Principles of Practice are a deliberate and thoughtful examination of learning that happens as communities of practice in the MAKESHOP. Through this practice, the space can promote the type of skills that they are interested in and provide effective professional development to prepare staff as well. Lindsey commented that learning artists in the space use techniques that more or less treat learners as peers in the space. He noted:

*Some of the facilitation techniques include asking, "Hey did you notice what they're doing? Check that out" or "They were having this problem, can you show them how to do that?" The facilitators actively engage the learners as being more competent peers and then teaching, which is great because when it's really crowded you can't not do that.*

During the summer and on weekends, when the teaching artists may be overwhelmed with the number of visitors in the space, they provide activities around a project (scratch programming or Makey Makeys) that will promote the principles of practice. These activities have a low floor for getting involved and a high ceiling for how far learners can advance their skills and knowledge in the project area. Each theme is selected prior to the activities for the week and teaching artists have the opportunity to be trained and gain proficiency so they can guide the program.

Another practice in the space to facilitate learning in communities is the design of the physical space. The height and size of the tables are purposely designed to have people face each other, but not too close, "not in their chili," according to Lindsey. Table corners are also very useful as a place for facilitation, away from the main happenings at the center of the table.

The MAKESHOP does not specifically recruit females into the space but does have practices in place to make sure the space is gender friendly. The space purposefully uses opposite gender teaching artists rather than what is traditional. Therefore, young female teaching artists are creating woodworking artifacts in plain sight of female visitors. In other areas, like sewing, a male teaching artist may be facilitating ways to mend or modify clothing. Again, there is a clear effort to rid the space of gender bias and traditional boundaries, such as females sew and males solder. Lindsey recounted a visit to the space:

*I walked in the other day and it made me laugh because there was sewing going on, and these kids were all making pillows and making whip stitches and these different things. They were all learning from each other, it was great. It looked like a sewing circle and then soldering was going on inside the workshop area, tearing apart old machines and finding the guts and soldering them back together. Around the soldering station were all girls, and around the sewing station were all boys and their moms. I said, "I don't know, I think we got to be more careful about making these gender-assigned roles and stuff," and the parents were like, "Look," and then they started laughing because it hadn't even dawned on us that something weird was happening here. It happens all the time at MAKESHOP.*

Lindsey also recalls how in 2000, the MIT Media Lab reached out to museums to try and figure out how to get scratch and programming into the educational system without being gender biased. MIT approached museums because when they developed the RCX robotics bricks they found they were in the hands of a lot of groups and it was a different demographic than they had thought would use the kits. MIT realized that museums have an important role in making the technology accessible to everyone. Lindsey stated:

*(MIT) realized that there's an opportunity to look at museums and non-formals to try to figure out the right way to get that out in a gender neutral way, in an easily accessible way to lower that floor of, "What do I have to know to get started," to a place where it would work, so one of the seminal moments for me was to think that, oh, museums and non-formal institutions have a role to play in lowering these thresholds of getting in contact with things that are tinkery or makery or programming, and so we still do that, and I think we're becoming smarter about how we talk about it.*

## THE MAKER MINDSET

MAKESPACE is working to create youth who have 21st century skills that are connected to their personal skills. Persistence, for example, is a skill that is found in the space, and visitors learn that they should not fear getting stuck on something because in this learning environment they will get through it.

*We encourage kids to fail and be stuck every day. The cool thing is that the staff of my friend at the Exploratorium would take pictures of those moments, and he kept getting these great pictures of parents and kids, and kids in those moments. He finally had to call everyone together and say, "I don't want to see one more picture of a kid who's on fire, with their eyes lit up."*

Lindsey explained that what is really telling about the space are those pictures that show children really bearing down and focusing on a problem. Parents and educators are often averse to this type of deep focus learning where children struggle until they find meaning from the process. Lindsey noted:

*I want to see pictures of kids really bearing down and learning. Because that's the thing that we as educators, as parents, we see that they're suffering. I say, no, that suffering is good. That's really powerful and educators try to do it – oh, they can't do it, great! And we try to eliminate the hardness of it. But what we as educators need to be more thoughtful about is how is it that we promote that really needy, gritty, uncomfortableness and then allow people to push through it and then revel in the fact that they made it through. But to also pause when they're really struggling and say, "It's hard isn't it? Yeah. This is driving me crazy." It's good to get that.*

The space also provides everyday experiences, those types of hands-on experiences that can be connected to academic (classroom) content. Classroom teachers may also benefit when students have these everyday skills because they have a wider base of knowledge and understanding of how academics and everyday skills connect. Students are using their hands, with real materials to make these connections between academic knowledge and everyday skills. Many stakeholders question what students are learning in the maker environment as it relates to specific academic bits of knowledge. However, the broader importance of what is happening in makerspaces is the learning experience that then connects to the academic content. Many times, students are impoverished, according to Lindsey, because they don't have a rich set of these everyday skills that connect with "academic knowings."

Lindsey described perseverance in the space this way:

*And what I see in the MAKESHOP here is that kids get this really rich way of thinking about everyday stuff that is powerful. That everyday knowing, that everyday learning, and everyday thinking about getting stuck and getting unstuck, and trying this out, and this out, and it works, so what about this? I just need to persevere a little bit longer and I can push through. Those are skillsets that help connect you to the academic stuff.*

Lindsey gave two more examples of how the MAKESHOP can connect everyday knowledge to the academic world. He stated:

*There's a really interesting book that talks about middle tech. What is middle tech? It's all this stuff that's older technology, like balloons. Balloons are interesting toys. You can take a balloon and you can write on it and blow it up and you see the writing expand and get bigger but it gets fainter. And when they started talking about the Big Bang and were trying to get people to understand what that is like and why everything is moving farther and farther apart, they talked about blowing up a balloon. Well, if you've never had an experience with a balloon, then that analogy is totally lost on you.*

*The one before the balloon was the raisins and the raisin loaf. Well, if you've never baked, how far apart the raisins are is totally lost. So, the fundamental, it's these everyday experiences that we're trying to cultivate that are ways that teach skills and perseverance and that sort of stuff but also fundamental ways of knowing that connect the everyday to the academic things that we want people to know.*

## FAMILIES IN THE SPACE

The space is accessible to families a majority of the time when the museum is open. During school days, only a few families with preschool or early elementary children attend. The space has adapted the making activities to engage these youngest of learners. The staff work with children as young as age two, and, according to Lindsey, it is surprising how much a young learner can accomplish in the making environment. MAKESPACE continues to push the boundaries of what is developmentally appropriate for these learners.

Parents are another area of emphasis for the space, and teaching artists learned over the years to help parents become learners. For example, a child deep in learning can be sidetracked by the parent acting as a chaperone with comments and instructions that may not allow learning to progress in the "natural and beautiful way." Teaching artists will try to involve the parents and encourage them to create their own project. In addition, they try to redirect parents when they jump in to attempt to complete the activity for the child. It's not uncommon for the teaching artist to point out to the parent that their child successfully "outsourced their project." Parents who have been outsourced may realize that they need a new strategy for learning with their child in the MAKESPACE.

## IMPACT ON THE COMMUNITY

One of the biggest impacts on the community for MAKESPACE has been its leadership in unpacking the Principles of Practice in the informal making and learning environment. This in turn means a lot of organizations are looking to MAKESPACE for help in starting their own makerspaces. Because of their experience, MAKESPACE staff can help new spaces figure out their goals and objectives and guide them in their investment of time and money.

Nationally, MAKESPACE provides training for all different types of spaces. In one experience, staff provided training for a technical institute in West Virginia that was a manufacturing training space full of CNC routers and milling machines. The space was meant for retraining of people entering their second careers in manufacturing areas. The instructional practice, according to Lindsey, was very direct teaching, the sage-on-the-stage type teaching. MAKESHOP used the card game to train facilitators in the space, according to Lindsey:

*[The training in the space] went like this, "Don't do this or you'll cut your fingers off. Don't do this, you'll wreck the work, don't do this; make sure to follow these steps and these procedures so that the template." ... And then you'll end up with something but it's all of the other stuff that you know is interesting. We did this with them, and they were like really skeptical. They played a couple of hands, and they went, "Can I get a set of these cards, we've got this guy who really needs it." It was validating for me to see that because it is such a direct teaching, that is outcome based. We don't want anybody damaged, we want to turn these people out in the world in six months, and they've got to know these things.*

Within Pittsburgh, five schools and seven libraries have started makerspaces with support and guidance from MAKESHOP. They also provide consultation in the design of physical spaces for schools, libraries, and museums, and provides follow-up training with facilitators by providing a summer boot camp, which is a summer professional development program for formal and informal educators.

MAKESHOP received a large grant for its part in the *Making Spaces* program, a nationwide project supported by Google, the Maker Education Initiative (Maker Ed) and KID Museum in Baltimore, Maryland. MAKESHOP'S part in the grant was to work with 10 schools to help them articulate their desire for a makerspace in their school and run a crowdfunding campaign to fund the space. As of this writing, seven out of the 10 schools established makerspaces in their schools. In the second part of the Google grant, MAKESHOP is working with museums and community organizations across the country that will be regional hubs. Each hub then will have 10 sites it organizes. MAKESHOP's exhibit team is working to design these spaces and, through the exhibit team leadership, 100 new maker sites will be established.

## DEFINING A MAKERSPACE

Lindsey defined a makerspace:

*Some qualities of it are social space. It is authentic tools. Authentic media. It promotes personal expression of ideas and values. It's divergent in its outcomes. It's a way for learners to experience technology, whole technology, and new technology, and it's a wonderful opportunity to cause people to fail quickly and not be upset by it. So, it's an investigation in failure and then ultimately success. We cause children to fail every day in the museum.*

## CURRENT CHALLENGES FACING THE ORGANIZATION

MAKESHOP and the Children's Museum of Pittsburgh provide leadership in informal learning and making. The museum is supported through generous donors, grants, membership fees, and their contract work with other partner organizations. Two issues that the museum is currently working through are equity and cultural competency, and the opportunity to grow the MAKESHOP to serve an older audience.

Equity and cultural competency issues exist, according to Lindsey, because museum attendance does not reflect the number of African-Americans who live in the community. Pittsburgh has a high number of African-Americans, especially in the North Pittsburgh area, but they do not visit the museum in high numbers. The challenge is for the museum to understand the cultural barriers that prevent these community members from taking advantage of what the museum has to offer.

Frequently, schools in the neighborhood, which are up to 95 percent African-American, visit the museum on field trips. To encourage the community to attend, the museum hosted a family night and invited school teachers, administrators, parents, and students on a night when the museum was normally closed. The turnout was very good, more than 450 groups, which was about 275 higher than anticipated. Lindsey commented:

*Everybody showed up. The thing we saw was kids coming in saying, "Come on, the museum is great," with the parent's kind of lagging behind. And then two dads walked in and one said, "Aw man, I haven't been in here since third grade." I interpreted that as a museum is the place that your teacher takes you on a field trip, end of story. Now, you and I would find that unusual because our parents took us to museums when we were kids, and when we're parents, we do those things that we know are the right things that our parents did so we're going to do it too. These families don't have a tradition of going to museums.*

The challenge then for the museum is to create a culture that is inviting to families and get them to explore the learning opportunities outside of the school day, as a family unit. Lindsey believes it will take repetition: having at least three family nights and three exposures to the museum to create the family culture. Another strategy is to provide scholarships for membership for a year, so families get unlimited access, in essence removing the financial barrier. Lindsey discussed removing other perceived barriers for family visits:

*We've removed the financial barrier, and they're here in the neighborhood, so there is not a transportation issue. Then it's just a matter of removing the perceived barriers such as, "I don't know where that place is"; "I don't know if it costs money" is gone. "I don't know if they like people like us" is gone. Getting rid of those barriers is sometimes the most difficult part but once they're gone, we have effectively changed the system because then they're thinking, "It's kind of rainy and cold, what can we do?" "I don't know." "Hey, let's go to the museum." That is good. Then we've won.*

The effect of these efforts included 40 to 50 families using their cards on weekends and holidays, which, according to Lindsey, is "a start." Dialogue with the schools continues in an effort to develop strategies to reach the families in the community.

The challenge, that is actually more of an opportunity for MAKESHOP, is the designing of a new makerspace (Museum Lab) in the building next door. Combining the MAKESHOP staff's knowledge and understanding of the physical space, the Principles of Practice, and their high-level thought process for the design of the space is intriguing. Primarily, the space will be for youth ages 10 to12, teens, and young adults, so it has to be welcoming and differentiated enough from the younger learning programs. The teaching artists and designers are using their knowledge and understanding of learning and making to question every step of the space design. According to Lindsey:

*It [the thought process] is not that no matter what I think, I just do it. That's not good enough. Let's talk about why it is that you did that because it's going to be a really good reason. That's allowed us to think very clearly about how we're going to build a physical space to support the learner-centered or learner-driven activities that go on there.*

The space will again use real materials and real experts doing real work. Lindsey believes that if it's not real work and the tools are not authentic, the visitors will "smell a rat" and the space will not be compelling. Longer duration projects lasting up to a week will also be part of the learning strategies of the new space. Lindsey believes these longer, deep-dive opportunities will allow "transformative" learning processes to occur. It is expected that there will be near-peer learning, with older members teaching younger members in the same way that experts, professionals in their field of work, will be transformed into teaching artists in the new space as well. Lindsey shared his experience of working with pilots that were very interested in teaching high school students about flying. The two pilots had just returned from a workshop and learned about "inquiry learning" and wanted to use the learning strategy. Lindsey commented:

*These retired guys were just on fire. They had a very clear vision of what they wanted to get—kids excited about flying. Totally cool. You've got the experts, you've got a target audience, and then you've got to figure out the connector point. The pilots didn't know teaching, they didn't know kids, but they knew flying. We know teaching, we know kids, and we can triangulate on that. They said, "They learn about flying patterns by doing models, and then you talk to the control tower, they learn that. They learn navigation, even flight simulators, so they get a chance to fly." They learned about aerodynamics, and the physics of flying. It takes a week. So, at the end of the week, do they get to fly - I asked? "Oh no, no, no, they can't fly." "Okay, I said, so if we do this, it's going to be a week long and on the last day they all fly."*

According to Lindsey, this flight activity was the most influential one he had ever engaged in. He watched these young learners be transformed because the activity was authentic. On the last day, the students got to fly. One young woman in the class stepped into the plane, which was sitting at a small airport with no other air traffic. She was strapped in and the plane took off, with her parents watching. The plane flew around and made a big loop around the area and landed. According to Lindsey, the conversation with her parents went like this:

*Her parents are like, "Pheww," after the plane landed, but when their daughter gets out, she's just like on fire. "Oh, my God! I know what I want to do for the rest of my life." This is a 13-year-old, right? And then the mom said, "Did you get to touch the controls?" And the daughter said, "I took off, I flew with the pilot. I made the landing approach and then the pilot took the controls."*

The goal of this new space then, is to figure out how to create these deep dives and authentic transformative experiences for visitors of the space. Also, keeping in mind that the activities in the space need to have a low floor and high ceiling for the professionals who will lead activities in the space. The museum has a tremendous number of partnerships in the community with which they can recruit professionals to lead these transforming and authentic experiences for youth in what Lindsey refers to as the "secret sauce" in the space. Overall, the idea is that the space will be an experimental platform for connecting the formal and informal learning environments. While free choice will be part of what happens in the space, it will not be without limits. As Lindsey explained:

*Yeah, it's going to be interesting because I think we're going to need a commitment ... I don't think it's completely open. I think we're setting pallets and then you got a free choice within that pallet of materials or that domain. What we will not support is that everybody's going to end up with an identical copy of a Les Paul you know, or whatever. It's not going to be that. There's got to be some way of allowing the individual to express themselves.*

## REFERENCES

Allen, S. (2004). Designs for learning: Studying science museum exhibits that do more than entertain. *Science Education*, *88*(S1), S17–S33. doi:10.1002ce.20016

Makeshop. (n.d.). *Studio*. Retrieved from https://pittsburghkids.org/exhibits/studio

Peppler, K., Halverson, E., & Kafai, Y. B. (Eds.). (2016). *Makeology: Makerspaces as learning environments* (Vol. 1). Routledge.

Samuelson, P. Wardrip, P. S., & Brahms, L. (2016). Taking making to school. *Makeology: Makerspaces as Learning Environments, 1*, 97.

## KEY TERMS AND DEFINITIONS

**Andy Warhol:** An American artist known for the pop art movement.

**Animateering:** A virtual world of puppets that mimic visitors through a Kinect system as they move.

**Children's Museum of Pittsburgh:** A children's museum in Pittsburgh, PA opened in 1983 with 80,000 square feet of space that has more than 250,000 visitors per year.

**Constructionism:** Theory of learning that states learning is most effective when part of a learning activity involves constructing a meaningful product.

**Constructivism:** Theory of learning whereby learners construct their own understanding and knowledge of the world.

**Divergent Outcomes:** Differing outcomes based on student choice.

**Fred Rogers:** Popular host of the PBS *Mr. Rogers' Neighborhood* TV show.

**MAKESHOP:** A Makerspace established in 2007 and consists of 3,000 square feet of space dedicated to DIY making by using new and old technologies with youth and families within the Children's Museum of Pittsburgh.

**Middle Tech:** Older technology.

**Ned Kahn:** Artists and sculptor that has developed a number of exhibits at the Children's Museum of Pittsburg.

**Principles of Practice:** Deliberate and thoughtful examination of learning that happens as communities of practice in the MAKESHOP.

**Scratch Programming:** A scripting language developed by MIT.

**Stay Time:** The amount of time visitor spends at an exhibit.

# Chapter 3
# Tinkering Studio at the Exploratorium


## ABSTRACT

*The Tinkering Studio is located in the Exploratorium Museum in San Francisco, California. The studio is at the forefront of research and evaluation on engagement and teacher professional development in the use of tinkering and making for learning. Divided into two spaces, a floor area for museum visitors and a learning studio for resident artists, allows scientists and exhibit developers to hone their craft and designs. Central to the visitor's experience is the problem space that permits deep engagement of a phenomena and the opportunity to devise meaning through the process of making or in this case tinkering. Tinkering, in the broadest sense, overlaps a great deal with making. Tinkering oftentimes does not lead to a tangible product, and at times there is focus on aesthetics at the cost of functionality as one tinkers. Learning communities can be a challenge in the space due to the drop-in nature of the visits. Learning communities are formed through a carefully designed learning environment that supports social interactions and educators in the space that connect learners. This chapter explores the Tinkering Studio at the Exploratorium Museum.*


DOI: 10.4018/978-1-5225-8310-3.ch003

*I think we're just trying to create a sense of joyful learning, and that learning can be fun and playful, and that sense of agency and that you can ask a question and develop a way of coming up with an answer to it. —Lianna Kali*

## ORGANIZATION BACKGROUND

The Tinkering Studio is housed inside the famous Exploratorium: The Museum of Science, Art and Human Perception, located in San Francisco, California on Pier 15. Opened in 1969, the Exploratorium has served as a learning laboratory to push the boundaries of inquiry-based learning and hands-on investigations for children (Exploratorium, 2018). The Exploratorium encompasses 218,000 $ft^2$ (20,253$m^2$) with 75,000 $ft^2$ (6,968 $m^2$) of exhibit space. The museum has a full-time staff of 245 employees, 250 part-time employees and 126 high-school-aged staff hired as 'explainers.' The Tinkering Studio consists of about 1000 $ft^2$ (93 $m^2$) of space and is located in the South Gallery of the Exploratorium. Lianna Kali, the Program Leader for The Tinkering Studio, and Deanna Gelosi, Project Coordinator for The Tinkering Studio, provided a tour and answered interview questions regarding the space. The studio, opened in 2013, was purposefully located adjacent to the Exploratorium's machine shop so visitors can witness museum staff create and work on exhibits in the space. The machine shop has a half-wall, allowing visitors to see and interact with staff in the machine shop, as shown in Figure 1. Kali noted:

*… the machine shop is visually accessible to visitors; you can peek over the wall and see people using tools. Especially for some of the ones that are up close, you can ask them questions about, "What are you working on? What's this machine do? What are you cutting there?" There's some really neat lathes and things; you can see chips coming off. It's beautiful.*

The machine shop models tinkering, as most exhibits in the space are built and maintained at the museum and, according to Kali, the process to develop exhibits follows the tinkering process. Developers of exhibits in the space get an idea, build prototypes, and then watch as people interact with the prototypes. The Exploratorium has a dedicated space for exhibit prototypes that allows developers to view their prototypes in action and if they break quickly, pull them back to fix. Kali explained:

*Figure 1. Looking into the machine shop*

*... that process that developers go through is what we hope visitors will go through too when they're in the Tinkering Studio. It might be a different scale of tools and of course, a different time length of how long you're working on an idea, but that process is really similar.*

An interesting observation about the exhibits in the space is that the signage requests that visitors interact with the exhibit. Signs will ask visitors to move a part or test a part of the exhibit. Kali pointed out the Tinkerer's Clock shown in Figure 2, as an example, has cranks at the bottom to move automata at the top of the clock. Kali explained:

*We have some art pieces, like the Tinkerer's Clock, which was built by Tim Hunkin, who's a collaborator and colleague. So, each of the figures on the clock is an automata, where you can turn a crank at the bottom and see it move up above. Then on the hour and half hour, it does a performance, which is kind of fun.*

*Figure 2. Tinkerer's clock*

Prior to moving into their current location in 2013, the Tinkering Studio was more of a prototype area where designers would take activities out into the space for a short time and then bring them back. Staff would cycle these activities periodically and over time it developed into the idea as a programming/floor space for visitors. Prior to moving, the studio prototyped many different activities and configurations. Kali noted that they painted the walls almost every other week. These iterative design and prototyping efforts prepared the group as they sought to move into the Tinkering Studio. According to Kali the reason for the move was, in part, from a grant from the National Science Foundation. She recalled:

*The directors of the Tinkering Studio, Mike Petrich and Karen Wilkinson, were part of an NSF-funded grant called the PIE, which stood for Play, Invent, Explore or Playful Inventive Exploration. It was them, as well as several other colleagues at other museums, so Explora in New Mexico was one, AVAM [American Visionary Art Museum] in Maryland was another, and there were others on the project as well. That was really about doing these playful and inventive workshops. So, from that grant, because the activity seemed really rich, people were very engaged with them. People loved this "learning through making" idea. So, they said, "What if we could turn this workshop experience into a floor environment?" That's how things like our marble machines area came to be. A lot of our initial prototypes with marble machines were on these two foot-by-four-foot boards that you could work on with a partner. We still do it that way in workshops, but we use a lot more materials.*

The Tinker Studio is slightly set back from the main museum corridor and is marked by beautifully designed gates, as shown in Figure 3. These gates are adorned with a number of hand-tools welded together and serve as a way to close the space to visitors when needed.

The Tinkering Tiles exhibit hangs on the wall and is another clear demarcation for the space. These tiles were created using different techniques and spell the technique that they are made with, as shown in Figure 4. A tile made from felt, for example, will have the word "felt" on it.

The workshop area is where the facilitated experiences occur. At the time of the author's visit, the area had an activity called Light Play, as shown in Figure 5, where visitors were experimenting with light and shadow. Gelosi expanded on the Light Play activity:

*… one thing we've been trying to experiment with is the different ways that people can experience Light Play. I know there's [sic.] a couple of stations that have these little screens and almost stages that people can build on, and then the two in the back have canvases so people can project their light play onto these walls. Those are really interesting, because I find that those*

*Figure 3. Studio gates*

*are very collaborative spaces. You'll see groups of three, four, five kids, especially on field trip groups, coming in and setting up in front of those screens, whereas the smaller ones are a little bit more intimate. It might just be two people or maybe just one person building in those sorts of settings. We'll find that certain materials have high value in the space. We have this giant boar, like a large pig, that's very popular. Horses are really popular. But also, certain material types. We use Mylar, which was new to me before I came here, but it makes this very cool effect that I just learned the word for today, which was caustic. It makes these really cool caustics that have a really nice feel to them. So, people will experiment with mood or feeling. Sometimes you'll have visitors come in and say, "I'm making this very dark scene," and they've got bats in the background, and its red lights and things. Some are like, "I've got a pony, and it has sparkles!" So, we also like to encourage that storytelling element as well in the space.*

Visitors will spend 20 minutes to two hours in the workshop area, which is an eternity when compared to a typical 30 seconds that visitors will give to a standard exhibit. Two staff members are usually in the workshop facilitating the activities in the space. During the week staff take the opportunity to

*Figure 4. Tinker tiles*

prototype different ideas for the activities. Adding programming elements to change colors of the light and control the speed on the motors for example. The staff will facilitate the prototypes in pairs and debrief each other on the effectiveness of the prototype. During busier times, the space will utilize their cadre of paid high-school explainers. The Project Explainers spend time at The Tinkering Studio and help facilitate activities with visitors especially on the weekends. Explainers receive additional training and preparation to be able to work in the Tinkering Studio. The core phenomena and associated activities in the main problem space frequently change. For example, prior to Light Play, the space had a lot of cardboard activities building automata and in the future it might be a totally different display.

*Figure 5. Light boxes*

Visitors can't take the Light Play models home, so the space allows them to display their creations in a cabinet. In other activities visitors have that option, as Kali explained:

*With Light Play, when they're done, the culminating thing is to put it into the display cabinet if they want. Other times, I'll just say, "You can leave that as an example for the next person who comes through," supporting that. With things like scribbling machines, we've done experiments with having a table with a big roll of paper that they'll test on that roll of paper, and then we can essentially roll it and pin it to the wall so that your drawings become this revolving test that fills up the space. So that's another thing to try.*

The space recycled a vending machine to sell common components to visitors. According to Kali the purpose of the machine is to allow visitors to continue to tinker after they leave the space. She noted:

*It [the vending machine] was actually donated to us by the guy who maintains the vending machines in the staff room. He was like, "Hey, I got this old one. Do you guys want it?" And we're sort of hoarders, so we said "yes." One of the reasons that it was important for us to have something like this is because we want people to keep tinkering beyond this space, but a lot of times, it's just like, you just need the hobby motor, you just need the conductive thread. "I've got everything else, but I don't have an LED." So we sell everything at cost, but it's a nice way so people can continue to keep tinkering outside the space. The machine's kind of funky and it only takes one-dollar bills, so everything's in our shop too because having seven one-dollar bills for buying LEDs might be kind of tough. And we try to put funny things on it too, like, "These are tools for tinkering! Please don't eat them."*

In a separate area is the staff workspace, amply named the Learning Studio (shown in Figure 6), where things are prototyped in preparation for use on the studio floor. The space is an active research and development area where new ideas are tested and considered. For example, Kali noted that staff might be interested in combining physical and digital tools in the space using a coding program and machine. The space is closed to the public but they do host professional development workshops for after-school educators, teachers, museum professionals and librarians. The space is also used for bi-monthly Bay Area Maker Educator meet-ups. Kali also explained other uses of the space:

*We also use it for artist residencies. So, if we have an artist-in-residence with us, they'll get a touch-down space in here to really develop their project. Every residency is super different, like Tim Hunkin who built the clock will come and do a residency with us. He tends to take over the shop, because that's his process. We had another residency who was an illustrator, and she did this amazing drawing of everything that was in the space at that time. It was amazing. She counted every single book, and then she'd draw a book and then do "X... " however many there are.*

The tools for making, located in The Learning Studio, are generally not accessible to the public unless it is part of the problem space in the Tinkering workshop area. The Learning Studio has ample storage space and a variety of bins, as shown in Figure 7. The space contains a cabinet filled with LEGOs, a materials wall and work tables throughout. There are wood tools, like a scroll saw, chop saw and drill press, as well as hand tools. Along the outer wall is a vinyl cutter, laser cutter, and 3D printer. Gelosi explained that these machines are used for prototyping:

*Figure 6. The learning studio*

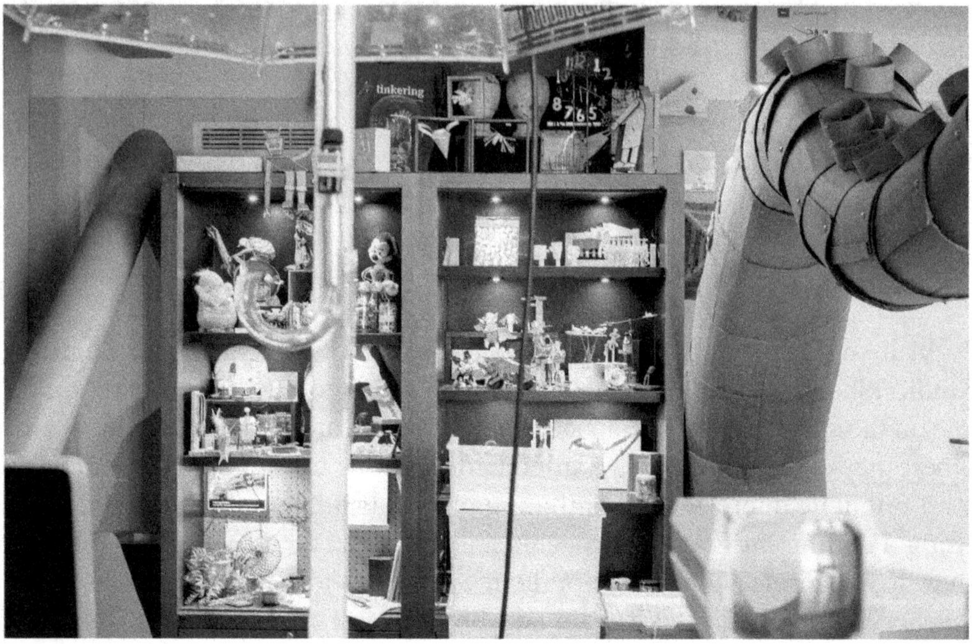


*So, these are often used for some quick prototyping type things. We'll use the vinyl cutter for an event, where it's like a baby shower. We were making stencils for little onesies. We'll use the laser cutter for just about any materials that we can use it for. The 3D printer, we'll use to make smaller little elements. We've used them to make pen-holders for a different type of art machine that was spinning around pens and things like that. It's a very used space, right here.*

Kali talked about the importance of prototyping in the space and how the tools lead to rapidly designing and testing ideas. She stated:

*What I also love about it is you can get an idea, you can test it out real quick, you can bring it on the floor with visitors. What I want to learn more about is how to make it not like we're doing an activity, so you can use the laser cutter, but we're doing the activity and the laser cutter is one of the many tools available to help you solve your problem.*

The overall equipment list is provided in Table 1.

*Figure 7. The Learning Studio bins*

*Table 1. The Tinkering Studio equipment*

| | | |
|---|---|---|
| **General workshop equipment** | Sinks<br>Shop vacuum | Dust/fume extraction<br>Workbenches |
| **General Hand Tools** | Drill<br>Jigsaw<br>Brad nailer<br>Dremel | Pin nailer<br>Hand sander<br>Hand router<br>Circular saw |
| **Woodworking** | Band saw<br>Chop saw | Drill press<br>Scroll saw |
| **Textiles** | Sewing machine<br>Hand needles | Knitting machine<br>Looms |
| **Computing** | Computers<br>Server | Tablets |
| **Plastics** | vinyl cutter | 3D printer<br>Vacuum former |
| **Glass** | Scoring tool<br>Grozing pliers | Shearing pliers |
| **Painting and Graphic Arts** | Screen printing materials | |
| **Digital fabrication** | 3D printers<br>3Doolder | Laser cutter |
| **Electronics** | Soldering irons | Multimeters |
| **Audio and Music** | Instruments | |

The Exploratorium has been around for over 40 years as an institution and tinkering has always been part of the inquiry learning process. When they decided to create the Tinkering Space for visitors, according to Kali, it was a seamless addition since the museum had adhered to the practice of inquiry learning for years. Having visitors go through the same tinkering process felt "natural." What staff had to confront as far as trust was the safety of their visitors. They had to be aware of and mitigate potential dangers through a documented safety plan. As Kali explained:

*... trust came up as something to be aware of, was in the sense of visitor safety. When we wanted to do spot welding or using drills or soldering on the floor, it wasn't that someone said, "No, you can't do that," but more, "Let's make a plan together so we know you're doing it safely." So, we have a documented safety plan for whatever the "dangerous" tool might be. We have a plan of how it will be facilitated, how we are addressing visitor safety concerns. For example, soldering, if we're gonna have two soldering irons out, that means we need at least two facilitators in the space. We set up fume extractors, we only use lead-free solder, we provide hand wipes for when visitors are done so they can clean their hands before they go in case they're going to lunch, because we don't want them to eat after soldering. Things like that. Ironically, the most dangerous thing in the museum is the stools. People fall off of them, because they're tippy. Our space is comparatively very safe, even when we're doing things that might be considered "dangerous."*

In previous exhibits the space has done spot welding and soldering in a number of different configurations, according to Kali. Some activities combine soldering with paper circuits, for example the Copper Crowns activity used soldering to attach LEDs to make headpieces or other things that can be worn. Glue guns are a staple in the space because of their usefulness. Woodworking tools like saws and drills have also been used in the space with visitors.

## SETTING THE STAGE

The space is open to anyone that has access to the museum and there are no specific membership options to join the Tinkering Studio. Daily fees to the museum in 2017 were $29.95 for an adult (18 to 64), $24.95 for seniors over 65, teachers, students and youth ages 13 to 17 and $19.95 for youth ages 4 to 12. Children under the age of three are not charged an entry fee. There are membership options to the museum starting at $45 for two adults and $149 for a family of up to four children, all the way to $249. Again, these are general memberships and fees and the cost to explore the Tinkering Studio is not an added cost but open to anyone in the museum.

The Tinkering Studio is well known for studies and dissemination of results conducted in the space. Once such study titled 'Learning Through STEM-Rich Tinkering: Findings From a Jointly Negotiated Research Project Taken Up in Practice' was published in 2014 by Bronwyn Bevan, Joshua P. Gutwill, Mike Petrich and Karen Wilkinson in the *Science Education Journal.* In the article the authors put forth a Tinkering Learning Dimensions Framework that is used in professional development for formal and informal educators (Bevan, Gutwill, Petrich & Wilkinson, 2014). Kali notes that the Visitor Research Team was looking specifically at what learning looks like in the Tinkering Studio and the Dimensions framework came for that effort. She noted:

*One thing that came out of it was something called Learning Dimensions. The way that product was developed is, our Visitor Research team took tons and tons of video footage of experiences in the Tinkering Studio at our old building. So, they looked at an activity called Circuit Boards, one called Marble Machines, which we saw out on the floor, and then another called Wind Tubes. They looked at it both in facilitated environments and when it was un-facilitated. From that video footage, they called out essentially four dimensions of learning that they observed, and indicators of what those dimensions look like in action.*

The four dimensions include engagement, initiative and intentionality, social scaffolding and development of understanding (Bevan, Gutwill, Petrich & Wilkinson, 2014). Each dimension has an indicator and a description of the learner's behavior. For example, within the learner engagement dimension an indicator would be "spending time in tinkering activities" and a description of the behavior would be "play, envision, make, explore materials over and over." An indicator in the initiative and intentionality dimension would be "persisting to achieve goals in the problem space" and a descriptor would be that learners "persist toward their goal in the face of setbacks or frustration within the problem space." A social scaffolding indicator would be "inspiring new ideas or approaches" with "notice, point out, or talk about others' work." Finally, the development of understanding dimension indicator could be "expressing a realization through affect or utterances" with learner's description of "show excitement when expressing a realization" and/or "claim to realize or newly make sense of something." (Bevan, Gutwill, Petrich & Wilkinson, 2014). According to Kali, the study was conducted at the Palace of Fine Arts, the previous location of the Tinkering Studio.

When asked if the learning dimensions would hold true for other learning environments, Kali and Gelosi noted that at the time of the interview they were actively researching the dimensions in an after-school program. Kali stated:

*We are also, in addition to the work we do here as activity developers and facilitators and doing professional development, we also do an after-school program roughly once a week-ish at Lighthouse in Oakland. Part of that, why we're doing that is to do a research study around research practice partnerships. Deanna [Gelosi] and I, as the educators in the space, are working with our colleague who is a formal researcher. We're doing an ethnographic study to look at what learning looks like in this after-school environment. Essentially, we're revising the dimensions of learning into another document that we're calling a cross-setting learning framework. So how learning in after-school might translate to in-school, how the dimensions of learning are or maybe aren't applicable to this after-school environment. That's under development right now.*

When asked if the Learning Dimensions Framework was compatible and comparable to the Framework for Design developed by Brahms & Wardrip (2014) that originated from the MAKESHOP makerspace located at the Pittsburgh Children's Museum in Pittsburgh, Pennsylvania. Kali noted that the directors of the Tinkering Studio were advisors on the MAKSEHOP project and there are some similarities and differences in the frameworks. Overall, Kali believes the main difference is the focus of the spaces and therefore the focus of the dimensions. She stated:

*I think there's a slight difference of focus of our spaces, where tinkering is the main focus of all the work we do, versus in Pittsburgh when you look at their dimensions, tinkering is just a line on one of their dimensions. They have a different intent in how they're designing their space. It's that we define all of our activity development within a tinkering framework, where we're saying it's art and science and technology and you're asking your own questions and making a personally meaningful artifact. We say all the attributes are part of what we call tinkering as a big umbrella, if that makes sense.*

The Tinkering Studio, on average, will see 250 to 1,000 total visits per month. As shown in Figure 8, 40 to 59% of visitors are female, 40 to 59% are male.

## LEARNING COMMUNITIES

Interactions in the Tinkering Studio are long, by museum standards, but short in respect to building community with other tinkerers in the space. One strategy for building communities is through the support of the high school explainers. These explainers, new to facilitation, are taught to guide and connect youth in the space. According to Kali, explainers, supported by facilitators, might say things like "Oh, you're working on this challenge and that person was working on a similar challenge. Go ask them what they worked on." The staff try to model community building behavior by working with youth in the space so that explainers can see and hear the facilitation. The intent is to support explainers by making them feel comfortable interacting and encouraging youth to build community in the space. Facilitators, also support people, noticing each other's work in creating community and interacting with visitors to learn from each other in different ways. In addition, staff facilitating learning in the space are very honest with both what they know and what they don't know. According to Kali: "I think telling a visitor, 'That's a great idea, I've never tried it before. Let's go for it,' giving that permission is really nice."

*Figure 8. Gender balance of visitors*

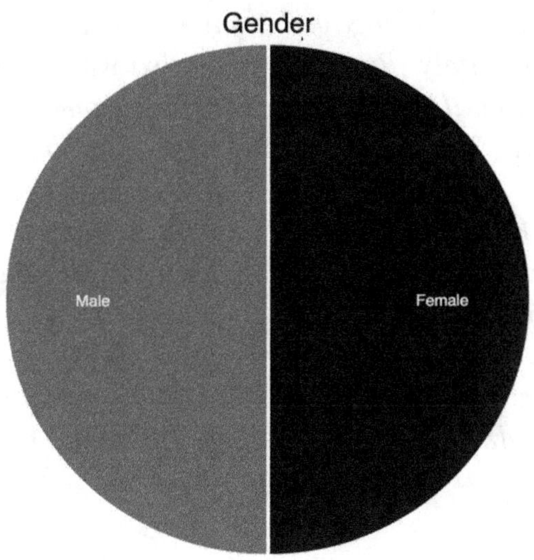

Another strategy for building community in the Tinkering Studio is to create an environment that supports social learning and interactions. The space is intentionally created to be inviting to novices. In addition, in this environment experts are less segregated from learners but more integrated, working alongside the visitors. Kali explained:

*Yeah, I think one thing that's challenging is it is a drop-in environment. So, people are coming and going. The community that happens is often quicker or smaller. We do try to think of how we address that. We try to use the environment to support that a lot. So, creating spaces that aren't hierarchical in the sense of, there's a place where the expert stands and you come to the expert. But rather, it's a table that's a little bit more curved and welcoming, where we're all sitting together, working side by side. So, I think that's one way we try to develop community, is by using space and creating spaces that are friendly and welcoming.*

Because of the drop-in nature for visitors to the space, it is difficult for communities of learners to form and for visitors to give back to the space. It is not an expectation that visitors give back by helping others, but it is a behavior that facilitators hope to see in the space. Facilitators do see visitors that have confidence in their abilities and are motivated to share their talents with others in the space. Unlike many other spaces, collaboration and community are encouraged and may not be as important as learner choice. The studio is designed for learners to choose the experience they have with the space. As Kali explained:

*I think we want people to be engaged in the space. I think we want people to be collaborative, definitely. But I think we also want to give people choice about their experience that they have. We have one woman who actually loves Light Play and will spend hours here. She's really the only person who comes back week to week to week. She enjoys working really independently, and we like giving her that autonomy to explore her ideas. I think maybe it might be subtle, but her dedication to the activity and the ways you can tell she's carefully noticing and observing her work, I think it gives back to the community in maybe a less tangible way where she's not telling other people like, "Oh, here's what I noticed," or "Here, you can do this," but I think her engagement is palpable. So, I think it does contribute in that way.*

Fundamental to the Tinkering Studio is the "problem space" which is the main interactive environment in the studio that rotates nearly every six months. At the time of the visit the problem space was focused on Light Play which explores light, shadow, and color to make a moving sculpture that projects an image onto a screen. Kali described it as:

*Often times, that's how I'll describe it to visitors when they come in. I'll say, "There's stuff that can bend light, there's stuff that can reflect light, there's stuff that can change the color of the light, there's stuff that can cast interesting shadows." And then I'll just encourage them to play and explore with those materials to develop a sculpture that is the way they want it to be. Within that problem space, some people get really interested in reflection, and they have Mylar and disco balls and all this stuff and they want to get things reflecting on the screen. Other people get into the narrative and they say, "I want to tell a story that when this thing spins around, you see these two things happen." Other people get really into the aesthetic quality of, "I want it to have this feeling when you look at it." There's a lot of breadth of what you can explore in that activity, but everyone in the space is exploring light, shadow, color.*

To become an expert in the space is a challenge because of the short duration and lack of follow-up outings for most visitors. The typical learning pathway happens in the problem space where visitors are able to start quickly and choose their learning path within the provided parameters offered in the space. Once visitors have started in the problem space they can obtain the knowledge and skills to create very complex structures. Kali explained the learning pathway:

*I think using that sort of structure of activity development does lead to ... you might have never used a glue gun, and by the end you feel really comfortable. Or you've never used a soldering iron, by the end you feel really comfortable. Or you may never have designed a mechanical component, but by the end you have some understanding of what pieces need to be fixed and what pieces need to move freely to get this thing to work the way you want it to. I think MIT, the lifelong kindergarten group, has the model or metaphor of the low threshold, wide walls, high ceiling. I think that's sort of how we try to design activities, with those in mind.*

When asked if visitors would need to have any prior knowledge of the problem space components, Kali indicated they don't expect visitors to come in with the knowledge or vocabulary to interact with the space. Facilitators will work with visitors to gauge their current knowledge and then share basic information. Kali gave the following example of this interaction:

*I would say we try to figure out what their prior knowledge is. So we might say, "Have you used an awl before, or have you used this?" and let them share what their experience is or isn't. They might make a connection that's not necessarily a direct correlation, but at least knowing what they've tried is cool. We definitely don't expect that you need to come in knowing how to use a glue gun or anything like that. Any tools we put out, we're prepared to teach them to whoever's using them. Even with glue guns, people will say, "Yeah, I've totally used a glue gun before." And I'll say, "Great. I'm gonna walk you through my safety steps again, just in case. You confirm if we're on the same page."*

To create a shared vocabulary, facilitators in the space use the appropriate vocabulary words either scientific or from the arts when it is relevant to the learning. The practice of facilitators using the appropriate vocabulary has the effect of reinforcing it for learners who in many cases will begin to use the appropriate words. In the following example Kali notes how vocabulary is used in the space:

*I think vocabulary's an interesting idea, and the way I like to think about it is, I like to use scientific or artistic, both vocabulary when it's relevant to the learner. I think this comes up a lot in our circuit activities, and I think like you mentioned with light and shadow. I wouldn't say to a visitor, "Today, we're making parallel circuits." But I would say, "Today, we're making circuits, and there's ways that you can light them that light up one light, or there's ways that you can light them to light up multiple lights." When a visitor has a series circuit but it's not working off of one battery, then it's like, "Oh, this is the time to insert that language because it's really relevant to their learning in this moment." Same with light and shadow. I might say, "That's a really interesting reflection," or "The light right there is refracting in an interesting way." Noticing like, "You've got some cool color mixing going on. What were you thinking when you were making this design? Tell me about your idea behind it."*

Gelosi noted that reinforcing vocabulary "by just casually mentioning it" with youth, especially in the after-school learning environment, is an effective way to create shared understanding of terms for learners. She notes that the practice is a subtler teaching method than the more traditional ways of defining and quizzing learners. Interestingly, the facilitators also pick up on the vocabulary that the learners are using. Kali noted:

*Yeah, and there's other times, likewise, I will pick up students' vocabulary. Like if they're describing a problem and they say, "It keeps jumping," or "It keeps sticking." I'll say, "Yeah, let's talk about this sticky point." I think it goes both ways in the space too, valuing the language students are bringing to the experience.*

In the space there is not a formal certification process for learners. In situations where a tool or piece of equipment needs some introduction the facilitators will offer instructions in a number of ways. Many times they will walk learners through the safe operation of the tool modeling and providing time for learners to step in and master the skill. This is a heavily scaffolded learning technique that becomes less scaffolded as the learners become more comfortable with the tools. Facilitators use their own judgment to determine the degree of help a learner may need in the tinkering process. Kali explained:

*On the floor, we don't do a formal certification process, but we do have something we go through. So, for example, if it's a drill, we'll say, "This is a drill. This is the part that spins. It's kind of sharp. This is the trigger that gets you started. When we're drilling something, it's important to clamp it down so it doesn't spin around." One thing I think I'm really proud of is how the space feels welcoming to girls. We have scrunchies, so we can be like, "Let's keep your hair out of the way, because that can be a dangerous thing when you're using a drill." So those are all things we consider. If we're using a saw, we'll be like, "Okay, let's put the piece in the vice. This is a push saw or a pull saw." We let people know what kind of saw it is. We'll do a lot of scaffolded facilitating at the beginning where it might be we're using the tool together, or you'll demonstrate and then the visitor will use it. Over time, as facilitators, we kind of judge how someone's doing. Are they really getting the idea and ready for us to step back a little, or do they need more support? It varies from visitor to visitor. We try to be aware of that in the space.*

In the space the high school Project Explainers are the acknowledged experts in the problem space. They are recruited by word of mouth and job postings around the bay area and through another department at the Exploratorium. The explainer program has been in existence essentially since the museum was founded 40 years ago. At the Exploratorium there are two types of explainers: Field Trip Explainers, made up of adults who have an interest in education and come from a variety of backgrounds, and the high school Project Explainers, many of whom work with the Tinkering Studio. The high school Project Explainers are part-time employees paid by the Exploratorium and attend professional development workshops prior to engaging visitors. Traits in explainers the space is looking for include a willingness to learn and an innate curiosity. Explainers are not expected to be experts in science or art but rather they have a strong interest in education and desire to support the inquiry learning process. Gelosi noted:

*I think honestly, they like to have people who maybe either have limited knowledge in certain areas or just different ranges of experience. I know that's something that seems really valued by the explainer program, to say they wouldn't want to fill the museum with a bunch of people who love science or just a bunch of people who love art; having people who have lots of different interests and interests that can then manifest in interesting ways in the museum. For example, like musicians. I think it's really interesting when I see explainers who are really interested in music running the sound station, because sometimes they'll bring out their instruments and they'll be playing music and they'll be talking about their musical instruments and how it works with the speaker.*

In addition, facilitators share with explainers the role of expert and novice in the space and how those roles constantly shift. For example, when a visitor is getting started the explainer acts as the expert in the relationship. However, in a relatively short time period the visitor may become really good at aspects of the activity and then the role of expert can be handed off to the visitor. Explainers are taught to support visitors to have agency, the sense of control of learning in the environment. Overall, the goal and expectation for the space is for visitors to have a fun and positive experience. Learning is under the visitor's control, utilizing the inquiry process to answer certain phenomena presented in the problem space. Certainly, this is accomplished through the help of explainers, facilitators and the design of the learning environment. Kali explained:

*For me, I think we're just trying to create a sense of joyful learning, and that learning can be fun and playful, and that sense of agency and that you can ask a question and develop a way of coming up with an answer to it. In our space, I think the questions, they might seem kind of silly. It might be, "How can I make a cardboard automata that looks like two basketball players defending a hoop?" But people are coming up with their ideas of, "Well, when I notice the cam spins this way, it does this. What if I make this change?" They get to try that in the moment and get feedback from these objects and from the materials, and then revise their ideas based on what they're seeing and noticing and feeling in these moments.*

Explainers are paramount in the development of the maker mindset for visitors to the Tinkering Studio. During training, explainers receive instruction around what are referred to as the three, sometimes four, Fs of tinkering including: Fun, Frustration, Failure and Facilitation. Each are present in the space and can create a quality learning experience for visitors. Explainers are expected to facilitate the experience by identifying indicators around the four Tinkering Fs of the learning experience, as Kali explained:

*We want people to be having fun, because that's a sign of engagement that they're going to stay and hang out. There's a million other things going on in the museum, so if you're not having fun, you can just leave and do something else. But we think failure and frustration are really rich learning moments. One way we talk about it is, when you're frustrated with something, you're really at the cusp of what you know and what you understand, and you're engaged enough that you want to push through that. I think a lot of the trainings we do with Explainers are to talk about supporting those moments of frustration and how we can facilitate. Maybe that's the fourth F; facilitation through that. Sometimes it's just reading people's body language and facial expressions to notice that something's tough or tricky. And I think a lot of the facilitation we do is around redirecting that. So, it's not about you failing. Like, you don't understand, you don't know how to use this tool, but rather these objects can do things and they're not working the way we want them to. How can we manipulate them or change them or impact those thing in some way, to get it to do what you want? So I feel like automata's a great example of this, where you might say, "You know, that cam ... " You wouldn't say, "Oh, you cut that cam wrong," but rather, "That cam is slipping and sliding around. What can we do to try to help keep it stable?" And redirecting failure and frustration to be object-based, not person-based.*

Kali also pointed out that the Tinkering Studio is really focused on creating excitement around learning. Creating engineers and development of talents for the STEM pipeline are not the primary mission of the space. She stated:

*I would say more specifically we care about people loving learning. I don't care if people come to the Tinkering Studio and then walk out and want to be an engineer. That's less important to me than the experience they had and how they felt about approaching learning through making something.*

When youth leave the Tinkering Studio there is an expectation that they will continue to be excited about learning. Not just STEM-based learning but a passion for open-ended learning. Kali noted:

*I think if they go home and they want to keep trying things in their kitchen, that internal motivation and excitement about this approach to learning is what I'd be looking for. But I think in terms of saying, "This will lead to a career in XYZ," is kind of a hard claim to make, first of all, but also just that I think people choosing to have this experience and then say, "I want to be an artist," or have this experience and say, "Now I want to be a teacher and I'm going to remember that feeling I had, and I want my students to have that same feeling." I think people can do these activities and take them in infinite directions that aren't just STEM fields.*

Likewise, Gelosi noted that the learning experience is intentionally open-ended so that learners choose a learning pathway that is relevant to their interests. She stated:

*I'd agree with just the fact that a lot of our projects are so open-ended that I feel like participants can come in and really make the project what they want to make it. For example, making automata with basketball players, maybe that particular person loves basketball and that was their way of being able to show their joy and passion for basketball, and then they go on to a career being a professional athlete or something. I think doing this sort of work in tinkering can really support people with however they seem themselves... But I think just being able to support them with whatever they would like to be able to do by giving them that agency to try out something new.*

The Visitor Research and Evaluation (VRE) department at the Exploratorium has examined female representation and in 2016 published the findings of a three-year National Science Foundation grant called the Exhibit Design for Girls' Engagement (EDGE) project (Dancstep & Sindorf, 2016). The project and subsequent publication examined attributes of exhibits to engage female visitors. In general, the project looked at four areas of exhibit development: (1) create experiences for interaction and collaboration, (2) ensure the experiences are low-pressure, (3) Provide meaningful connections, and (4) the exhibits should represent girls and their experiences. According to Kali the findings from the EDGE study resonate with the Tinkering Studios design approach, and they have considered them more explicitly in the environment and activity design. Kali pointed out, when asked about females in making, that the act of making is not a new phenomenon:

*... this idea that the maker movement is something new, when in fact, humans have been making things since forever. I think personally, what I try to do a lot is just broaden the idea of what counts as making. In our after-school program especially, we share things that are made all over the world as examples. We recently did tin art and we talked about Mexican Hojalata, talking about there's lots of different types of Hojalata and some of them are really functional and some of them are really decorative and beautiful, just showing those examples of that and connecting it to cultures outside of the U.S. I think is important.*

For females specifically, the problem space and overall environment is used to make girls feel welcome. Much of the space adheres to the most important design attributes for females found in the EDGE study. Kali reflected on their practice:

*I think in our space, we try to use the environment to do a lot of how we make the space welcoming to girls. So, I think our color palette is fairly neutral. We're not going to paint things pink, necessarily, and actually, our research team did a study that shows that doesn't work anyways. For example, as you approach the experience, there's a place to watch what's going on and sort of establish and notice before you're asked to dive into it. That's something that really helps support girls' engagement. Another is having multiple stations of things so that you don't feel like you're kicking someone out to then have that experience. So, like with Light Play, we have four stations set up right now. You can walk up to the tube wall, see what's happening in the space, decide if that's something you want to come into, and then have your space within a greater collaborative context to be working. I think modeling is super important, and our staff is fairly balanced in terms of gender representation. That means a lot of our facilitators out on the floor will either be two women or a man and a woman when we're facilitating. I think having women in the space does make a difference.*

In addition, the studio showcases different artists work and has "a lot" of female representation in the work that is selected for display. Gelosi stated:

*Also showcasing other women makers and artists that are doing things that we find interesting and exciting and engaging. For example, although you can't see them from the inside because we have curtains to block the light, on the outside of the space, there are all these 'Cabinets of Curiosities', that are a mix of objects made by makers and tinkerers and artists and objects made by visitors. We highlight the inspiration of where our project ideas come from, and they come from all sorts of folks. I do think representation in the maker movement is a huge issue, and one that I'm personally really interested in.*

## YOUTH IN THE SPACE

The Tinkering Studio is an inviting place for youth and adults of all ages to explore and create. The majority of visitors to the studio are family units. While Kali noted that they would like larger groups to access the space, the logistics involved make it difficult:

*I'd love for our space to be more accessible to field trips, but field trips have their own set of pressures and restrictions that they have when they come. There's a larger group with only one chaperone and they have to fill out a worksheet and they can't fill out the worksheet if they're hanging out with us. So, we do try to support field trip groups as much as we can, and I love it when they're in the space, but the majority of our visitors are families.*

The space is designed so that parents and youth can learn collaboratively and yet youth still have agency over their learning. An interesting dynamic that the museum faces is the role of parents and their tendency to "take over" the projects. During these encounters facilitators work to help parents see their child's creativity and contribution to the learning. Kali explained:

*I love it when parents and kids build side by side. I think it's great when they collaborate together, but I also think it's great when they do their own thing. I think the greatest challenge of families is the parental takeover. A lot of the facilitation we do around that is just re-voicing the children's ideas or supporting parents to be like, "Here's your set of materials," but also acknowledging that those dynamics are powerful and they existed before us and they will continue to exist long after we have this interaction. So, just trying to balance supporting families to work in ways that feel collaborative and positive.*

Gelosi added that in some projects parents will hang back and be less engaged because they are less comfortable with the activity. She noted:

*That's also really nice to notice, that we've designed an activity sometimes where the parent's stepping back and they're not really sure. Maybe their kid is a little bit more adventurous or has a little bit more gusto with just trying something out. Sometimes there isn't even that facilitation necessary in the sense that the activity's set up in such a way where a kid might dive into something, where a parent's like, "I'm not sure what to do yet."*

## IMPACT ON THE COMMUNITY

Kali believes that the Tinkering Studio has provided the community with a positive learning experience, using familiar materials in an unfamiliar way. Visitors also are provided choice in learning and the opportunity to ask questions and test their ideas in the space. The biggest impact of the studio is not on the museum visitors but on the community of educators who are interested in tinkering as learning. Kali thinks of the space as a research and development group testing and refining and disseminating ideas around learning engagement. Kali expanded on this idea:

*I think in terms of publications, we have a book called The Art of Tinkering [Wilkinson & Petrich, 2013] that has community impact because it's out there in the world and people buy it. Or we do things like MOOC, Massively Open Online Courses. We have one called Fundamentals of Tinkering that's all about circuits. We're publishing another one now that's going be a follow-up on motions and mechanisms. The audience for those, we hope, is teachers and after-school educators who might be inspired to try this work in their spaces by getting to participate in those opportunities. Or the Bay Area community of educators who come for events here. It's both an opportunity for them to try an activity as a learner for themselves but also interact with their colleagues and get to know what's going on in other people's spaces too. I think in that sense, when you think of a community of maker-educators, I think this space supports that larger community.*

The impact of the space on learners is more difficult because the space rarely sees them more than once. On occasion they will receive emails from families with messages like, "I loved this so much, I went home and tried it again." According to Kali, "That's a peak experience for me. If a visitor is excited enough about what they did here that they want to keep doing it, that's fantastic."

## DEFINE A MAKERSPACE

When asked to define a makerspace, the conversation was interesting since the focus of the studio is on tinkering more so than making. Kali and Gelosi discussed the differences between tinkering and making.

Kali stated:

*I think they're definitely parallel things. Sometimes when you're making, you're tinkering, and sometimes when you're tinkering, you're making. I think the difference is, maybe when you look at something like a Make Magazine, you might see a project that was like, "This was developed by someone else, and it's to make this thing at the end. You could follow these steps to end up with this object." And I think for us, we're not so interested in everyone ending up with the same thing. In fact, when we do activity development, if everyone is making the same thing, that's an indicator to us of, "Maybe we need to tweak our prompt or our materials or our framework of how we're thinking about it a little bit." So, we really think of tinkering as a process that you can go through to support learning at this intersection of art, science, and technology.*

*I think maybe another slight difference from capital M making is that the aesthetic portion of this is really important to us. We believe people's ideas around how something looks and why you're making those decisions around the aesthetics are just as valid and important as the process of making that thing. If someone's making a light play and they want to tell this story, we're really interested in that story that the light play is telling. Or when they're making a sewn circuit, the reasons behind why it's a bear and why it's important the stomach lights up, and all those choices and details that go into making it really personal and meaningful. And also, just not to say, we don't think one is better than the other. We just choose to use a different word because there are qualities about tinkering that we value, that we think perhaps aren't captured when people think of making.*

When asked to define a makerspace Kali responded:

*I would say it's a learning environment that supports collaborative learning, based on working with tools and materials and objects. I would say it can happen in a garage, it could happen at a kitchen table, it can happen in a library or in an after-school program. It can be something that is permanent, like the Tinkering Studio, or it can be something that's ephemeral and gets set up for an afternoon and then goes away again. I would say the things that it needs to have are materials to manipulate and work with and space for you to cognitively or emotionally ask those questions of, "What can I do with these materials? What is my interest with them, and how can I take my idea and make it real with this stuff?" I try to really not define them as: "It needs a 3D printer, it needs these digital tools, it needs really expensive or large equipment." I think you can make with hand sewing, just like you can make with a CNC router.*

Gelosi added:

*I really like that. One thought that I had was the types of materials that are used. I think they can really range from things that are super familiar, like things that you'd find in your house and that you might be repurposing or re-imagining in a different way, or it can range to materials that are totally new to you and that maybe you're experimenting with and trying to learn about through making with them. Having what Lianna [Kali] was saying, a rich material set and having that variety is really important as well.*

## CURRENT CHALLENGES

The Tinkering Studio at the Exploratorium has done a remarkable job informing the field about exhibit design, teaching the tinkering process, and developing practices to engage females. The studio's main interaction space, referred to as the problem space, is a unique way to present a specific phenomenon to be explored and allows visitors to express agency over their engagement processes. Careful planning, iterative design and precision are hallmarks of the space and items found within it. An exhibit on the floor will have gone through many cycles of test and retest before it is made available to visitors. Even then, facilitators will continue to enhance the experience by using common objects in an uncommon way. Coupled with the premiere researchers at the space, it is no surprise the Tinkering Studio is at the forefront of the tinkering/maker movement.

Unique to the space is the reduced emphasis on STEM skills and career exploration, and more of a focus on creating excitement around learning. As a drop-in space it does not necessarily expect learners to return for a prolonged series of interventions. Visitors take with them an experience that gives them a feeling of accomplishment through the process of tinkering and making.

Central to the openness of the Tinkering Studio is learner choice and ensuring visitors have the time to immerse themselves in the problem space. With this model the relative number of learners that are served is small compared to other museum-based exhibits. Kali noted that it is a challenge to provide access to large groups such as those that often attend the museum. Visits from school groups often try to bring school learning into the space. Worksheets to complete and predefined learning objectives don't intersect well with the learning model in the Tinkering Studio. Overall, there seems to be tension between engagement level and number of visitors. In the Tinkering Studio there was a conscious decision to allow visitors an immersive experience at the expense of overall numbers of visitors. It's not clear how such a model would work in other smaller, less well-funded museums who for the most part rely on numbers of visitors as the most important metric for success and impact. Another wonderful attribute of the space is the propensity to share activities developed in the space. For example, they have on the Tinkering Studio web site teaching guides and hardware lists to recreate activities, thereby providing other institutions the ability to have their own inquiry learning problem space.

## REFERENCES

Bevan, B., Gutwill, J. P., Petrich, M., & Wilkinson, K. (2015). Learning Through STEM-Rich Tinkering: Findings From a Jointly Negotiated Research Project Taken Up in Practice. *Science Editor*, *99*, 98–120. doi:10.1002ce.21151

Dancstep, T., & Sindorf, L. (2016). *Exhibit Designs for Girls' Engagement: A Guide to the EDGE Design Attributes*. San Francisco, CA: Exploratorium.

Wilkinson, K., & Petrich, M. (2013). *The art of tinkering: Meet 150+ makers working at the intersection of art, science & technology*. Exploratorium.

## KEY TERMS AND DEFINITIONS

**After-School:** Informal education programs that are conducted outside of the formal school day.

**Agency:** The capacity and propensity to take purposeful initiative of one's own learning.

**Automata:** A mechanical device that functions in a predetermine set of actions.

**Explainers:** Part-time employees that help facilitate activities with visitors especially on the weekends.

**Exploratorium:** The Museum of Science, Art, and Human Perception located in San Francisco, California on Pier 15.

**Learning Studio:** A workshop within the Tinkering Studio where things are prototyped in preparation for use on the studio floor.

**Light Play:** An exhibit which explores light, shadow, and color to make a moving sculpture that projects an image onto a screen.

**Problem Space:** The main interactive environment in the Tinkering Studio.

**San Francisco, California:** Large metropolis located on the west side of the San Francisco Bay.

**Tinkering Studio:** Makerspace housed inside the Exploratorium.

# Section 2

# Educational Spaces/ Libraries

# Chapter 4
# Assemble

## ABSTRACT

*Assemble employs a "pay-what-you-can" revenue model in an attempt to reduce financial barriers for youth in Pittsburgh's East End to attend maker activities in the space. Assemble is a community-based makerspace centered on developing high levels of self-efficacy around making in youth served by the space. Assemble runs a number of different after-school programs at its main location and at various schools around Pittsburgh as well. Staff in the space consists of contract teachers and high-school interns all trained to help build learning communities by connecting students. Youth in the space are encouraged to help teach each other through specific learning activities embedded in the course offerings. The space is well known for their building of the Burrito Cat robot, a project completed by female students. Assemble relies on a cadre of contract teaching artists to provide programming. Since these teachers have a great deal of autonomy, it presents a unique set of challenges especially providing a consistent learning experience for the students. This chapter explores Assemble.*

## ORGANIZATION BACKGROUND

Assemble is located in Pittsburgh's East End where the Friendship, Garfield, and Bloomfield neighborhoods converge. Like other neighborhoods in the area, by the mid-70s these neighborhoods suffered from long-term decay and began a decades-long rebound to lift up the residents of the communities (Fanzo, 1993). Founded by Nina Barbuto in April 2011, this community-

DOI: 10.4018/978-1-5225-8310-3.ch004

based makerspace was created to foster confidence for making. While open to makers of all ages, the space primarily caters to youth. Assemble relocated in 2016 to its current home on the ground level of the newly built Penn Mathilda Apartments. The apartments were developed by ACTION-Housing and have 39 living units in the building. The management company provides housing preferences to U.S. veterans for half of the units. The ground floor includes 6,000 $ft^2$ (557 $m^2$) dedicated to neighborhood-oriented commercial spaces. Currently, Assemble occupies roughly 1,500 $ft^2$ (139 $m^2$) of the commercial space.

According to Barbuto, the old building had its share of challenges therefore, staff members were very happy when the new space, which is more accessible, became available. However, during the lag between moving out of the old building and moving into the new building, Assemble had no home. Staff moved out on June, 2016 and started camps on June 20, 2016 but did not have an official new space until July 1, 2016 so they moved the equipment and supplies into Barbuto's house.

Assemble is located in a relatively small physical space with a prominent work area located in the front section of the room with one wall being made of windows like a typical storefront. There is also a special area for youth to relax and chill, called the "chillax zone", which contains books and games as seen in Figure 1. This area has a wall painted a different color that demarcates the zone as a special place for youth.

Every month the space hosts a different art exhibition as part of Penn Avenue's First Friday Unblurred Gallery Crawl featuring different Pittsburgh artists, technologists, and makers. There is a homework bar for youth, and they are to complete their homework as they arrive during the after-school programs. The space is laid out with the less dangerous items closer to the main work area. Deeper into the space is an increased level of tool sophistication. For example, pencils are located close to the workroom so that youth can grab them easily, but scissors are further back because, of course, youth tend to run when they are excited. Also, further back is "messy art stuff." Another area is the "snack land" where healthy snacks are stored. The next area has sewing materials and other dangerous/messy art supplies, like glitter. Separated by a door is the danger room that contains the laser cutter and other tools. The danger room is not available to students unless they are trained on the laser cutter and 3D printer. Table 1 lists the tools and equipment in the space.

*Assemble*

*Figure 1. The Chillax zone*

*Table 1. Tools and equipment*

| | |
|---|---|
| **General workshop equipment** | Vacuum<br>2 saw horses<br>6 folding tables<br>2 folding work tables |
| **General Hand tools (powered)** | Various tools |
| **Metalwork** | Soldering equipment |
| **Fabrics** | 3 sewing machines |
| **Painting and graphic arts** | Painting supplies |
| **Science, Synthetic Bio, Chemistry** | Microscopes |
| **Computing** | Chromebooks<br>Microsoft Surfaces<br>iPads |
| **Digital fabrication** | (3) 3D printers |
| **Electronics** | Soldering irons |

## SETTING THE STAGE

Assemble runs a variety of programs (formal and out-of-school programs, summer camps and homeschool) in the space and at other school locations around the community. Other events include Maker Nights and Saturday "Crafternoons" held at Assemble. The largest area of concentration is after-school programming. It mainly takes two forms — one that meets at Assemble and others that take place in schools scattered throughout the city. At Assemble, after-school programs run Monday through Thursday, as shown in Table 2; each night caters to a different audience.

Within each after-school program, Assemble, has rotating themes and project areas. For example, Girls' Maker Nights had four themes during February 2017: DIY Fashion and Patternmaking; Fabric and Printmaking; Introduction to Sewing; and Shrinky Dink Jewelry. The Girls' Maker Night is geared towards girls and those who identify as girls, as well as fourth-graders, but is mainly attended by middle-school-aged youth.

Themes for youth in grades 6 to 8 in February focused on robot biomimetics. In the biomimetics course, youth start by designing their robot in session 1, build and program in sessions 2 to 3, and then test the robot in the final session.

Youth in grades 3 to 5 and 1 to 2 have a more varied experience in the after-school offerings. For grades 3 to 5, example session topics include coding, circuits, polymers, tessellations and kaleidoscopes. Grades 1 to 2 also experience tessellations and kaleidoscopes, then take a more art bend with painting and engineering. During the weekdays, youth are welcome to hang out in the space even if they are not part of the after-school theme or if it's targeted to another age group. Guest makers sometimes help with the program. Barbuto explained:

*Table 2. After-school programs at Assemble*

| Program Name | Grade Level | Day of the Week | Time |
|---|---|---|---|
| Girls Maker Night (girls only) | 5–8 | Mondays | 4–6 P.M. |
| Tuesday After-school | 6–8 | Tuesdays | 4–6 P.M. |
| Wednesday After-school | 3–5 | Wednesdays (except 2nd of the month) | 4–6 P.M. |
| Thursday After-school | 1–2 | Thursdays | 4–6 P.M. |

*Mondays is for Girls' Maker Night. Tuesdays are for middle schoolers, so we have a lot of these girls come back. We have some kids that are on the cusp, the sixth grade-ish cusp that will come to all three. They're different things, because it's technically a different program. If they really want to work on what they did the day before, that could happen, but typically, it's like, 'I know, I'm going to give you something new.' Girls' Maker Night, middle school, our third to fifth grade, and then our first and second graders are completely amazingly wild and awesome.*

Assemble is also a Pittsburgh Public School partner and is able to work within schools both in the classroom and during out-of-school time. Currently, there are programs in the following schools: Arsenal, Woodland Hills, Community Day School, Urban Academy, Allegheny Traditional Academy, Propel Charter Schools, and the Environmental Charter School.

Each program delivery is a little different. For example, Assemble has a "combo" program providing in-school and after-school programs at Arsenal Public School. Two days a week Assemble provides programming in the Woodland Hills School District, which is in Allegheny County just east of the Pittsburgh Public School District. Assemble also runs an after-school program at Community Day School, a parochial school just south and east of Pittsburg.

In some cases, Assemble works through the science department of a school to help "actualize their lessons." Another set of programs happens at the Environmental Charter School, which is a school that teaches from an environmental-themed program. The first program is the exploratory program that is a 10-week class taken by middle school students. They also work with the first-grade teachers on their Invention Convention projects, providing expertise for the unit and providing PD for teachers. Barbuto also discussed working with second-graders on the insect unit at the Propel Charter School. She recalled:

*All of their second-graders are part of the insect unit. We'll go in three days, and we work with every second grader. It's a chain of charter schools, and we help them to expand their knowledge of insects, learn about biomedics, and then turn themselves into superheroes. Ultimately, the deliverables are some prototypes and costumes, and then students have a parade, which is so adorable. These kids that are like 'I want to be able to do this,' and then you have to be able to think, 'What am I taking inspiration from and copying from.' You're covered in recycled materials and LEDs and potentially googly eyes. They're using this idea of method acting to even build empathy for what they want to become ... a spider.*

Most Saturdays, Assemble runs the Crafternoon program for youth in grades kindergarten to 5 from 1:00 to 3:00 P.M. Again, the themes rotate from creating emoji pillows, glass mosaics, locomotion, and even open craft times on some Saturdays. 'Learning Parties' occur every second Wednesday of the month and are open to all ages. Guest makers, scientists, artists, and engineers lead hands-on activities.

During the summer months, Assemble runs a number of different camps over a nine week period. In the summer of 2016, they ran a course on DIY Youth Media Storytelling through the Community Mixtape Project. The project combines media and technology arts to allow community members to tell their own personal stories. Additionally, Assemble runs the M3 Materials, Media, and Me program for youth ages 6 to 10. In the project, youth are guided through the design processes that are led by guest artists and technologists. Each Saturday during the summer months, youth experience a different material to work with, including light, paper, fabrics, electronics, and recycled materials. Barbuto explained:

*We have a Saturday program called M3, Materials, Media, and Me, and that is the only government-funded thing that we have. It's through the PA, Partners in the Arts. We get a grant for $1,200 a year to do that one, so we have a lot of government funding ... not so much. That's one of the first funded programs that we ever did, and we are still doing it.*

Assemble does not have a membership fee and does not charge for after-school programs during the school year. During the summer, camps are free to youth that live in the Garfield neighborhood and there is a cost for youth outside of the neighborhood. Assemble provides scholarships to other youth in the pay-what-you-can model.

On average, Assemble will see 250 to 1,000 total visits per month. As shown in Figure 2, 60 to 79% of visitors are female, 20 to 39% are male, and 20 to 39% are "other."

The ethnicity of students is shown in Figure 3. About 20 to 39% are white, 40 to 59% are black or African-American, less than 20% Asian, and 60 to 79% are two or more races that may be included in the other ethnicities.

***Assemble***

*Figure 2. Gender balance of visitors*

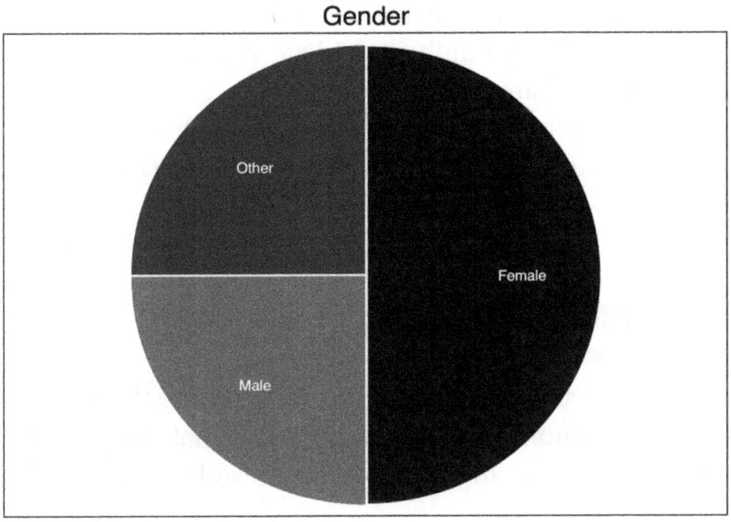


*Figure 3. Ethnicity of membership*

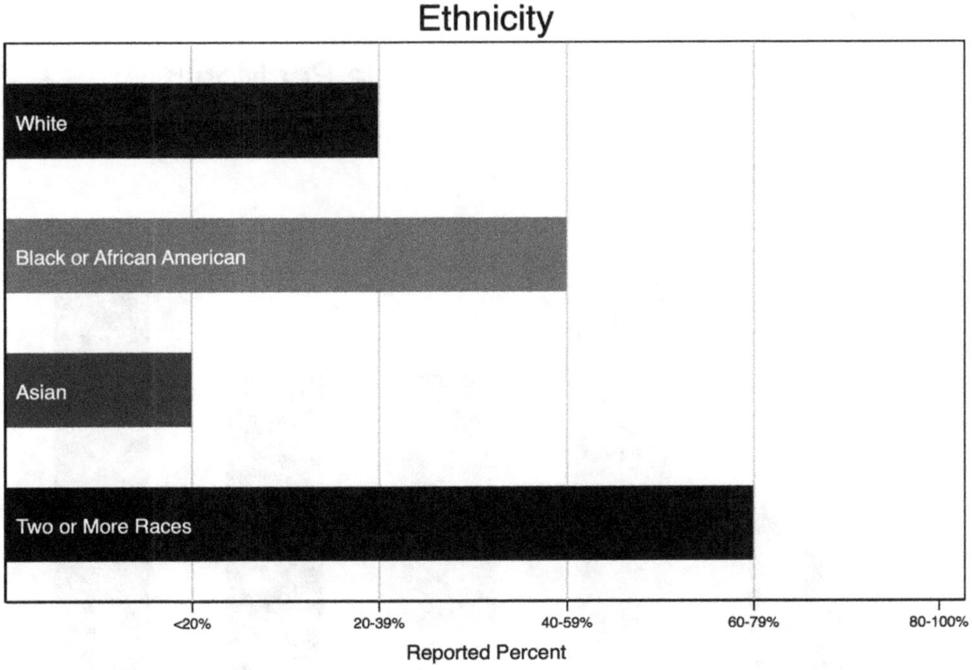

The types of users that visited the space are shown in Figure 4. An estimated 20 to 39% of users are visitors or just observing, 60 to 79% are youth under the age of 13, 40 to 59% are youth ages 13 to 18, another 40 to 59% are aged 18 to 24, and 60 to 79% are teachers.

In general, the purpose of visits to Assemble as shown in Figure 5 was an introduction to making, to make something specific, to make one-off pieces, and to socialize.

## LEARNING COMMUNITIES

Learning communities form through the programming that occurs in and out of the space. For example, the Learning Parties that happen once a month are drop-ins at no cost for all ages. During these learning parties, Barbuto explained:

*Figure 4. Types of visitors per month*

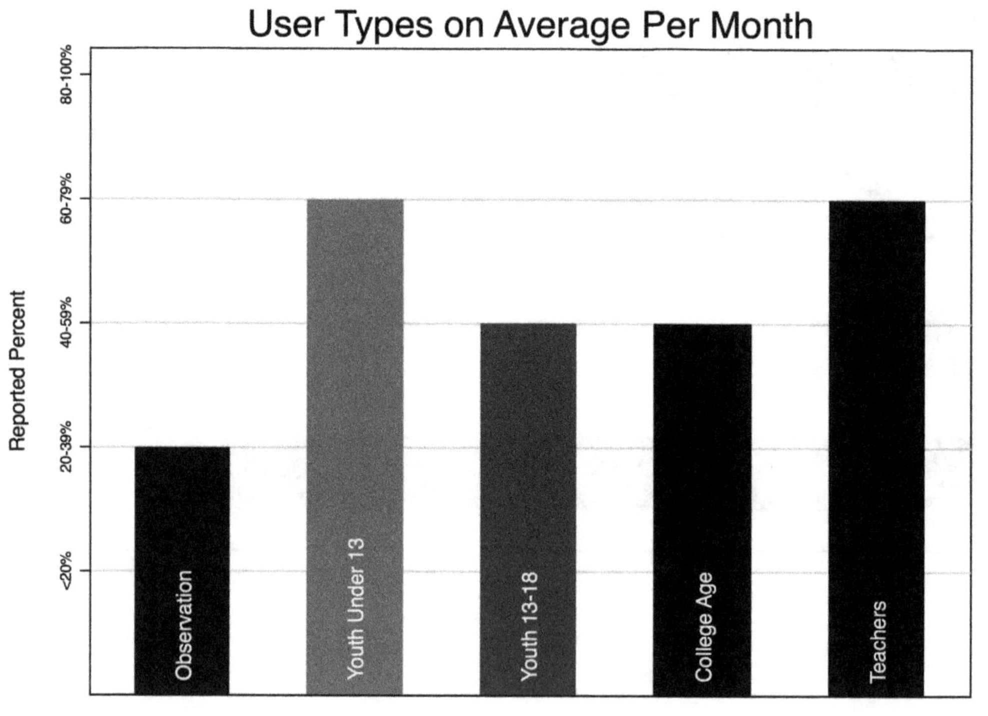

*Figure 5. Purpose of visits per month*

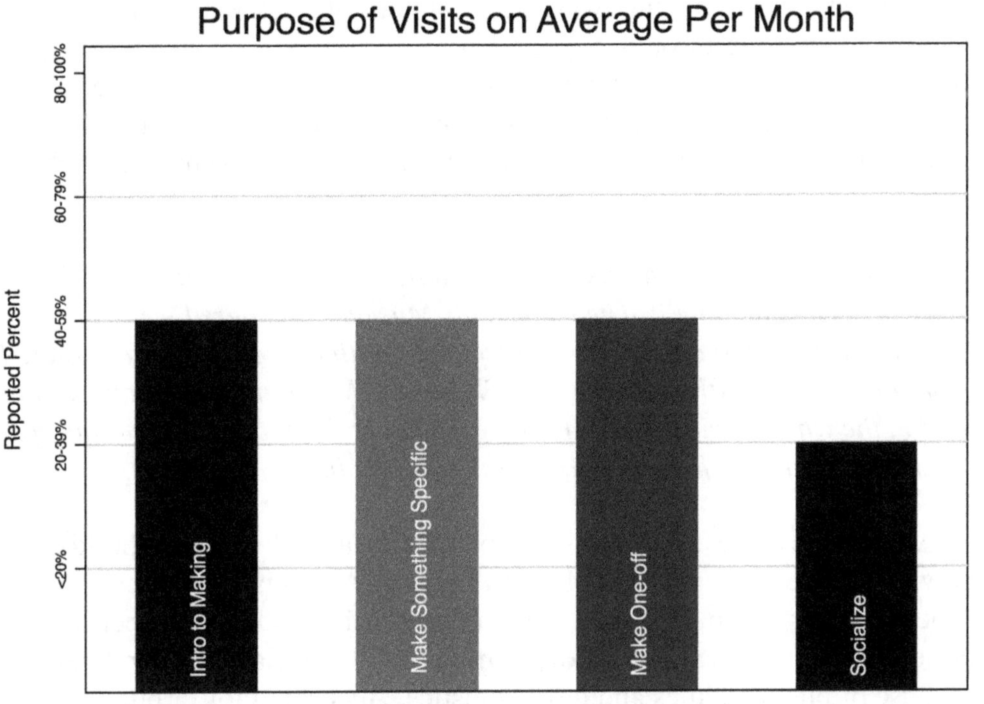


*In each one [learning party), we have a different guest maker, and it's also based on this idea of the chillaxing or homago (hanging out and geeking out). There's a bunch of pizza, there's different steps. This class was a little bit of a challenge skill-wise, because there was some soldering. It's like, how can you get everything done in an hour-and-a-half timeframe because by the time you eat your pizza and/or show up, you have an hour-and-a-half (for making).*

Through these activities and being present on the site, the participants make connections and learn from each other. In the space, youth are encouraged to teach each other. Barbuto explained:

*There's parts of it that work, and then there's parts of it that's like, oh, you know this will help teach your friend. That's always something to influence the kids. If you know this already, you should teach the person next to you. Building community within your learning community and doing icebreakers and stuff like that are important.*

Families and school groups, as well as current attendees of the site, are encouraged to visit. In this way, members are able to join in a hands-on activity, all moving through the same project area. All the courses that are taught at Assemble and in the school-based programs emphasize building confidence in making. Another practice of Assemble is to partner with other organizations, which allows youth to go from one space to another. Barbuto commented:

*We bring in different guests from organizations, companies, academic departments, you name it. The Children's Museum was here for the last one ... it was circuits and contraptions. Also, the Youth Maker Night was created in tandem with Youth Make at the Children's Museum. They have youth, food ... the whole series. We started that together. The idea was that the kids potentially could go from one to the other in the future.*

Attendance in these programs is important because the projects build upon previous content over the month. In this way, Assemble provides a richer experience for youth, allowing them a deeper dive and more experimental projects. Conversely, after-school programs in schools have shorter durations because of bus schedules and other logistics. According to Barbuto:

*You get everyone, eat a snack, try to do something for half an hour, and so it's a lot harder to get into deeper things. But we can get into bigger, heavier projects here [at Assemble]. We also have the storage to make sure that a project will be there next week, as long as someone puts a label on it.*

Teachers are not on staff but are contracted to facilitate courses both at Assemble and at the area schools. Each year teachers survey participants to determine what they would like to learn over the course of the year. Teachers will then script themes and learning activities throughout the school year. For example, during the Hour of Code, which is a national program, they will focus on providing activities on coding. In April, they will facilitate learning around environmental issues. In addition, Assemble relies on volunteers and fellows. Barbuto commented:

*Things more like edible science stuff... ice-cream will happen in the springtime versus the winter ... Last month was all about animation, so each week was a different form of animation. We also brought in some [college] students from Carnegie Mellon who are building this online platform that kind of uses a similar methodology as Flash, so understanding how to program in-time using buttons, but then also being able to use the code behind it to take a stop-motion movie that they made and add all these other fancy things to it.*

There are a number of teaching artists interested in working at Assemble and many of them are from the neighborhood. A number of qualified teachers have an interest in the after-school and in-school programs and Assemble has developed a relationship with a number of teachers who contract with them each year. To recruit teachers, Assemble, will post announcements online and through the different maker communities. A number of the teaching artists come from other maker sites in the city, including places like the Pittsburgh Children's Museum, Carnegie Museum of Art, TechShop, and the Pittsburgh Center for the Arts. This crossover benefits the spaces but also expands possibilities for children. As Barbuto stated:

*We try to help send kids on their way after they do our programs too, or if they're like, 'I'm really interested in this,' we'll be like, 'Hey, let us help you get a scholarship to do this other thing.'*

High school students working in the space are part of a grant program sponsored by the Three Rivers Work Investment Board program and the Bloomfield Garfield Corporation. Some of these students come up through the program and teach, but they are not given the responsibility of attendance or other logistical considerations. They are more like content experts facilitating learning in certain areas.

Assemble provides professional development training to teachers but it can be difficult to get them to attend the training since they are on contract and not required to attend. For example, Assemble will bring in different experts on germane topics for youth in the neighborhood. In the past, they have brought in experts from the *Centers for Victims* who provided training on trauma and working with those who are suffering from different forms of trauma.

Assemble is able to pay teachers to attend the training through the Healthy Out-of-School Time (HOST) alliance nonprofit organization. HOST is a partnership between United Way, Children's Hospital, and a number of other out-of-school time groups. Teaching artists are also provided curriculum and encouraged to use what is provided, but they are also free to modify their delivery plans and content. Barbuto talked about other fundamentals for teaching in the space:

*We already tried to think of how; are you incorporating the different learning styles, so it's not just healthy eating but healthy moving. We're not a gym, and so a lot of out-of-school time places might just have a rec center, where it's like 'Go play in the gym.' It's difficult, but if you're programming each other to move across the room, you're getting each other moving and active, and you're not just sitting at the computer through a period of time. One of our teachers a few years ago made sushi with the kids, and so talking about how to prepare a bowl and everything else, stuff like that, and making sure you are always revealing the science and the technology and engineering and math and art that you're already utilizing. How we define STEAM also is part of it.*

Assemble has impacted the community by providing access to making equipment and supplies and giving them a space to learn and socialize. Since 2011 more than 20,000 youth have been served by Assemble. Impressively, nearly 90% of those that visit the space are from the Garfield or adjacent neighborhoods. In 2015 Assemble estimated that it reached over 6,000 people through outreach events. Barbuto described the impact of Assemble:

*Youth being jazzed about robots and everything else, and everything in between. They can come and hang out if they just want to paint ... that's also fine ... with glitter, and then hopefully clean up after themselves. I'm kind of just re-visioning moments. I think just being a space that's not coming in and leaving.*

The impact on youth in school and learning is hard to gauge, but parents report that they see improvements in grades and attitudes towards school. Barbuto warns that Assemble cannot take credit for these improvements; she stated:

*Parents have definitely said that their students light up and their attitudes change, and they see improvements in their approach to learning, which we all know that it takes just one person to ruin it all.*

## FAMILIES IN THE SPACE

Families are an important part of what happens in Assemble. Their role is to be a "platform manager," to help build the programs that work for the families of the youth that attend courses in the space. The space supports events like *New Dad Night*, an effort to help fathers prepare for raising children in the community. Older community members from the neighborhood have also requested courses to learn after watching the youth in the space. While an exciting idea, Barbuto commented:

*Okay, we have to figure out how to make that happen. Also, having someone who can have that time to make those conversations and to say, okay, this is what we can do, this is how we can pay for it ... that's my role, is figuring out how to pay for it ... but not making it up just ourselves, but being able to listen and then expand upon it.*

There is also interest from Veterans groups that would like to utilize the space as well, and Barbuto is working on ways to provide them access to the space. The learning parties also serve as family events in addition to a celebration of learning ceremonies that occur at the end of each school year. The space runs day camps during non-school days as a way to help families. Barbuto believes this is an important role for Assemble:

*Helping out families with their child management is important. We do day camps ... we've started doing day camps more this year, where when kids don't have school, especially kids from public schools, we're offering a day camp. For example, for MLK day, we had a day camp for 8- to10-year-olds centered on African-American scientists.*

## YOUTH IN THE SPACE

The space primarily serves a youth audience during the out-of-school time hours, with different age groups during the week. Each day a different age group is served, mainly due to space limitations but also due to differences in behaviors. As Barbuto noted, the 2nd graders are more manic and loud, which makes it difficult for older learners in the space.

The battle between equipment and supplies storage and having adequate workspace also is at play at Assemble. With limited space, the solution to limit class size works well and also allows youth to schedule their activities around Assemble themes. Youth also are able to drop in and out of the program as other things like sports or school activities require absences from the space.

When asked how Assemble benefits female learners and how they are recruited, Barbuto noted that the space attracts a lot of females. The majority of visitors to the space identify as females. Barbuto reflected on why they may have more females than males and concluded that it's well-known that Assemble is a female-run organization and a lot of strong females have been on the board and in volunteer roles. She noted:

*Well, it's funny, we actually attract a lot of females. I don't know if it's because it is identified as a female-run space, but even on our board ... there's been a lot of really strong women that come through this space. Let us just say that, through teachers and others, and by trying to be conscious of that too to balance things out. That hasn't been too much of a problem because I think of how it's laid out. I mean, it wasn't something I was like, "I'm going to make a space that's specific to girls."*

Barbuto noted that she is uncomfortable with the "pink-ifying" of activities and the learning environment to attract females. She believes that science and the arts can be approached in a "genderless" way. For example, one of the most famous artifacts from the space is Burrito Cat. Burrito Cat, as shown in Figure 6, is a genderless robot cat made by an all-female team in the space. Barbuto believes that youth should be able to express their individuality. She noted: "You can still be you and do all these other things, and that's something that we really try to help kids see that."

The purpose of the Girl's Maker night is to provide a safe space for girls to express themselves and to "explore and be goofy" without fear of being judged. For Assemble, this model works well and more girl-exclusive learning opportunities are being offered. One female learner who had an amazing time learning about science during a summer camp, convinced Barbuto that the camp experience was fantastic but would be even better for the female learners if it was exclusive to females. The reason, according to Barbuto, was:

*... because these rambunctious boys ... it's not so much that they're distracting because they're cute. They're distracting because they're annoying. I got to give her props for that, and let's have an all-girls summer camp.*

*Figure 6. The Burrito Cat robot*

The role of females in science is also a featured design consideration during instructional time in the space. For example, when talking about DNA, the important contributions of Rosalind Franklin and Henrietta Lacks are highlighted as a way to "understand these heroes that have come before."

It's not only women but also African-American and people of color in general who are showcased in the site. Experts from the community are also brought in to help make youth understand and overcome barriers to entering STEM fields. Especially seeing experts that look like the youth can help overcome the barrier of children thinking that a career or interest is not for them because the experts don't look like them. Barbuto noted that Assemble is always working to build trust in the community to recruit youth and families into the space. It's an ongoing process and something that is never finished. An interesting strategy of Barbuto's is that she has moved into the neighborhood. As she described it:

*In the process of, or in the time span of starting Assemble, I bought a house in the neighborhood, and I live down the street. Kids know me. They know me and my dog who wears a tutu. If there's something that's going on, they know that they can ... especially my neighbors ... they can come and reach out to me. Some of our early Assemblers were kids that happened to live on my street anyway, because I'd be like, 'What are you doing?' They're like, 'I'm bored.' I would say: 'I have something for you, and I have snacks. Get over here.'*

Other strategies include walking around and putting up flyers in the neighborhood so community members understand who is running the space and what services they are providing. A bigger storefront, which for Assemble is a wall of windows, has been another way to increase trust with the community. As members of the community pass by the space, they can see what is happening and many times it will pique their curiosity. Barbuto described these interactions:

*People are like, 'What's going on?' They get stopped at the light here, and they're like, 'Oh, I have to come in. Looks like you're doing cool stuff.' 'Well, come on in.' I also just run after people when I see them walking down the street. I'll be like, 'Do you like robots? You should come and hang out with us.' Or if you're at the pizza place down the street, it will be like, 'Come hang out.'*

A lot of the artifacts created in the space deal with taking apart and reassembling stuffed animals. Probably the cleverest artifact to come out of the space is Burrito Cat. The Burrito Cat is a genderless cat in the shape of a burrito built with Hummingbird Robotics. Burrito Cat also contains motors and sensors as well as a speaker. Burrito Cat has the ability to greet youth with: "Hi. I'm Burrito Cat and we are going to be best friends forever."

The idea was conceived by youth and the final design was unanimously approved by makers in the space. Originally, the first drawings were of a dumpling cat, a cat with the body of a dumpling, but then morphed into a burrito on the request of another student in the space. The drawing of the burrito cat is shown in Figure 7. When asked what they learned through the making of Burrito Cat, youth responded:

*Figure 7. Drawing of the Burrito Cat*

"It takes a long time to make."
"I learned that coding is awesome."
"We learned about servo motors and other motors that can turn 360 degrees, which are just called motors, and servo motors just go 180 degrees."
"We learned from each other as we built it. We learned coding from each other and helped when we got stuck."

## DEFINING A MAKERSPACE

When asked to define a makerspace and the core components of a makerspace, Barbuto responded:

*A makerspace is a space that has access to tools, supplies, humans and danger, but also a first-aid kit is not far. How's that? That safety net.*

## CURRENT CHALLENGES

Assemble is a noteworthy space that provides programming for many young people in the community, usually for little or no cost to the families. What is remarkable is that this has been done with a small staff and the vision of one person. The current model is good for keeping down costs and serving the community. There are downsides, including the challenges of coordination in the programming, sharing values of the space and promoting fully, those maker habits of minds through programming and some dated equipment.

A significant challenge in the space is the reliance on contract teachers. In this model, the teaching artists have a high degree of autonomy in what and how education is delivered in and for the space. Because the teachers are contractors for the space, it is difficult to require them to attend meetings and professional development trainings. Moreover, cross communications amongst the contractors is also less than what would be expected with employees. Barbuto has a plan to move from the contractor model to more of a part-time teacher model by bringing on teachers as part-time employees. This change will help in the areas of content coordination and also help reflect the values of the space in all programs on and off campus. According to Barbuto, the underlying ethos of the place is:

*Building confidence for making is what this is about, because if you don't think you can, well, you're never going to do anything. But if you think you can, no matter what that thing is, you can do it.*

According to Barbuto, Assemble will be hiring a program coordinator to handle the logistical considerations for the myriad of learning experiences offered in the space. In the current model, Barbuto does a lot of the program coordination in addition to running the other aspects of the space. A program coordinator will also free up Barbuto's time to develop a well-conceived professional development program that is able to convey to teaching artists the ethos of the space. Barbuto explained:

*Our value is an open-ended invitation for people to know that they're always welcome, being welcoming and having ... what does that mean, how do you define this, how do you act and say hello to people when they walk in the space, number one, 'Hi, my name is ...' No matter what your personality type is, this is what you have to do as someone who is working here, from board member to volunteer. We're in the process of taking these and putting them into action steps, or even being like how do we produce the professional development for ourselves or for others to catalyze and crystallize what is the DNA of Assemble, and that's part of the next step.*

Current practices around the maker mindset include the challenges of an area that has a small staff and a large workload. Also, contracted teachers may approach teaching the fundamentals of the maker mindset in their programs differently, so it is not consistent. The understanding of the need is present but there have been starts and stops to implement it. Badges were one mechanism to recognize learning, as Barbuto noted:

*We were doing badges ... we haven't been doing anything like that lately outside of certain set programs. Especially when we're going into schools, then that is on the teachers here, but we always want to bring in how you take it to the next level, maybe elsewhere if it's not with us. We want to be doing this more, but it's having someone who can work with everyone, with all the teachers and what they're doing on a regular basis.*

*Within our own programs, we haven't done that per se, because it's so age-versus-skill. The idea is that you are an expert while you're working with other people in your age group, because it's more based on social skills and child development, I guess, than what you can do. I mean, we do have a pretty firm rule about being 11 to use the glue gun yourself, even though many will say they can ... but it's for safety. It's okay to use it with a teacher ... We want to be doing maker portfolios better. We've had start, stop, start, stop. It's just finding the right way to do it and having someone who can stay on it always.*

The 2017–2020 strategic plan for Assemble identified some of the maker mindset practices and values of the space. One value is *Learning through Making*: "Our hands-on environment recognized that everyone learns in different ways. We encourage learning through making, doing, listening and touching."

In addition, failure as opportunity, an important maker skill, is included in the values of the strategic plan. *Failure as Opportunity:* "We view all successes and failures as opportunities to learn, grow, and try again. We understand failure through play and inquiry."

Another important value that aligns with the maker mindset is collaboration. In the plan, it states: *Collaboration:* "We unite communities of artists, technologists, makers, and learners because collaboration leads to unique problem solving and overcoming barriers."

Through the strategic plan, it's clear that instructional practices that encourage aspects of the maker mindset will become part of the learning environment at Assemble.

An annoyance amongst any technology space is the shelf life of equipment, and those who make the equipment. Assemble purchased 3D printers from a company called Solidoodle, that is no longer making printers or supporting those they made in the past. A real struggle is to continue to operate the 3D printing machines with software from a third party or even open source software. Another major piece of equipment not working is the laser cutter. The software is current but Assemble is getting assistance from another makerspace to use an air scrubber on the vented air.

## REFERENCES

Fanzo, M. (1993). *Ethnography Study 1993: Bloomfield, East Liberty, Friendship, Garfield, Morningside, Shadyside.* Retrieved April 8, 2018, https://www.riversofsteel.com/_uploads/files/bloomfield-east-lib-friendship-garfield-morningside-shadyside.pdf

## KEY TERMS AND DEFINITIONS

**After-School:** Informal education programs that are conducted outside of the formal school day.

**Assemble:** A makerspace in the East End section of Pittsburgh, PA.

**Chillax Zone:** A special area for youth to relax and chill.

**Henrietta Lacks:** Doctors and scientists used her cell line called the HeLa for many medical treatments.

**Homago:** Hanging out and geeking out.

**Pay-What-You-Can Model:** A payment model that allows patrons to pay only the amount they can afford to participate in the program.

**Penn Avenue's First Friday Unblurred Gallery Crawl:** A rotating art event where people from all over the East End neighborhood visit Penn Avenue between the 4800 and 5500 blocks to meet with artists and local business owners.

**Pittsburgh's East End:** Area of Pittsburgh, PA where the Friendship, Garfield, and Bloomfield neighborhoods converge.

**Robot Biomimetics:** Robots that borrow characteristics and abilities of insects, birds, and other animals.

**Rosalind Franklin:** A female scientists who contributed to the understanding of molecular structures.

# Chapter 5
# Digital Harbor Foundation


## ABSTRACT

*If not for stolen computers, the Digital Harbor Foundation may have been a very different learning environment, focused on computer technology more than making. As it turned out, the staff in the 5,000-square-foot space works with students from around the Baltimore area to develop their skills in technology and making. Several students from the space have been invited to the White House to showcase their knowledge and projects. Learning communities are developed intentionally through physical seating arrangements and layout of the learning spaces, and through the course material. In the middle and high school room, all students complete a 14-week basic maker course to familiarize them with the machines and processes of making. The space follows a "pay-what-you-can" model for all courses and materials used for the projects. A separate Nano Lab caters to younger students in 3rd to 5th grades. Digital Harbor Foundation believes in building students' problem-solving abilities and ability to self-direct their learning. This chapter explores the Digital Harbor Foundation.*


DOI: 10.4018/978-1-5225-8310-3.ch005

*Then through repetition, because you're going to do that six or seven times as we go through different topics, by the end you start to feel you've journeyed into the unknown six or seven times and come out the other side unscathed and maybe even very successful. - Shawn Grimes*

## ORGANIZATION BACKGROUND

Digital Harbor Foundation (DHF) briefly started as a technology center. In its original form, the space would have been used to teach mobile app and web development, and other types of coding to students in the South Baltimore area. Basically, the space would have been used as *an educational program that involved a lot of time sitting in front of a computer*, according to Shawn Grimes, the foundation's executive director. The inauspicious beginning causing the transformation from a technology center to a makerspace happened like this:

*About three months after we opened, we had someone break in and steal the limited number of laptops that we had. We had programs starting the next day, and we had been here all night with the police and the crime lab and everything else thinking, "What are we going to do when these kids get here?" We happened to have remembered some goofy project that involved an electric toothbrush and a pool noodle. That was an art bot, so we ran down to the local Dollar Tree, got all the supplies, came back, and we're like, "Okay, this is time over for today, let's just try and stretch it out through today and then we'll figure out tomorrow, tonight." It ended up they (the students) wanted to keep going back to that project over the next two weeks. Every day they did not want to move on from art bots, and that made us realize it doesn't need to be technology focused. At that point it was like, it needs to be hands-on, maker-focused, and that was our awakening to the maker movement versus being a tech space, of being a makerspace.*

From its inception in January of 2013, the 5,000-square-foot Digital Harbor Foundation space has been in the Federal Hill area of South Baltimore just south of the city center and near the Inner Harbor of the Patapsco River. The neighborhood is very affluent, and Grimes considers it part of South Baltimore more than the Federal Hill area, which makes it a little more generic and inviting to underserved youth. The physical space is connected to the Federal Hill Preparatory School through the school's gym and was once a recreation center for the community. DHF can be accessed through the school's gymnasium but also has a dedicated entrance so that visitors do not have to enter the school.

Prior to having a physical site, the Digital Harbor Foundation was a scholarship fund run by entrepreneurs around Baltimore City. Once the recreation centers were closed down in Baltimore, the Digital Harbor Foundation, with seed money and fundraising, moved from a scholarship fund to a physical space. Currently, the space is run as a 501(C(3)) non-profit and relies heavily on grant donations to fund the program.

The financial operation for the physical space is somewhat of an anomaly because Baltimore City Recreation and Parks owns the building and title, and leases it to the Baltimore City Schools, which permits Digital Harbor Foundation to operate in the space rent free under a memorandum of understanding. The arrangement is jokingly referred to as the *Bermuda Triangle where responsibility goes to die.* DHF serves students across Baltimore City from 88 different schools, including 51 private and 37 independent or home schools.

Inside the space, two maker areas are divided by a main hallway that eventually leads to the school. Immediately to the right as you walk in the main entrance is the Nano Lab, the smaller of the two spaces. It is designed for the Mini Makers program, catering to students in grades 3 to 5. While the original roots of the space as a recreation center are apparent, with industrial-sized concrete block construction and high ceilings, the Nano Lab has nice purple and white coloring along the wall in a block-like pattern, as shown in Figure 1. The Nano Lab contains a 3D printer farm consisting of five networked 3D printers and an oven for form molding.

The other major piece of equipment in the Nano Lab is a laser cutter. Work areas include tables and chairs and many storage areas around the walls. As shown in Figure 2, the walls display colorful posters about manufacturing (subtractive and additive), how a 3D printer works, and some tips on being a SUPERMAKERS, which stands for:

**S:** Students
**U:** Understanding their
**P:** Peers
**E:** Everyone deserves
**R:** Respect

*Figure 1. The Nano Lab 3D print farm*

**M:** Manners
**A:** And
**K:** Kindness
**E:** Everyone is
**R:** Responsible for
**S:** Safety

The middle high school room, which is across the hall, is twice as large as the Nano Lab. This room is completely open with different studios and storage along the perimeter of the space, as shown in Figure 3.

Like the Nano Lab, the middle high school room contains multiple 3D printers and a laser cutter, plus a 3D scanner, Computer Numerical Control (CNC) mill, and an assortment of hand tools. Hand tools are stored on custom-built tool carts that were designed in-house. In these carts, as shown in Figure 4, every tool is labeled and outlined in one color. This, according to Grimes, helps create a shared vocabulary so students know exactly what the name of the tool is because it is marked on the tool cart. In addition, he stated:

*Figure 2. Nano Lab space*

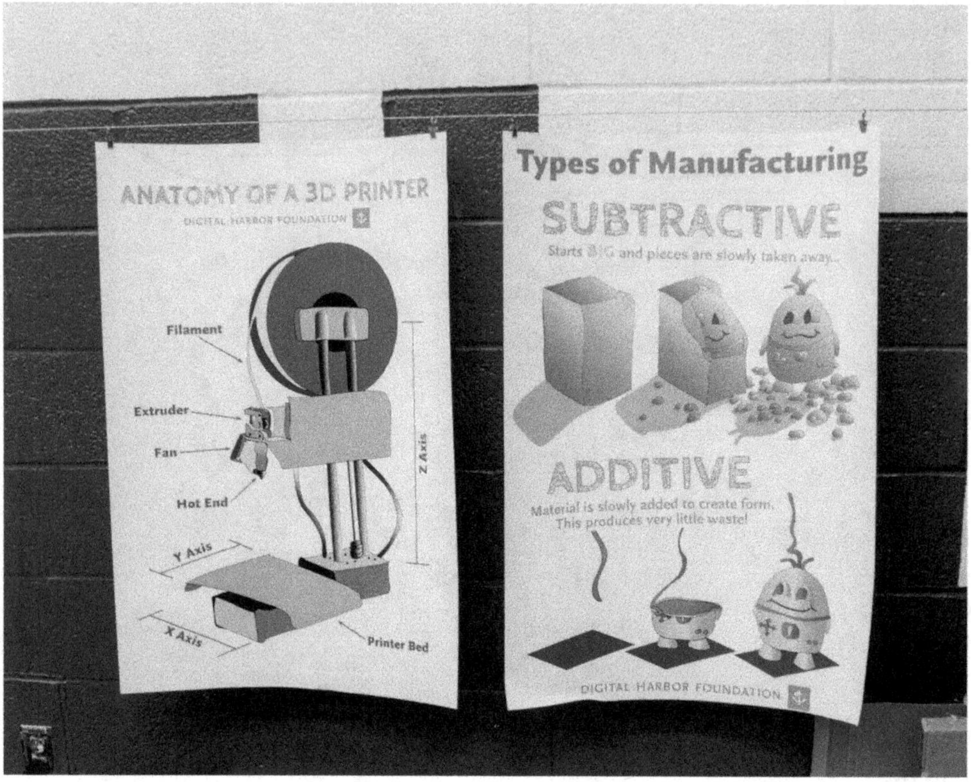


*I like it because I can see exactly which tool is missing from the cart. Or if I find a tool laying on a table, I know that it goes to the orange cart. The screw driver here goes to the yellow cart. That has helped our organization. Otherwise, we would just have our screw drivers in a drawer, and we would never know if we were missing one.*

Power tools include: drills, belt sander, orbital sander, router, miter saw, and a scroll saw. The space also has a vacuum former, vinyl cutters, and an electronics area with laptops, servers, Kinect sensor, Oculus Rift, Raspberry PIs, and Makey Makeys. Of note in the middle high school space is the 3D Assistance area run by 20-year-old Darius McCoy, who was recently a student in the space and one of the first students to participate in DHF. As a student, Darius built a 3D printer from a kit and was then invited to build a 3D printer at the White House. Now a DHF staff member, he runs the 3D Assistance

*Figure 3. The middle high school room*

*Figure 4. Tool carts*

lab as a community college student and provides printer repair for teachers and people in the community.

Grimes noted that Darius received a National Science Foundation (NSF) grant to create the 3D shop and has around eight employees. In addition to 3D printer repair, the 3D Assistance lab also provides services such as small batch manufacturing and on-demand 3D print jobs. The lab has done jobs of up to 2,000 items for a local university. The 3D Assistance lab is a separate entity from the middle high school room's 3D printer farm and is not used by students unless they are employed by Darius. Beginning at age 14, students, with appropriate training, are eligible to apply to work in the lab.

When asked about gaining the trust of the community, Grimes said that trust within the community had not been a challenge for the space. DHF looks like a school from the outside, and the space doesn't give off an opulent vibe until visitors actually venture into the space and see what the students are making.

Grimes stated:

*I don't feel like we're very glitzy or glamorous in here. Our tech is off to the side and more of what you see at first glance are the ordinary trinkets or little things. Then you get closer and find out that it was a youth project.*

Another interesting comment from Grimes is about the neighborhood-centric attitude of Baltimore. Grimes, being from Baltimore's east side, may not be fully accepted into a community of people from the south side of Baltimore.

*A good bit of us are Baltimore natives. I've been here my entire life. It's very siloed; they [residents] don't like outsiders telling them how to do things in Baltimore. Even neighborhood to neighborhood, it can be very ... the new term I'm using is "neighborhood-centric." If you grew up on East Baltimore, which is where I grew up, you have no idea what it's like to live in West Baltimore. That is very much held against you.*

However, since trust was not an issue as the space started up, one can assume that even being from East Baltimore provided some credibility to starting the space in the Federal Hill district. Moreover, the idea that students pay-what-they-can to be a part of the space also lends credibility and trust to the space. The pay-what-you-can membership model asks families to pay what they are able for the services and programs.

## SETTING THE STAGE

Digital Harbor Foundation is a youth-based educational makerspace that caters to young makers in grades 3rd through 5th in the Mini Makers program, and middle and high school students through the Maker Foundations program. Additional programs are also offered during the summer and reach students starting in the first grade.

To join the space, students are recruited and attend what is called an *Anchor Night,* which is an orientation for students who are interested in the space. At Anchor Night, DHF staff talk to students about the commitment that's involved with attending the program, which includes showing up two days a week for two to three hours a session. Also, during Anchor Night, students work on a hands-on activity while the staff observe students as they progress through the activity.

Staff are particularly interested in interactions and collaborations between students as well as their overall level of excitement about being in the space. Then students are invited into the program. Students cannot join; they must be invited to participate. However, Grimes stated: *Right, you have to be invited. The dirty secret is, we've never turned anyone away.*

The Mini Maker program in the Nano Lab is primarily an after-school program that is run twice a week while school is in session. DHF runs a number of innovative maker-type activities during the sessions. Steph Grimes, the Director of Education at Digital Harbor Foundation, spoke about the different projects that students make in the Mini Maker program. One seven-week program immerses students into toy manufacturing in a program called *Tinkering Toys.* In the program, students learn about additive and subtractive manufacturing processes through the development of their own toy and toy company. They learn how to use sewing machines and to hand stitch and fill to make stuffed animal toys. Then they have to develop packaging to sell and transport their creations. Within the same Tinkering Toys program, students also have the opportunity to cut laser tiles for a matching game as shown in Figure 5. Steph explained the project as follows:

*Sean [Grimes] developed an app in-house that allows you to create a simple SVG [Scalable Vector Graphics] from a pencil sketch. It uses the computer's camera and then they just transfer it over. These are some of their laser cut tiles. They're watching the laser cutter in action and seeing how their game pieces are being made and then they're using water color and painting them to give them color or not.*

*Figure 5. Laser cut game tiles*

In the project, students are free to choose their designs and a template is provided for the size, but it is not standard across the board.

According to Steph Grimes, the most famous project to come out of the Nano Lab is the *Bubble Wand* project. The wands are custom 3D printed and allow students to experiment with design, with the purpose of creating a wand for blowing soap-based bubbles into the air, as shown in Figure 6. Students are able to use the same in-house app as the laser tiles to create their wands. Students draw them out on paper and then scan and 3D print their wands. One of the Mini Makers blew bubbles with the U.S. President at the White House Science Fair, according to Steph Grimes:

*One of our mini makers, one of our third graders, actually got to go and blow bubbles with the President at the White House science fair. That was a big hit. Again, they're using the same app that they use to create the laser cut tiles and drawing out what they want to have and then just 3D printing it and then making bubbles to test it. That's the fun part.*

Another project within the toy manufacturing activities is the creation of sticky toys. Steph Grimes defines the project as:

*Figure 6. A custom 3D printed bubble wand*

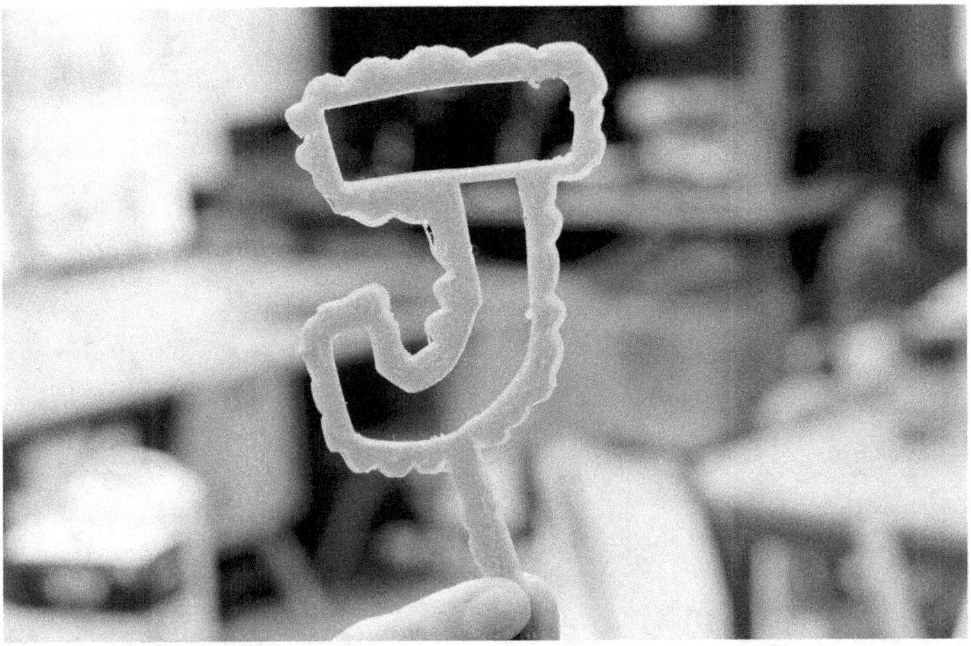

*These are those hands, the sticky things that you throw, against window planks really. They're doing molding and learning molding basics through that. They're mold designing that and then 3D printing and going through the manufacturing process to actually create the sticky part of that. Then they cook it in the toaster oven.*

As shown in Figure 7, the slime solidifies in the 3D printed mold and then students can remove it from the mold and use the slime to stick to windows. Again, these projects are teaching students traditional fabrication methods through accessible toys and games.

Another project in the space is the Interactive Games program. In this program, students are creating one-off arcade games using a cardboard component with a digital game. Steph Grimes described the program as the following:

*They're programming games in scratch. This is one of the games that was built; it's got these three little pom-poms. The whole idea is that this is then connected to a Makey Makey and then paired with a scratch game that they've developed to interact in a certain way. That's really looking at programming.*

*Figure 7. Slimes in mold*

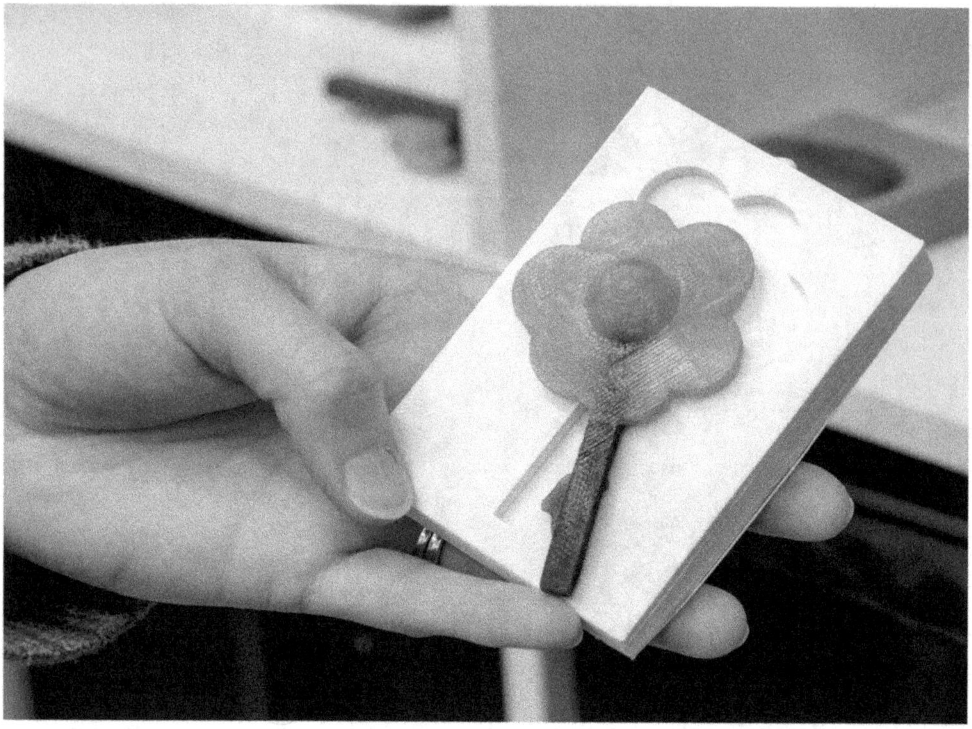

*One aspect of it is researching. They start with: let's research our arcade games, let's play some games, what are the mechanics that happen in board games or card games or games you might play with your family?*

*Then translate that into let's do some research in arcade games. What's skeet ball? What are the mechanics of that? What does a claw machine look like? Those types of things. Then really starting to base ideas and then programing it in scratch so they've got a digital component. Then they've also got the hands-on cardboard construction component.*

The Interactive Games program is one program that readily bridges the gap between digital technology and the making processes.

From a pedagogical standpoint, direct instruction mixed with inquiry learning activities is used for the students in the Nano Lab. Moreover, the students use a scaffolded engineering design type of notebook where they are prompted in the design and planning of each project. The notebook consists of seven pages and contains prompts for each project. The first activity in the workbook is intended to support students as they design and develop their toy company logo. The notebook starts with criteria for what is needed in a logo, including: it must be simple, memorable, timeless, versatile, and appropriate. Next, students work through a series of self-reflection questions and write the answers in the notebook:

- *Is your logo simple?*
- *Are you able to easily remember your logo?*
- *Will your logo still look good in 10 years?*
- *Does your logo look big or small? How about black and white? In color?*
- *Does your logo look like it should represent a toy or brand?*

Once the self-reflection questions are answered, students select by circling one of the choices for the purpose of the logo (specific toy, toy brand, your personal logo as a designer). Students are then instructed to sketch at least five different logos in the notebook and circle their favorite design when complete. Next, with the logo design narrowed down, students are instructed to draw it three more times using different color schemes. To finalize the project, students are prompted to draw their logo two more times in black and white.

The notebook allows students to record their progress from an idea all the way to a final project. The Bubble Wand task introduces students to creating a prototype and again has probing questions in the notebook. Students begin by drawing three versions of their bubble wands and then are asked for a peer review before selecting their final design. Next, using the in-house conversion app, the drawing is converted to a 3D (SVG) print file and then printed. Finally, students are asked if it worked (yes, no). The notebook has space for them to reflect on what they would change about their bubble wand. Other activities with similar scaffolds are also included in the notebook.

The idea behind Tinkering Toys is that students are working on toys for their very own toy company, and at the end of the unit students receive an opportunity to present their projects at a showcase. There are two showcases per year, with the first in January and the other during spring. The showcase can be a large public event or sometimes it's smaller with parents, family, and friends attending, depending on timing of the event. During the showcase visitors walk through and visit each student's area to learn about their projects.

Across the hall from the Nano Lab is the middle high school room, which again is roughly twice the size of the Nano Lab. The expectation is that students graduate from the Nano Lab and make their way to the middle high school room where they will start with the Maker Foundation program. Of course, it's not just the Nano Lab graduates but other students from the Baltimore schools joining the middle high school room. The Maker Foundation courses are 14-week introductory courses that meet twice a week for about three hours a day. Middle and high school students take the course together as one cohort. Shawn Grimes described the course as:

*That course, it's a survey course. You'll do 3D printing, electronics, game development, web development, graphic design, I think those are the big ones. Then once you've completed that, you are eligible for our member programs, which are more advanced topics. You'll take a seven or a 14-week course on one topic. Might be intermediate 3D design or 2D fabrication.*

The course is facilitated by program specialists at Digital Harbor Foundation. The content for the Maker Foundations course is online. Students are able to progress through the program at their own pace with support from the program specialists. While the program is self-paced, the courses have specific start and end times, and students are required to manage their time so that they can complete the course in the allotted time. Students have the flexibility to choose to spend more or less time on a project, depending on their interest.

Once students have completed the Maker Foundations course, they can attend the open nights and also work on other projects. Content in the space is constantly being created and updated as program specialists teach and learn from the students. Teachers in the space are hard to spot, according to Grimes:

*That is our goal. I want to have to look for you because I don't want to be able to say, you're just sitting at the presenter station. I want you embedded and working hands-on with the kids.*

As previously mentioned, the Digital Harbor Foundation works on the pay- what-you-can model and that includes materials and consumables that are used in the middle high school room. Students do not have to pay for anything while using the space. DHF also has a budget for students' special projects. Students with an idea for a project can apply for the funds by writing up a proposal that includes a budget. Grimes commented about past projects:

*We've had a lot of kids want to do, for whatever reason, maglev (magnetic levitation). They want to do maglev shoe or a maglev skateboard. It's like, okay, show me what you're going to do differently than the three kids before you who failed.*

Other projects that have been done in the space include large letters with lights that are controlled by a Raspberry Pi computer. The letters change color when a certain hashtag is tweeted. Grimes recalled that Adam Savage, co-host of MythBusters, the popular Discovery Channel television show, found out about the letter project and wanted to create a larger version for the White House's South by South Lawn event. Savage's team visited DHF and built 7-foot versions of the letters with the help of about 50 students in the space.

Other items in the middle high school room are power tools like table saws and drills. Grimes commented that they don't intentionally teach the use of table saws or power drills. That equipment is not built into the course, but if a student needs to use the equipment, a program specialist will provide an introduction to the equipment, including required safety gear like glasses and gloves.

On average, Digital Harbor will see 250 to 1,000 total visits per month. As shown in Figure 8, males and females are equally represented in the space.

*Figure 8. Gender balance of visitors*

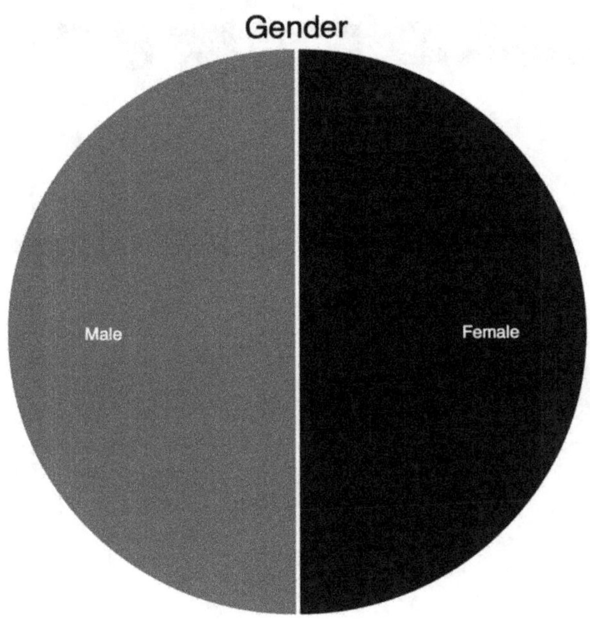

The ethnicity of membership is shown in Figure 9. About 40 to 59% are white, 60 to 79% are black or African-American, less than 20% are Asian, Native American, Alaskan Natives, Native Hawaiians and other Pacific Islanders, and 60 to 79% are two or more races that may be included in the other ethnicities.

The types of users that visited the space are shown in Figure 10. Less than 20% are visitors or observers, hobbyists, startups, and college age (18 to 24 years of age). 40 to 59% are youth under 13 years of age or youth 13 to 18 while 20 to 39% are teachers.

The purpose of visits to the space are shown in Figure 11. 60 to 79% of visitors were there to receive training, while 20 to 39% were there as an introduction to making and to socialize. Less than 20% were there to make something specific, make one-off pieces, small batch production and to network.

*Figure 9. Ethnicity of membership*

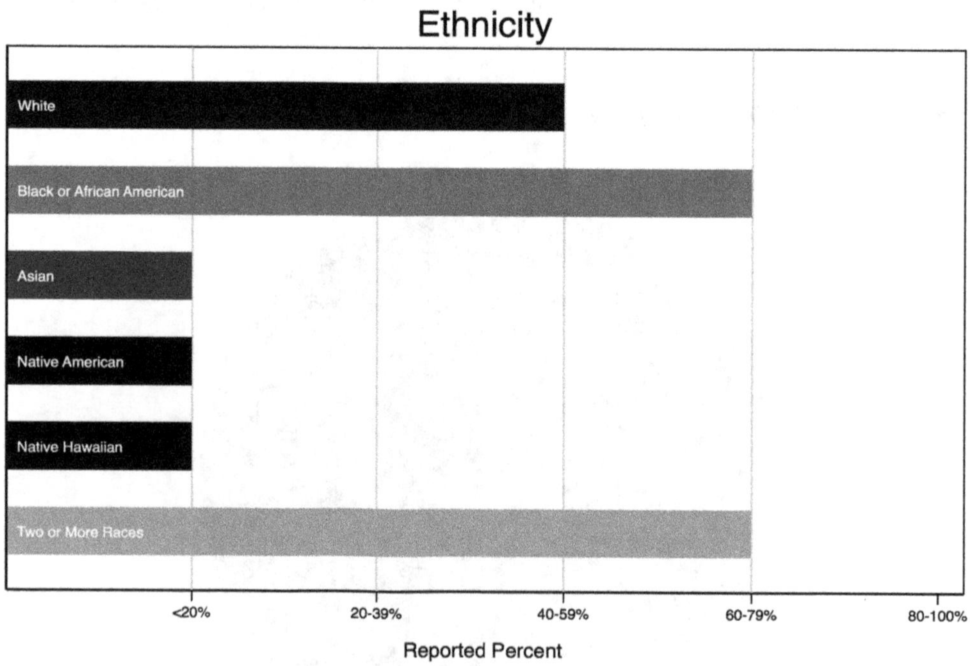

*Figure 10. Types of visitors per month*

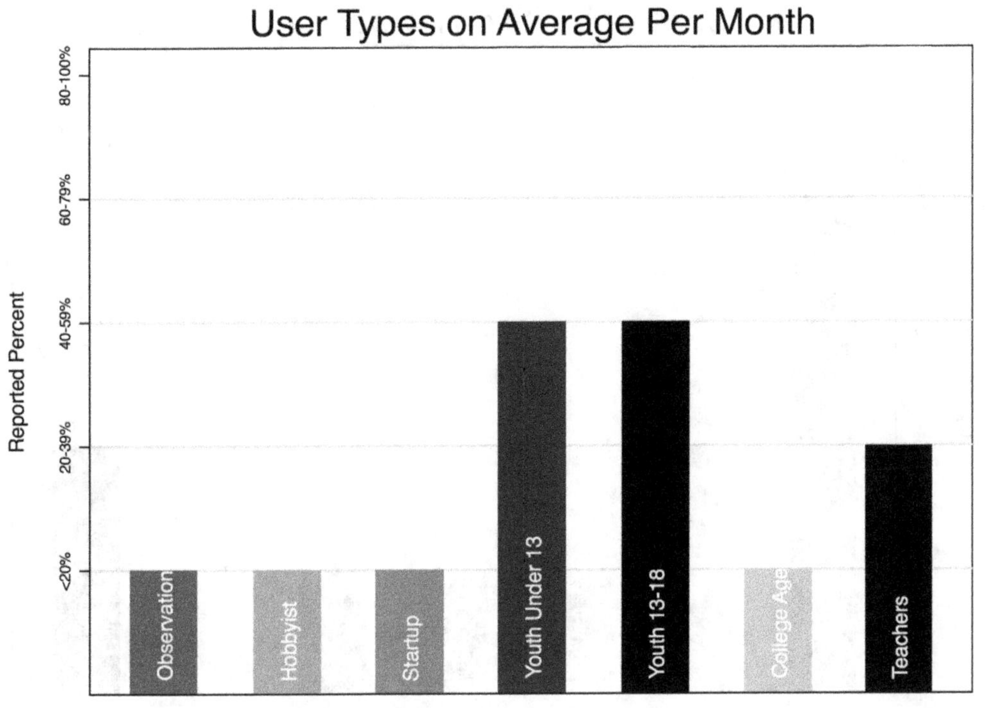


## LEARNING COMMUNITIES

The development of learning communities in DHF is very organic as Grimes explained it:

*We've done some interesting social network mapping evaluations. In the beginning of a program we're looking at connections between youth. You give them a roster of kids and have them check off which ones they consider to be a friend. In the beginning, very few. By the end we're seeing clusters of the youth, the spread of the map is much more close together with very few outsiders. Then what's also interesting is that we noted 75% reciprocity. I say you're a friend, 75% of the people that I marked say that I'm a friend as well.*

To encourage students working together and establishing community, DHF set up the learning environment in a specific way to find the right configuration that encourages collaboration. Grimes commented:

*Figure 11. Purpose of visits per month*

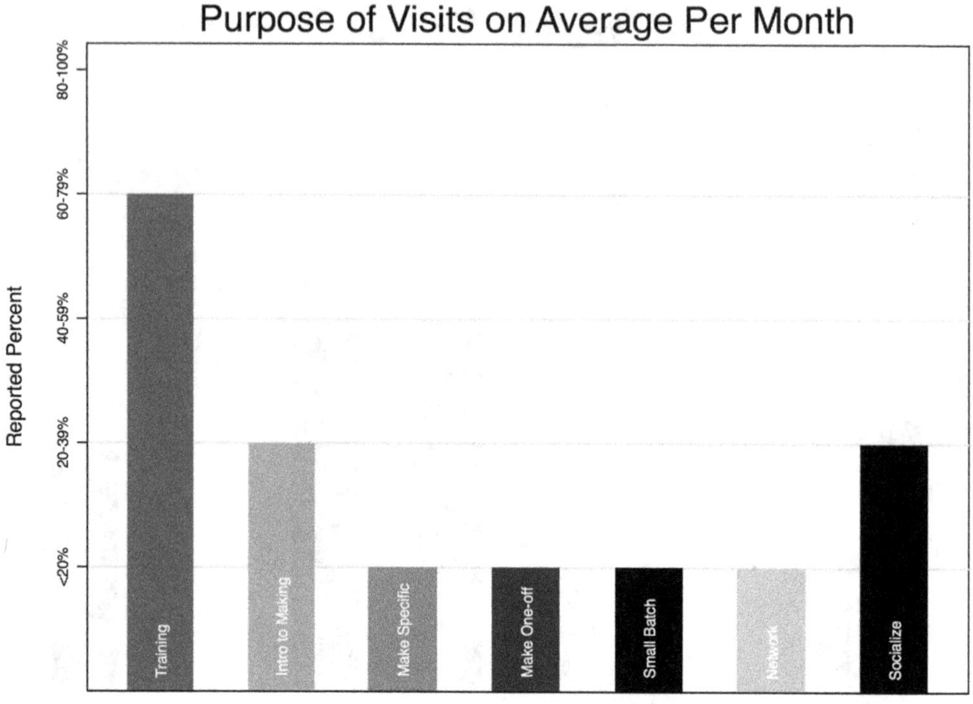


*All the tables are on wheels, so we spent a lot of time with different configurations. We found that having two students face each other provided the most collaboration and indirect collaboration. Kids sitting next to each other may talk about what they're working on, but they might also just glance over, see what someone's doing, and they're like, that's really cool, I'm going to do that too. With the physical builds, they can do the same things looking across the table. Sometimes they will talk to each other, sometimes they don't. We have some youth with some anxiety and things like that, so they don't want to interact with other people for a while. Eventually they seem to come around.*

At each table there are seats facing each other, with four students at a table. In addition to the physical layout, learning communities are established through the creative work that is done in the space. The use of digital manipulatives in a social context lends itself to the formation of communities, as opposed to utilizing a worksheet. Grimes mentioned that even students who are not comfortable with social interaction find themselves comfortable working in the space. Indirect communication is also possible, according to Grimes:

*Even if it is what we call indirect collaboration, or as one youth with severe social anxiety calls it, human adjacent, he can be human adjacent. We do have some courses that focus on group dynamics more intentionally.*

Digital Harbor Foundation has also experimented with a Minecraft course as a way to build community within the middle high school space. Students build a colony in Minecraft with members deciding on the governmental rules and job roles of each community member. The roles (farmers, builders, and even politicians) were self-defined and assigned by the students. Surprisingly, educators found that the students scored lower on a posttest self-efficacy towards communication and teamwork than they scored on a pretest. Grimes explained the results this way:

*When we brought that to our program quality committee, we were, yeah, looks like their communication skills went down. Their point was they're actually more aware of what good communication skills are before and after. We do some work with some researchers and when they talk about self-efficacy, I'm like, yeah, but if a kid says that ... most of our kids are so confident they'll say they can do anything but that's not actually true.*

Not a typical artifact but one that needs to be recorded is the Weekend Hackathon printer queue project that is located in the 3D printer areas for the middle high school room, as shown in Figure 12. It is somewhere between an art wall hanging and a command center. The project hangs prominently in the 3D print lab area of the space. The project was created by a learning community consisting of a staff member and six students who had gone through the Maker Foundations course.

The team had 36 hours to create the artifact and show it at the end of the hackathon. According to Grimes, the group went through the entire design process in 36 hours. The 3D print queue is an amalgamation of 3D printed purely decorative pieces, some with a purpose; a computer screen; an Arduino microcontroller to record the print jobs and filament usage; a Raspberry PI computer to run the screen; and circuitry to support everything, including LEDs around the project.

The project was part of a larger community event, and the team competed against other adult teams. During the competition, the students had three minutes to present the project. The student team ended up winning their division of the hackathon. Grimes commented that the project brought together the students as a team, and they learned a great deal from the entire

*Figure 12. The printer queue*

design process: programming, circuitry, 3D printing, and public speaking and presentation skills. Students who were a part of the Hackathon continue to be members of DHF, but the team no longer works on projects together.

Close to half of the members at Digital Harbor Foundation are females. Grimes believes that the social connections are what keeps the females in the space. An all-girls group called the Makerettes was established by a team of students and an educator. The all-girls group meets every other Friday and, on occasion, will develop site-wide projects like the ugly Christmas sweater project. The Makerettes' main function, however, is to provide community amongst the girl makers. Prior to establishing the group, many of the female attendees would not continue to be members of the space until one of the youth came to the realization that it was her connections to the staff and other female makers that kept her coming back. On occasion DHF will also run female-only cohorts of the Maker Foundations courses. Grimes also commented about male students in the space:

*The guys don't have a problem coming. We changed a good bit of our marketing to include girls on the marketing. This is our Maker Foundations program, then on the back we have some guys, but our main photo is the girls.*

*We found out when we changed this that the girls appeared more ... enjoyed seeing themselves in a photo; the guys did not care who was in the photo.*

In DHF the maker mindset is taught through practice. Not only practice but teaching students how to learn. Students are encouraged to be self-reliant when it comes to gaining the knowledge they need. According to Grimes, this is an important skill:

*I think that one of the most important things that we can teach them is that learning does not come from a person (lecturing) in front of the room, because as soon as that person's not in the front of the room, your learning is not stopped. Again, this is why a lot of our content is web-based and self-driven.*

In the space students have a *three-before-me* rule, which, simply stated, means that a learner should ask the person on her left, the person on her right and Google (perform a web search) her question before asking a staff member for an answer. A staff member will ask students what they Googled to see if they have used appropriate parameters in their query. Accordingly, this builds up the student's problem-solving abilities and ability to self-direct her learning. Members also have some choice when it comes to selecting their projects.

Built into the Maker Foundations course is a structure that consists of two weeks per topic area. In the first week students develop their skills and knowledge. The second week is developing a project that implements that skill and knowledge. The project is up to the student to choose and complete.

When asked about the keychain syndrome, which means that all the youth create the exact artifact, Grimes explained that they provide free choice not in the keychain itself but what goes on the keychain. He stated:

*I think the key on the keychain is independent choice. It's what goes on that keychain. We do a field trip, where kids can come to our space during the school day and do 3D printing. They make a keychain, but they can put whatever they want on that keychain. It could be mom, dad, puppy, mummy, whatever ... And I always use the analogy of my name is Shawn, S-H-A-W-N. When I was a kid and I wanted a toothbrush with my name on it, they always had S-E-A-N, but never S-H-A-W-N. I'm sure there's all kinds of S-E-A-Ns who have the exact opposite happen to them. The reason we do the keychains for the field trips is because we have a time commitment. In the actual programs, they don't have those sorts of instructions.*

Staff also help instill confidence and resilience for students through their modeling of behavior. Most staff in the program have little experience in making and digital fabrication but attend training just a few weeks before the session starts, to teach the same way the students are learning. Staff model the ideal of tolerating the unknown, which is a foreign concept to many. Grimes describes a teacher development exercise:

*That's not their background, so they're bringing their own experience of having gone through the unknown. We do an exercise in their educator workshops where we say, "Make a robot that draws with the supplies you have." And during the first three minutes some teachers get right to it, but some teachers sit there and like, "What in the world is he thinking?" Then we put up a slide with an example of an art bot. At that point, even just with the example, they're like, "Oh, okay, I see what he did."*

Teachers are modeling this behavior, and students are learning to tolerate the unknown as they repeat in each lesson, delving into areas that they are not totally comfortable working in. In the training, teachers experience the frustration and uncomfortableness that the students will have during their courses. Teachers are instructed to use scaffolds to allow students to get more comfortable with the content and the unknown. The practice of reaching into the unknown multiple times is one-way DHF instills confidence in their students. Grimes stated:

*What I think we need to do is instill confidence, and I think from that you can at least increase your tolerance for not knowing or your tolerance for the unknown. That's what we try to do, you have this one week of building skills, but then you have this week of, I don't know what I'm going to do. Then through repetition because you're going to do that six or seven times as we go through different topics, by the end you start to feel you've journeyed into the unknown six or seven times and come out the other side unscathed and maybe even very successful. Maybe that's how we're impacting the stick to it-ness, is that we're making the unknown more comfortable.*

According to Grimes, paid staff in the space come from three different backgrounds: creatives, like art school teachers or art school graduates; formal educators; and technology-related professionals. Each background represents roughly one-third of the total staff, which Grimes refers to as the magic triangle. Grimes himself comes from a technology background but prefers to hire creatives. He states:

*Through my experiences here, I favor hiring the creatives. It's something that I value more now than actually valuing the technology. As a technologist for 20 years, it's not that that's a hard pill to swallow, but it's tough to realize that you've been an idiot for the last 20 years so that's more of it. I always thought, "It doesn't matter what it looks likes as long as it works." No, that's completely wrong.*

Digital Harbor Foundation provides youth leadership roles and the possibility to move from student to mentor to a paid staff position. As mentioned before, Darius is one example of a student who has risen to be a staff member and is running the 3D Assistance area. Nathan is another student who will graduate and work in the space full-time. One other student, who is a senior in high school and leads some of the teaching in the space, is now working at a software development company five days a week as a quality assurance tester. Students in the space are provided leadership opportunities by presenting to groups on behalf of Digital Harbor Foundation at various events throughout the year. Grimes explained leadership development in this way:

*… the cream starts to rise to the top in very unexpected ways, and actually what I find, a lot of the [students] who are not as outgoing are the ones who end up being the most responsible and trustworthy. We don't have any direct mentoring constructed coursework. It's more sort of woven all throughout. If you build a really remarkable product per project, then you're going to get invited to show it off at National Maker Faire or submit it for TED-Ex Youth. Then that's when coaching starts to come in. If a youth doesn't want to do it, let's figure out why. Is it a confidence issue? Then we're going to work with you and you're going to get over that in a positive way, not like we're going to throw you out there no matter what. We look for those to come up organically from our program, then focus our attention.*

When hiring, DHF is looking for candidates who value young people and feel that they have as much to learn from them as they do to teach them. Grimes asks candidates what they can learn from youth, and if the candidate thinks youth have nothing to offer, then they are probably not a good fit for the space. The more candidates understand that students come into the space with a specific skillset that they can learn from, the better fit they are to work in the space. Grimes gave the following example:

*Just a very minimal example, I drive. I have a car. I drive all the time, but we only have one car and so when Stef [Grimes] needs to go somewhere, and I need to go somewhere different, we have to figure something else out. Uber's a really easy option, but I decided I wanted to start riding the bus more. I've no idea how to ride the bus. I haven't ridden it since I was a kid, so I asked Darius to help me. I had to humble myself and be like, "Darius, how do I ride the bus?" He was happy to teach me, and I recognized that riding the bus is an experience that he's done his whole life.*

In the space, staff are encouraged to facilitate and not lecture when delivering content. The space holds a professional development workshop every semester right before the programs start. In addition, when teaching standard logistics like fire drills and rally points, staff are taught to match the level of the students. When a student has a question, a staff member is taught that he or she should be at the level of the student and not talk down to them at all. Also, they are encouraged to co-work with students whenever possible by putting their laptops next to the students and working alongside them. For example, when students are working on programming, staff are expected to be working on programming also. This creates synergy, while encouraging and inspiring the student. Grimes stated:

*They (students) are not treated as equals, but they're treated as peers, because you can't ask kids what they want for dinner, it's always going to be candy. It's knowing when you have to be an adult and when you don't have to be.*

## FAMILIES IN THE SPACE

Surprisingly, or maybe not surprisingly, families are not that involved in the space during the week. The younger students in the Nano Lab have more involvement from their parents since they are the main providers of transportation. In the middle and high school programs, DHF does not see much family involvement. The students mostly walk or use public transportation to get to the space. Staff rarely interact with the parents. Families are invited to public events like the showcases, but Grimes speculates that many of the parents are not able to make it because of jobs and other responsibilities.

Grimes shared an interaction with the mother of a member:

*A lot of times the youth that we're working with, for instance, Darius, I've met his dad once, and his mom I met once through a car window. I never actually face-to-face interacted with her. She yelled through a car window and said, "Can you tell Darius to come out?" I was like, sure.*

*And that's Darius's thing. His mom worked the night shift and she was never around. She had to trust us with his care or at least know that he was somewhere he was supposed to be. ... I know she has never been to a showcase, but his little brother is about to sign up for our spring programs. I guess maybe inter-generational families are not as important, but generational families can definitely have an impact.*

One program to engage families is the Family Make Night that is held once a month. The program is open to the public, but it's usually attended by a different audience of parents than those of the students who come to the space during the week. The parents of these students are, of course, invited to the Family Make Nights but usually do not attend. Most families that attend are from more affluent areas like Baltimore County, Frederick County, and surrounding areas, and can drive to the space for the activities. Families are invited to come in and are provided a laptop with the directions for the evening's project. Families can work on their project at their own pace. While staff are around to help facilitate as needed, they do not generally provide direct instruction for the project. Families are free to arrive between 6 and 8 P.M. and can work and leave when they are done. Like all programs in the space, the Family Make Night follows the pay-what-you-can cost model.

## IMPACT ON COMMUNITY

Grimes indicated that DHF is having a positive impact on the community. People are talking about the space as a positive place in Baltimore that has sent nearly a dozen kids to the White House and has been featured in the media. Moreover, student members in the space from different backgrounds are being portrayed in a positive way, representing the community in a positive light. DHF is also providing youth with confidence so they can pursue careers related to what they are learning in the space. Students are gaining work skills.

The space has also had some impact on sustainability for its members. While not all will go into the STEM fields, most will be able to sustain themselves and their families upon leaving the space. Grimes stated:

*I think one of the main causes of any sort of unrest or crime here is a feeling that there is a lack of options; that it doesn't matter if breaking into this car could get me arrested, because I'm not going to end up with a job that will be impacted by me being arrested. Whereas now they're starting to see more options.*

The high school student working at a software firm wanted to be a photographer when she started attending courses in the space. She was encouraged to learn more about technology as a backup plan, which was not well received by the student. After a year and a half Grimes asked her:

*"Do you still hate technology?" And she said, "Yeah," and I was like, "But wait you're here every day." She's like, "But this isn't technology." I was like, "What do you think technology is?" She said, "Word documents and spreadsheets." I was like, "Okay, okay." Now, she wants to be a mechanical engineer. That's what she's applying to colleges for.*

The impact of the space on the individual learners is reflected by the stories that Grimes shares. None are more potent than the story of Darius and his very good friend Eric. The two were inseparable during their early years at the space. Eric was a member of the DHF and convinced Darius to join in the beginning. In the intervening years, Darius continued to be a member of DHF while Eric ended up dropping out of the program. As Grimes explained:

*Before they graduated high school, Eric ended up being incarcerated for fighting and then never graduated high school and has been on a downward trend; whereas Darius has graduated high school, is enrolled part time in community college, and he's employed. These guys were basically inseparable. If I was taking one of them someplace, I had to take both of them. I think the difference was that Eric got into the wrong crowd and stopped coming, but Darius kept coming. He was never able to pull Eric back in, and I don't think that Eric saw the opportunity as much as Darius did.*

Darius is an example of a student that has come through the DHF program and developed skills that have enabled him to support himself and his family.

Grimes also feels that DHF has had an impact on students' attitudes towards school. More to the point, it has impacted what they think school should be like. With learning choices and hands-on activities, many students have thrived at DHF, whereas in the formal educational system those supports do not exist. Moreover, problem-based learning centered on personally relevant learning activities appears to be a very powerful learning tool. When students have to figure out payroll and profit margins for their business, math may have a whole different level of engagement than what is found in the formal educational system.

## DEFINING A MAKERSPACE

When asked to define a makerspace and the core components of a makerspace, Grimes responded:

*I first have to define making for me, and I think that making is the intersection of creativity and productivity. Then to take that into makers are the ones who produce creative and productive projects, and then a makerspace is a space that allows a community of makers to share tools, share experiences, and share projects.*

## CURRENT CHALLENGES

If you had a checklist of everything a makerspace should be, Digital Harbor Foundation would meet 99% of that criteria. Like many successful makerspaces, DHF found a way to bring value to an underutilized building in the community, in this case a recreation center connected to the Federal Hill Preparatory School that had closed. This benefited both the community, by not having a vacant building, and DHF, by not having the burden of meeting a monthly rental fee. Because of this, DHF has adopted the pay-what-you-can model, which starts at zero. Every event that is hosted adheres to this payment model, including the Family Maker Nights. Even supplies used in the space are low cost or free to student members. However, this model also means that funds must be raised to support these initiatives. Digital Harbor is always on the hunt for grants and other revenue streams to keep the doors open.

One challenge is the location of DHF, which is in the more affluent Federal Hill neighborhood. It is a challenge to recruit underrepresented youth because they most likely do not live in the neighborhood. While public transportation does serve the space, it is unlikely that younger students are able to attend programs if they have to arrange their own transportation. This makes an interesting challenge if the idea is to have a continuum of maker-related experiences for students starting in the late elementary grades and moving all the way through high school.

It's a solid plan for students to spend two years in the Nano Lab and then move across the hall to the middle high school room, but staff are struggling to figure out a way to bring in younger makers and their families from underrepresented groups. During Family Make Nights, the typical attendees are driving to the space from nearby counties, and these events are not generally attracting the targeted underrepresented students' families. Because these families typically are struggling with jobs and other responsibilities, involvement for them is difficult. However, family involvement and support for students in the space might take other forms. Grimes reflected back to Darius' family support:

*Family support of the space is not communicated to us. It could be happening at home. Like Darius's mom could be saying, "No, this is really important. You need to keep going with it." But we're not collaborating on that. Or, just thinking of some of the other youth, there's not much collaboration between us and the parents. Their message is hopefully in support of us when the students are at home, but I don't know.*

## KEY TERMS AND DEFINITIONS

**3D Assistance Lab:** A lab area in DHF that provides printer repair for teachers and people in the community.

**3D Print Farm:** A collection of 3D printers.

**3D Printed Bubble Wand:** A 3D printed object used to create bubbles.

**Anchor Night:** DHF orientation night.

**Baltimore Federal Hill:** Area of South Baltimore just south of the city center and near the Inner Harbor of the Patapsco River.

**Digital Harbor Foundation:** Out-of-school makerspace in Baltimore, Maryland.

**Interactive Games Program:** In this program, students create one-off arcade games using a cardboard component with a digital game.

**Maker Foundations Course:** Fourteen-week introductory course on making that meet twice a week for three hours a day.

**Makerettes:** Female maker group at DHF.

**Makey Makey:** Hardware controller.

**Middle High School Room:** DHF area for middle and high school students.

**Mini Makers Program:** DHF program catering to students in Grades 3 to 5.

*MythBusters*: A popular Discovery Channel television show.

**Nano Lab:** Area at DHF for students in Grades 3 to 5.

**SVG:** Scalable vector graphics file used in 3D printing.

**Tinkering Toys:** A maker program for Mini Makers at DHF.

# Chapter 6
# The Fairfield Makerspace

## ABSTRACT

*The Fairfield Makerspace is located in the green belt corn growing area in the southeastern portion of Iowa, USA. The town hosts the Maharishi University of Management (MUM), which is unlike any university in the Midwest in that most members of the university community practice transcendental meditation (TM). This practice has led to a general misunderstanding between the university community and those that do not practice TM. MUM opened the Fairfield Makerspace in response to the mistrust between the town and the university. The role of the makerspace is to find commonality between communities in the areas of making and sustainable living. The space was finding its footing as it began their first year of operation. Learning communities are formed through workshops and special meetups called Transformation Tuesdays, where members upcycle items. This chapter explores the Fairfield Makerspace.*

DOI: 10.4018/978-1-5225-8310-3.ch006

*From my interaction with people in the community, like at the hardware store or similar environments, I hear them say, "Oh, you work for the university? They don't like us over there." People in the community think we don't like them. I try to tell them, "I don't think that's true. You need to just come and check it out." But there is that preconception that they are not welcome, so we're doing everything we can to change that. — Lyndi Ouellette*

## ORGANIZATION BACKGROUND

The Fairfield Makerspace is a university-based site open to faculty, students, and staff of the Maharishi University of Management (MUM), as well as the public in the small town of Fairfield, Iowa. The non-profit and privately-owned MUM started out as Maharishi International University in 1971 and the name was later changed to Maharishi University of Management, to reflect the school's role in preparing students "to successfully manage all areas of life—both personal and professional" (Schmidt-Wilk, Heaton, & Steingard, 2000). To understand the Fairfield Makerspace and its unique set of challenges, it is necessary to briefly visit the history of the school and its teaching practices. The story of MUM starts with its founder, born in India around 1917, whose given name was Mahesh Prasad Varma or Srivastava (Lowe, 2011). At some point after studying in India with a Hindu monk, Mahesh took the name Maharishi Mahesh Yogi, which means great (maha) sage (rishi), and yogi, which is reserved for practitioners of yoga (Lowe, 2011). Maharishi developed and later taught the Science of Creative Intelligence (SCI), which in 1972 became a course at MUM (Schmidt-Wilk, Heaton & Steingard, 2010). At the center of SCI is the practice of Transcendental Meditation (TM) which, according to Maharishi, leads to enlightenment (Wallace, 1974). SCI and TM are both rooted in the ancient Vedic Hindu scripts (Schmidt-Wilk, Heaton & Steingard, 2000). Wallace (1974) noted that Transcendental Meditation "is a systematic procedure to gain enlightenment, which is the development of one's consciousness to the fullest potential." The TM movement is grounded in ideas and ancient texts from India called the Veda which means knowledge (Lowe, 2011). Maharishi taught participants of TM to use simple mantras from a Vedic text called the Rig Veda, which is perhaps the oldest of the Veda texts (Lowe, 2011). In addition, it is said that the Vedic texts describe a systematic approach to achieving heightened consciousness.

TM is central to the teaching at the Maharishi School of Management, whereby students understand the field of heightened consciousness through awareness and experiential learning (Schmidt-Wilk, Heaton & Steingard 2000). Transformation of society is another important learning goal for students at MUM. Throughout their education, students are taught the importance of creativity and sustainability to advance the quality of life for everyone. Through TM and their education at MUM, students are able to implement and refine practices that help others. In addition, TM is said to, "lower stress, enhance mental clarity, and support overall health" for students (MUM, n.d.). MUM offers undergraduate and graduate degrees in the following academic areas, in addition to other certification programs.

- MUM Academic areas:
    - Art (BA and BFA) and MFA in Studio Art
    - Business (BA, MBA, Ph.D.)
    - Computer Science (BA, MS)
    - Literature and Writing (BA)
    - Maharishi Vedic Science (BA, MA, Ph.D.)
    - Mathematics (BS)
    - Media and Communications (BA, MFA)
    - Physiology and Health (BS, MS, Ph.D.)
    - Sustainability (BA)

Unique to MUM is that courses are taught in a block schedule where subjects are taught for one month. Concurrently, with their one course per month, students also take the "Research in Conscience" course where they learn TM practices and meditate twice a day (Schmidt-Wilk, Heaton & Steingard, 2000). MUM is interested in developing students intellectually and spiritually, as reflected in the block scheduling of TM courses, all the way to the food served at MUM which is organically grown vegetarian food.

The Fairfield Makerspace was started as a passion project by MUM's sustainable living graduates and professors. The physical space for the Fairfield Makerspace is located in the Sustainable Living Department building on the MUM campus, spread across three different rooms for a total of 1,900 $ft^2$ (176.5 $m^2$). Prior to becoming a makerspace on January 1st, 2017, the space was used as an electronics lab, a student lounge and a workshop. During the author's visit, three members of the Fairfield Makerspace participated in a structured interview at the site. Two of the interviewees, Lyndi Ouellette and Leslie Hollis, are administrators working in the space and are employed by

MUM. Ouellette is a graduate of the sustainable living program at MUM. The third interviewee was Pam Ryerse, who serves is an entrepreneur and expert in textiles and sewing. Ryerse also donated industrial sewing equipment to the space to get their sewing studio started.

The main workshop, as shown in Figure 1, is a typical looking woodshop with a myriad of equipment and tools scattered about the space. In addition, there is an area for larger scale metalworking and welding. The shop also has a large bay door that can easily fit a vehicle or larger piece of equipment. As shown in Figure 2, along the walls are hand tools, storage, and tabletop space for working. At one time the shop was used to create tiny houses as part of the sustainable living program.

In a former iteration, the sewing studio, as shown in Figure 3, functioned as a student lounge prior to being renovated. The space is dominated by a large sewing table and smaller sewing stations set around the room.

Across the hall from the sewing area is the digital fabrication studio, as shown in Figure 4. The studio was once an electronics laboratory for student and is being overhauled to allow for additional equipment. Ouellette brought in her personal 3D printer to be used in the space. When asked why she responded:

*Figure 1. The Fairfield Makerspace shop area*

*Figure 2. Tools in the shop area*

*Figure 3. The sewing studio*

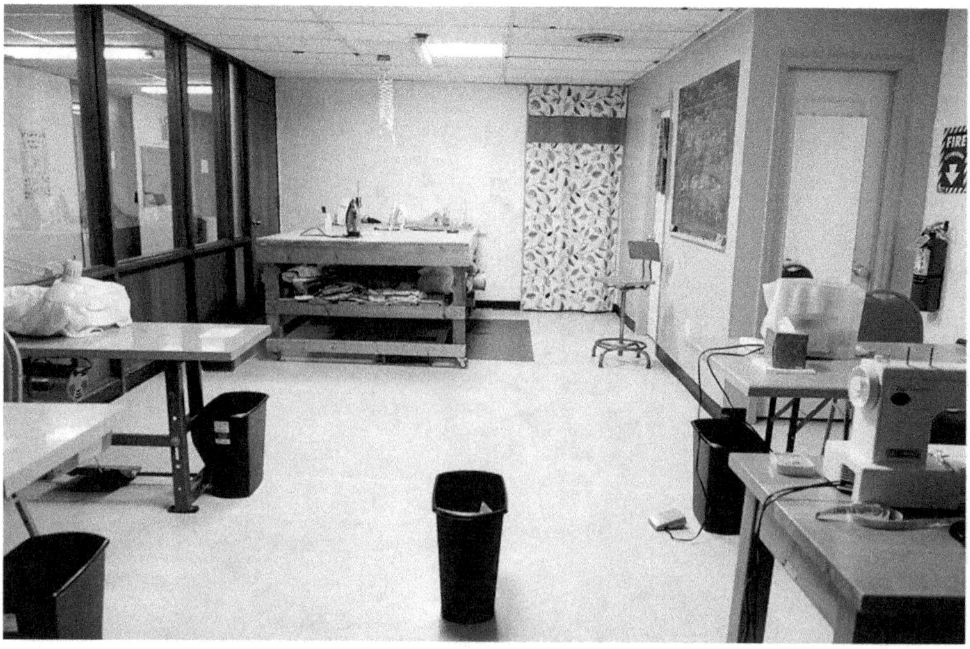

*I don't know if you've used 3D printers at all, but sometimes you have a print that can take a really long time. If someone else wants to print anything, they have to wait for that print to be done and we're like, "Maybe we should see what it's like to have two 3D printers." Also, the noise at our house ... He [Mike, partner] was printing something, I think the print time on it was 24 hours and I didn't want to listen to it overnight. We decided to just house it at the makerspace because we're here all the time anyways, and people can use it.*

The bike shop, as shown in Figure 5, is another space in the building that is also available to makerspace members. The bike shop was started by MUM students that were fixing and reselling bikes. They also supported the MUM campus bike program, where bikes were located across the campus for students to take, use and return for no fee. In the space, there are a number of bike frames, wheels, tires and bike stands, much like a commercial shop.

True to their mission as a program of sustainability, the space works diligently to re/upcycle material. Ouellette stated:

*Figure 4. The digital fabrication lab*

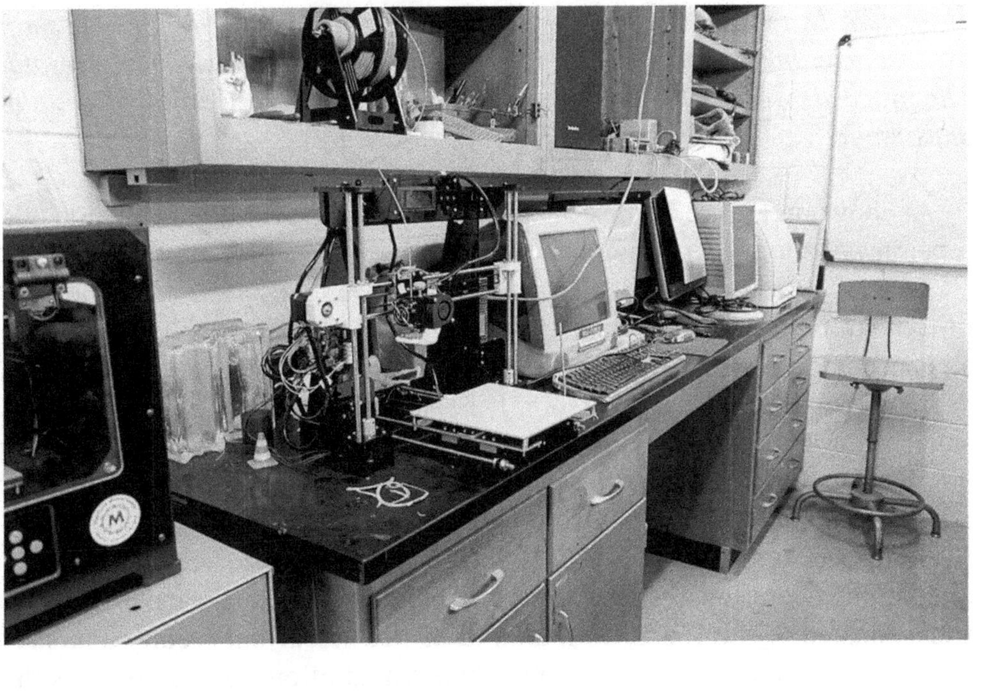

*Figure 5. The bike shop*

*It's hard when you're in sustainability, you don't want to throw anything away. It's always like, "We can use this. We can upcycle it." In the bike shop for instance, bikes would be donated to the space refurbished and resold. The proceeds were divided between the members working on bikes and the makerspace.*

As shown in Figure 6 a box of caulk and an angle grinder of questionable repair await adoption by members of the space.

There is a sense of optimism in the space, surrounded by a vision of helping the community of Fairfield and MUM students to better their lives. There is an expectation that as people develop their skills in the space, they will also develop a sense of entrepreneurship. The space has an eye towards developing small business incubators or micro-businesses. The idea is members can create products or ventures and give a percentage back to the space, much like the bike shop model. Members would have access to the equipment and space to create their products and in turn the space would receive some support to continue operations. A great deal of the current materials and equipment were donated to the space from alumni or MUM current faculty and staff members, as well as community members. In addition, MUM provides the

*Figure 6. Donations to the space*

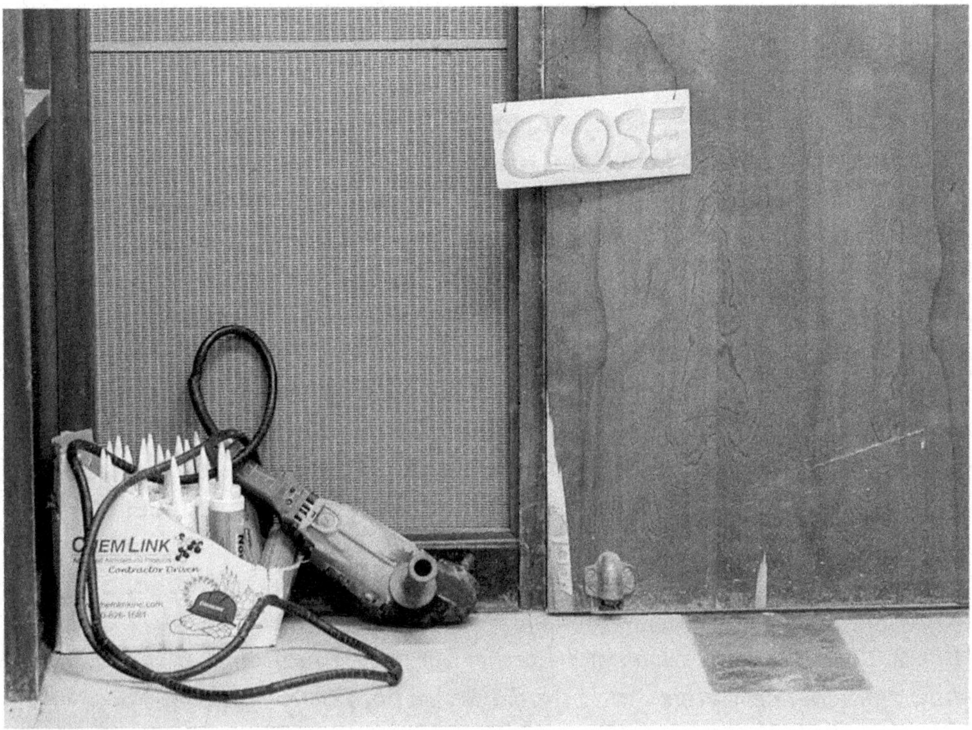


space free of rent and covers the salaries for two administrators. Ouellette noted that the space needs to be run somewhat like a business. She noted:

*We're creating an area where we can sell really high-quality lumber and quality—other pieces that might be donated to us, or that we find, or that we have, and then give people access that way. But if you went to another lumber shop you would pay a premium, so we want to have it [the lumber price] somewhere in between.*

Ouellette noted that the makerspace is in a precarious position, as a small town they have limited access to supplies. According to the 2016 U.S. Census Bureau Fairfield has a population just over 10,200. The nearest large population center of Iowa City is over an hour's drive from Fairfield (ACS,2016). By necessity many people in the town, and in more rural areas in general, have their own shops according to Ouellette. She stated:

*That is their background. They're more ... blue collar, I would say a lot of them have their own woodworking shop. I feel like with the welding, maybe not so much.*

The Fairfield Makerspace is focused on sustainability and trade skills, according to Ouellette. They want to help members learn to create things but also to mend and recycle items as well. The idea for trade skills is to allow members to use those skills to make a living. In 2016, it was estimated that Fairfield had about 19 percent of its residents living in poverty, therefore anything that can be done to help the community provide for their families is an important endeavor (ACS, 2016).

Organizationally, the space is run as part of the Sustainable Living Department of MUM. The department offers an elective course for MUM students around making, where they learn the different pieces of machinery in the space including woodworking and metalworking. Students in the course built a tiny house, according to Ryerse. When asked why MUM and the Sustainable Living Department wanted a makerspace, Ouellette stated:

*I think their hope is, at least from my degree standpoint, it was a lot of philosophical knowledge. And I think they're hoping to substitute some more, practical skills. A lot of students that come here, they don't want to just learn about it. They want to put it into action and see it from start to finish, and that way they have more tangible skills when they graduate.*

When asked why MUM wanted to invite the wider community to be a part of the space, Hollis noted they wanted to help the relationship between MUM and the larger community. There exists tension and misunderstanding between the MUM community and the residents of Fairfield. Ouellette does not think it was the official position of MUM to improve relations with the wider Fairfield community, but it has been seen as an opportunity to do so by people running the makerspace. Ryerse commented that in the past others searched for a building to locate a makerspace in but rents were high, or the buildings were in such disrepair that they could not be used. MUM has invested in the space and provided staff to make the space a reality, which is a substantial investment in a community that to some extents has some deep seeded misgivings towards the university. Ouellette shared her understanding about the 'interesting dynamic' between the community and MUM. The university attracts students from a wide range of backgrounds not typically found in a rural agricultural-centered community like Fairfield. MUM students often look 'non-mainstream' and practice TM twice a day. The central focal point of the 272-acre (Barnett, 2004) campus are two 35-foot-high golden domes. Outside of Fairfield structures such as these are not found in the middle of the United States. Ouellette and Ryerse both commented that the people of MUM are less structured, and perhaps less conventional, than what is found in a typical small town in Iowa. The practices of MUM are not conventional and perhaps difficult to appreciate without proper contextualizing from members of the MUM system. Ouellette commented:

*From my interaction with people in the community, like at the hardware store or similar environments, I hear them say, "Oh, you work for the university? They don't like us over there." People in the community think we don't like them. I try to tell them, "I don't think that's true. You need to just come and check it out." But there is that preconception that they are not welcome, so we're doing everything we can to change that.*

An uneasy existence lies between MUM and the town and it is the vision of the makerspace to ensure everyone feels welcome in the space. The makerspace expects to attract many of the community members that have an interest or career in the hands-on trades. They expect to bring in those community-based experts and have them teach classes and recruit others to take classes as well. But again, as Hollis points out, there are stark differences between the average town person and someone from MUM. The sense of time is one area that divides the two groups. At MUM a person practicing TM is called an RU (pronounced rew), short for guru, and RUs have a very loose sense of time. RU time is elastic and flexible which, when offering classes in a makerspace, can lead to issues.

The makerspace may be the ideal place to build up trust between the two groups, as Ouellette and Hollis are working to bring the idea to fruition. To begin to build trust the space has hosted a number of workshops and invited the community to participate. Ideally, they post the adverts for the workshops in as many places as possible in the town and at MUM. Teachers and others are invited into the space to offer their skills as well. Ouellette stated:

*We invite teachers from both communities and say, "Hey, would you like to offer a skill? Is there something you would like to teach or is there something you would like to give a talk about?" Because there are a lot of entrepreneurs in this town. Maybe because of the size of the town, but there are so many entrepreneurial people per capita. It's pretty fascinating. We had an open house when we opened our sewing space, and that definitely attracted some people that were more of the town folk side, and they were like, "Oh, I didn't realize we're welcome here, and I want to come here." "Didn't know this was here," I think just having personal relationships when they can see that you're just a normal person is important, you're just like them.*

The space is also looking to build trust by identifying and interfacing with strategic partners in the community. For example, they envision working with the local lumber store to help offset costs of banners and printing in return for the lumber yard receiving some promotion in the space. In this way the lumber store would benefit from increased sales and the space would have a partner that has the trust of the town. The space successfully formed an important and beneficial alliance with a local art gallery owner. Hollis recalled how the partnership began.

*The event was an artist and makers mashup. There's a local gallery owner here who owns the Icon Gallery, Bill Teeple, who's very much a community builder. And he thought it was a great idea to get dialogue going between, "fine art, capital "A" Art, with craft art," and to get those communities together. I would say that it was successful. People were really excited about that. He wants to visit the idea, because one of the questions that came up that evening was, "Can I come back and see the show tomorrow?" And he was kind enough to let us squeeze in between shows. So, it was just a one-night event, but he'd like to revisit that concept and have us have maybe a month-long show connected with a contest for the MUM community, where a student would create a piece for the show and then we'd have someone in the community do something else. It's starting to pull those communities together and have it be not just an exhibit, but an interactive event show. Which is what we had, because Mike had the 3D printer there and Lyndi designed some pieces, and we had 3D printed jewelry there available for sale.*

The overall equipment list is provided in Table 1.

## SETTING THE STAGE

The Fairfield Makerspace is open to the general public and MUM staff as well as students. Costs for staff and the public are $40 per a punch card for 10 visits, and $20 per four months for students. The space is open four days

*Table 1. The Fairfield Makerspace equipment*

| | | |
|---|---|---|
| **General workshop equipment** | Workbenches<br>Shop vacuum | Dust collection |
| **General Hand tools** | Hammers<br>Shears<br>Rulers | Wood claps<br>Rotary cutters<br>Tape measures |
| **Woodworking** | Milling machine<br>Drill Press<br>Planer<br>Joiner 8"<br>Scroll saw | Stationary belt sander<br>Band saws<br>Table saw, Craftsman<br>Table saw, SawStop<br>Table saw, Protech |
| **Metalworking** | Milling machine<br>Drill press<br>Bench grinders<br>Cut-off saw<br>Torch, Acetylene/Oxygen<br>Stationary belt sander | Clark metal worker<br>Metal band saw<br>MIG welder<br>Blacksmith forge<br>Metal sharpener |
| **Fabrics** | Singer 190 straight stitch machine<br>Brother serger<br>White serger<br>5x8 fabric cutting table<br>Steam iron<br>Pancake compressor | US blind hem machine<br>Consew serger<br>Elna sewing machine<br>Printing blocks for fabric<br>2 Kenmore sewing machines<br>Staple gun<br>Brad nailer<br>Sleeve board |
| **Digital fabrication** | Flash Forge Creator Pro 3D printer | |
| **Electronics** | Arduino kits | 4 Computers<br>Raspberry PI kits |

a week: Wednesday through Saturday with hours varying depending on need. For the general public and MUM staff, the fee amounts to $4 a visit, which is about the same price as a good cup of coffee according to Ouellette. The space has really tried to keep costs low, as Hollis noted.

*It's a super deal for students. That means they have access, once they're trained, to all the spaces. If you get the $40 punch card, this is just for the community at large, you have 10 punches. So, I don't know how more accessible we can make it, other than saying "It's free, just come right in."*

Setting an appropriate fee has been under considerable debate in the space because they need to have operating capital to replace and purchase new equipment and tools, yet they recognize the need to serve the community thereby keeping the fees manageable for students and those with fixed income. Hollis recalled the debate:

*We've gone back and forth within the core membership, does the fee match the equipment we have? So, we have to have the value. In fact, if all of our machines were in tip-top working condition, then we can say "Yeah, it's worth every penny." Because you have access to this. And if we could do five days a week, then it would definitely be worth it and we could do an annual membership, because that would be great for people. Especially, when there are different communities that have 10 to 3 P.M. free. Then you have the students that can't do anything before 3 P.M. because their days are obligated until 3:30 they have class. So, things for them would be scheduled in the evening. And even for us, we work all day, normally. I just left work early. It's even more difficult when you work for yourself. This is definitely a labor of love or insanity. I can't figure out which one.*

The space also has a drop-in program that allows anyone to use the space for a $5 flat fee per use.

*People pay $5 and they have access to all the crafting materials. The cutters, things that are kind of expensive if you get it for yourself. That's the beauty of the makerspaces. Somebody might have a drill press or a band saw, but they might not have all this stuff. You can have a cache of equipment that not one person could accumulate and give people access.*

Ouellette reiterated the issue of trust:

*Pretty much, it's open to anybody. It's open to the entire community. It is kind of a weird dynamic because we're located on campus. This school has a unique relationship with the town, and there's a little bit of hesitation to come here because it's on the MUM campus, so people who are outside the paradigm of the school are like, "Oh, I don't know if I can come here and utilize the space."*

Members are required to bring in their own wood, fabrics, and other supplies which are not offered by the space. Some smaller items however, like screws, are supplied. Recruitment of members is an ongoing process for the space. The connection with the art gallery was an important event for the space in that it reached a number of community members and also created a strategic partnership with the gallery owner. The makerspace showcased a number of items made by members during the gallery event, to plant the seed of making.

To join, potential members complete a liability waiver and indemnity agreement and a membership information form, then they have access to the space. Participants of workshops must also complete a liability waiver and indemnity agreement which is specific to that workshop. Hollis noted:

*We were discussing, loosely, the terminology for that. What would it all be called? Workshop member? People do sign the membership waiver and that's why I separated that out for one that says "Workshops." So, when a person is signing it, it's saying "I've signed it for this workshop specifically." Not a membership. When people come just to take your workshop, but don't necessarily want to be a member, that liability form is specific to that workshop. There's always that with any university, safety and liability and all that stuff.*

The workshops are designed to help non-members that may have a particular piece of equipment already but are looking for additional training. Ryerse commented on the importance of the workshops:

*That helps the person that already has a sewing machine at home, but they want to learn some technique and they saw a class advertised. So, they'll just come for that. We may see them once in a while. They already can sew at home, why would they pay to come here unless we have something they don't have. They're just going to pay for the workshop, they're not going to be a member.*

Past workshops offered in the Fairfield Makerspace include the 'Crafts for Cats' which was focused on basic sewing skills. In this free workshop participants created cat toys and blankets for cats housed at a local animal shelter. Another workshop, called 'Drapery Panels' explored basic techniques for the development of window coverings. The workshop fee was $10 and ran for four hours. The course was described as a demo course providing instruction on techniques and consultation on fabric choices.

On average, the Fairfield Makerspace will see 10 to 50 total visits per month. As shown in Figure 7, 60 to 79% of visitors are female and 40 to 59% are male.

The ethnicity of membership is shown in Figure 8. About 80 to 100% are white, less than 20% are Black or African-American, Asian, and two or more races that may be included in the other ethnicities.

*Figure 7. Gender balance of visitors*

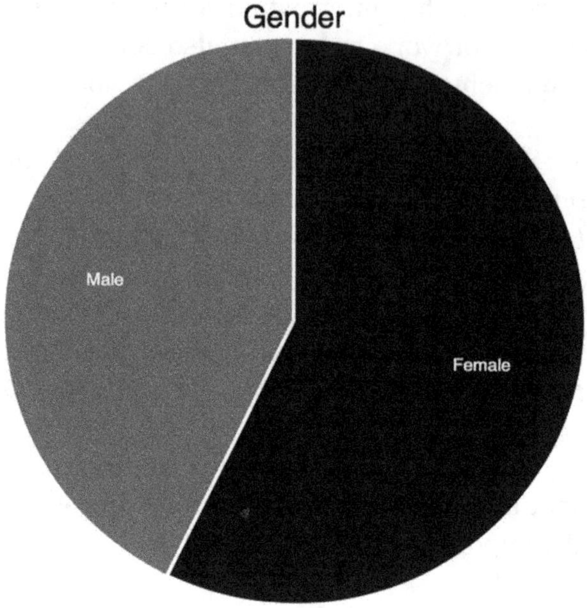


*Figure 8. Ethnicity of membership*

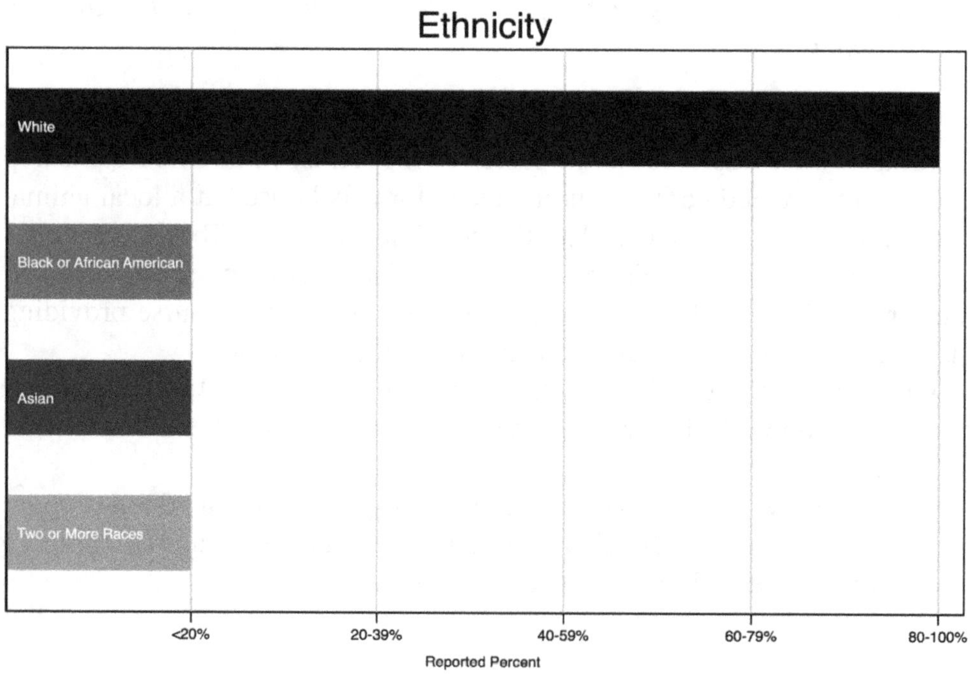

In general, the purpose of visits to the space are shown in Figure 9. The purpose of the visits were: 60 to 79% to receive training, instruction or learn a skill and introduction to making, 40 to 59% to make something specific.

## LEARNING COMMUNITIES

Operating in the first year of existence the space has pondered how to encourage learning communities but is still in the early stages of establishing their makerspace. One strategy to develop learning communities was through workshops that enabled members and potential members to meet and share interests. Another effort to create learning communities was the establishment of a program called 'Transformative Tuesdays.' Working within the spirit of sustainability, Transformative Tuesdays brought makers together to transform or upcycle items like furniture. In this way, the textile members cross interests with woodworking and metalworking as they bring new life to old objects. Hollis described the program:

*Figure 9. Purpose of visits per month*

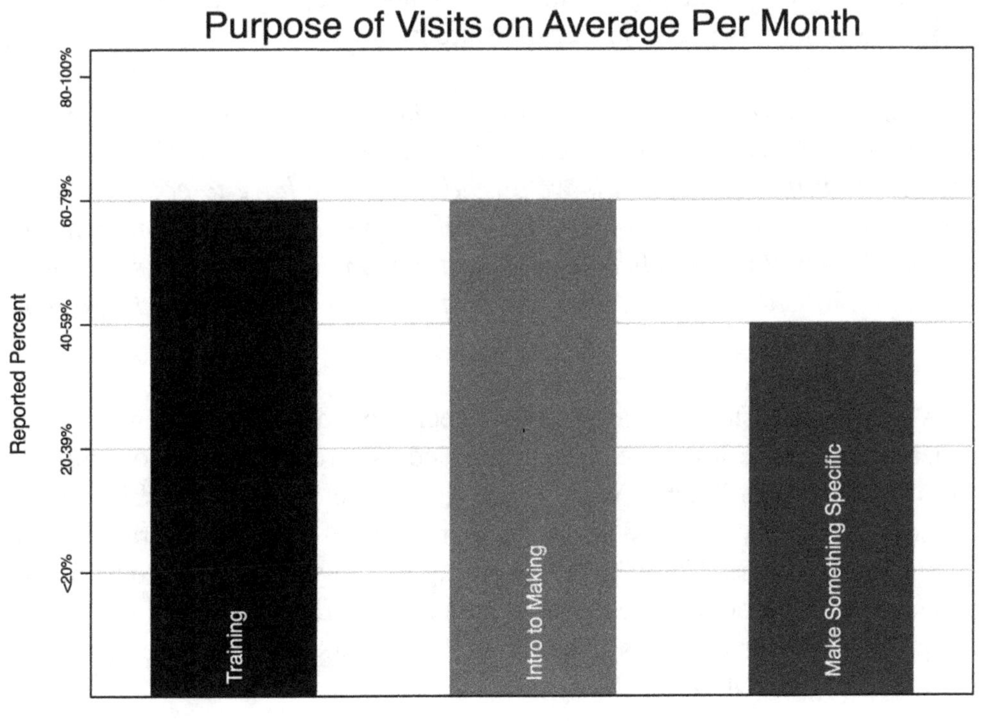

*[Transformative Tuesdays] where people can take some ratty thing that they're just unhappy with, like the bones of the chair, and reupholster it. So, how do they make sure that the frame is okay. If there's a loose bit, tighten that up here, and then go into the sewing room and reupholster it. There was that collaborative project with recovering the cushion top for that piece you found. What do you call that? Not dumpster dive, but it was roadside. A roadside find.*

Fairfield Makerspace has organized ways to develop volunteers that will act as experts in the different shop areas. The core members of the space are faced with a lack of capacity to effectively offer the courses and learning pathways needed for the space. The makerspace has a core group of members that meet regularly bi-weekly to work through space logistics, staffing, equipment and machine needs. In addition, the financial system to track membership dues and other considerations is another core member responsibility. Core members are not necessarily instructors in the space since many times the instructors do not have the time to meet bi-weekly. At the time of the author's visit core members were the only ones that were actively teaching workshops. Most instructors were volunteers and did not wish to be paid. However, the core membership is considering a plan to compensate instructors for workshops. Ryerse mentioned that paying instructors and keeping track of costs are important functions in the space, she stated:

*Anyone that we've asked to teach, we ask them, what would make it worth your time, and then we build the class fee around that. What do the materials cost? Even if they're materials we already have, we have to consider what would it cost us to get them again. Even if people are like, "I don't want to be paid," we build that in because the next person might want to, so we have to have a realistic picture of what the costs are. I want people to be paid, to have something.*

A number of different strategies have been looked at to identify and recruit experts. At a basic level the website is used as a recruitment tool with the message: 'Ready to Teach a Workshop at The Fairfield Makerspace? Everyone has something they are good at, and teaching classes allows us to transfer that knowledge to others. If you have something you love, we would love to help you share it! You could teach people how to solder, sew or build a bobsled, the possibilities are endless. The Fairfield Makerspace will even promote your event!' (MUM, n.d.).

The website has a link to contact a core member to set up the potential workshop. It is expected that these experts will come directly from the Fairfield community. An exchange program has also been explored with the University of Iowa to identify experts from both spaces. In this strategy, there would be an exchange of faculty, students and volunteers from both entities. Opportunities within MUM also exist to identify and recruit experts. Hollis explained:

*We just had a tour of the Art Department to figure out what kind of things to dovetail. So, we're trying to figure out some curriculum of a few small workshops that people could really get their hands on the equipment. Like aluminum anodizing is something simple that people could do just with a sheet, to learn, what does the anodizer do? How do you paint, dye? How you dye it and how do you seal it? It's doable in a day. We're learning how to use the CNC machine. They may have to take a few classes and understand some of these design programs.*

Certification is required on the machines before members are allowed to use them. The process in the metal and woodshop is controlled by a work study student who certifies people on the machines. Training on the individual pieces of equipment is informal and was "in flux" at the time of the author's visit. In general, training on a machine lasts one hour and sometimes it is done in groups, other times it is on an individual basis. When asked how member certifications are verified Hollis reflected:

*You're catching us at a time when we're getting our system solidified. Now we know we have to have a separate color-coded card for students, because they're $20 for the semester, versus a punch card. So, we know just by ID. We can say, "Okay, they've got the blue," or whatever color we choose, card, and that way Rhett [the shop manager] doesn't have to constantly say, "Hey, are you supposed to be using that machine?" We'll know that they're in a file system. Certifying people was also a learning experience because we're like, "Oh, we'll have a class, and we'll teach everybody how to use the chop saw." And we had 10 people, and one person shows up and that was a little bit too much.*

It safe to say that in the space the shop manager plays a vital role in teaching and certification. While, Ouellette and Hollis are the only key holders, the space operates according to the shop manager's and work study students' availability. The space is working to train additional members with equivalent skills as the current shop manager. This could be a challenge since the shop manager not only supervises safety but also consults members on the process of making, derived from vast experience as a maker. Members, especially those core members, contribute vast time and talents to the space. When asked if this was an expectation of all members to give back to the space Hollis mentioned the members are encouraged to spread the word and bring a friend to the space. The space does offer an 'exchange' program to members who can't afford the price of membership. These members exchange work in the space for their membership. Hollis clarified that the space does not offer services:

*We need to make it clear to people that it's not necessarily a service center. We'll teach you how to service your bike but we're not going to sit in here and fix people's bikes. We'll show people how to give their bike a basic tune-up.*

Ouellette advanced the idea that members need one of two things to become involved in the makerspace. Either they need to invest their time in the space or they need to have a financial commitment to the space.

There is also a sense of community derived from the attachment of the space to MUM. As a MUM entity, and because of the diverse project areas, MUM community members contribute to the space whether or not they are members. For example, contributions of equipment from an angle grinder to sophisticated electronic equipment is a common occurrence for the space. The MUM or RU community has supported the space largely since the makerspace supports their mission of sustainability.

Training in the space, especially on the machines, has transformed from a lecture-based experience where everyone makes the same artifact to a more dynamic choice-based one-to-one tutoring delivery method. Hollis explained:

*When we had our initial class, each person had to get a board and make these certain cuts so that they could tell that you knew how to adjust the machine. We had our initial woodworking class, was a bench making class. And we realized that some people learn differently. Some people are project-based learners and some people just want to know how to use a machine. So, you just get a raw piece of something or weld a bunch of things together just to know the parameters of the machine.*

The certification process has been debated amongst the core group and no clear answers have emerged. Hollis explained:

*We've discussed, how do you certify someone. Do you do it via a project? But it doesn't give the person a clear understanding, it gives them an understanding of how to cut a leg to stick it on that bench, not, "Okay, we're going to set you out and you want to create your own project. How would you go about it?" There needs to be a little bit more in-depth training. We're going back and forth with that within the group. It seems that the one-on-one certification is the more thorough.*

Gender balance in the space is about 60% males to 40% females. When asked what strategies are used to support female makers in the space. Ouellette noted that the intentional hiring of female staff is one strategy that the space has employed. The previous coordinators of the space were all females as well.

*When they [MUM] were trying to find people to replace the coordinators I was like, "Can you please have a female?" Even with the lab supervisor position, I'm still working on them to have or find somebody with the skill set who is also female.*

Ouellette believes, at least from her own personal experience, that some females are not comfortable publicly demonstrating machine techniques. She felt this form of learning and public demonstration of a particular skillset was too intense, and she did not want to learn new skills in that type of environment. Hollis described the learning environment during the chop saw certification course. During the course Ouellette was a class participant and Hollis observed the course. Hollis recalled:

*And Lyndi [Ouellette] is like "I don't like an audience, I don't want to do this," but she did it. It wasn't the most comfortable learning environment. We're trying to have multiple strategies for people who learn differently. Lyndi and I, in our core group there was a discussion between learning skill based on a project versus learning—like when I was learning to sew, I just wanted a bunch of samples. This is how you do a ruffle. This is how you do whatever seam. With cutting, we're like, "I just want a welding sample." And some of the guys stated, "It's a waste of my time if I don't come out of there with a thing, a finished thing." A lot of people feel like, "I want to leave with something."*

Core members as instructors have worked to provide varying participant numbers in the workshops, based on the needs of the learners. In other words, some workshops are more of the traditional *learn a skill and demonstrate it* to the class while others are more individual based. Hollis explained:

*We're trying to offer both, and that's what the training sessions are for, when people sign up for training session, you can get a little more one-on-one where you can focus without a bunch of eyes on you and make yourself a sample. Here's a mitered corner. That's how we taught at the university. We made people do a sample book because you don't want to, with some materials, start out and go, "Oh, I just screwed up my entire project," that puts too much pressure on you. Whereas if you have a piece of muslin and you're just messing around with it, who cares? Get the seam ripper out and tear it.*

Ouellette remarked another strategy for all makers is to have a variety of instructors from all walks of life. Crossing stereotypical gender lines helps put the learners at ease and can diversify the audience for a particular maker area. For example, having a female in woodworking may allow other females to gain the confidence to be involved in the space. Likewise, a male instructor leading a textiles course is another effective way to promote learning in the space. Ouellette revealed:

*I also think having instructors of different genders in the different spaces, not just having all female-taught sewing classes. So, we have the rustic bench class and soon as we had some females take it that were not part of the core membership, they felt really empowered. To me, that was super important. That was what the Makerspace is to me. It's empowerment through those skills, especially in terms of gender because I've always been in more masculine trades. So, it's empowering to see the makers realize these skills do not belong to one gender. They can do it just as well as anybody else.*

## YOUTH AND FAMILIES IN THE SPACE

The Fairfield Makerspace does not specifically cater to youth/families but the space is open to youth over the age of 13, as long as they are trained on the machines. Families are welcomed in the space as well and there have been some family specific programs, like the LEGO building and craft builds including card making. These activities were initially developed to bring families into the space. Since the initial family-based workshops, there have been a few families that work together in the space. For example, a father and son duo designed and built a rustic bench.

Philosophically, according to Hollis, promoting the space to families and youth is an important step in the development of the makerspace and learning communities. She remarked:

*I think it would be great. The whole family can come and say, "I'm going to be in the woodshop, you can be doing Arduino, and I'll be over here," and everybody's in the same vicinity. Talking to some faculty that have children, we're always looking for something interesting and fun and sneakily educational for the kids to do.*

In addition, there is a feeling in the space that making can supplement learning in the public schools, allowing for children to be more creative. Making can also fill in the gaps in public education as programs are getting cut. Ouellette surmised:

*I think more to supplementing the public school, or the idea of education. It's very systematic now and I like the idea that the makerspace can be a place for families or adults to let their kids be creative out of that mainstream environment. Here's a skill that you can actually have or you can create something. Helping to fill in, too, where a lot of schools are getting cut. What used to be creative programs. A big part of it was Home Ec [Economics]. You don't have the option anywhere; nobody has those skills anymore. It's so sad. Also, I think you can gear things both ways, where the kids are like, "I want to go do my own thing,", and we don't have to worry about childcare or whatever. Everybody is having fun. It's more of a village mentality.*

Ryerse commented, when asked about the maker mindset and how they prepare members for the process of learning and how to learn from failure, that in her sewing workshops she wants to make sure learners have the required prerequisites. These prerequisite courses prepare members for more advanced courses and she explained that learners want a return on their investment and they need to feel satisfied with the course. For Ryerse, that means the learners walk away with a completed project. She explained the pillowcase workshop in this way:

*That was a way to wrap in a pre-requisite ... with very basic beginning skills. A pillowcase is essentially a series of straight seams and some pressing. And a little serger. So, two different kinds of machines. You learn how to measure and fold. If someone has taken that class, then if a more advanced class has a pre-requisite, like some experience necessary, you can say, "If you've taken this class you have the experience to take this next class." We'll definitely put that there is a prerequisite.*

In the space members are taught through hands-on learning experiences with real world artifacts which the core staff feel reduce the angst of failure because the making experience is done is a safe and controlled learning environment. Learning in the workshops is highly scaffolded in the beginning and then the scaffold is slowly removed as members develop their skills and take advanced workshops, armed with the appropriate prior knowledge. Hollis went on to explain how they have put together courses for novices:

*But most things that we've put together have been for people that we say, "No previous experience necessary," just to get people in. I try to, though when people are working on things, remind them or ask them, "Is this your first time working with wood equipment?" It needs some work. That's kind of the beauty of a makerspace. That is the whole point. It is like the learning, reflective process.*

The space encourages the maker mindset through the support of the members. The purpose of the space is for members to hone skills, get better and work on more advanced projects and to become tradesmen. Or for members to discover a skill that they did not know they possessed: one reason for the existence of the Fairfield Makerspace. Hollis recalled the experience of a member using the wood tools for the first time:

*One woman who was in, I think she's an engineering major, that we met at student orientation. She left with her bench and she was just staring at it. She's like, "This is so cool." And that was the first time she'd ever used scary woodworking equipment, and she's like, "Wow, I made this." That was the same with the gal that, she walked out with her little pillowcase. It was going to be a gift for a very special little girl, and she was like the same way, because it was done. It's the most empowering thing to see something from start to finish, and know you actually made it. And going in thinking, "I don't know if I can do this." Then it's like, you just did it. Now you can do it again, switch it up. It's also just about reassuring somebody psychologically, "Hey, you did it; you were capable."*

A discussion on showcasing failure ensued when asked if the space ever talked about or displayed failure. The group discussed a wooden bench project that Hollis built and could perhaps be classified as a failure in some ways.

**Ouellette:** *Leslie [Hollis] won't let us display her failure though. That is a good idea. I never thought about that. Displaying failure.*

**Hollis:** *Just don't try to sit on it. We could put it out there and just say ... Well, no. We don't want people to see that when they start. If they want to see it after they finish and say, "Don't worry, you did a great job."*

**Ouellette:** *Yeah, it's a hard line, because if you are the people who are the core members instructing, you don't really want to admit that you can fail, because people are trying to learn from you.*

**Hollis:** *Yeah, I'm not teaching that class and I feel I have no problem. Now, if it was metalsmithing, and it was janky looking, I would not show it to them.*

**Ouellette:** *We can't ask a member, "Hey, you made a really bad something. We'd really like to display that as our failures." It's not really something people would like.*

**Hollis:** *Because I know next time what I would do differently, and why. But it also gives people a visual, too. "Okay, this looks interesting, but why doesn't it work?"*

**Ouellette:** *That's a really good idea though.*

## IMPACT ON THE COMMUNITY

The Fairfield Makerspace had been open for only four months at the time of the interview and believed that it had some impact on the community, but it was too early in their existence to really talk about impact. Ryerse explained:

*You're really just catching us as at the beginning. We're paddling out on our surfboards, and the wave is starting to build up. And we're like, "Let's catch it!" Literally, our open house was April 8, 2017. We've been treading water, getting events. And it took two months just to get that little room fixed up. Before, you would not have recognized it. The before pictures, it had mustard, some natural wall covering. Which was, again, an experiment. Which is nice about sustainable living, because they're like, "Let's see what this material looks like when we spread it on an interior of a wall." It was some kind of mud stuff. And then we learned how to work with that.*

Ouellette and Ryerse both felt that they had gained more community from the space. Both got involved for the community aspect of making. Ryerse in particular had been living in Fairfield for a dozen years and realized her social connectedness was sparse. Ouellette stated:

*From what I've heard from people, like we said earlier, hearing the feedback of those ... At least for me it was women that had said it. But that they had felt empowered, that they had learned these skills. I don't know. I feel like it's been positive so far. It's still been a very small community sample.*

The space has made connections between members and helped at least one entrepreneur in the town create a prototype, which would not have been possible without the 3D printer. Even more important was the support and learning community to provide valuable instruction on how to use the machine and build the prototype.

## DEFINING A MAKERSPACE

When asked to define a makerspace and the core components of a makerspace the group built an answer from each other's responses.

***Ryerse:*** *A place where people can let their imagination and creativity be supported by access to tools and access to knowledge.*

***Ouellette:*** *For me, it's a community-based resource for people that don't necessarily have the equipment or means to do something on their own. I feel like makerspaces offer that community support, basically.*

***Hollis:*** *It's to support people's creativity. Unless it's really dangerous, we would try to support most any project that someone brought in here. Try to find a way, let's see if we can help you do that. We'll try.*

***Ouellette:*** *Just a place to experiment. Whatever that experiment is: woodworking, biology, 3D printing.*

***Hollis:*** *I want it to be a space where anyone can use it and create and do whatever they want, basically. And I don't want it to be like, "This is just for people to prototype." I think it'd be good for them to also utilize it* *like that. I think a good question would be, how do you measure success? I don't really know how to answer that, but I've thought about it a lot.*

## CURRENT CHALLENGES

The Fairfield Makerspace is tied to the MUM institution of higher education and is also acting as a community-based makerspace. This model has a number of challenges and yet the payoff is to unite individuals associated with the MUM community and the residents living in Fairfield. As mentioned, MUM is unlike many traditional universities due to its teaching and practice of transcendental meditation. Twice a day students and staff practice meditation as derived from ancient Vedic scripts. MUM draws an international cadre of nontraditional students and faculty to the small Iowa town. As explained by Ouellette the lack of understanding on both sides has caused mistrust. The core MUM group envisioned the makerspace as a bridge between the two communities.

Gurus or RUs who practice transcendental meditation have a fascinating view of time. According to Ouellette, it is referred to as RU time, which is a more 'elastic' or flexible view of time. This view can be difficult when scheduling workshops according to Ouellette. She has observed:

*Honestly, it's been good in the sense that we've really had to make protocols around things like that, because sometimes there's a flexibility with paying as well. Some people won't show up. And we found with our rustic bench we could only fit so many people, so we immediately said, "Hey, we're closed. The class is full." But then some people who didn't pay ahead of time took up those spots when we could've had other people come in. And they didn't come. It's been a learning process in that sense. We're like, "Okay, now we know we have to have certain systems in place for that community that needs a little bit more structure."*

Time is just one exaggerated example of the differences between the two communities. It's likely however, that both communities have more in common than what is seen on the surface. Sustainability and creativity, as well as self-reliance, are strong themes for both communities and are represented in the maker environment. In addition, the idea of entrepreneurship and the development of 'blue collar' skills for employment is another synergistic area. The space has done some important groundwork in developing relationships with residents of Fairfield and one would expect the space to add town members. Developing a larger member base is dependent on the Fairfield makerspace being able to meet the needs of both communities, while at the same time securing commitment from experts to share their knowledge and expertise. Organizing workshops and coming to grips with training and certification is another challenge for the space as they grow. In addition, as a mostly volunteer run space they need to recruit additional volunteers to help extend the open times of the space to meet the needs of members.

## REFERENCES

American Census Survey (ACS). (2016). *2012-2016 American Community Survey 5-Year Estimates*. Retrieved from https://www.census.gov/quickfacts/fact/table/fairfieldcityiowa,US/BZA010215

Barnett, A. (2004). *Trouble in transcendental paradise as murder rocks the Maharishi University*. Retrieved from https://www.theguardian.com/world/2004/may/02/usa.theobserver

Lowe, S. (2011). Transcendental Meditation, Vedic Science and Science. *Nova Religio*, *14*(4), 54–76. doi:10.1525/nr.2011.14.4.54

MUM. (n.d.). *Consciousness based education*. Retrieved from https://www.mum.edu/about-mum/consciousness-based-education

Schmidt-Wilk, J., Heaton, D. P., & Steingard, D. (2000). Higher education for higher consciousness: Maharishi university of management as a model for spirituality in management education. *Journal of Management Education*, *24*(5), 580–611. doi:10.1177/105256290002400505

Wallace, R. K. (1974). *Neurophysiology of enlightenment*. Paper presented at the 26th International Congress of Physiological Sciences, New Delhi, India.

## KEY TERMS AND DEFINITIONS

**Business Incubator:** Process to support new businesses as they go through the steps of starting up.

**Fairfield, Iowa:** Town located in Jefferson County, Iowa with a population of about 10,000.

**Fairfield Makerspace:** Makerspace in Fairfield, Iowa located on the Maharishi University of Management (MUM) campus.

**Maharishi Mahesh Yogi:** Founder of MUM.

**Maharishi University of Management (MUM):** A university located in Fairfield, Iowa that practices transcendental meditation.

**Rig Veda:** One of the oldest of the Veda texts used for transcendental meditation.

**Sustainable Living Department:** A department at MUM that houses the Fairfield Makerspace.

**Trade Skills:** Skills and careers which require specific training.

**Transcendental Meditation (TM):** A systematic procedure to gain enlightenment, which is the development of one's consciousness to the fullest potential.

**Upcycle:** A process of transforming unwanted materials into new materials.

# Chapter 7
# Nebraska Innovation Studio


## ABSTRACT

*The Nebraska Innovation Studio (NIS) is a university-based makerspace built on a membership model open to the faculty staff and students from the University of Nebraska – Lincoln (UNL) and community members at large. The space is located in the newly developed Innovation Campus that sits between the two established university campuses of UNL. Consisting of 17,000 $ft^2$ (1580 $m^2$), the space is large and modern with idea strips consisting of TV monitors, peg boards, and white boards running throughout much of the space. NIS has received a number of donations to enable the purchasing of equipment including laser cutters, 3D printers, a long arm quilter, as well as a number of work tables and computers. Overall, the space is very welcoming to new members, with few rules and policies to distract from the making experience. Learning communities are formed through the hard work of NIS staff, which keep track of individual members' projects and interests and work to ensure they connect with like-minded makers in the space. NIS has impacted the community by opening a shared university space, with the community focused on innovation and entrepreneurship. This chapter explores the Nebraska Innovation Studio.*


DOI: 10.4018/978-1-5225-8310-3.ch007

*A big reason that women do not come to makerspaces is because of mansplaining ... It's generally a male dominated thing. No mansplaining. The best description I've heard of it [mansplaining] is explaining something in great detail assuming ignorance of the other party. When you think of your dad explaining to you when you're a kid about how things work. It really comes off more as parenting. Most people think it's really uncomfortable or like getting unsolicited advice. — Brett Kennedy*

## ORGANIZATION BACKGROUND

The Nebraska Innovation Studio (NIS) is part of the University of Nebraska-Lincoln (UNL) and is open to the University community (faculty, staff, students) as well as the residents of Nebraska. The space is approximately 17,000 $ft^2$ (1580 $m^2$), located on the former Nebraska State Fair grounds. The host building for the space is the former 4-H building that was built in 1931. The former 4-H Building was rededicated in June of 2014 and is now part of a contiguous building complex with a conference center and a business accelerator area. The current reconfiguration of the building started around 2010 and the first phase of Nebraska Innovation Studio was completed in 2015 and opened in October of that year. NIS was conceived as a place that permitted university students the use of real tools (wood, metal, laser cutting) to express their creativity. The University of Nebraska-Lincoln has an agreement with NIS to pay for the rental costs of the space and salaries for the two current employees for a period of five years. The equipment was acquired through external sources such as grants, private donors and membership fees.

Brett Kennedy, the Director of Nebraska Innovation Studio at the time of the interview, answered questions about the space and provided a tour. Kennedy, who graduated from Arizona State University with a Bachelor of Fine Arts (painting), worked at a small makerspace called MakerBench until his graduation in 2013. He then worked for TechShop Inc. as an instructor and member ambassador for a few years before coming to Nebraska in August of 2016 as the director.

Newly completed, NIS is modern and yet retained a little of the old 4-H building, with curved barned doors and brightly colored concrete columns, holdovers from the days when 4-H projects lined the walls. Entering the space there is a large gallery to showcase maker projects, which rotates every few months. During the author's visit custom-made furniture and other art pieces were on display in the gallery. Each artifact displayed a short biography of the inventor, as shown in Figure 1.

Past the gallery and reception area is the woodworking studio which houses a large air handling system and a number of laser cutters, drills, and other woodworking essentials, as shown in Figure 2.

Down the hall from the woodworking studio is a computer lab (Figure 3) photography and ceramics studio, screen printing press (Figure 4) and a sewing studio (Figure 5). The multi-use area is separated from the rest of the space by large glass garage doors.

The electronics and rapid prototyping lab is cordoned off by a door and houses a number of 3D printers, electronic tools, and a workspace. An interesting feature in many of the studios throughout the space are the TVs that are built into the walls. These idea strips, controlled by computers, are ways

*Figure 1. Maker gallery*

*Figure 2. Woodworking studio*

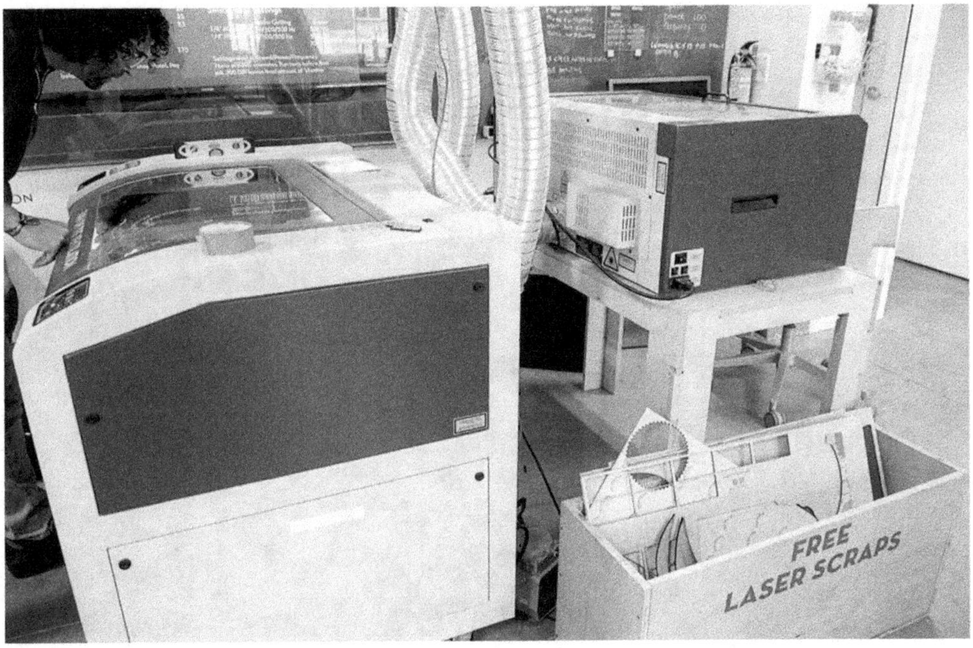


*Figure 3. Computer lab*

*Figure 4. Screen printing*

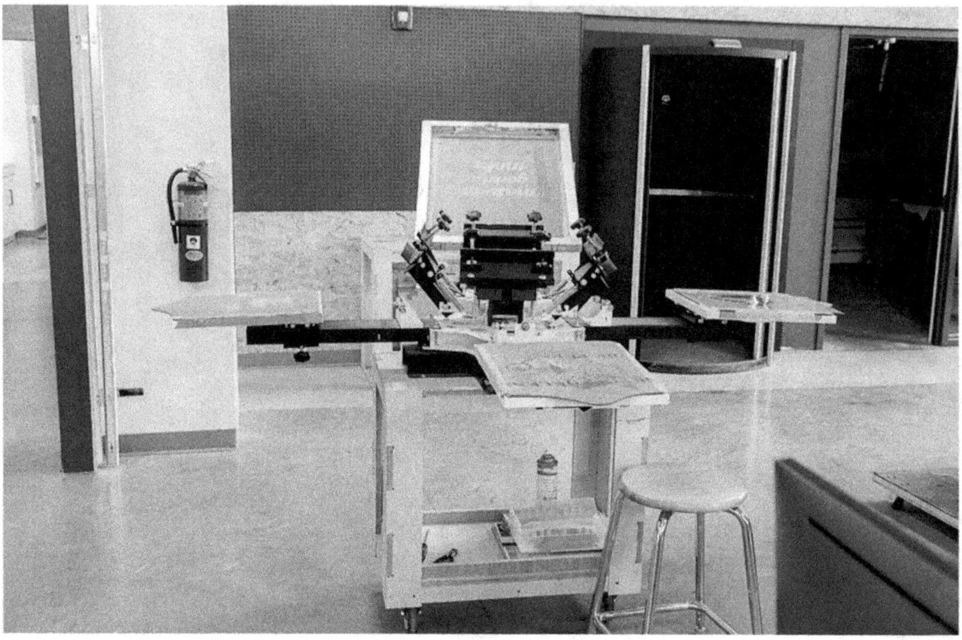

*Figure 5. Sewing area*

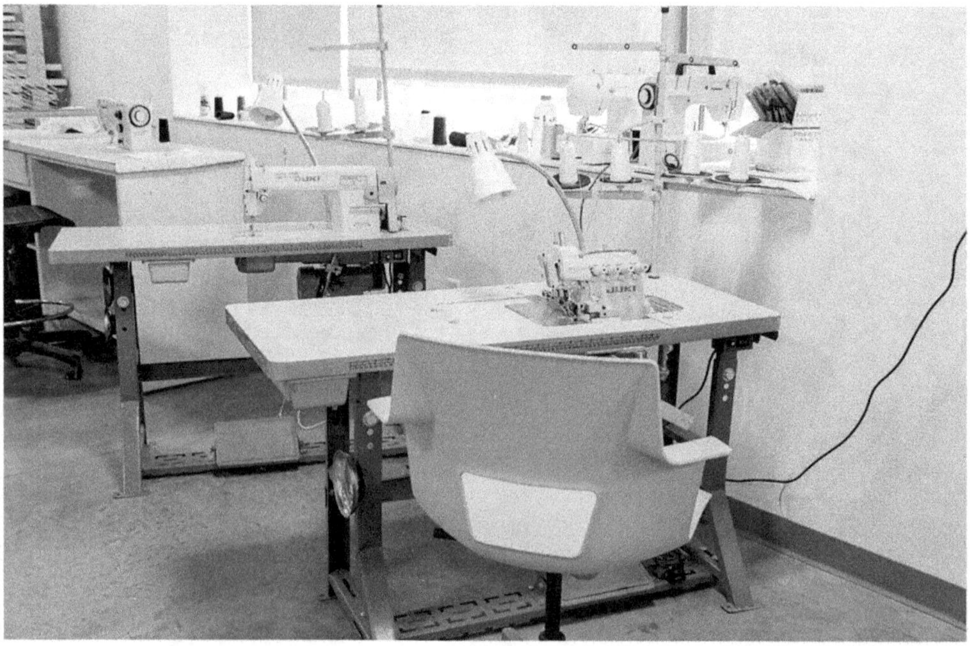

*Figure 6. Idea strip*

to communicate with members on a host of things like the cost of supplies or request for members to volunteer to lead a workshop, as shown in Figure 6.

The space has a dedicated room near the gallery for a ShopBot Alpha CNC Router with a 4' x 8' (1.2 m x 2.4m) area, dedicated computer and air handling system. The final area of the makerspace is an unfinished open area with worktables, limited storage area for member projects, and additional woodworking tools. The space can be used for classes and for a work area for many of the member projects, as shown in Figure 7.

Kennedy reflected on his previous job and how trust played an integral part in many people leaving the space. Trust in the space starts with staff supporting members and creating a welcoming space. He noted:

*At my last job, finding out why people leave makerspaces, it's a big customer service issues where they feel like they're being parented or something like that. It seemed like a lot of people that look on their resume to work at a makerspace had an attitude where they want to control the space and tools need to be used in specific ways and they need to always do this. I think trust has to come from the staff specifically. Something that we do here is we never talk bad about member's mistakes. We always expect to fix stuff. We*

Figure 7. Member project in the workspace

*budget in tool fixes and they're fairly predictable. It's just part of the game. We want to encourage an environment of making mistakes. Overall just have a welcoming space.*

Negativity in the space can quickly spiral out of control according to Kennedy and it is important that the staff in the space provide expectations of behavior amongst staff and members and between members. NIS expects members will at some point break items in the space and the NIS staff will fix them. Kennedy stated: "I'm very confident that they can't break anything more than we can fix it."

Within the community of Lincoln, Nebraska there is a great deal of support for the space. It is rare, according to Kennedy, that community members question the university funding of the space. What is more of a factor for the space is the requirements of the university to meet certain funding and growth goals.

The overall equipment list is provided in Table 1.

*Table 1. Nebraska Innovation Studio equipment*

| | | |
|---|---|---|
| **General workshop equipment** | Tables<br>Sinks<br>Shop vacuum | Dust collection<br>Cutting mats |
| **Woodworking** | Festool compound miter Saw<br>Laguna 18" (45.72cm) Band saw<br>Jet 10" (25.4cm) disc sander<br>Jet 6" (15.24cm) belt sander<br>Jet oscillating spindle sander<br>SawStop table saw<br>Panel saw<br>Scroll saw<br>Table router | Clausing drill press<br>Felder 19" (48.26 cm) planer<br>Woodmaster 38" (96.52 cm) Drum sander<br>Powermatic 8" (20.32 cm) Jointer<br>Festool domino jointer<br>Festool manual router<br>Festool track saw<br>FesTool orbital, eccentric, Rotary sanders<br>Wood clamps & vises<br>Powermatic 36" (91.44 cm) Wood lathe |
| **Textiles** | Juki MO-6700 serger<br>Silver Reed LK150 knitting machine<br>Screenprinting screens | Juki DDL-5550N Straight Stitch<br>APQS 14' (5.18 m) longarm quilter<br>2 Bernina regular sewing machines |
| **Computing** | Computers | Design software |
| **Plastics** | Graphtec 24" (60.96 cm) vinyl cutter | |
| **Digital fabrication** | Epilog 50 watt laser Epilog 60 watt laser<br>2 Ultimaker 2+ 3D printers | Stratasys Mojo 3D printer<br>NextEngine 3D scanner<br>ShopBot Alpha CNC router |
| **Electronics** | Soldering irons<br>Solder pot<br>DC power supply<br>Hot air rework station | Oscilloscopes<br>Reflow oven<br>Dual channel function/arbitrary waveform generator |
| **Ceramics** | 30" (76.2 cm) Slab roller<br>Ceramics hand tools | 22" x 22" (55.88 cm x 55.88 cm) Skutt electric kiln<br>10" (25.4 cm) wide x 12" (30.48 cm) deep Skutt<br>6 VL Whisper & Brent C electric throwing wheels |

## SETTING THE STAGE

As previously mentioned, the space is open to anyone including members of the university community and the general public. New members are required to take a 60-minute new member orientation course to learn about the available equipment, logistics and culture of the space. These orientation courses are offered frequently (2 to 3 times per week) and potential members can sign up online for no-cost. At the time of the visit there were 223 active members at NIS. Membership costs for the space are broken down by affiliation with the university. The costs in 2017 US dollars were as follows:

- **UNL Undergraduate Students:** $15 per month
- **Students (non-UNL or graduate):** $20 per month
- **UNL Staff, Faculty, Alumni:** $35 per month
- **Others:** $55 per month

Once members join they are sent an email with instructions to sign up for an orientation session and to bring a form of payment (not cash). In addition, members are given access to the Innovation Studio Manager software that was built for the space by the UNL information technology group. The Studio Manager system permits users to log in and sign up for classes. Youth must be over the age of 12 to have access to the space. Members between the ages of 12 and 17 have limited access to some of the tools, especially the woodworking tools, and must be accompanied by an adult while at NIS. Members 18 and older can access all tools if they have completed certification training on the particular tool. Recruitment of members is accomplished mainly through word of mouth, articles in the university press and a number of community events that invite the public to view the studio.

Kennedy noted that training and certification is required for any computer-controlled tool or "anything that can cut off a finger." These include most woodworking tools, the laser cutters, and the 3D printers. Once members sign in they are able to see and enroll in the course offerings. Occasionally, a member will offer a special course in topics like silk screening or quilting, and a special announcement will be sent via email to all members.

Curriculum in the space is comprised of a set of printed Standard Operating Procedures (SOPs) that are contained in a binder and located at each machine. The binders are used as a training resource during the certification process and also used as a reference for members when using the machine. The SOPs contain general safety and usage guidelines developed by the space as the minimum threshold of knowledge needed to use the equipment and not get hurt. The SOPs do not have project ideas or any sort of tips and tricks. Once a member has signed up and attended a certification class, Kennedy or the lab manager opens up the Studio Manager software and checks the member off as being certified. Most certification courses are conducted by Kennedy and the lab manager, and it is their responsibility to approve the certification on the machine. In addition, it's up to staff at Innovation Studio to know each member and what equipment they are certified on. Members don't have an electronic sign-in to the space or the machines. Kennedy tries to make a conscious effort to talk to each member of the space:

*So far, we haven't had any bad interactions. If somebody doesn't know how to use a tool, normally they look like they don't. A lot of times people will just stand by the tool and look at it in a weird way. Really, we just go up to them and ask them if they want to learn how to use the drill press or something like that and then we can approve them on the tool there.*

Kennedy noted that the brief interaction or a mini-class will count as a certification as well.

Courses offered in the space are listed in Table 2.

On average, the Nebraska Innovation Studio will see 1,000 to 5,000 total visits per month. As shown in Figure 8, 20 to 39% of visitors are female, 60 to 79% are male.

The ethnicity of membership is shown in Figure 9. About 80 to 100% are white, less than 20% are black or African-American, Asian, Native American, Alaskan Natives, Native Hawaiians and other Pacific Islanders, and two or more races that may be included in the other ethnicities.

The types of users that visited the space are shown in Figure 10. Less than 20% are visitors or observers, 80 to 100% college age students, and less than 20% are teachers.

The purpose of visits to the space are shown in Figure 11. 20 to 39% of visitors were there to receive training, an introduction to making, and small batch production; 40 to 59% were there to make something specific; while 60 to 79% made one off pieces. Less than 20% were there to network or find a maker/partner/designer and socialize.

## LEARNING COMMUNITIES

The most important consideration in the development of learning communities at NIS according to Kennedy, is allowing members to follow interests when making projects. Allowing this freedom of choice and personal expression naturally permits the establishment of learning communities. He described the importance of choice as:

*I think the most motivating thing is for members to come here and make what they want to make. I really try not to get in their way to do that. I think something that all makers have in common is this uncomfortable rambling for stuff they really like. As long as I can help them make their projects that they're interested in, those communities normally form pretty regularly. Something*

*Table 2. Courses offered at Innovation Studio*

| Course Title | Description |
|---|---|
| Band saw, Miter Saw, Drill Press & Table Router Training | • 1-hour training<br>• Required before gaining access to the band saw, miter saw, drill press and table router<br>• Learn how to set up the router table, learn various bits, learn to operate machines safely and effectively. |
| FesTool Hand Tool Training | • 1-hour training<br>• Basic information needed to correctly operate and care for all our FesTool hand tool |
| Epilog Laser Cutter Training | • 1-hour training<br>• Required before gaining access to the Epilog Fusion 40, 32 and mini laser cutters<br>• Learn the basics of generating a file to send to the lasers, how to operate the lasers, the differences between the two, and the basic use of the rotary tool. |
| 3D Printer Training | • 1-hour training<br>• Required before gaining access to the Mojo and the Ultimaker 2+ and 3-extended printers<br>• Learn how to upload files and operate the equipment. |
| Table & Panel Saw Training | • 1-hour training<br>• Required before gaining access to the table and panel saws<br>• Make several cuts on both saws and understand their basic operation |
| CNC Router Training | • 1.5-hour training<br>• Required before gaining access to CNC router<br>• Learn to code tool paths for the router in VCarve Pro |
| Wood Jointer & Planer, Belt, Disc & Spindle Sander Training | • 1-hour training<br>• Required before gaining access to the wood jointer and planer as well as the belt, disc and spindle sanders |
| Silk Screen Training | • 1-hour training<br>• Required before gaining access to the silkscreen equipment.<br>• Learn to print image, apply emulsion, set up screen, apply ink, clean and remove image from the screen, and operate 4-station press. |
| Lathe Workshop Phase 1 — Pen Turning & Bottle Stopper | • 2.5 hour workshop<br>• Required for certification on lathe (3-sessions) pen turning & bottle stopper - mini lathe, spindle (rolling pin) - large lathe |
| Adobe Illustrator for the Laser Cutter | • 1.5-hours<br>• Learn Adobe Illustrator for laser printing. |
| Celebrity Selfie Mini Quilt Workshop | • 7-hours<br>• Learn Adobe Photoshop and quilting. |

**_Nebraska Innovation Studio_**

*Figure 8. Gender balance of visitors*

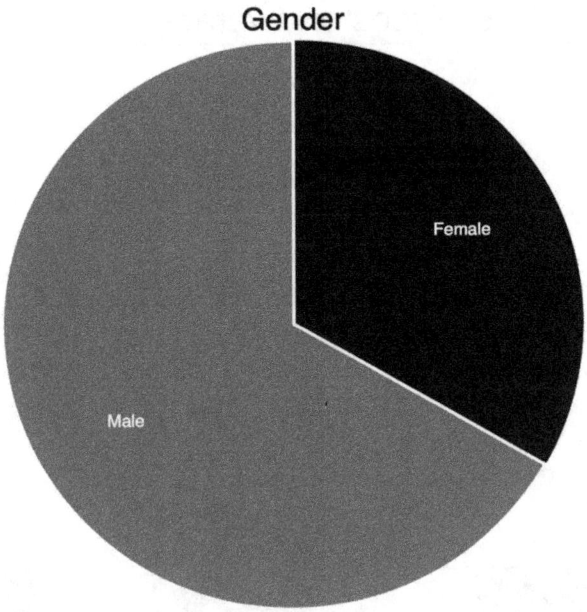


*Figure 9. Ethnicity of membership*

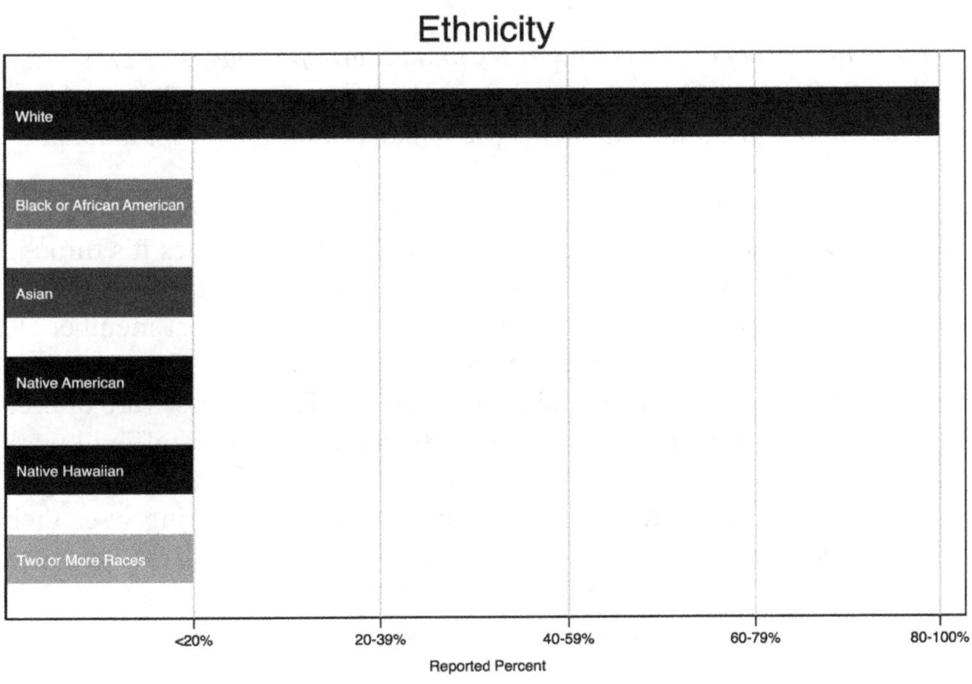

*Figure 10. Types of visitors per month*

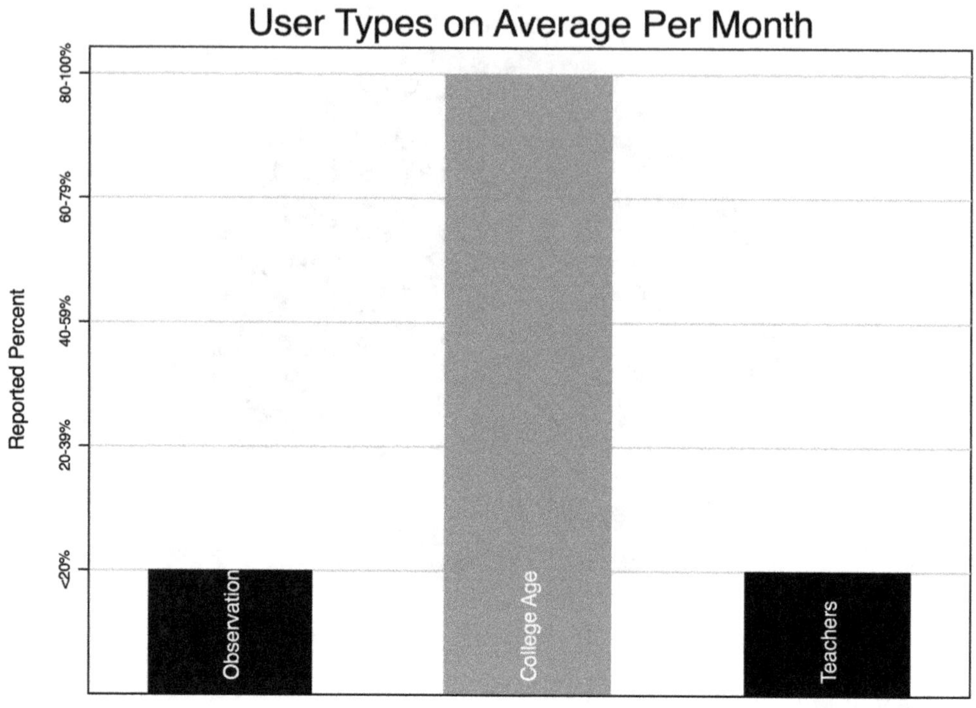


*I've seen other spaces do, is they'll try and do group projects or classes on harder projects or promote a certain area by buying a tool. It's just always come down to how do we enable people to make what they want to make.*

When asked how the space encourages or enables members to create following their interests Kennedy responded that a lot of times it's through convenience. The space will keep in stock materials like high quality birch plywood, a variety of screws and other items that they expect members to use. Another way is by providing a number of different classes on the tools in the space to allow members to make their projects. These classes are offered on a frequent rotation and if there is interest by members the staff will work to provide the classes promptly. Staff in the space make it a practice to give members space and as Kennedy describes it as "not hovering over their [members] shoulder and telling them what to do constantly." The staff will provide instruction when asked or when members look frustrated, but they shy away from providing instruction on how to complete a project.

*Figure 11. Purpose of visits per month*

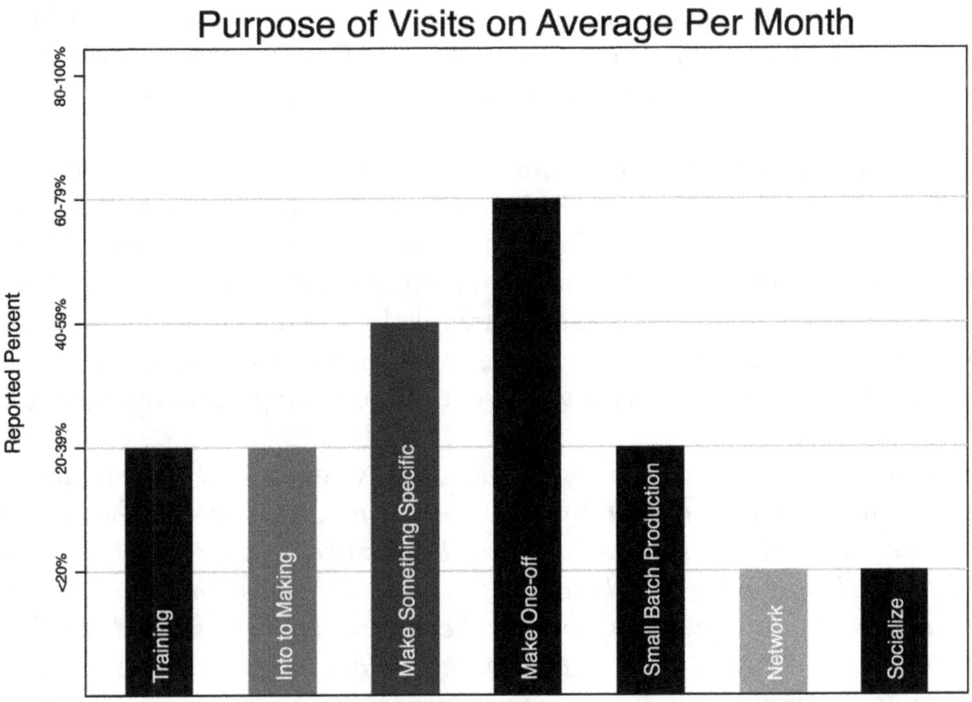


Kennedy had another observation around the formation of learning communities centered on specific machines/tools in the space. These *Super Tools,* like the long arm quilter or wood turning tools, draw people together. Kenney stated:

*I think the biggest one [learning community] we have here is a quilting group that comes in. They're people who have never met each other but they're all united by this one super tool. I think these happen the most around single tool communities if that makes sense. The wood lathe, that happened really well. The long arm quilter, the laser cutter that happens. It's less common with say, just the general woodshop.*

The super tools may provide members with a powerful way to connect, based on shared knowledge in the use and deep-seeded interest in the tool. Kennedy suggested it may be that,

*... they [members] feel more connected to that tool and they want to share the quirks with each other. I think it's a specific enough of a project to where almost every project made on it has something in common with something else, whereas the woodshop you can go a bunch of different ways.*

Kennedy also noted that learning communities occur across machines and interest areas. Often times these collaborations are short-term and don't last more than one or two sessions but are useful to makers as they work on their own projects and receive help from other members of the space. Like all learning communities, these are transactional exchanges of skills and knowledge between members. Kennedy recounted his observation of an architecture professor working within one of these temporary communities:

*Collaboration, it doesn't always happen on those single tool communities. I would say those are more totally across the shop. As an example, we had an architecture professor. He was making a robot to make these large architectural features. He was using a fairly simple stepper motor system that you'd find in a 3D printer or another CNC tool but there were electronics people talking to him about different ways to control the motors, different codes to make them do different things. Just because they saw an electronics project that seemed interesting to them, they didn't necessarily form a community, but they formed a two-hour, super meaningful concentration of knowledge that might make up for a weekly meeting. I think they definitely take from each other. The professor gets electronic knowledge and different parts that he can use. The electronics people break out of their shell a little bit and think about not such a specific electronics project, something that's relatively easy to work on for a non-electronics person but how much better it can be made by an electronics or electrical engineer. I think there's a benefit for both people there.*

Staff in the space are instrumental in helping new members find their interest area and like-minded members in the space. Kennedy noted:

*As far as joining learning communities, I would say it starts with me and Jerry [staff member] being uncomfortably friendly with them and introducing them to other members around the studio that I think they'll get along with. Then sort of feeling out their interests and usually suggesting workshops that we have. We have a lot of member taught workshops here. Long arm quilting is one that has a lot of those, which I think is a reason for its strong community.*

Again, the staff at NIS take it upon themselves to assist members in making connections and forming communities. In a conscious effort, the staff brings members together by providing details on individual projects and interests in an attempt to connect and learn from each other. Kennedy cautioned that the practice can backfire when a member feels like the NIS staff just 'tossed' or outsourced a project to another member and they are now obliged to help them out. In most instances the method works, and members will connect. This process requires the NIS staff to keep track and understand what members in the space are working on. When asked how this is done Kennedy responded:

*I just talk to everybody and track everything and talk to them about what they're making. That's the easiest icebreaker for us, is just to ask people what they're making or if they need help. We normally interact with everybody at least one time during their project. They're normally memorable experiences. They're not the same project and we just remember them and I write them down in a spreadsheet.*

Facebook is another mechanism utilized by the space to share members' projects. Facebook successfully draws a lot of attention from members and Kennedy notes as soon as a project is posted, it will generate a surprisingly large number of hits. In addition to Facebook there is project storage in the space for members, which is another way to share what they are working on. Kennedy noted that open storage is not always the case in makerspaces.

Certification classes and workshops are additional ways for members to find their learning community in the space. Certification classes are typically one hour long with each member taking turns on the machine making a particular object, in order to demonstrate one aspect or another of the machine. The classes connect members but are limited because of time and members typically don't have the option to explore and learn from each other. Workshops on the other hand can last up to six hours and allow members to connect and form deeper learning communities. Kennedy noted:

*I think those [workshops] are one of the biggest connectors for members making meaningful interactions with each other. I think about when I teach a class and trying to get everybody to talk to each other and how that doesn't always happen and how odd that is, but when a member teaches that class it seems to be much more of a social thing. That's just a note for myself to think about that more when I structure classes without doing cheesy icebreaker activities, right?*

While there are some explicit learning pathways for members to improve their skills beyond the basic certification courses these pathways are not widespread. Tools like the laser cutters and 3D printers have certification courses and usually a specialized course covering the supporting software to create designs on these machines, but rarely will members be able take courses to move their skills beyond this elementary level. To acquire advanced skills members, create projects and learn through the making process and join learning communities to learn and teach others.

Because there are two full-time staff members in the space they typically serve as experts on almost all of the machines. As new machines are added to the space others will work with and learn how to use the machines properly. As previously mentioned, the space purchases machines that have high reliability rates and staff can easily fix each piece of equipment. Kennedy explained they are still working on identifying experts from the member community. He stated:

*As far as bringing in experts from the community, I wouldn't consider any of our members necessarily experts. I'm still working on that. Even something just barely beyond basic is something worth teaching a workshop or class on and a lot of people don't realize that. There's a huge intimidation factor that goes into learning a new tool or new technique. A lot of it is just getting in there and doing it for the first time and seeing somebody else do it. When I ask people to teach workshops, they're usually nervous or they're not sure about it or they've never taught a class before. I always tell them, just talk for an hour about stuff they like and other people will like it and that's it. Those classes always fill up. They're always really popular. We always get great reviews for them.*

Often, members will approach Kennedy to host a workshop and they will usually schedule and announce the workshop in the Studio Manager software and add it to the calendar function of the program. Other times Kennedy will ask a member to lead a workshop on a specific topic. The selection process is usually based on content knowledge and the workshop leader's ability to connect with learners. Kennedy stated:

*Otherwise if we're looking for somebody to teach a specific workshop, we normally ask the most outgoing person. I wish it was a little more complicated than that. I don't necessarily look for a good teacher or anything like that.*

*I think almost everybody here is a very visual learner so even if you suck at explaining things, they can see you do it and that's pretty powerful.*

The Nebraska Innovation Studio has more male than female members and when asked about this Kennedy brought up the idea that one of the issues for this phenomenon in makerspaces is called "mansplaining." He defined it as:

*It is explaining something in great detail, assuming ignorance of the other party. When you think of your dad explaining to you when you're a kid about how things work. It really comes off more as parenting. Most people think it's really uncomfortable or like getting unsolicited advice.*

Rothman (2012) published the following definition, "mansplaining — explaining without regard to the fact that the explainee knows more than the explainer, often done by a man to a woman." In practice mansplaining has been around for centuries. As Rothman noted in a letter dating back to 1776, John Adams, who would become the second president of the United States, explained in essence to his wife, Abigail Adams, that he had more knowledge of what it was like to be a woman than she did.

The term was first referenced in 2008 by Rebecca Solnit in her collection of essays *Men Explain Things to Me,* as noted by Lewis, 2014. In the essay, Solnit describes a situation where she, an author who had just written a book on a particular subject, had the subject explained to her by a man. Lewis (2014) captures the effect of mansplaining as having a women's expertise instantly dismissed because of the "lady-shaped package it came in."

Mansplaining in a makerspace, where in most instances there is a large male majority, may in effect silence the female voice and expression. It's not hard to imagine the frustration and feeling of exasperation when being silenced or taught in a degrading manner simply because of your gender. Kennedy noted:

*I think they all start to create a boy's club sort of thing and then there's weird comments that they say to a woman. There's actually a Facebook thread that came up a while ago of a lot of women members at our last makerspace that just listed off stories and stories of comments they've gotten or just generally uncomfortable experiences of guys explaining things in very uncomfortable ways or hitting on them or something like that. It was really eye-opening for me.*

Kennedy goes on to explain that mansplaining is not accepted at NIS and they work to mitigate it through their instructional practice and through the rules and regulations of the space. Instructionally staff members at NIS do not tell members how to build stuff nor treat members differently based on gender. Organizationally, the space does not tolerate the practice from members and will give warnings and ultimately remove a member if they continue the behavior. Kennedy explained:

*I think Nebraska is generally full of very nice people and we have a good mix of young people versus old people. I hate to say this, but it tends to be more of an older guy thing. I came from a makerspace where we were in the suburbs. We were next to Intel and a lot of old engineering firms. We had a good crowd of men between the age of 40 and 70 that were pretty much all of the conspirators, I guess. I don't know. That sounds like such a weird word. Controlling it is difficult, other than just not supporting it or not bringing it up in any way. We don't do any special women events. We don't do a girl's night. I think we just encourage everybody equally.*

Institutionally the practice is hard to monitor since most females will not report the infraction to staff. Kennedy will listen to conversations and provide feedback to individuals. For example, Kennedy will ask the member in question if they were in a similar situation would they feel comfortable with the conversation. He noted:

*Almost everybody feels very sorry right away and fixes their actions and is very understanding. If they don't, that's usually a clear sign to me that they're not probably a good person for the makerspace.*

To encourage the maker mindset in the space Kennedy has streamlined the experience in the space. From getting certified to signing up, it's all a simple process and meant to be informal and convenient for members. When asked about how the space encourages other aspects of the maker mindset, like those of learning by failure, Kennedy noted:

*I think that goes along with budgeting fixes into your budget and trusting members. I have to say I trust them to break stuff and I trust them to break stuff in very predictable ways. We've never had a large fix, I would say over $200 in the year and a half of being here. Our members are very responsible I think. I'm really just not worried by their mistakes at all and I see that as* *a huge thing for people trying to start their spaces. I almost always just say we expect people to break stuff and we expect us to fix it. That's the maker mentality, just being able to fix everything.*

Preparing people to fail at NIS is difficult and staff help members move to the next step immediately when faced with failure. Members are not given time to dwell on failure, even if it is cataclysmic and a ruined project. Kennedy gave the following scenario:

*It might be, "Wow. I just spent two hours laser cutting that. It didn't cut all the way through." My next sentence would normally be, "Well, we can get the next one going and we'll fix it this time," and just take their attention away from it and whisk them away.*

When asked what a typical artifact is in the space Kennedy responded that woodworking is very popular in the space and that a lot of people make tabletops. The space has a variety of sanders and a nice planer, and clamps that allow members to create beautiful table tops with a variety of woods. In the electronics area members make CNC machines, controlling stepper motors with an Arduino microcontroller. Quilting is also another typical artifact found in the space with members making eight to 12-foot quilts using the long arm quilting machine. Finally, creating t-shirts is also another very popular activity in the space, according to Kennedy. He continued:

*They're not necessarily showing a great innovative use for the studio, but they do a good job of getting people excited and feeling accomplished. It's [screen printing] a project that they can do in a few days and everyone around them, all their friends, are going to love it no matter what.*

## YOUTH IN THE SPACE

The Nebraska Innovation Studio occasionally provides space for youth outreach events with other entities within and external to the university. Schools and summer camp groups come to the space and work on small projects. Children over the age of 12 are allowed in the space if they are accompanied by an adult. Kennedy has observed that parents will bring in their children and work on a project together and learn and grow at an equal pace. In addition, he rarely sees a parent outpace a child in skills and knowledge acquisition, "that's always good to see" he noted.

When asked if he thought school makerspaces were interest driven, especially when looking at current examples where students all make 3D keychains, Kennedy noted that he prefers youth are able to choose their making pathway but there is definitely interest from kids in making. Kennedy reflected on his own experiences growing up:

*When I was in school, I was still interested in making stuff. At that point in my life it was skateboard ramps. Those were done with all hand tools and not very expensive things but when I was in high school I didn't have $300 to buy some saws and stuff like that. Those can go a really, really long way. I think a big part of that is getting the teachers interested in making and finding the appropriate educator to sell these tools. I think a big thing that I see now is a school gets a 3D printer. It's nobody's job to maintain it and teach on it. What happens is you download files of key chains or knickknacks. You print those out and then everybody goes, "Well, that was $2,000 that we might never get back." There's so many cool things that you can do if the person teaching it is interested in it.*

Kennedy believes it's important to let youth choose their projects in some ways. While he thoroughly enjoyed art classes he recognized that it was not for everyone. However, all learners have an innate creative and innovative ability—it's finding the right tool that permits the expression of these abilities. Some students are not going to like woodworking or electronics but once they find their area of passion they will unleash their creativity.

## IMPACT ON COMMUNITY

Since the space opened in 2015 the Nebraska Innovation Studio has fulfilled the need of people to come and make stuff, according to Kennedy. It came about at a time and a place when the university was creating a new campus based on innovation and entrepreneurship. The creation of a state-of-the-art makerspace was a perfect addition to that vision. Kennedy noted:

*I think in the long term you think of this super shop class where people fix things themselves and [are] not intimidated by doing stuff themselves. A lot of people think to invent something, you have to make this super complicated project that is the next iPhone but a lot of those are relatively simple projects that are just made well or done in a slightly different way or maybe they refined a process on how to make something a little bit easier. Just showing people what they can do with the tools and how they can do it easily and in a repeatable way is very, very powerful to put this entrepreneurial mindset in people.*

The impact of the space on learners has been their ability to innovate and make new products in cheaper and quicker ways. In addition, the space raises skills and knowledge of all members regardless of their backgrounds. Kennedy added:

*They [members] are making new products and cheaper ways and quicker. I think that's just because you can't have anybody come in here and know the tools right away. Really, you're building everybody from the ground up. Even if they're an engineer or an artist, everybody's skill levels rise a little equally. I've maybe met two or three people out of thousands that come in and they're like, "Oh yeah. I've been an inventor for 20 years and know how to use this stuff." Those people are super awesome and cool to talk to but how do we get the other thousands of people to be the same?*

Members have experimented with selling their products made in the space. According to Kennedy more people are selling their first products and seeing others in the space doing the same, which they thought would be much more difficult to accomplish. Members have begun to figure out how to create their own ways of selling and are very successful at it. Kennedy also talked about how he believes entrepreneurs will begin to invest their ideas more heavily in manufacturing and making than service ideas. Kennedy stated:

*I work with entrepreneurial students on campus that come in here, almost all of their business ideas are service based, or app based or something like that. I think that has to do with not having these resources or shop class or art class being cut in schools and that used to be such a huge, huge thing in part of our country to be makers and specifically hardware people. I think there's a bubble that's going to burst there soon and will go back to making stuff with our hands.*

Nebraska Innovation Studio caters to a community of learners that are beyond the age of typical learning. Kennedy believes the space has allowed non-typical learners to continue to learn and practice these skills from a very basic level to an advanced point, capable of creating products that people will purchase. Kennedy noted:

*I don't think that exists anywhere else. If you were to take a woodshop class, you normally take a project-based class of making a cutting board. There might be a series of other classes that are a lot of money that rarely anybody ever pays. Here we very much put the ball in your court and it's up to you to learn and you'll save a ton of money and you'll be very proud of yourself and have a lot of projects that you're very happy with. I think many, many more people prefer that route.*

## DEFINE A MAKERSPACE

When asked to define a makerspace Kennedy responded:

*I think a makerspace should be the creative hub of a city really. I want it to be the most motivating, inspiring, creative space for all fields to come in and do whatever they want and do what they're interested in and make that happen. I think universities traditionally really suck at that. There's a statistic about art school, how 95% of art students don't continue making stuff outside of college. Part of that is making art is hard on your own but also, it's picking up a paintbrush and you can paint your living room if you really wanted to. I think it should just be creative and motivating and inspiring. Not necessarily innovative or technical or other words that usually follow makerspace. I think those things organically happen if the other things are met.*

He noted that the components of a makerspace included:

*Convenience and customer service goes a very, very long way there. A lot of people in an educational setting don't like that or they don't really talk about it. That was my main thing when I came in here. The tools are here. There's education here but it's not customer friendly or it wasn't convenient and that resulted in having about 15, 20 active members whereas now we have over 200. Then, I think it needs to be welcoming and educational and willing to make mistakes. That's a big one. Trust. We brought that up right away. That's a huge one.*

*If members don't feel like they're trusted, they won't feel like they're a part of this space and they won't trust other members as well, so they don't want to talk to them, they don't want to create those communities organically. If I say something like if we have a rule on the 3D printer only use this brand of 3D printing filament. Somebody asked me why that happened, and I would say another member came in and they used this kind of filament and it didn't work because of this. They might go, "Oh, that member's stupid. Why did they use that?" They project it onto other members and then they think everybody's stupid. It's that negativity bouncing around.*

## CURRENT CHALLENGES

The Nebraska Innovation Studio Makerspace has a lot of positive momentum and was founded as part of a new university campus focused on innovation and entrepreneurship. The space has attracted a large number of students and faculty but even more impressive was the number of community members from outside of the university that use the space on a daily basis. Within the space the NIS staff has worked diligently to develop communities of learning based on machines and interests of members. In addition, NIS has taken a critical look at how communications happen between members, and fiercely police "mansplaining" to prevent members from feeling disenfranchised.

Its unique relationship with the university does present some challenges for the space. Primarily, members cannot become key holders nor are they able to take on logistical tasks in the space. The University has paid staff that direct all logistical operations and while members are trusted, they are not allowed to operate in the space without a staff member present. The university also has strict membership goals and financial targets that the space is required to meet in order to continue its existence. One can imagine during a financial downturn how the university could view NIS as a non-critical component of student education. NIS is not tied to a specific department and therefore would not be considered part of the three pillars of the land grant university (teaching, research, and extension).

While not a challenge, the current configuration of NIS does not cater to youth and families. Additional programming in this area would perhaps help recruit students to UNL and also provide a space for families to connect with university students and experts in a way they would otherwise not have the opportunity to connect with. In addition, it would be intriguing to witness K–12 students joining learning communities with university students and faculty. What might the impact be on K–12 youth and other community members working, accessing technological knowledge to create and innovate in their own backyard.

## REFERENCES

Lewis, H. (2016, April 22). The Essay That Launched the Term 'Mansplaining.' *New Republic*.

Rothman, L. (2012). A Cultural History of Mansplaining. *The Atlantic*. Retrieved from https://www.theatlantic.com/sexes/archive/2012/11/a-cultural-history-of-mansplaining/264380/

Solnit, R. (2008). Men who explain things. *Los Angeles Times*, pp. 1–2.

## KEY TERMS AND DEFINITIONS

**Entrepreneurship:** The capacity and process to design, develop, organize, launch, and manage a business to make a profit.

**Facebook:** Online social networking site.

**Innovation:** The process of inventing or making something new.

**Lincoln, Nebraska:** City located in the southeast section of Nebraska, home to the University of Nebraska – Lincoln and is the seat of government for the state.

**Nebraska Innovation Studio:** Makerspace located at the University of Nebraska – Lincoln.

**Standard Operating Procedures:** A set of procedures for the safe operation of a machine.

**Super Tool:** A tool or machine that draws in a community of learners.

**University of Nebraska – Lincoln:** Land grant university located in Lincoln, Nebraska.

# Chapter 8
# Lighthouse Creativity Lab


## ABSTRACT

*The Lighthouse Creativity Lab, a program of Lighthouse Community Public Schools (LCPS), is a school-based makerspace dedicated to serving the student population of Oakland, California. LCPS is a family of two schools, Lighthouse and Lodestar, which opened in 2002 and 2016 respectively. The schools were founded with the mission to provide a high-quality education to the largely Latino population, following the expeditionary learning framework that emphasizes community and critical thinking skills, both important factors in making. Over the last 5 years, making has moved from a high school course into a school-wide endeavor, with all K–4 classes hosting a mini-maker space in the classroom. Moreover, the Creativity Lab works closely with teachers to incorporate making into learning expeditions as well as offering making as an elective in the middle and high-school grades. Learning communities are created through the social aspect of working on specific projects and through preparation for events like the Maker Faire. This chapter explores the Lighthouse Creativity Lab.*


DOI: 10.4018/978-1-5225-8310-3.ch008

*We are a firm believer that the low-tech tools and supplies are just as useful as high-tech supplies. And we are a fan of them because they're accessible, they're cheap. There's not an issue of students feeling like they don't want to mess this thing up. — Amua Camargo*

## ORGANIZATION BACKGROUND

The Lighthouse Creativity Lab, a program of the Lighthouse Community Public Schools (LCPS) located in East Oakland, California, serves an ethnically diverse population consisting largely of Latino students. Charter schools in the United States operate independently of traditional public schools and usually have flexibility and choice in curriculum and educational approaches. In 2016, Lighthouse enrolled 450 students in grades K–8 and 260 in grades 9–12 (Lighthouse, 2017). The school is diverse: 72% of the student body is Latino, 5% Asian, 11% African-American, 3% white and 9% other. The school actively recruits students from the East Oakland neighborhood, part of Alameda County, which includes several adjacent neighborhoods to the north and east of the Lighthouse Community School. Eighty-three percent of students at Lighthouse qualify for the free or reduced lunch federal program and 78% are English language learners (Lighthouse, 2017). As of 2012, the Latino population of East Oakland was 53%, the African American population was 26% and Asian/Pacific Islander population was 15% (Marcelli, & Pastor, 2012). In another study from 2012, 17% of the 90,000 residents living in East Oakland were unauthorized immigrants to the United States (Oakland, 2012). In addition, 18% of residents were unemployed and 5% were low-income (HealthPolicy, 2017).

The Lighthouse school was founded in 2002 with a Charter to serve underrepresented students in the Oakland City area, specifically addressing inequality in education especially as it exists for students in the East Oakland area (Lighthouse, 2017). According to Camargo the school was started in an abandoned storefront in 2002 and after several moves landed at the current location in 2009. The current home of the Lighthouse Community Charter Public School is located in a sprawling two-story building with large atriums throughout to house both the K–8 and 9–12 student populations. Unlike many school buildings, the Lighthouse building, which started out as a carpenter's union hall, has an abundance of natural light, with plenty of open spaces. According to Camargo the design of the building fits one of the tenets of

Expeditionary Learning (LE), which is to create a learning environment that learners feel good in and will enrich their education. Camargo described Expeditionary Learning:

*Expeditionary learning is something that came out of Outward Bound. So, we study through expeditions. They'll study one topic for a really long amount of time and study all of the other curriculum through that lens. For example, one of the expeditions in our middle school is around gun violence, so they've used that in their math classes, in their humanities to write opinion pieces. And then another one is sharks. So they looked at that across disciplines as well; actually went out and took photographs and also wrote books about it. So basically, just looking at something really in-depth for a long period of time.*

Camargo noted that because the school started out as an Expeditionary Learning school the implementation of making was relatively seamless. According to Ikpeze (2013), the Expeditionary Learning (EL) Outward Bound model pairs real world projects with difficult academic content, which are referred to as academic expeditions. The EL model grew out of a collaboration between the Harvard Graduate School of Education and Outward Bound, USA (DiCamillo, 2015). Learning expeditions "encourage students to engage in original research; develop critical thinking, problem solving, and literacy skills; and build character" (DiCamillo, 2015). Other components of the EL model include a learner-centered focus, an emphasis on knowledge authentic to the learners, assessment that is formative and continual, and a focus on learning that is community-centered. The EL model can be seen in the published instructional stances of LCPS, which includes purposeful understanding that is deep, learning that happens in community, and learning that is personalized and driven by the learner (Lighthouse, n.d.). With Lighthouse's roots in the EL model, it is not a surprise that in 2009 the school began its foray into integrating making into the classroom and it was relatively seamless.

Making was first introduced by Aaron Vanderwerff, a science classroom teacher who integrated making into his physics classroom and started a robotics course in 2009. The robotics course was expanded in 2010 to include making and was the start of the Lighthouse Creativity Lab, which at the time of my visit was directed by Vanderwerff. Camargo, who recounts the beginnings of Creativity Lab:

*Aaron [Vanderwerff], who is our director, he was our physics instructor, and he wanted to take some students to the Makers Faire. So, he got a grant to do a project in his class. I think it was the next year they started having a club after-school. And then he got buy-in from other teachers in seeing how interested the students were. Then it was built into an after-school program, and we started electives. So it has been slowly since 2009, growing to what it is today. It initially was funded through separate grants but now it's part of our normal operating budget. And we do have to do, sometimes, separate grants for particular things that are outside of our regular yearly expectations.*

Vanderwerff described how he was inspired by events at the Tinkering Studio located at the Exploratorium Museum in San Francisco, which in essence were mini-Maker Faires occurring on a monthly basis. Vanderwerff, inspired by his visit to the Tinkering Studio, sought permission from the building principal to integrate making into his classroom. He recalled:

*First, I went to the principal and I said, 'Can we do this making thing?' He said, "okay," he said sure because he was kind of a yes guy. I came into class and like, here are some Make magazines; we are bringing something to Maker Fair in five months. Get ready. What do you want to make? We started just coming up with project ideas. Most of their projects for the first few years were electronics and programming based, kind of Arduino based, and that's because of I think what was in Make magazine.*

Vanderwerf noted that since that time the *Make* magazine is no longer used "because kids don't see people like themselves in the magazine, because most of the makers and people in the magazine are men, or boys, and they are white for the most part, which has been a critique of the movement as a whole."

After the success of the first class the next year (2010) a combo class titled Making and Robotics was offered where students would do one week of making and two weeks of robotics and programming and would then switch back and forth. Vanderwerff noted he grew up in a contracting (building structures) family and did a lot a woodworking, which led him to the woodworking based making activities in the 2010 class. He stated:

*All of it is making from my perspective. We would actually do a one-week project. Here is a chair, build this chair, you have a week, at the end of the week, we would take a look at the chairs. Next couple of weeks would be programming challenges, make your robot do this, follow-the-line, who can get theirs to go the fastest, whatever it happens to be. There would be a built-in piece around, you are learning to program a loop, or you are learning to use a sensor or whatever it is.*

The Creativity Lab officially opened in August of 2013 and in that year the program offered a high school elective course in making and a course in robotics, began an after-school making program for K–8 students, and offered professional development for teachers. From there additional course electives were offered in grades 7/8, a high school level after-school program was started and in 2016 the Lodestar K–8 school was opened, which integrated making into the curriculum. In 2012 Vanderwerff transferred teaching responsibilities to Ed Crandall, who is the 9$^{th}$ grade Science & Making elective teacher.

There are two Creativity Lab spaces on the Lighthouse campus; one space is 600 $ft^2$ (56 $m^2$) and 300 $ft^2$ (28 $m^2$). In addition, all K–4 classrooms have a mini makerspace, as shown in Figure 1.

Camargo noted that in kindergarten students start using woodworking tools. She noted:

*They start doing carpentry, and every Friday morning they do some sort of Making ... some sort of projects. One project that our Kindergartners do is they get paired up and they interview a partner about what their favorite things are and what their favorite colors are, what do they like to do, and then use that information to create a toy that they think their partner would like. It's a good exercise in them becoming sensitive to different aspects of an object, sensitivity to the design, and learn empathy. You know, they're not making the toy that they want- it's for someone else. So, they start using saws and hammering and printing and whatever the tools they want. Also, they start sewing in Kindergarten as well. Starting in middle school there is Soldering and Robotics elective in the middle school.*

During the author's visit the Creativity Lab was providing 3D design instruction to students in the lab. As shown in Figure 2, the class began designing on graph paper and then moved to the software program Tinkercad.

Figure 3 provides a glimpse of a LEGO designed structure and a student's drawing of the structure on graph paper.

Another important and yet whimsical item in the creativity lab is the injury log, as shown in Figure 4.

*Figure 1. Classroom mini makerspace*

Outside of the Creativity Lab Camargo pointed out the cardboard city made by students, as shown in Figure 5. She said that the Creativity Lab uses low-tech tools and supplies because of their accessibility and their ability to put students at ease while they make. She noted:

*We are a firm believer that the low-tech tools and supplies are just as useful as high-tech supplies. And we are a fan of them because they're accessible, they're cheap. There's not an issue of students feeling like they don't want to mess this thing up. And so, they sort of limit their ideas or what their plans are. Also, for the teachers too. That is also a big consideration, but we do*

*Figure 2. 3D design course instructions*

*Figure 3. 3D design student work*

*Figure 4. Injury log*

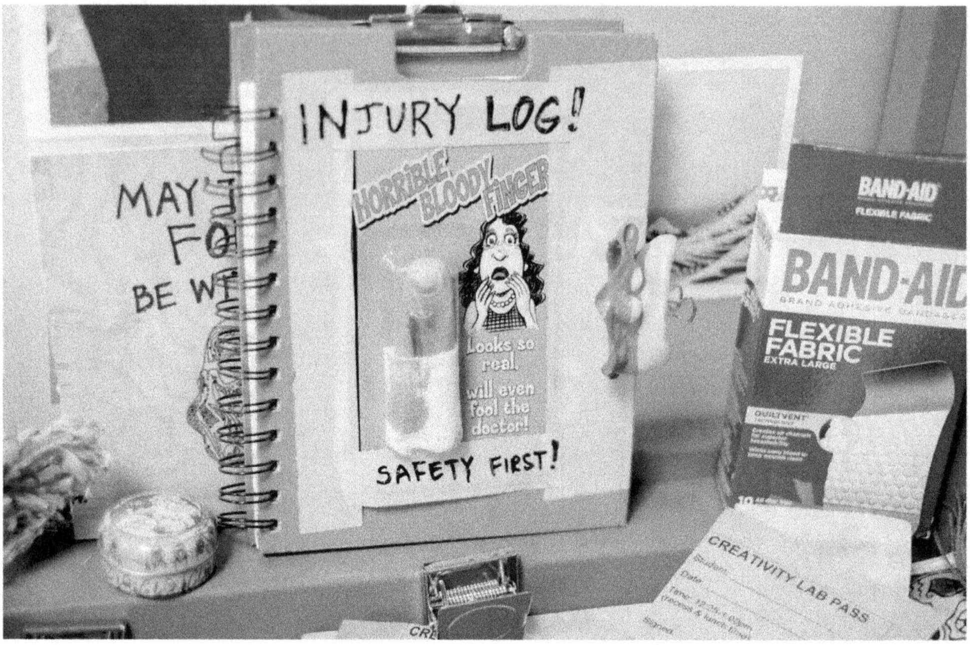


*have 3D printers. We do have those high-tech items. But we got those over the course of many years. And it was always in response to a student who needed that particular tool for their project.*

Camargo next showcased chairs made by students in the space, as shown in Figure 6.

In Figure 7 there is an example of a robot that was built as part of the robot class, which is also part of the robot petting zoo. According to Camargo the robots can be plugged into a power source and have LEDs as eyes and motors to move. She noted:

*They're [robots] made to be touched, but they will actually move, once they have the motors ... But you can attach it to a power source. And then when you hit certain levers or whatever the action step is to create a response, they'll move their arms. Different robots will do different things depending on how the student designed them.*

*Figure 5. Cardboard city*

When asked about issues of trust Vanderwerff focused on the process of introducing making into the school. He noted that in the beginning, in the first physics class, he and the students built trust over the course of the year as they built robotics. One of the benefits of being in a formal learning environment is that students assigned to the course had to participate in the making activities. Students in the formal learning environment sometimes have the perception that the making tasks are not something for them or they are not capable of the task. Vanderwerff believes this perception is why it is important to make, he noted:

*I think the biggest issue there for kids is the perception that this is not something that they want to or can do, which is actually why I think it's super important that we do it, because I think it shifts…students' perceptions of themselves and what they are capable of, because I'm a physics and chemistry teacher and so just like physics and chemistry, robotics is perceived as a difficult thing. If I don't generally do well in my classes often, I do not think that I am capable of difficult things.*

*Figure 6. Student made chair*

Vanderwerff also spoke of building cultural capital around new STEM content areas. For example, in East Oakland there are not many people working in the computer science and programming fields, but the Creativity Lab has managed to expose and create interest for students. He noted:

*It [programming] is not something that in our community you bump into. Most of our students' families are doing more blue-collar jobs, hands-on work. The year after the programming class started in December, so like a year and a half in. I actually went to a Young Makers' event where [the leaders of the event] were talking to teachers, but mostly it was parents who wanted to start little maker clubs. It'd be awesome if we see students who go into that field, and as an example we have seen kids. There were two graduating classes before me and they mostly studied things in the humanities, and then*

*Figure 7. Robot*

*in life science. I think just because they were exposed to physical science and engineering, there have been a number of kids who have decided: I want to study programming.*

The Creativity Lab has also built trust with teachers, administrators, families, and ultimately students. To build trust and community with parents the school holds weekly meetings where parents and staff discuss a pertinent topic. Once a month the Creativity Lab does a workshop for parents. Vanderwerff described parents involved in the workshops:

*... you put the activity out and they look at each other like, 'Are we gonna do this? Really they are gonna make us do stuff?' Then eventually they jump in and, but the point there was for them to see this is a type of learning, why we want to be able to do this. You see the same gender things like you do a sewing projecs and the guys kind of want to keep back, as you do with the kids.*

Building trust with administration was more of a grassroots effort done by seeking assent from administrators to talk with teachers about potential projects and activities. Then, as Creativity Lab staff meet with the classroom teachers there is a collaborative effort to determine how to implement maker-based projects into the classroom. According to Vanderwerff:

*What we learned is in first through fourth grade, teachers have so much [to teach] that there is no room for another thing, then the question has become, 'What were you doing this year and which of these things do you feel like would benefit? Which would help kids to learn that idea more deeply?' Obvious ones are like electricity. If I build a circuit, I actually know what's going on. If I can then explain the theory behind it, great, that's also knowing what goes on. There are some teachers who are excited and don't know what to do to get started. The admin is feeling like we have all these things going, how does this fit into that? If it doesn't fit into that why are we doing it? Then this process we are going through now, where I'm trying to bring things back together, kind of weave them - into a rope kind of way, where expeditionary learning, which is the network we belong to, and then we have these instructional stances, which is how we think teaching and learning should look. It's a relationship based purposeful and learner driven.*

Lighthouse has many flexible spaces like the Creativity Lab. Camargo indicated the lab is only used as a classroom for a few hours a day and the rest of the time it can be used for other classes or for professional development training for teachers including a workshop called *Design Making Experiences*. She went on to describe the workshop:

*We also do Design Making Experiences, which is professional development for teachers and it's actually free for OUSD [Oakland Unified School District] for Title I schools and it's a two-day workshop that Aaron [Vanderwerff ] does with [Angi Chau from Castilleja School] down south, It's a private all girls high school but they alternate the location for those trainings, so the first day is sort of understanding making, understand what impact making has on your education and then ... And sort of forward thinking to what sort of projects they want to project to their classroom or their school and then the second day is more focused on independent work actually creating that curriculum to bring back so the goal is you leave with a lesson plan.*

On the high school side of the building is another maker lab that also serves as a science classroom. Most of the machines and storage units in the space are wheeled so they can be easily transported into other spaces or moved about the room. Even more impressive is that the wheeled devices were all built by students. Camargo noted:

*The kids built them [wheeled containers] for one thing. You can hang tools on the one side. Whiteboards for the science class on the other side or just ... After-school Making is using this to track all their ideas. You can have long-term thinking. We've got storage for welding equipment underneath. It's all stuff the kids built and it's all mobile and multipurpose. Which, for making it for a school, you need. The rooms have to be used for other stuff too.*

The science/makerspace is an impressive classroom that boasts power cable drops from the ceiling so that power tools and other equipment can be easily moved around in the space. Crandall mentioned the importance of the power cables on the ceiling. He also noted that they have a laser cutter and a 3D printer and it is his belief that the laser cutter is the better investment. Because the software to control a laser cutter is much simpler than the software to build 3D objects. He noted:

*In the four years we've had this stuff, the 3D printer I've had one student actually use and get good enough at using the stuff so he could build his own 3D devices. Lots of kids use that laser cutter. You don't even need that to start. You need scissors, cardboard, and hot glue. As a start.*

The space also has a number of power tools and 'heavier' pieces of equipment like chop saws and table saws that get used frequently with adult supervision. He noted that the drill press was not used as much and he would not consider it a good investment for the space. The Creativity Lab supports students in prototyping, using cardboard, LEGOs and K'nex kits. In the space the only piece of equipment off limits to students is the table saw.

The overall equipment list is provided in Table 1.

## SETTING THE STAGE

As a public-school, enrollment is free and open to all students in Oakland City California. Each year there is an enrollment period from November to February and then if there are more students than spaces available, a lottery is held in March. Accordingly, there are no tests or other qualifications to enroll in the school. Students living in Oakland are given priority. Camargo noted

*Table 1. Lighthouse creativity lab equipment*

| | | |
|---|---|---|
| **General workshop equipment** | Tables<br>Sinks<br>Shop vacuum<br>Overhead power<br>Computers | Dust collection<br>Cutting mats<br>Workbenches<br>Whiteboard<br>Digital projector |
| **Woodworking** | Drill<br>Circular saw<br>Chop Saw | Drill press<br>Router<br>Hand-held sander |
| **Metalwork** | Welder | Grinder |
| **Textiles** | Sewing Machines | Sewing cart |
| **Computing** | Computers<br>Arduino<br>Flora<br>Paper circuit materials<br>Sensors | Hummingbirds<br>Probots<br>Mbots<br>Botball robotic parts<br>LEGO EV3 kits |
| **Plastics** | vinyl cutter | Heat press |
| **Painting and Graphic Arts** | Screen printing materials | |
| **Science** | Biology, Chemistry, Physics labs (school based) | |
| **Digital fabrication** | 3D printers<br>CNC mill | Laser cutter |
| **Electronics** | Soldering irons | USB Oscilloscopes |
| **Audio and Music** | Instruments<br>Microphones | Computer-based editing<br>Sound booth (portable) |

that the schools usually have a waitlist and that it is approximately equal to the number of students that are enrolled. In 2017 the waitlist was about 700 students. Many of the students that start in the elementary school will stay through high school. Camargo noted:

*We do have some students that leave us in high school, because they want to go to a school that is more of a sports school, but typically, the only openings we have are for our kindergarten class. It was in response to that, that we opened up Lodestar. Basically, also took that as an opportunity to say: Okay, what are the things that we're doing really well here, at Lighthouse, and where are areas that maybe we can tweak a little and see ... Where can we improve. That's sorta what happened at Lodestar.*

The school actively recruits students from the East Oakland neighborhood that have been traditionally underserved by the school system. In general, the school is supported by regular tax sources as well as private donations and grants. According to Camargo, the school received a special financing and backing from the community to start the school. She indicated:

*It was a loan that was specific to education. Jenna, [Stauffer] who's our founder and CEO, I've heard her say that she threw a long pass and it landed. It all miraculously worked out.*

The Creativity Lab defines maker-centered learner as hands-on, student-driven learning. The model of instruction as previously mentioned follows the Expeditionary Learning (EL) Outward Bound model where students explore real world problems and reflect on their observations. The Agency by Design framework is also subscribed to in the Creativity Lab. In this framework learners are empowered to design their learning and engagement with the physical environment. Learners then develop a sensitivity to design whereby they are capable of looking closely and reflect on their design, explore complexity and finding opportunity to build and iterate objects or systems (Agency by Design, n.d.).

One of the core missions of the Creativity Lab is to work with teachers to implement making into their classrooms and integrate the activities in the core curriculum. To help with this effort the lab hosts two AmeriCorps Maker VISTAs each year. Teachers are supported with the help of Vanderwerff and the VISTAs, with ways to implement making, within what they are already teaching. Teachers have existing curriculum and lesson plans for the year and the lab supports placement of maker activities that will support that academic content.

Camargo noted that there are a number of projects and courses available on the Creativity Lab website, which have been developed by the lab and also by the Tinker Lab at the Exploratorium in San Francisco. The Lighthouse Creativity Lab integrates making into the classroom through work with teachers and through activities developed in the lab. At the school there are a number of elective courses that students can take at the middle and high school level (Lighthouse, n.d.). These include the middle school *Making Course* that incorporate a variety of making activities from cardboard prototypes to 3D printing integrated into the core subject areas. The middle school programming elective course focuses on coding using different off-the-shelf open sources hardware to create projects like the cardboard robots. The high school electives include *programming/robotics* and *making*. In the programming/robotics program students compete in the Botball robotics competition in the second half of the semester. Likewise, in the making elective at the high

*Figure 8. Gender balance of visitors*

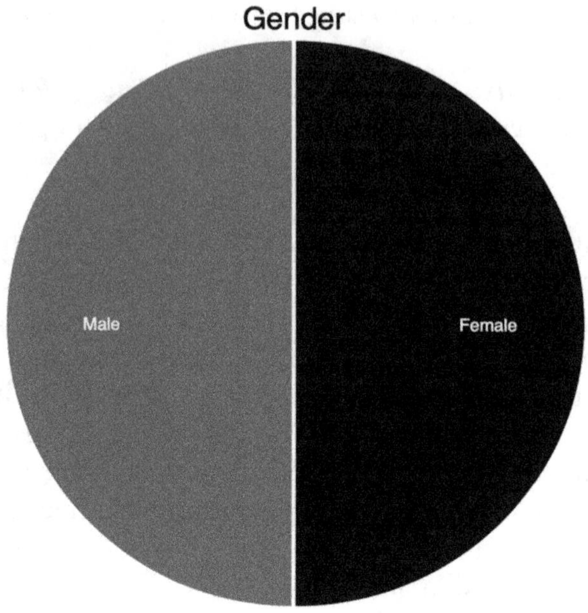


school level students prepare a project for the Maker Faire. The after-school programs are divided between K–4, middle and high school. In the middle school program students are free to choose the interest areas while students in K–4 design and build using different media once a week.

On average, the Lighthouse Creativity Lab program will serve 250 to 1,000 students per month. As shown in Figure 8, 40 to 59% of visitors are female, 40 to 59% are male.

The ethnicity of membership is shown in Figure 9. About 20 to 39% are black or African-American, less than 20% are white, Asian, Native American, Alaska Natives, Native Hawaiians and other Pacific Islanders, and two or more races that may be included in the other ethnicities. Between sixty and seventy-nine percent of students in the space are Hispanic or Latino.

The types of users that visited the space are shown in Figure 10. Sixty to seventy-nine percent of users were youth under 13 years of age, 20 to 39% are ages 13 to 18, less than 20% are teachers.

The purpose of visits to the space are shown in Figure 11: 60 to 79% of users were there to make something specific, less than 20% to receive training, instruction or learn and skill, as an instruction to making, and to make one-off pieces.

*Figure 9. Ethnicity of membership*

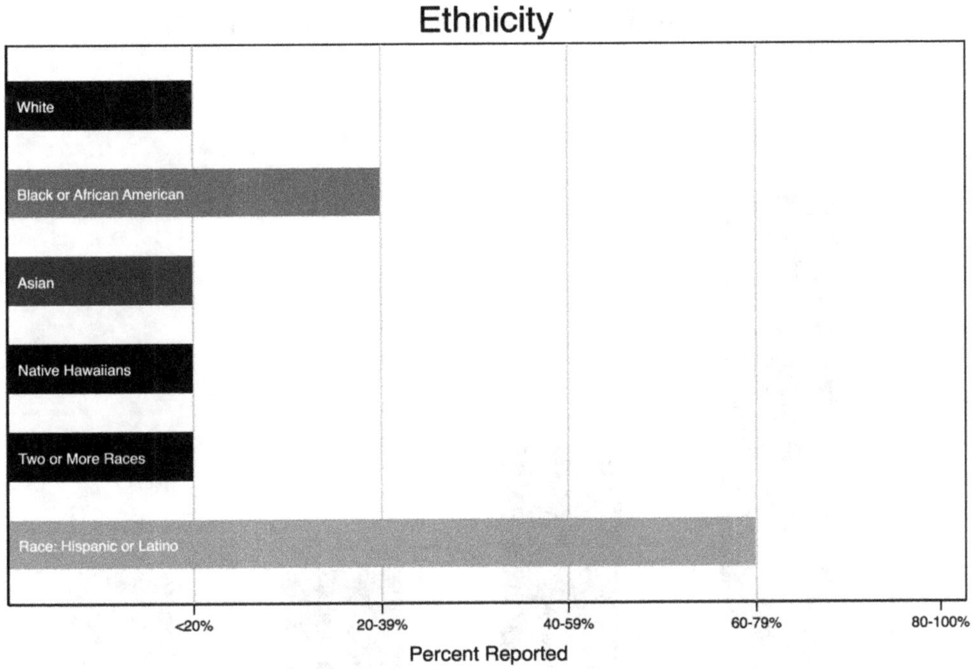


## LEARNING COMMUNITIES

In general, the Lighthouse school promotes learning communities through the Expeditionary Learning Model, which includes mechanisms for social learning and sharing and giving back to the community. Communities of learning are informal in the school according to Vanderwerff, he noted:

*... we are building towards at this point as well, in particular giving back to the community. I think that there are informal aspects of that that are happening. The students figure things out; they definitely are asked to share what they are thinking, what they are learning with each other when they figure things out in particular.*

Professional development and teacher education are important topics since it is difficult to hire a teacher with extensive knowledge in all aspects of making. New teachers typically don't have all the required maker knowledge, but what they do have is a desire to learn those things. During the author's visit there was a course on architecture and dimensional drawing, where

*Figure 10. Types of visitors per month*

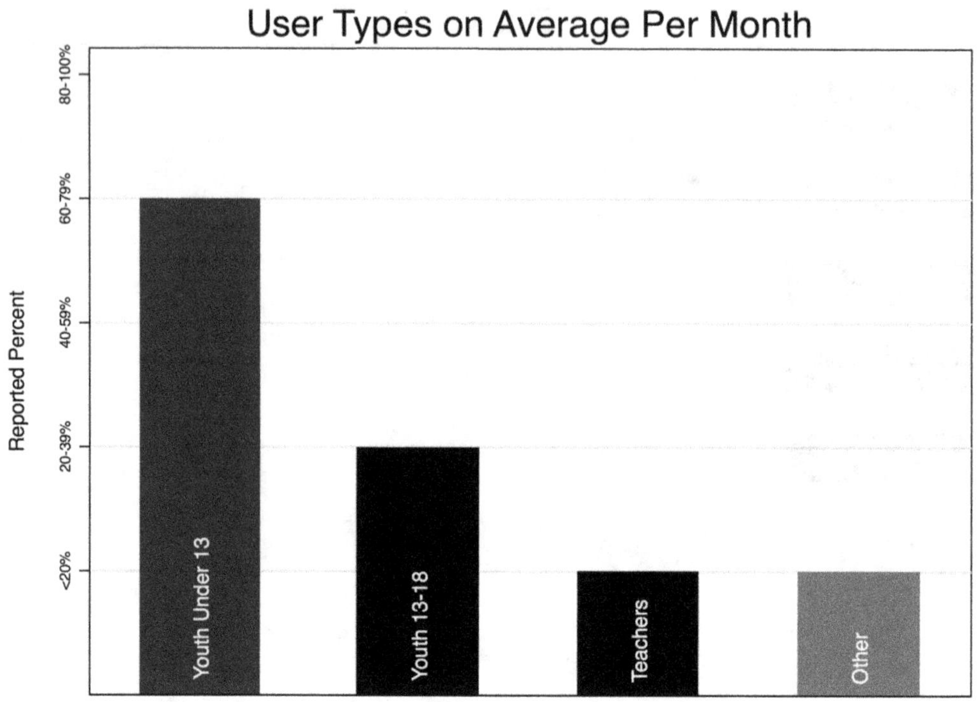


students created architectural models from LEGO bricks and then drew it in two dimensions. The next step was to create 3D versions of the model using a program called Tinkercad. The teacher in this case was working from several projects that were combined to create a course. She did not have a 3D design background but was able to learn from other teachers, trainers, and, in some cases, the students themselves. Vanderwerff noted:

*As they [students] are learning Tinkercad, the teacher doesn't necessarily know everything. She might have a few hints that she throws out, but then as kids are figuring things out, I definitely have heard her say things like, 'That's really great. Can you show everybody else?' Even with sewing or a variety of different things. There is that aspect which just comes from experience as a teacher of being able to pull things out of kids and learn things alongside the kids, in a way that doesn't, that feels positive.*

*Figure 11. Purpose of visits per month*

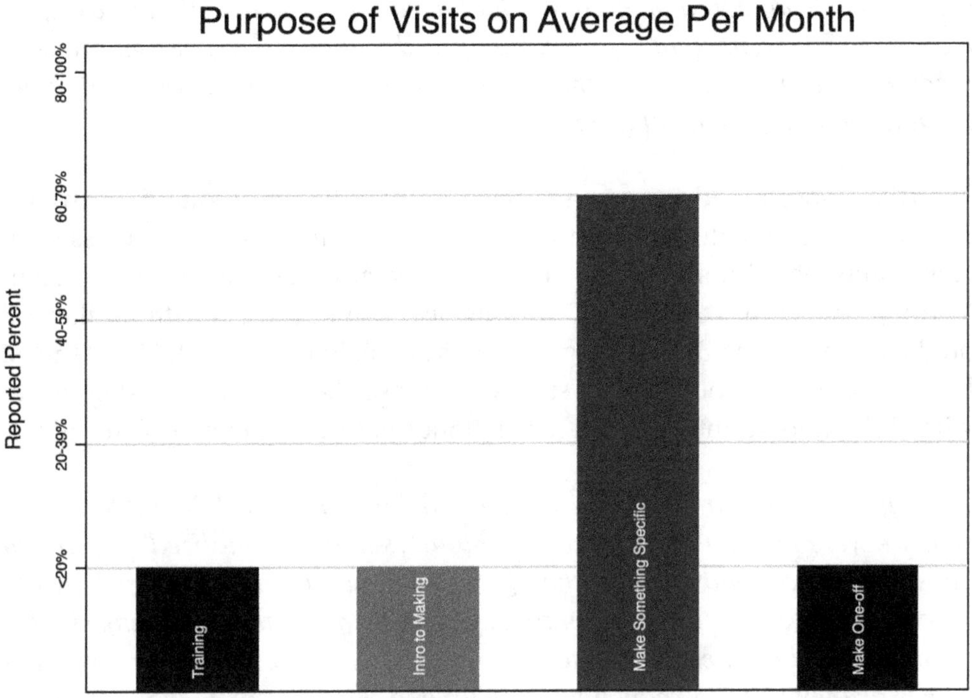


In the high school courses students will work on independent projects in small groups. Each project, students work on is completely different from the others. For example: one group will be making a trophy case while another is creating a 3D printed phone case. Most of these student groups have mentors from the community who help advise and teach the students about making and their particular project. The student groups share their projects with their mentors every Friday to receive feedback and improve on the project. The purpose of engaging the broader community is to let the students see the community members as part of a smaller community; individuals with particular skills and knowledge they engage and learn from. The learning expeditions are content heavy, project-based units that are local and focused on issues that are relevant to the community. Vanderwerff explained that these expeditions ideally create connections with the community because students are expected to be out in the community:

*The final project and then product, kind of our ideal is to find a need in the community. That could be an individual need for yourself, all the way up to the world. Find a need in the community and then use some design process, it could be design thinking if there are people involved that you need to get input from, to create a solution.*

In the school-based makerspaces, especially in the classrooms, it's difficult for students to create community around a machine as was witnessed in community-based makerspaces. For students, at times, they have choice in learning, other times they are all working on the same project with similar end products, like in the 3D printing course previously mentioned. Other times, like in the high school course, students choose the end product they make with skill building interspersed throughout the year. Vanderwerff recalled:

*There have been years where we do a month and a half of skill builders. This year we were trying to insert the skill builders in a personalized way. If you are going to do woodworking, then [participate in a focused lesson], just to get comfortable with using power tools. I have seen kids that are doing similar projects, helping each other out. We are going to use these woodworking pieces or they need to know how to weld, and they'll help each other out.*

The Lighthouse Creativity Lab has developed a number of strategies to support gender equity. In the middle school for example, all students are required to participate in all making activities including programming. Often they even pair same-gender students together so that the students can't opt-out of a particular experience. Like a "wheel," all students participate in making, computer programming and music classes. The activities are mostly introductory for students and it is meant as their first experience in the different areas. Educators are purposeful in selecting a variety of media that have traditionally been seen as gendered, like sewing or welding. Circuitry is another area that is explored as Vanderwerff explained:

*We make sure when we are doing circuitry that we do some sewing circuits, but what we don't do, [and] I actually just had this misunderstanding come up, is say this is the girls' thing, and this is the boys' thing. What we do is we put it all out there. And then we make everybody do all the different things a little bit, and then we let people choose what they want to do. Yeah, when we would do the skill builders in high school, I think that was the clearest example, everybody is building a chair, everybody sews a pillow for the chair and embroiders it, and we all do some soldering, and we all do some Arduino programming and circuit building.*

In the Arduino programming activities youth choose from a series of mini-independent projects. Working in same-sex pairs youth are not able to opt out of projects or to outsource their work to other students. Vanderwerff noted:

*We also put them in for the chair and the pillow in particular, we put them in same sex pairs. There is none of the like, here is a saw, I'm going to pass it off to the other person, because I don't do that. Then, you are embroidering your pillow cover, this isn't your job. And so, I just remember enjoying after-school on those days seeing all these young men, and they are out there with their embroidery, getting tips from the moms. One guy in particular sewed these six-inch stitches, and it doesn't work, it's getting caught. [The student is] like "whatever man, I'm just doing it this way". He goes outside and somebody else's mom is like, 'You can't do that.' And so she helps him take them out, and then before you know it, he was doing it the right way. It helps when as the adult in the room you are also doing the sewing and the woodworking and the different pieces and showing folks.*

Another practice in the space is to have a mix of genders and race for the teaching faculty. Hiring maker teachers has been a challenge for the school. Many candidates who apply for maker jobs are white men and therefore represent a narrow vision of the maker movement. The school has actively attempted to target and recruit selected teachers as Vanderwerff recalled:

*… we do actively reach out to people. We've had in-house folks, women of color and I'm like, 'You should [apply], what do you think about this role?' They are pretty intimidated by all the things that they feel like they need to know. I'm always like, 'This other person who is teaching the making class, she came in knowing something like woodcarving and sewing, that's it [to start]. You know, at least that much. There is also an internal piece, our after-school staff tends to be more diverse. How we can kind of start from there and cultivate people. [One way we do this is] the Tinkering Studio, comes once a month, and we do our [after-school educator] inquiry group, showing that there is importance in that after-school space, through learning together. How we can build people's self-confidence up, so that they might be interested in teaching in the Creativity Lab program. Some people just aren't so interested, but I think that is a goal.*

When asked how the Creativity Lab encouraged the maker mindset, especially the idea of learning from failure, it was revealed that it starts with teacher professional development. One strategy with teachers is push them through a rapid prototyping activity that lasts approximately 20 minutes. One activity, for example, is to build a chair out of cardboard, which many educators fail in their first attempt, a likely outcome based on the short time line. Teachers will then go through the process again. The purpose of the exercise is to allow teachers to go through the iteration process and to allow them to fail, but in this case they are "failing forward", learning from their previous iterations on the project. From these activities teachers are able to help students iterate and fail forward. Prototyping and modeling are also strategies that help with learning from failed projects, as Vanderwerff explained:

*I've heard criticisms where it's like, in communities where kids are looked down upon by society or seen as failures by society, maybe the word fail isn't the best. I think this idea of failing to learn or prototyping possibly is a different way to think about it. Then we figure out, what do we learn from that? So, it crumpled, great! Move on, and I think also modeling, that piece and then the other piece that I've learned through the coaching in particular is that if we have a rubric to describe what a good project is, most of the rubric has nothing to do with it succeeding. Most of the rubric is, did you design something? Did it follow the criteria that we had stated? Did you collaborate with your partner to create that thing? Did you reflect on how it went? Here is all these other things we want kids to do. Let's give them some feedback on those things, and sure there might be one line in the rubric that it did hold 150 pounds, great. You met on four out of five of these things? Awesome, how are we going to get the fifth one? And keep doing that. I think that short time piece, and then I think also support, for a longer project, getting support at the right time is really important, because I've seen kids, if you back off from the project, that can be healthy, but then if you give up, that's actually bad in the long term, for their brain development.*

There is a bit of an art to varying the level of teacher intervention for students to succeed in making. It requires that the teacher understand where students are and take action steps based on this assessment. If, for example, students are at the end of their ability to persevere without help, the teacher can work with students one-to-one to help push through the challenge. Other times a teacher can ask the right question to redirect or focus youth towards their goal.

The typical learning pathway for students is in K–4 is very much formalized, starting with woodworking. Students learn subtractive manufacturing processes by shaping wood with files and sandpaper. Other skills taught in the woodshop include using saws, drills and hammers to create projects. Vanderwerff described the following student project based on woodworking skills:

*Then they do a small design project where they ask a partner what they like in a toy and then they build them a toy. And then they do similar things with sawing. And then they use robots to do a little bit of programming. It's like the thirds of the year. The other grades don't really have space to do a standalone. This is 45 minutes a week, and then each day there is choice time at the end of the day. Kids could do these things on their own as well. The first through fourth grade, or first through 12th grades don't have a standalone time, except in the electives or enrichments.*

Certification on the machines is done in a hands-on skill building way. Unlike the traditional lecture followed by a whole class quiz, students make projects and are incrementally introduced to the tools and machines to help them complete the projects. The knowledge and skills are introduced in a just-in-time format taught as the students need or request the tool or skill. As an example, students will build a chair in small groups but everyone builds a chair. The students are allowed to devise their building plan and make measurements. They are then slowly introduced to the tools sometimes as they are using them, as Vanderwerff explained:

*Then while they are measuring we'd say, 'By the way, here is this thing that's called a square, here is how you use it.' They don't need to be certified but we ask, "let's see your tape measure, you are a little off, we need to be more precise". We might give them little hints. Then when it's time to use the saw we are like, 'Okay, looks like this group, these two pairs are ready for the saw.' I'm going to demo how to use it safely and then you are going to do it in front of me. That's the certification process we've used. They are usually really nervous. There are so many variables in how you hold it and all these things that you can't explain in a lecture. We start by sharing "If I say stop, just stop, don't freak out. The only way I can give you feedback is standing in front of you observing and providing feedback for example, 'You are not holding [the saw] flat, hold it like this.*

## YOUTH IN THE SPACE

Understandably, the Creativity Lab is meant for K–12 students and is designed to give them the opportunity to participate in making. The lab is a place where teachers are coached and trained to provide student ownership (agency) of their learning and provide the means for students to express their creativity. Youth experience making through activities coupled with the Learning Expeditions, as well as electives courses and after-school programs.

Families play a role as well in the school. In addition to parent supporting the learning of children they also support faculty at the school during events like the Maker Faire. In addition, family members support the space by building supportive materials like circuit blocks for the Creativity Lab to be used in the program.

## IMPACT ON COMMUNITY

The project has given students a better understanding of what is possible in their lives through making. They have a better sense of what they can do in their lives, according to Vanderwerff. The true power and potential of the Creativity Lab to change the lives of children in the city of Oakland has not been fully realized but there have been small successes. More students, according to Vanderwerff, are pursuing technical outlets.

When asked what stakeholders, like policymakers and others, are interested in the impact of the maker activities on student learning Vanderwerff noted that there is interest in the impacts but it is more along the lines of test scores, attendance, and graduation rates. Measuring these impacts are very difficult. Vanderwerff explained:

*But it's hard to actually measure that outcome [increase in attendance]. I'd love it if we could do that, but then there is also how much time kids spend already doing assessment and surveys and other things. Adding another thing becomes too much. I think we see it more like the Agency by Design Project mostly does, like case studies and qualitative work, that kind of thing.*

While measurable outcomes are difficult to collect there are many stories of students succeeding at the school and beyond. Vanderwerff shared the story of two seniors at Lighthouse that were failing humanities [English and History], which is a requirement to graduate. These seniors were not going to graduate in part because they were reluctant to meet with staff during office hours to improve their writing skills. Then the two got interested in converting a gasoline truck into an electric truck and were surprised to find the school supportive of their efforts and interested in the project. According to Vanderwerff, within two weeks of starting the project the seniors started to turn their grades and writing practices around. He related the story:

*First, they [seniors] didn't think that we [the school] would let them do it. Then when we did, I think that they felt that the school cares what we care about ... They started this truck project and then two weeks later they started going to office hours and then a couple of months later the humanities teacher comes to me and she's like, 'That truck is making them pass, which is going to let them graduate, which is great.' Then they ended up going to Laney College, which is one of our community colleges here. Laney college staff came and saw their truck and recruited them to go get their certifications there. Unfortunately, they didn't finish their certifications. The story is not perfect, but they passed high school and they were definitely in danger of failing and it was highly likely that they would have to take their senior year again. If that's true here, where they are getting all the focused attention, they possibly would have fallen through the cracks in a larger school.*

## DEFINE A MAKERSPACE

When asked to define a makerspace Vanderwerff responded:

*We're more focused on the program than the space itself. I think that the core components are the people, that they are someone who is welcoming and makes people feel at home and can support a growth mindset and anything that's here, you can figure it out.*

*Something that really draws me to the Agency by Design work is that students see the things around them, and the systems around them, see how they were designed and then think about them. Learners become sensitive to the design of the world. And then think about where they would like to see change and use the stuff to make change in their world. Whether that's change for themselves to get themselves out of a situation that they don't really want to be in anymore.*

*I heard this podcast of this developing group in Chile. They would build a house, and then they'd only finish half of it inside, and the other half, it's up to you, finish it. They said that people took ownership over these houses, because it was their house.*

*They got to figure it out. And then staff-wise, I think anything. It could be a sewing circle, it could be all the high-tech stuff. I was pretty resistant to getting a laser cutter and all those pieces because I actually just, in particular 3D printers, do not find them terribly useful.*

## CURRENT CHALLENGES

The Lighthouse Community Public Schools are one of the first public schools to integrate making into the classroom. Using the Expeditionary Learning Framework teachers and the Creativity Lab trainers are able to collaborate, and design learning has components of choice, community and hands-on learning. The school serves a K–12 audience and is very purposeful in scaffolding learning for the younger K–12 students and then providing more open choice-based challenges for middle and high school learners. The mini-makerspace found in the K–4 classrooms also reminds children that creativity and innovation can be found everywhere, not just in a makerspace or laboratory. Indeed, Lighthouse provides students many opportunities to innovate and create through the after-school program and elective courses. The annual Maker Faire is a way for the school to celebrate and motivate students to learn new skills and showcase their designs and inventions.

The Oakland California community that the school serves has more of a blue-collar economy that is rich in diversity but, as Vanderwerff pointed out, it's hard to capture and honor what the families do and make in the community and translate it back to the makerspace. Many family members in the community "make stuff" for a living but those particular skills are hard to bring into the makerspace. The Creativity Lab is interested in developing ways to bring in community members and honor those skills.

Gathering and measuring data is particularly hard in a formal school environment, where students frequently face a myriad of tests leading to test fatigue. The space has in the past had others perform evaluations on students but Vanderwerff said the data was not very informative. He also notes that they are changing so many variables at once it would be hard to determine what exactly is leading to change in the students. Overall, the school has been very successful in preparing students for post-secondary education, with 88% of graduates being accepted to four-year colleges and universities, and 90% of these students being the first in their families to attend college. Of the students enrolled in college 59% finished the first two years and 41% graduated with a bachelor's degree (Lighthouse, 2017). More research is needed to determine what factors have led to these successes and to tease out the impact the Creativity Lab has on student learning at the school.

## REFERENCES

Agency by Design. (n.d.). *Educator Resources.* Retrieved from http://agencybydesign.org.s219538.gridserver.com/edresources/

DiCamillo, L. (2015). Exploring an interdisciplinary expedition in a global history class. *Journal of Social Studies Research, 39*(3), 151–162. doi:10.1016/j.jssr.2014.12.001

HealthPolicy. (2017). *BHC fact sheet east Oakland.* Retrieved from http://healthpolicy.ucla.edu/chis/bhc/Documents/BHC_Fact_Sheet_E_Oakland.pdf

Ikpeze, C. H. (2013). Increasing urban students' engagement with school toward the expeditionary learning model. *Journal of Urban Learning, Teaching and Research, 9*, 55–64.

Lighthouse. (2017). *LCPS School Profile.* Retrieved from https://lighthousecharter.org/wp-content/uploads/2017/04/LCPS-school-profile.2016-17.pdf

Lighthouse. (n.d.). *About our program.* Retrieved from http://lighthousecreativitylab.org/about/our-program/

Marcelli, E., & Pastor, M. (2012). *Unauthorized and uninsured: East Oakland and Alameda county.* San Diego State University and the University of Southern California. Retrieved from https://dornsife.usc.edu/assets/sites/731/docs/Web_11_East_Oakland_Contra_Costa_Cnty_Final.pdf

## KEY TERMS AND DEFINITIONS

**After-School:** Informal education programs that are conducted outside of the formal school day.

**Agency by Design:** A learning framework whereby learners are empowered to design their learning and engagement with the physical environment.

**AmeriCorps Vista:** The domestic counterpart to the Peace Corps (Volunteers in Service to America).

**Arduino:** A small microcontroller used for rapid prototyping.

**Expeditionary Learning:** A learner-centered pedagogical model that encourages students to engage in original research; develop critical thinking, problem solving, and literacy skills; and build character.

**Lighthouse Community Public Schools:** Located in East Oakland, California, serves an ethnically diverse population consisting largely of Latino students.

**Lighthouse Creativity Lab:** Makerspace that is a part of the Lighthouse Community Public Schools.

**Lodestar School:** A K-7 school established in 2015, part of the Lighthouse Community Public Schools.

**Maker Faire:** An event created by *Make* magazine to celebrate making.

**Oakland, California:** A large metropolitan city located on the eastern side of the San Francisco Bay.

**Tinkercad:** An online 3D design and 3D print software product.

# Chapter 9
# Johnson County Library Makerspace


## ABSTRACT

*The Johnson County Library Makerspace occupies 1700 $ft^2$ (158 $m^2$) of space in the Central Resource Library in Johnson County, Kansas. Originally intended as a modernization of the small business services resource area within the library, the vision for the space quickly pivoted towards a community-based educational experience centered on making. In its original form, the space had one 3D printer and an idea to create a series of summer, mobile maker experiences dispersed amongst the 13 branch libraries. The widely popular mobile makerspace program paved the way to a permanent space for library patrons young and old. The space adheres to the central mission of the library to provide educational experiences for the public. Accordingly, the library has democratized creativity and innovation by providing free access to the equipment and information to the public. The space has reached out to incarcerated youth to inspire them to take up making and use it as a way to build job skills. In addition, the space provides patrons with a pathway to connect and form learning communities around making skills and interest. This chapter explores the Johnson County Library Makerspace.*


DOI: 10.4018/978-1-5225-8310-3.ch009

*People always come in and they're like, "Why would you even have this; what is this used for?" They don't have any idea and then you start to tell them what's possible and they go away, they think about it for a while, and suddenly things change and they come back and they don't stop having ideas. That's when it sort of starts. The first time they see something, they're just sort of, "Who knew you could do this?" — Meredith Nelson*

## ORGANIZATION BACKGROUND

Meredith Nelson, the founder of the Johnson County Library Makerspace, recalls how on her first day of work in 2012 as a business librarian she was thrust into the world of making when her supervisor asked if she had heard of a 3D printer. She commented:

*My first day of work my boss sat me down and said, "Have you ever heard of a 3D printer?" Of course, it was my first day, so I said, "Yes, of course I have! What a great idea!" Then I ran back to my desk and started googling stuff and the first 3D printers hit, one of the, I forget which library it was, but someone was talking about 3D printing in libraries. Then very slowly over the next year, we started developing a plan. At the same time, everybody else was sort of developing plans as well. Towards the end of that year we started construction on a very small space that was at the time being unused.*

Nelson was originally hired to make changes to the way the library supported business in the community. She shared a vision that would permit the library to support entrepreneurs and business people by providing co-working spaces and providing access to different kinds of software. From modest beginnings in 2013, the first iteration of the makerspace was very small: the size of the current sound booth in the space with a 3D printer and a few Macintosh computers. With no IT support Nelson cobbled together equipment like cameras and microphones, usually purchased online. Once the first space was open, the library immediately set out to great a larger space which opened in March of 2014. According to Nelson they began offering programs just before the opening of the new space and then with the opening in March, the popularity of the new space skyrocketed. Nelson was quickly overwhelmed with visitors to the space, who in turn appreciated the ability to print in 3D and not have to pay for the materials.

As she explained, as a librarian she spent half her time on the reference desk and was only spending 20 hours a week at the makerspace during this period of meteoric rise in popularity. Within the first six months of opening additional staff were added to the space and Nelson began working on outreach programs. She commenced the mobile makerspace program, visiting the other libraries in the Johnson County system and setting up all-day drop-in programs for youth. The mobility involved taking supplies from the main branch and using them to deliver programs in the various other branches. The space did not have a physical vehicle nor trailer that they used to deliver the program, as is common in mobile makerspaces. Nelson recalled:

*My first event was okay, it was fine. The second event, over 300 kids showed up and parents were complaining. I was on my own and the parents were complaining mightily that it wasn't at the right time and their kids couldn't come. It's one of our sort of high maintenance branches, but it went over really well. The kids loved the projects, the branches loved having somebody come in and do this extra stuff to what they were doing. That first year we took little vibrating motors and put them onto coin cell batteries. We were supposed to do brush bots but I did run out of tooth brushes, so kids were using all kinds of stuff or they would just decorate them and have little bugs and stuff. Then we did little bits and we had the stomp rockets, with PVC pipes and two-liter bottles. That year, projects kind of moved throughout the summer because I would run out of supplies. I had no idea. I was expecting 30 or 40 kids and when 200 show up you just run out of stuff.*

In addition, during the mobile maker program, the 3D printers were used. At first, the program was held outdoors but as Nelson soon discovered the summer humidity played havoc on the 3D printer extruders and filament. It was interesting to hear Nelson discuss how she kept 200 youth occupied with one 3D printer. She noted:

*We would just try to do the little robots. I would try to do a plate of 20 of them and it would take 45 minutes. I've never seen, the one branch, I've never seen kids wait so long for stuff. Each of the ping pong balls, just for the egg bot, took five, six minutes for it to get set up, for them to pick something, for it to go and color on it. Finally, a plate would be done with the 3D printer, and I would say "Who wants a little robot?" And 25 kids would raise their hands, and it was like, look, I got six. You guys are going to have to fight.*

*So, it was challenging, but I also told them come back to Central [Central Resource Library] and we'll print something then.*

After and because of the overwhelming success of the mobile makerspace, the library commission began to plan for a grander makerspace as part of a building wide renovation to the Central Resource Library. During this time of renovations, the makerspace received a grant from the Kaufmann Foundation to purchase the initial equipment for the new space. Also, during this time, the mobile makerspaces were getting positive press coverage and one news story in particular, published in the *Kansas City Star*, ran the story: 'Kansas teen uses 3-D printer to make hand for boy' (Williams, 2014), which propelled the visibility of the space. Nelson recalled:

*Then we got the biggest piece of press we could possibly ask for: a kid helped another kid print a prosthetic hand on our 3D printer. He helped design it, came in and printed it. It wasn't even our first hand, it happened to be like a high school kid helping his neighbor, so it was a huge press story. It hit the Kansas City Star and people started really picking up on it. I know a lot of libraries ended up using it as justification to build their own makerspaces, because look at what can happen. A kid who couldn't have a prosthetic before now has one. It was a great story, people were like, "Are they sturdy? Do they break?" And of course, it had broken and we just printed another one, because after a week of having one he was playing racket ball and it broke, and we were like, "We'll just print another one." So even the fact that it broke was big news, it was huge. With all of the press and everything, things started to just sort of build and build and build.*

Another outcome of the success of the mobile makerspaces caused the team to rethink the original vision for the space. Originally intended as a way to provide small businesses with co-working space and allow access to training on software. It was their vision to have small businesses and entrepreneurs come in and learn the skills to gain or increase their employment. Nelson talked about how there was a change in their vision:

*I wasn't expecting the whole kid's thing. Other people though, were building makerspaces almost completely either for kids or for teens, and that was not on my radar. I'm not a children's librarian. It's not that small businesses didn't use it, we still had tons of freelancers, tons of small businesses, but the thing that overwhelmingly hit was full families. This wasn't really programming for kids, parents come in and they listen to story time but it's not really for them, right? They're there for their kids. That's how we've always done programming: we have parents who bring their kids in and then we have programming for adults. But this was not that. It was everyone together. Parents would come in and design stuff with their kids and print it. The parents were just as excited about it as the kids were.*

The early years of the makerspace also changed how the library interacted with the community and how the community viewed the library. Patrons saw an opportunity to utilize the equipment and space in ways they had not done before. The opportunity to experience innovation and creativity in a relatively safe environment changed their viewpoint of the library. The mission of the library, according to Nelson, is not just to provide information but to also create experiences for visitors. Establishing the makerspace helped in their mission to create those experiences.

The new goals for the space included providing creative maker-based programming for youth in the Science, Technology, Engineering and Mathematics, often referred to as the STEM areas. Regarding the new goals Nelson noted:

*The goal was to reach kids when they were little and teach them that crafts are something. Making something is work, is play, and it is science. We have this really academic idea of what science is and by pulling maker stuff into it, it's not just science education but it's maker education. Parents don't have to think that crafts are useless for kids, right? They're really not. They're very important for them. But we don't think of it that way, and so we think they're sort of busy work, but they're not. They're good for kids.*

The current Johnson County Library makerspace is located in the Central Resource Library and is separated from the main part of the library through a set of doors. The space occupies 1700 $ft^2$ (158 $m^2$) and is, for the most part, an open floorplan with much of the equipment and computers running along the outer walls, with workspace located in the interior of the room. Each area of the outer wall has a specialized function; starting immediately past the entry doors is the CNC router area, as shown in Figure 1. The Carvey CNC router and computer station are the first work area as patrons enter the makerspace.

As shown in Figure 2, the laser cutters are immediately adjacent to the CNC station.

*Figure 1. Carvey CNC router station*

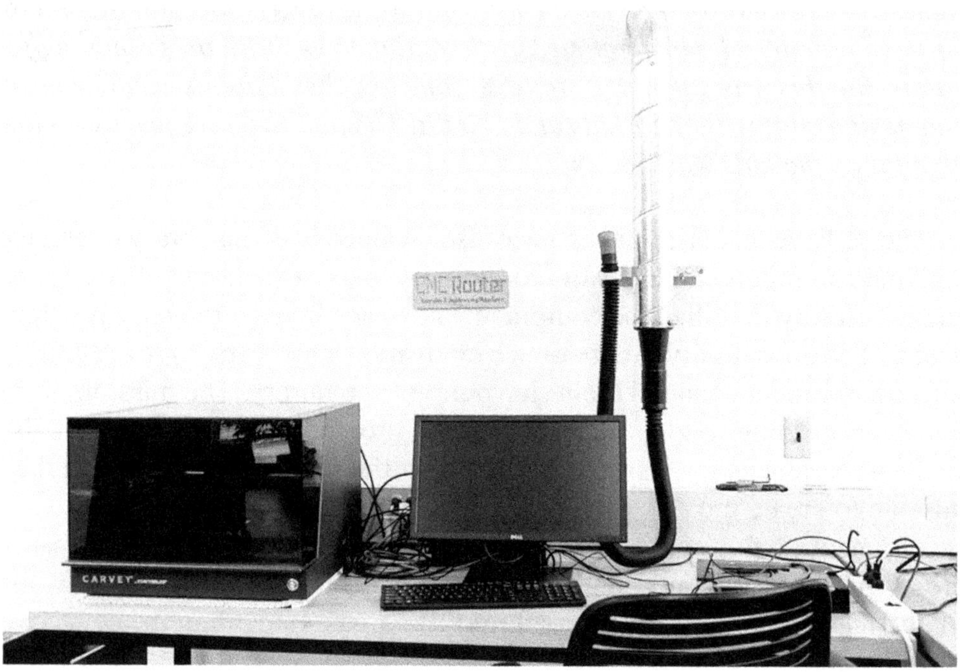


*Figure 2. Laser cutting station*

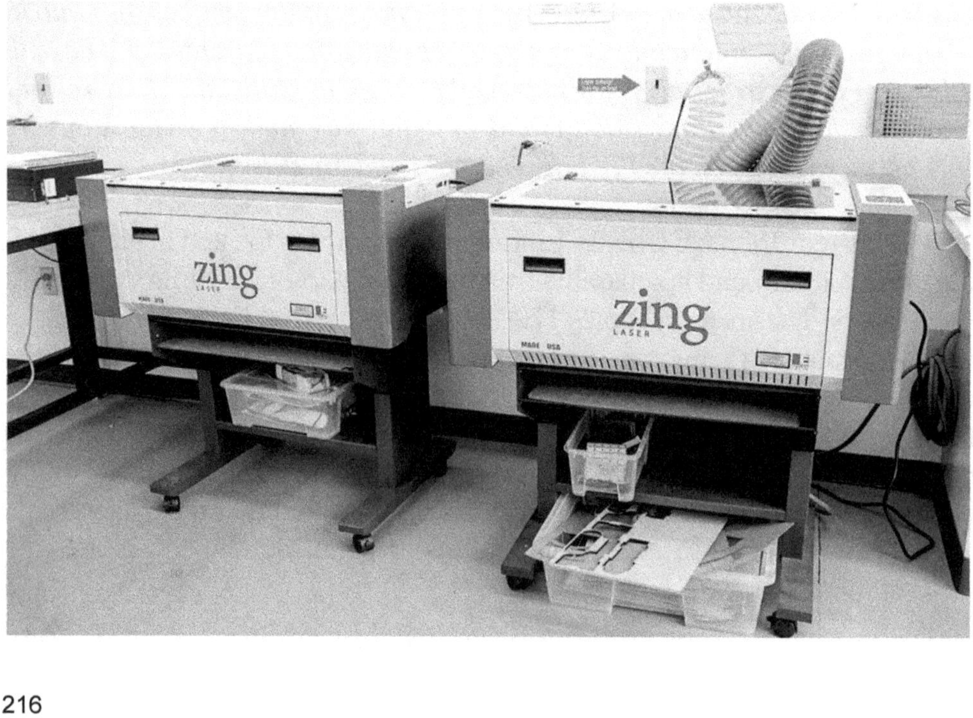

Moving deeper into the space along the outer wall, the next station is an electronics area with an oscilloscope and other tools, as shown in Figure 3.

Just below the windows, along the back wall of the space, is a wood storage area and the dedicated textiles area, as shown in Figure 4.

Moving past the textiles area on the next outer wall, as shown in Figure 5, is the 3D print farm area.

Nelson expressed that patrons don't always understand what can be done in the space. One of the main reasons for providing patrons the 3D printer filament, according to Nelson, is so they can see how the machines work. She noted:

*Someone wanders in, they don't really laser cut something, because we're like, "You have to bring in your own materials." And they get that, they say, "Oh, okay, so if I wanted to do something I would just bring it in?" Yes. Then we refer people to our website where the lists are and things like that. 3D printing is a little bit different, some people just want to come in and see it work. That's partly why we have so many 3D printers. We have one that's reservable and a walk-in. These little guys, one thing that I hated and that goes back to that queue. For a long time, we had one printer and we*

*Figure 3. Electronics station*

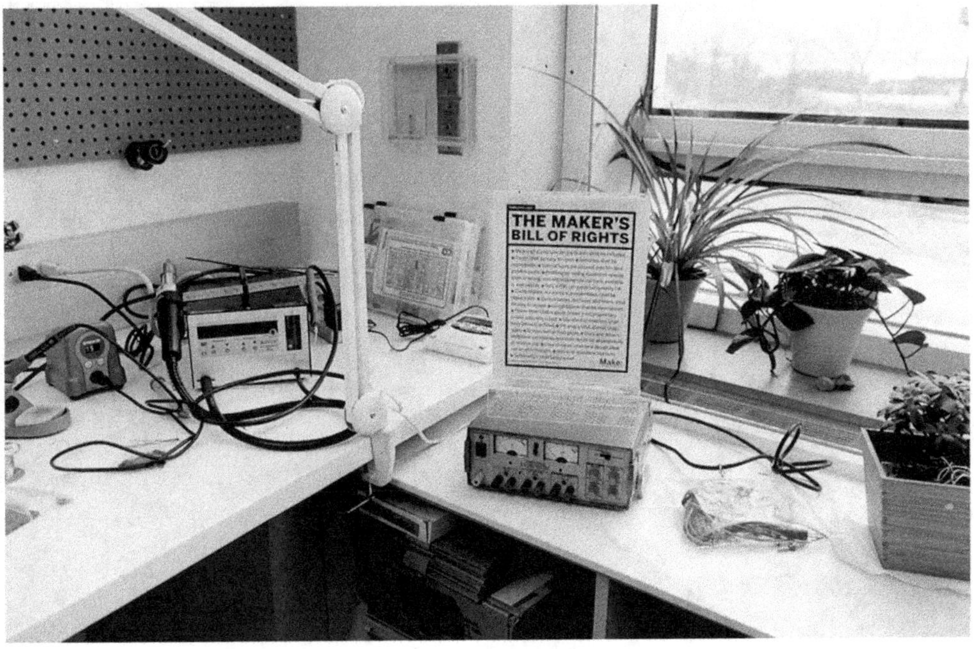

*Figure 4. Textile mannequin torso*

*Figure 5. The 3D print area*

*had more people that wanted to print stuff than we could print. So, we had a queue. It started out on a piece of paper but then it would just sit next to the printer and people would cross out people above them like they'd already been printed, and we were like, "Okay kids, we've had enough of this." So, I moved it to a Google form and people went on and submitted.*

*But then people would just sit there and put in 15 things, so that was problematic. Right before I left on maternity leave, I think, we were down to about 100 prints in the queue, and then it's really hard because then you get a five-year-old who wants to see it and wants to print something and you're like, "That's fun, kid. Come back in three weeks and you can pick it up when it's done." And that's no fun. So now we always try to make sure we have at least one of the little guys for 15, 20-minute jobs for kids. Adults are a little more patient, they'll wait. But it's hard to tell a five-year-old to come back later.*

The interior of the Johnson County Makerspace provides a work area for creatives, as shown in Figure 6.

*Figure 6. The interior workspaces*

Separated from the open areas is the music recording studio, which has a door in order to reduce noise in the open area, as shown in Figure 7.

When asked about gaining the trust of the community, Nelson noted that as a long-standing institution dating back to the 1950s, the community has been very supportive of the Johnson County Library System and, most recently, the movement towards making. Moreover, the library is situated in an affluent and well-educated area pocketed with high-tech industries that see the need to develop a workforce with matching skills. In her own words Nelson stated:

*I'm actually really lucky. And there are a couple of reasons for that. One is Johnson county is well educated and mostly affluent community. We do have poverty and things like that and they are starting to, they have been rising, but for the most part we have good schools and high confidence in our schools. Citizens here vote overwhelmingly to increase funding to libraries, parks, and schools. That's our deal. So that's partly a community thing. My starting in a library, I was sort of already encapsulated in that little trust, we have great libraries. So, I had that going for me. If you're an outsider and you're starting a new space, you don't already have that sort of association with a*

*Figure 7. The sound booth*

*larger institution that is already considered a center of the community. That is probably why it was so successful.*

*There are tech companies around here. A lot of them are in tech and programming, like, we have Sterner, which is a health care IT industry. We've got Garmin and Sprint. We have lots of these kinds of companies that employ people who are both interested in the sciences and technology and education and have those educational backgrounds.*

The community supports the mission of the library to provide the experiences to patrons and they have received feedback that the community would like to see more of these programs. Nelson explained:

*I did a LEGO robotics thing on Monday and the mom was like, "So, do you do this every night?" No. I can't. There's always requests for more. There's never a lack of "Why aren't you doing more?"*

With the current configuration of the makerspace at the Central Resource Library they have discontinued the mobile makerspace after its three-year run. The mobile spaces served as a mechanism to excite youth and the community about making. However, with the permanent space built out they desired to have patrons visit and use the equipment in the space. In this way, the learners can choose their projects and connect with other makers in the site. Nelson did acknowledge that by discontinuing the mobile makerspaces that they will reach less youth because of transportation issues.

As a library, one may notice that the equipment does not include overly loud or dirty tools. Aside from the CNC router, which actually won't run unless the lid is closed, there are no power woodshop tools in the space.

The overall equipment list is provided in Table 1.

## SETTING THE STAGE

The Johnson County Library Makerspace does not charge a fee to join. Visitors are free to walk-in and ask for help or instruction on any of the machines, as long as they are available. The makerspace subscribes to a do-it-yourself (DIY) model of making whereby people in the space decide what and how they are creating and innovating. The library staff will provide instruction on a particular machine but they do not create curriculum for patrons to follow.

*Table 1. Johnson County Public Library Makerspace equipment*

| | | |
|---|---|---|
| **General workshop equipment** | Tables<br>Sink<br>Shop vacuum | Dust collection<br>Cutting mats |
| **General Hand tools** | Drills<br>Sanding blocks<br>Measuring tools (tapes, calipers, rulers)<br>Screwdrivers | Pliers<br>Wire cutters<br>Box cutters<br>Knives<br>Scissors<br>Digital calipers |
| **Fabrics** | Sewing machines<br>Needles<br>Dress forms<br>Pins | Scissors<br>Cutting mat<br>Thread<br>Bobbins |
| **Computing** | Computers<br>Drawing tablet | Kinect scanner<br>Flatbed scanner |
| **Plastics** | Vinyl cutters | |
| **Digital fabrication** | 3D Scanner<br>3D printers<br>3D Printers (multiple) | Laser cutter<br>CNC router |
| **Electronics** | Rework station<br>Fume collector<br>Raspberry Pi<br>Arduino<br>Power supply<br>Oscilloscope | Soldering stations<br>Breadboards<br>Jumper wire<br>Wire cutters<br>Wire Strippers |
| **Audio and music** | Keyboard/Midi board<br>Microphones<br>A/V editing software | C-stands<br>Music holder<br>Green room<br>Sound booth<br>Audio interface |

In addition, there are no certifications or safety briefings required to use the machines. Nelson commented:

*There's always someone in here so we're always watching. We don't have ... Like at the wood worker's guild, you know, when you're walking around there are blades all over the place. We just don't have that kind of machinery. Everything that we have, if you mess something up, you're really just going to piss off the person that's working on it but no one's going to really get hurt. We do have things that can hurt you, we've got knives and things like that. There are enough of us here and people do watch out for each other.*

According to Nelson the space is meant as an introductory space to making. With the digital fabrication and associated software, visitors can learn the basics of CAD or graphic design and then, if they are so motivated, join another space that has the specialized fabrication tools they may need. The library is fully supportive of visitors graduating and moving on to more advanced makerspaces in the area.

Nelson also noted that they are a large organization spread over 13 buildings and therefore are trying to build capacity within all branches of the library system. As new buildings are planned and others are set for renovation, Nelson advocates for designated makerspaces. Each branch serves a different community therefore the design of the future makerspace must take into consideration the populous it will serve. Nelson stated:

*… it depends on the population. Right now, we have a Monticello building and we had advocated for the computers, a couple of computers to go out there with software. A 3D printer, I think, and we had originally also advocated, mostly for like media stuff to go out there. Ideally the media would be separate from the fabrication. It's hard to get loud when you have the sound booth right here. It's hard to work on graphic design on the computers over here when all of these machines are humming, so, ideally, I think we would want to separate those out into two separate spaces or multiple spaces. But, given the constraints and the sort of expertise of all of us here, that's what we're stuck with right now. But I'm still continuing to advocate, like in that building, they'll get some computers, maybe a 3D printer. We're also redoing our one [library] down south and they will almost certainly get a 3D printer. If the Glowforge (3D laser printer) ever gets up and running, hopefully they'll get one of those. They will almost certainly get a whole media room. Maybe a smaller sound booth, but a sound booth. Maybe a green screen.*

Nelson commented they won't be able to replicate the Central Resource Libraries Makerspace in each of the branches because of space and based on the needs of the community. In some cases, they will not have a dedicated space but will have computers and a 3D printer or laser cutter. She noted that the library staff maintains all their own equipment, so they have to ensure they have capacity to keep each branch operational, with a dedicated full-time person just to oversee the equipment.

Because the library does not have a membership fee nor does it charge for 3D printing filament, sustainability is an interesting topic for the space. The library sits in an affluent area that supports the library year to year through taxes. In addition, the space has secured grant funds from local foundations to purchase equipment and supplies for the space over three years. Nelson explained:

*I think we've been very good about telling our story and the story of the people who come in here which is certainly important for gaining, I don't want to say legitimacy, but for gaining money from donors, from administration or whatever because we have the stories to tell and we've been good about that. Long-term, our goal is to continue with the new buildings, placing the equipment in the new buildings, sort of expanding that stuff. Possibly removing the media from here. Long term, removing media stuff from here and ferreting that out among the other branches.*

The Library offers a number of courses taught by library staff. The courses are run for all age groups and some cater to families and youth. For example, the *Talk Teeter-Totter* course provides learners with instructions for the building of a custom teeter-totter (mechanical balance scale) as a communication tool to resolve differences. The course is one hour and, like all library courses, is free. The Makerspace Beginner's Night is a two-hour course for adults that introduces the machines and software found in the space. There are other monthly scheduled meet-ups as well, including the Drop-In Sound Studio Help meetup. This monthly three-hour session recruits local artists to work with visitors in the visual and audio areas. A month Maker Meetup is described as: 'Maker Meetup is a perfect time to chat and tinker with other makers, entrepreneurs, engineers, hobbyist and designers (Johnson County Libraries, 2018). Explore other people's projects and share challenges or goals you have with yours. Knowledge, connections, inspiration and community involvement - that's what we're Making!' In addition, the library offers a 3D Thursday meetup hosted by a maker-in-resident, exploring CAD and modeling.

On average, the Johnson County Library Makerspace will see 1,000 to 5,000 total visits per month. As shown in Figure 8, 40 to 59% of visitors are female, 60 to 79% are male.

The ethnicity of visitors is shown in Figure 9. About 60 to 79% are white, less than 20% are Black or African-American, Asian, Native American, Alaska Natives, Native Hawaiians and other Pacific Islanders, and two or more races that may be included in the other ethnicities.

The types of users that visited the space are shown in Figure 10: 60 to 79% are visitors or observers, 40 to 59% are hobbyists, 20 to 39% are youth under the age of 13, and less than 20% are startups, college age students, youth ages 13 to 18, and teachers.

*Figure 8. Gender balance of visitors*

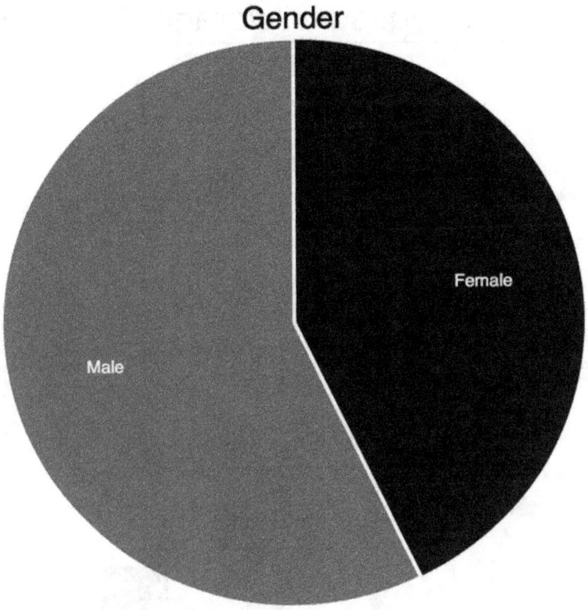


*Figure 9. Ethnicity of membership*

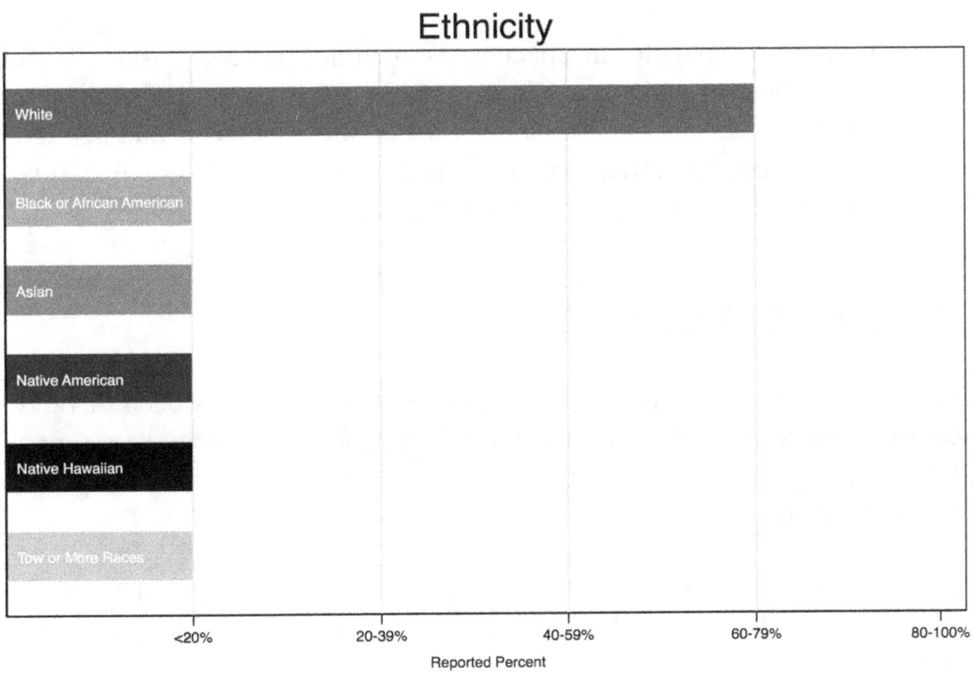

*Figure 10. Types of visitors per month*

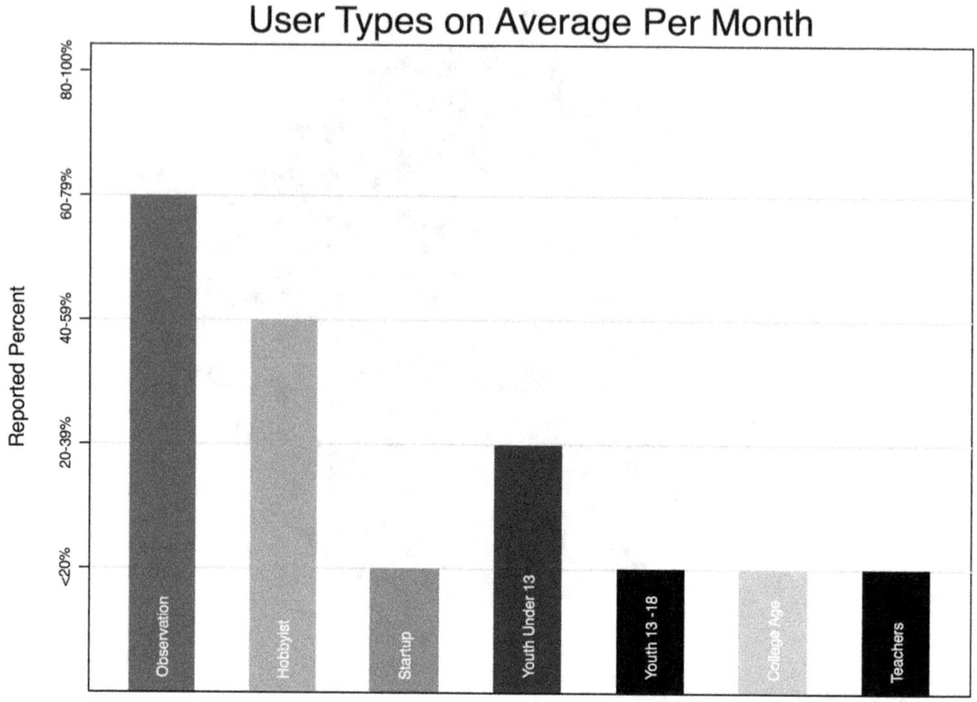


The purpose of visits to the space are shown in Figure 11: 40 to 59% of visitors were there to make something specific, 20 to 39% of visitors were there as an introduction to making and to make one-off pieces, and less than 20% were there to receive training, instruction or learn a skill, socialize, small batch production, and to network or find a maker/partner/designer.

## LEARNING COMMUNITIES

The development of learning communities in the library has been difficult, according to Nelson. For adults, it's difficult because there are so many different things happening in the space. Nelson claimed that learners do find each other:

*The people who regularly use the laser cutter, you know, they're all regulars and they come during the day so they run into each other and they talk to each other.*

*Figure 11. Purpose of visits per month*

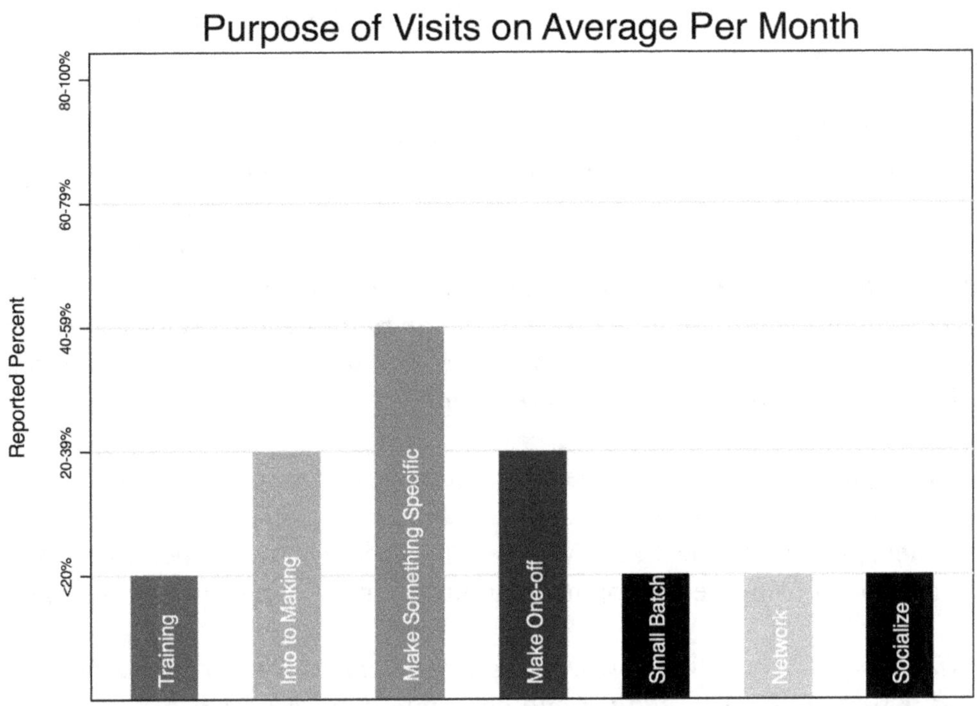


In general, visitors connect and share interests based on the machines that they use. As Nelson pointed out, the regular visitors that use the machines often know each other and will "hang-out and talk." There is also some movement among the community of learners as the 3D modeling visitors will interact with those using the laser cutters. Communities of learners are helped by the openness of the space. Without walls between the different making stations interactions occur organically with free barriers. Youth especially benefit from the fluidity of the space and openness of the communities. Nelson noted:

*And people do that [talk to others in the space]. Especially kids. That's why there isn't a kids' community kind of a thing, because it's not like kids are into woodworking, they're into everything. Literally. So, they'll bounce around all over the place and ask people what they're doing. They'll come in, I've had kids actually open the studio door while people are actively recording something, if they don't either lock the door or put the sign on, and ask them what they're doing. We always have to be like, "No, no, no, talk about it later." That's just what they do. Especially the kids. The adults do it too if they see something going on. If someone's sewing something over here, they'll talk to each other all the time about something that they sewed three and a half years ago.*

An additional learning community that has formed in the space is what Nelson refers to as the retiree community. She explained:

*We have a lot of retirees from Black & Veatch, who have heard about us and they come in and connect with each other. We also have sort of a new, we've been getting some volunteers lately and it can range from, "I just moved here and I'm unemployed and I'm bored," to retirees who were engineers to teens who are really super interested in this stuff.*

The space also works to connect communities that are outside of the library makerspace. Nick Ward-Bopp, a staff member and makerspace facilitator, runs another space called the Maker Village. This space is a wood/metal shop that focuses on housing, redevelopment, and restoration. According to Nelson:

*[Nick] does a lot of networking with the larger Kansas City Maker community and is sort of able to establish and negotiate those relationships. We have free laser cutters but if you really get into it or you need to do commercial stuff, you need to go somewhere else. So, we know where to go, and that's part of what the maker movement is for, so, you know, congratulations, you've graduated beyond the beginner makerspace, now, scoot.*

The library does not shy away from its purpose to provide an entry level experience for visitors. With that, less emphasis is put on learning communities and more on getting people to just experience the space and get started. The 'scoot' mantra is important for learners if they want to enhance their skills and abilities. Scoot means they need to seek out additional sites, like the Maker Village. The library's exuberance for getting makers connected is apparent, as they continuously provide visitors with options to connect with other spaces in the area. Nelson explained:

*We had another gentlemen, who came in and did lots of stuff and he just hung out all the time. Eventually he made his way to the Kansas Wood Workers Guild. So, you know, our community is small and just starting to learn and so when they go beyond us we encourage makers to grow up and go away.*

*It's not that we don't want them here it's just that we don't have wood turning equipment, we don't have table saws. If you want to make furniture, we're going to send you somewhere else. If you want to do more of the electronics we're going to send you to the Cowtown Computer Congress, and that's the hacker group in town.*

As previously mentioned, the library offers meetups: monthly meetings open to both experienced members and neophytes to help create learning communities. The meetups run the gamut of general making information to meeting on the 3D printer and laser cutters. During the meetups makers work on projects and usually will have a speaker. The speakers represent various facets of making including furniture making to equipment monitoring representatives that allow learners to see new equipment in development. The maker meetups have been successful in engaging visitors and create communities of learners for the adults. However, the model of meetups did not work for teen visitors to the space. Nelson described the barriers for teens to participate in the meetups:

*We tried doing a teen maker meetup for teens and reserving the equipment because it's harder for teens to, you know, adults can take a day off work, kids can't really do that. So, we tried to do that. It did not go over very well so we're still trying to figure out. We have a teen librarian who is on our committee and we're still trying to figure out a good way to engage them.*

Not resting on their laurels, the Johnson County Library Makerspace began a program to reach youth in the nearby juvenile detention center. Many of those incarcerated at the detention centers are being treated for alcohol and drugs. The goal of the outreach program is to provide those teens with potential hobbies, skillsets and job skills that they can use for future employment once released from the detention center. The juvenile outreach program does not have much history but Nelson is excited about its potential. She stated:

*We're just getting started into that. We've only done a little bit so far. It was well received and so we're going to be trying to do some more. We're pretty limited in what we can do and a lot of the kids are more interested in music and movies and filming, things like that. So, we're going to start introducing some of those things.*

When asked how they will measure the success of the program. Nelson noted that the group from incarcerated services would follow-up with the youth and report back to the library. The staff does try to do some evaluation of their maker activities and their classes. Nelson noted that evaluation is a mixed bag in the makerspace:

*But when we're in here we're actively talking to them and it's hard not to know if they're not having a good time. It's pretty easy for us to see, well, everyone came in and then immediately left, or everyone was really actively engaged. So, we haven't done as many paper evaluations as we probably should.*

There is another community of learners that has formed around music and recording but, as Nelson described it, the library staff have not been able to reach them. In her words:

*We have a music librarian but he mostly works with established local musicians. We get a lot of young people, who are interested in sound booth, recording, sound mixing, stuff like that. They've been a community, they come they go, a lot of them know each other. We haven't actively engaged with them as much as we would like to … It's a community where I think they feel like they're on their own and they can talk to each other about it, but talking to us outsiders is kind of odd for them? I don't know. We've been working on how to do that.*

It's an interesting conundrum with a tight knit community of learners that presumably are working together on projects, yet they are not open to being mentored by experts from the community and the library. When asked if the library is worried that the community of learners is not taking full advantage of the makerspace resources Nelson noted that the concern is they have no communication with the group. They do not respond to emails, according to Ward-Bopp, he stated:

*Nobody responds to emails, so we're going to try potentially a text service that takes just a message and then they can accept whether or not; they get notifications via text from us for those programs. Just something that's used by our incarcerated teen librarian. Zero responses to emails. We've never gotten a response to an email I've sent to a teen and I've probably sent 15 or 20.*

Ward-Bopp noted that there is interest from outside groups as well to try and help this particular group of sound people. There are experts from the greater Kansas City area that would like to offer classes on sharing platforms, copyright law, sharing services and provide general information on the music industry. They had even proposed different tracks for producing and engineering music, and tracks for artists and musicians. However, enticing these learners to attend classes has proven very difficult. The group, according to Nelson, operates in a vacuum and does not communicate with the library as to what they are doing. She stated:

*We know they're making music and they're posting it, but that's about it. They don't tell us, they don't share with us the links, they don't tell us how it's benefiting them, what progress they're making, if they're releasing an album.*

Nelson and the library staff feel that if this sound community is going to use the recording software they should learn to use it correctly. She stated, "If you're going to do it, learn how to do it right and then we can help you with that stuff." Conversely, there is a feeling from members of the group that the library staff may be an obstacle for them to create their music. Ward-Bopp summed up their attitude this way:

*When we go to engage with them, we are an obstacle for them to make music. They're like, "Dude, get out of here. I want to make some music." And I get it! On face value, I probably can't offer them a lot, but if they really want to do it we're here to help. They see us as obstacles, and we're like, no, but no! We know all kinds of people! We're the librarians trying to push our services on them. So, anyway. We'll get there.*

As previously mentioned, visitors are free to choose their projects. New visitors to the space can wander in and find a staff member or volunteer working at the site and ask for instruction. Nelson recalled the process goes something like this:

*They come in and they'll talk to us and say, "I don't know what I'm doing." Then we'll go over and actively help them out with their first couple of projects. It usually takes two to three times before they're completely on their own, depending on the person. Some people never really catch on, but we still help them. That's what we do … If we're busy helping another patron, sometimes the person on the other machine will actually kick in and help out and tell them, "This is how you need to arrange your file." We introduce them to CorelDRAW, we input files. I will often do a lot of example stuff where I'll just pull out the chip board and run something off really quickly, like this is how you type if you're just looking for a name. If you want an image from a website you can just go to google images and do some searches if you want a mascot on something, stuff like that.*

In addition to the one-to-one training, the space also offers tours to new visitors. As people peruse the space a staff member will engage the visitor, give them a tour and answer questions. Frequently, visitors will have perused the website and will inquire about a particular machine or technique and its capabilities. Often these sorts of questions are fielded by volunteers in the space or regular makers in the space that enjoy helping others. Neophytes to the space usually need time to reflect on their visit and digest the capabilities of the machines. Nelson stated:

*I discovered this when I opened up the first makerspace. It started with the 3D printers, you can do this with all of the machinery as well. People always come in and they're like, "Why would you even have this, what is this used for?" They don't have any idea and then you start to tell them what's possible and they go away, they think about it for a while, and suddenly things change and they come back and they don't stop having ideas. That's when it sort of starts. The first time they see something, they're just sort of, "Who knew you could do this?"*

*They're sort of blown away and then, like I said, it just takes a little bit and then they're like, "I do have something I want to 3D print!" And then they come back. That's when we really start on the education process because there's the idea of it and what's possible, then there's, "I have an actual project now! I want to engrave glasses for Christmas!" And that's when we really actively [engage], this is the software that you use, this is the thing. Because then they're interested. You start that in the beginning and their eyes glaze over, they're still trying to figure out what they could possibly use it for.*

Teaching in the makerspace is very informal. Nelson talked about her experiences teaching children:

*I've taught kids as young as five to solder, you know, use the soldering irons with them and if they get burnt their parents are like, "That's why she said not to touch that part." I've only ever had one kid run away crying and her mom came back and was like, "She's more embarrassed than anything." We're not worried about those things because we've never really had an issue. I think a lot of people over worry about the litigiousness of patrons here.*

There is a formal training program for Youth Services (YS) staff. Once the mobile makerspace program was discontinued, Nelson wanted to provide making experiences to youth in other branches. To that end they began a train the trainer program teaching YS staff how to use maker kits that travel from branch to branch. Nelson, for example, trains YS staff on educational robotics and then sends out the robotic kits to the staff to conduct the learning experiences at their library branch. Nelson noted:

*Some of the YS staff is really great at it. We've had one in DeSoto who, she's in this tiny, tiny little branch library. There are not a lot of people in De Soto. She has really successful coding classes. She had the little bits out there for months because she had a couple of families that would just bring their kids in to play with the stuff. I try to support them that way because I also have to be here.*

Library staff do not know, for the most part, when and how many people will wander into the space nor do they know what interests they will bring to the space. Therefore, they have worked to train staff and volunteers to help visitors. These volunteers have the dual purpose of providing finite knowledge of the machines but also how to engage visitors within the space. Nelson related:

*We do train them on this stuff so that they can show people the basics of 3D printing or laser cutting. I wouldn't say that they're experts. They come in for a couple hours a week and they help patrons when it's busy. There's one of us on duty, there's usually another one of us hanging around and then we have the volunteers.*

Volunteers are important assets in the space, especially as the number of visitors rise. During peak times the space may have over 30 visitors at one time. In those instances, the volunteers are vital in keeping the space running. Volunteers greet visitors, provide a tour of the space and equipment, and help with logistics and even troubleshoot a machine. Documenting their importance, she recounts a story of a volunteer interacting with youth:

*We've had kids who were kind of lost. Young kids who were bored, mostly, come in and find a box cutter and they decide they want to cut stuff up, and all of our retirees and other patrons will be like, "You want to cut away from yourself, not towards yourself." So, we're not the only ones who kick in. People who are here often share their stuff. There will be kids just looking at the laser cutters and they'll pull stuff out and show them what they've been working on and how it works. They'll show them their files, so, it's a generally helpful environment.*

While Nelson stated that there is not an explicit expectation that users of the space give back to the community, she recounted a number of instances where users did give back to the space. Recounting several of the stories Nelson stated:

*One of our guys makes puzzles, sort of board animal puzzles, and he actually makes them and sells them for the Make-a-Wish Foundation, but he also helps other patrons. He's a Black & Veatch retiree so he's also an enormous advocate for them to keep giving us money.*

*We have Lon who does jewelry and other creative kind of things. She works with leather and some other stuff. And she will often pull patrons aside and give them some of her materials to make stuff. We don't expect it but they tend to do it anyway. Shelley is a wood worker, he used to work for Hallmark. A creative at Hallmark, which is based here in Kansas City. He does all kinds of really cool stuff. He shows people around and he's one of the people who will help the younger kids: we have kids that come after-school. All libraries do. A lot of kids are drawn to the books and the TV and the friends and the computers.. But all of the ADHD kids come in here. And that's the way it is. And it's fine!*

*So, it's not really even an expectation that they teach other people how to use their stuff, but just participate in the room and sort of what's going on. If they see that we're crazy busy with something, they will help somebody else.*

When asked about how positive youth/adult relationships are created in the space Nelson noted that the relationships form in the space naturally and the dedicated makers can't help but share their knowledge. Nelson provided an example of how those relationships form and how they follow the ethos of the space: we share, we're nice.

*We actually have a lady, she has a catering business, and so she creates these really cool things on the laser cutter. She's an older African American lady and she actually has helped us talk down some of the kids who want to fight in here, because she knows that we're just like the white frumpy librarians over here but also just because she's part of the community and I doubt that she knows them personally, but she's part of this makerspace community and so are they. Even though they don't always fit in with the fabrication stuff and all of that. You know, she talks to them and other kids talk to each other. Everyone just talks to each other. We encourage all of the relationships, it's not just the younger and the older. We encourage everyone to be nice and talk to each other. Those are the rules. We share, we're nice. That's it.*

The library does not have curriculum for the machines but does a good job posting reminders on the wall. For example, on the laser cutter there is a switch to turn on the air handling system that says "Laser Cutting? Turn me on first!" In addition, there is a sign noting that a line that is a hairline width in the software program Corel Draw will vector cut (cut all the way through the material) and a line larger than .00 will raster cut (engrave on the surface), as shown in Figure 12.

*Figure 12. Laser cutting tidbits*

In her words, Nelson justified that lack of curriculum:

*But most of our machines are fairly easy. We also don't have complex machinery, I mean we don't consider it complex machinery. There's no set process, you open up the laser cutter, you put your thing in, you hit go. There's a very small amount of things that you have to do. It's not like a bit CNC Carver where you turn on this and then you go to the next step; there's a whole process of steps. There aren't very many. "Did you turn on the ventilation because it's starting to smell like wood in here." "Oh! I forgot!" And then they turn it on. That's it.*

When asked if there was a learning pathway to the space Nelson noted that there is not a typical pathway available to visitors. The space does not have a path of classes to take in order to advance users in their skills. In the Johnson County Library Makerspace the typical learner develops skills and knowledge through repetition and through their own projects. The space is a DIY space in projects and DIY knowledge as well. While a pathway does not exist the staff and volunteers in the space are working to improve their skills. Nelson commented that they end up moving past how to use the machines to more of helping with ideation and design. She noted:

*And sometimes it gets to the point where we're not helping them with their projects so much as we're helping them through the ideation process and the creative process. Like, "I just need another set of eyes, is this even, is this a good font?" Things like that. But eventually, we're not here to compete with makerspaces that make money, who have more materials and things like that. So, it's sort of like school. You come here, and you learn and you're like, "Oh my gosh, this is awesome." And then you leave. You learn how to do stuff and then you move on. Sometimes that means getting a job and that has happened, where people are just coming in bored and they work on some skills and then they actually get a job and we don't see them for a while, and they're like, "It's because I got a job."*

Again, the space is meant as a spring board to other making endeavors. In another example, a frequent visitor used the space to hone his 3D printing skills to a point that he was able to find employment. She described his story:

*We had one gentlemen who came in for a while. He was in every day and randomly 3D printing. Then he started to get into 3D modeling. He had done some programming before and he was kind of, I don't know for sure, because we're a library. We don't ask personal questions, but I think he was kind of struggling with, not just unemployment but struggling with personal stuff. Like I said, he was here a lot and he was helping other patrons design their models and come up with ideas for how they could change their models and stuff. Then he stopped coming and we were a little bit worried because he had personal issues. He came back one weekend and was like, "Oh, no, I got a job." It's always great news. He still comes back every now and then.*

Nelson said that although the library could not claim he received his job skills from the library makerspace they did feel that it contributed to his overall social development. His time in the library allowed him to polish not just his 3D design and modeling skills but also allowed him to interact with other learners, providing him with much needed social skills.

When asked how they teach the maker mindset and, in particular, how they instruct visitors to deal with failure and persistence Nelson suggested that the staff and volunteers provide support for visitors who need help. She mentioned that when people struggle, if they talk with a staff member or volunteer they will find help. Staff also model failure by simply working on their own projects and through that show how to persist, iterate, fail and ultimately succeed. Nelson provided the following example:

*I always talk about the failings like, "This didn't print quite right so I have to make a new enclosure," or, "Yes it works, but…" And we talk about that with patrons. When things fail some people get really frustrated but we're just like, "That's part of the process!" Especially with kids. A print fails and I'm just like, "That's the way it goes, come back another time! We'll try it again."*

When possible, visitors are instructed to bring extra materials, for example, if they will be working on the laser cutter, this warning to bring extra materials is a soft way to prepare visitors for failure. For new visitors, it's important for the staff to rein in expectations that the project or cut is going to be perfect the first time. Nelson described the library staff as "dream killers," in the early part of the creative process. While the dream killers' moniker is extreme, they attempt to temper expectations and help visitors recognize that making requires a certain mindset. Accordingly, most visitors accept the possibility of failure if they have been prepared and indeed have the extra material to iterate their designs and try again. There have been instances however, when visitors do get 'irritated' when things go awry. As visitors spend more time in the space and acquire experience on the machines, their efficacy is slowly built up. In the end, if visitors are open to embracing the maker mindset they can successfully innovate and create. Limiting expectations is not always successful in the space and Nelson provided the following example:

*For me it's when they mess up materials then they get really mad because they paid $3 for that glass or whatever and I'm always like, "Don't put fine china in there, that's the way it goes." We've had a couple of incidences where, the one guy that tried to break the glass on his way out. Another guy who got really mad because he forgot to send a print job and it was clearly my fault. He had a cut in the MDF that we caught. "The whole sheet's ruined! 24 by 12!" And I was like, "Okay, I think you're overreacting a little." But that's pretty rare. Most people expect that. Just the expectation that this is a DIY space, I think also does that. Most people are accustomed to failing at something in their lives.*

As reported, the gender divide in the space is about 40% females and 60% male visitors. In a move to attract more females they have incorporated experiences in textiles. Several females in the space create jewelry using the laser cutter and share their work with other visitors at the site. Nelson observed that most of the older youth that wander into the space are almost exclusively males. Nelson admits she struggles with the gender issue. She noted:

*I struggle also with that because I started this space and I hired three men. So, we struggle with finding people who want to participate. Thomas is our resident relater, trying to get everyone to come in and participate. He also works incredibly well with kids and younger people.*

When asked what affordances are made in the space to specifically recruit female members, Nelson suggested that it was something that they are working on. The activities in the space are open to everyone and no-one is excluded. Nelson feels that one of the most powerful actions they can take is to have female mentors and role models. They have been successful in the past, recruiting makers-in-resident that are females that work with visitors on specific projects and showcase their own projects. Nelson explained:

*I feel that's a very important thing. It's one thing if a dude tells a young female patron that this is a space for her, it's another thing entirely if someone like her tells her this is her space. I teach a robotics class for the Boy Scouts, and them learning from a girl, because most of the Boy Scout experience is from fathers and other males.*

The staff agreed that there is a variety of typical artifacts that are created in the space. These typical artifacts include: glassware engraving, laser cut boxes, 3D printing of game and game pieces, cases for Arduinos and other electronics. Vinyl cutting is a popular project in the space, as are wedding themed gifts and cake toppers. Nelson said that a lot of what visitors are doing is iterating:

*So they've got an idea or they're taking someone else's design and augmenting it for a project and they're just going through that classic, bringing it, measuring. Then the first one doesn't fit or is not good enough and they come back and they're slowly iterating. That could be to fix a knob for a home appliance.*

In addition, a lot of visitors use the 3D printers to prototype. One visitor created a Raspberry Pi case and another developed aa RFID (radio frequency identification) tag for cattle. Youth in the space typically build Pokémon items, figures and items like the fidget spinners.

The makerspace is an important resource for visitors to learn and create these typical artifacts. Through the community of learners and through the guidance of staff the visitors create an awareness of what can be done with the equipment. While creating a wedding topper might not be earth shattering, it is both a creative outlet and a way to build a knowledge base around CAD design and modeling. Without the makerspace many visitors would not even attempt to create these objects but would go online or to the nearest store and outsource the project.

## YOUTH IN THE SPACE

The makerspace does not have a minimum age limit but they abide by the library policy that states that kids under the age of eight have to be accompanied by an adult. When young visitors come into the space they are treated like an adult, according to Nelson. Of course, they are more lenient on some things. Many times, these young visitors want to see how to print a 3D model and the staff or volunteers will show them how it is done.

There are special considerations for youth as well, especially if they are struggling on a project or piece of machinery. The staff recognizes that youth are not taught how to fail and failure in the space can be hard on their psyche, if not put into the proper context. In most instances, a young visitor will not create an intricate artifact from start to finish but they need encouragement and extra attention from the staff. Nelson talks about their process when working with a young maker:

*... if it's a kid by himself and they're in here, I treat them differently than I would an adult. Typically, I would handle a family the same way I would handle anyone, where I kind of lower expectations to start and talk about what we can do. I just let them know from the get go: this is an iterative process. The first thing that you do is going to build towards your ultimate goal. It's probably not going to be exactly what you want right away. I think with that, kids don't come up with a big goal.*

## FAMILIES IN THE SPACE

The Johnson County Makerspace is welcoming to families, although they don't offer 'family' type programming. Like all other visitors they are left to create and choose their own personally relevant projects. Typically, the learning experience is led by the parents working alongside their children to create specific projects. The most popular family activity is creating and printing 3D models. A frequent father-daughter pair of visitors spends time creating items on the CNC router. Other families work on the laser cutter to create projects. Many families bring in young children just to provide them with exposure to the technology. There are instances, as Nelson recalls, where the parents attempt to outsource the learning to library staff. She described the following:

*I've had a few instances of parents coming in and being like, okay, teach my kid this science project and I'm like, "Okay, we'll try to make something." We do have a few parents who, every now and then, they believe this to be a kid space, so they're like, "Okay guys! Have fun!" And we're like, "Do you have a project, are we supposed to help them with something in particular?" And they're like, "Oh no, just let them do their projects." Like we already have stuff in mind. We have to explain that's not how it works.*

## IMPACT ON THE COMMUNITY

Nelson indicated that the makerspace has provided the community democratized access to tools and information around digital fabrication and other making areas. Once these skills are unleashed on the community they are easily transferred to other projects and spaces. The library provided inertia for the entire makerspace movement in the Kansas City area. As Nelson suggested, community members don't necessarily have to come to their library but they can check out other spaces based on what they want to create. She believes another important impact on the community has been to empower the populous to use technology without fear. She mentioned:

*Another thing that I hope that we're empowering or teaching people to do is not to be afraid of stuff. We still get people in the library, even, that they're afraid to touch a computer because it will break: they will push one button and the whole thing will explode. And when we explain stuff like the 3D printer, it's not magic. If I can take it apart and put it back together, anybody can. I'm a librarian. It's simple mechanics. Just teaching people the idea that they can actually do this stuff.*

The space has also brought about awareness of the maker movement to schools in the community. Especially through the success of the mobile maker project. A lot of the schools in the area are buying and building their own equipment and makerspaces. Nelson remarked:

*I'm confident that their parents are going into schools and saying, "What are you doing like this? These are fun projects, these are good for kids." And encouraging, giving teachers the tools to also tell their administrations, "I have kids coming in every day who did LEGO robotics at the library, and we should be doing them here. We should be coding here."*

When asked what impact the space has had on individuals Nelson went on to name a litany of positive impacts. These include allowing people with disabilities to come to the library and make and feel productive. Again, Nelson feels that the space has democratized making and especially provided visitors access to software they would have never used before. In general, people are just more aware of making because of the library makerspace. Nelson believes patrons now have the agency to make. She stated:

*"This isn't unreachable for me. This is something where [we] can come in with small project to get started. The more I get comfortable the more I start learning." We have tons of patrons who come in with one specific idea to do one thing and they may or may not do that one thing but they end up learning almost all the tools. Then become regulars. That is a normal path for a lot of the people that walk in here. They might come in with friends on a regular basis, parents, their kids. That has in-roads and if you have an idea you're like, "Oh, I can actually maybe do a small batch run. Here in the states. I don't have to know Chinese and stay up all night and work with a firm." Youth are going to grow up not afraid of machinery, either. They're going to grow up not afraid of lasers and cutting themselves and things like that. I still have to tell parents all the time, it's okay if a kid uses a drill. It's fine. I still get parents, because I talk about the 3D printer like a glue gun. Have you ever used a glue gun? I still get parents who are like, "No, that's way too dangerous." Really? He's twelve.*

Females also have benefited through the space as they can see that small batch manufacturing is not a male-only occupation. Gender is not as important as personal interest and patrons are free to pursue creativeness and innovative work. Nelson recalls:

*We have groups. I gave a tour to a group of women who were all silversmiths; who do traditional goldsmith[ing] and they were like, "Oh my gosh, I can expand my practice in so many different ways." They're seeing more tools and resources and three of them have come back since then. They come in and they find it pretty easy and then they're regulars. Now he wants to engrave everything he owns now; he brings his girls with him and they all get to engrave stuff and it's been the thing that they do on Saturday morning. They come and engrave everything they own. That's cool, now he feels like this is a space for him to come and use, not just to spend time in, but more ideas flow the more that you do stuff.*

The library makerspace stands out as it pertains to the impact on learners. As Nelson recalled the library is a safe space, it is owned and operated by the county tax payers and everyone is welcome. In some instances, people may not feel comfortable in another space. Nelson noted:

*We're not in a clique where you have to know somebody to come in, so, in some of the makerspaces there is that kind of, this is the type of people that are here that they will help people like them but not really anybody else. We've heard that from a lot of people who come in. Sherry is one of them. She's a middle-aged, African-American lady and she's got really good projects and she's told us, "I get treated horribly at other places and I love this place." She helps other people and she gives her material; she has stuff in her car, she'll give her material to someone who's walking in here who just mentions that they want to learn to use the laser cutter. She will give her material to that person; show them how to do it.*

*She's actually a perfect example of someone who would walk into a regular makerspace that wasn't in a library and just not be taken seriously. People would be like, "Yeah, you just don't know what you're doing." They're not going to take her seriously. She asked me the very first time she came in to show her something on Corel. Sometimes we get patrons who really pick up on it quickly and sometimes they just never quite pick up on it and we just end up doing all of the work. Instantly, she picked up on it; you would not have expected especially a middle-aged woman to pick up on software so quickly. Most of the time that's where we struggle.*

## DEFINING A MAKERSPACE

When asked to define a makerspace and the core components of a makerspace, Nelson responded:

*I struggle with this one because people think of a makerspace as a space, but as a librarian it can just be a cart of tools. I would define a makerspace as more of an experience of having a community place in which to make stuff where there is some kind of help or assistance. Sometimes not necessarily help or assistance but some kind of community where people actually come together and communicate on projects, on making things. I obviously have included digital creation in that, some people would not. One person told me that "If you don't have a drill press you're not a makerspace." So, I think that definition varies widely but you know, I started out with programming and went from there. It's resulted in a space but it may not have just as easily. I still define it by my rules of share, help other people, and that's about it. Sharing, helping other people.*

## CURRENT CHALLENGES

The Johnson County Library Makerspace has a lot of positive momentum and many components that make the space a success. Located in a trusted public institution that is in an affluent area has permitted the space to build capacity and establish a permanent location in the Central Resource Library. The space has a clearly defined mission to provide learning experiences to its patrons while at the same time not trying to be more than an introductory space. That is, they don't expect visitors to be members of the space with specific responsibilities. Nor do they try to provide learning pathways that go beyond the basic maker abilities offered in the space. At the time of the author's visit they had a track record of grant funding and had secured additional foundation funding to continue operating the space.

What are the challenges then? An area that did not come up in the interview is how the space caters to underrepresented youth and adults. The subject was not broached but it's not clear who the patrons are and what their usage patterns are in the different branches of the library system. There are no subways or light rail systems in the Kansas City area therefore busses would be the only public transportation option to the Central Resource Library. It seems that patrons in other branches, those within walking distance, would not necessarily benefit from this makerspace. Nelson did share plans to build capacity of the system to have a smaller version of the makerspace, which is commendable. A recommendation would be to outfit those libraries, with less mobile patrons, first with the maker equipment since they are less likely to have access to the Central Public Library.

## REFERENCES

Johnson County Libraries. (2018). *Events*. Retrieved from https://www.jocolibrary.org/events?age_group=All&event_location=4&event_type=4215&terms=&start_date%5Bdate%5D=08/01/2017&end_date%5Bdate%5D=07/31/2018

## KEY TERMS AND DEFINITIONS

**Agency:** The capacity and propensity to take purposeful initiative of one's own learning.

**Arduino:** A small microcontroller used for rapid prototyping.

**CAD:** Computer-aided drafting for project design.

**Central Resource Library:** Main Library in the Johnson County Library system that houses the makerspace.

**Glowforge:** A 3D laser printer and engraving machine.

**Iterating:** To do again, to repeat.

**Johnson County Library Makerspace:** Library-based makerspace located in the Central Resource Library in Kansas City, Kansas.

**Kansas City, Kansas:** Metropolitan area on the eastern side of Kansas spanning into Missouri.

**Maker Education:** Using the concepts of making as an educational practice.

**Prosthetic:** An artificial body part.

**STEM:** Science, technology, engineering, and mathematics.

# Section 3
# Community Spaces

# Chapter 10
# Open Works


## ABSTRACT

*Open Works is a newly established community-based makerspace in the Greenmount West Neighborhood District of Baltimore, Maryland. The space, located in a completely renovated building especially designed as a makerspace, encompasses 34,000 square feet and has an impressive array of new equipment, specialty shops, public spaces, and 140 micro-studios for creatives and entrepreneurs in the community. Open Works offers a variety of face-to-face courses to certify makers in five out of the seven studio spaces and relies heavily on the six full-time staff and fellows to run the space. Open Works is grappling with the need to increase paid memberships as a mechanism for sustainability and at the same time trying to meet the needs of a disadvantaged community. This chapter explores Open Works.*


DOI: 10.4018/978-1-5225-8310-3.ch010

*The walls are intentionally low so people actually get to know their neighbors. It's meant to be a shared open space, hence the name Open Works, it's that we really want this to be a space of collaboration and working together. — Laura Cohen*

## ORGANIZATION BACKGROUND

In September 2016, Open Works became a fresh face in the Baltimore Maker community. Founded in the Greenmount West Neighborhood of Baltimore, it is in the southeast corner of the Station North Arts and Entertainment District (Greenmount West, n.d.). These state-designated arts and entertainment districts are designed to foster economic development by offering property and sales tax incentives to arts-related businesses (Maryland State Arts Council, n.d.). The community-based makerspace, which contains approximately 34,000 square feet (3158 $m^2$) spanning two floors, is located in a building that was initially built in 1930 as a distribution warehouse. In recent times, and before the $11.5 million renovation of the building, it had been used as a food bank, a thrift store, and then as a makeshift nonprofit space for storage and workshops. The building renovations and the current operating costs are funded by the Baltimore Arts Realty Corporation (BARCO), which is a nonprofit organization started in 2012 to create working spaces for artists, performers, makers and artisans in Baltimore. BARCO acts as the parent company for Open Works and handles the marketing, finance, and human resources for the space. The author was granted access and spoke mainly with Laura Cohen, Educational Manager for Open Works, who has a Master of Arts in Art Education and has a background in community organizing and teaching, as well as pottery and community arts.

In terms of space, Open Works is gigantic, with two floors of machines and tools, three classrooms, 140 micro studios, which can be found on both floors, and a sweeping front lobby area combined with a coffee shop. The front areas of the space are open to the public, and people with paid memberships can receive training and access to the many studios in the space. The front lobby area also acts as a venue for public programming, with a large drop-down screen and the ability to host workshops and lectures. Open Works has used the space to present a series called Workshop Wednesdays, where professionals offer talks about several different aspects of the maker world including copyright, social media, ownership, and issues relating to patents. The space sees 250 to 1000 visitors on average per month. The space contains an impressive number of tools, specialty shops, and classrooms. Table 1 provides an overview of tools and equipment found in the space.

The shops and classrooms are not shared spaces but rather separated by walls and doors. The upper level of the building houses the main entryway, coffee shop, and lobby area. In addition, there are two classrooms and one

*Table 1. Tools and equipment*

| | | |
|---|---|---|
| **Woodworking** | 14" (35.56 cm) bandsaw<br>18" (45.72 cm) bandsaw<br>12" (30.48 cm) compound miter saw<br>Drill press<br>DF500 Festool Domino joiner<br>12" (30.48 cm) jointer<br>16"x42" (40.64 cm x 106.68 cm) lathe<br>panel saw<br>20" (50.8 cm) planer | Router table<br>12" (30.48 cm) disk sander<br>40" (30.48 cm) edge sander<br>Spindle sander<br>2 SawStop table saws<br>Scroll saw<br>Tormek water-cooled sharpening system |
| **Metalwork** | 4" (10.16 cm) angle grinders<br>7" (10.16 cm) angle grinders<br>5" (12.70 cm) horizontal band saw<br>19" (18.26 cm) vertical band saw<br>Bench grinder<br>14" (35.56 cm) abrasive chop saw<br>9" (22.86 cm) cold saw<br>Disk sander<br>Hammer drill<br>Drill press<br>40" (101.6 cm) English wheel<br>30 amp plasma cutter<br>Multi-process welders | Oxy/acetylene torch<br>50" Pan and box brake, 16ga capacity<br>16 ton pipe bender<br>4'x4' (121.92 cm x 121.92 cm) CNC plasma cutter<br>Pneumatic riveter<br>24″ X 37″ (60.96 cm x 93.98 cm) Sandblast cabinet<br>12 ton shop press<br>Syncrowave TIG welder<br>Universal bender<br>52" (132.08 cm) shear 16 ga. capacity<br>50" (127 cm) slip roller 16 ga. Capacity |
| **Fabrics** | 8 Juki industrial lockstitch sewing machines<br>2 Juki industrial walking foot sewing machines<br>Juki industrial serger<br>Juki portable pearl line serger | 8 Juki portable sewing machines<br>Computerized embroidery machine<br>2 cutting tables<br>Dress forms<br>Juki industrial Coverstitch with cylinder arm |
| **Painting and graphic arts** | 36"-wide full-color Epson roll plotter<br>2 18"-wide Epson photo printers<br>Scanner | Photo backdrop and softbox light<br>6 Mac workstations with Adobe Creative Suite<br>Vinyl cutter |
| **Computing** | 16 Dell Precision workstations with 27" monitors<br>SolidWorks<br>AutoCAD product suite | Rhino<br>3D Studio Max<br>Microsoft Office<br>Sketchup Pro |
| **Digital fabrication** | 8 Ultimaker 2 Extended 3D printers<br>2 CNC routers<br>4 computer workstations<br>Filament recycler | 2 4'x8' ShopBot PRS Alpha CNC routers<br>Tormach Personal CNC 1100 mill<br>2 laser cutters, 18" x 24" bed<br>1 laser cutter, 28" x 40 bed |
| **Electronics** | 8 soldering workstations<br>Regulated DC power supply<br>Fume extractor<br>Oscilloscope | 3rd hand clamp stand<br>Soldering iron<br>2 desolder pumps<br>Assorted precision hand tools |

computer classroom with 16 computers. Labs include a digital media, textiles, electronics, and a 3D print shop. The digital media studio is designed as an area for graphics and printing and contains a vinyl cutter, 36-inch (91.44 cm), full-size roll plotter, 18-inch-wide (45 cm) photo printers, a scanner, and computers with digital media software. Across the hall the 3D shop contains 8 networked Ultimaker 3D printers as shown in Figure 1. and two desktop CNC routers plus four computer workstations.

Of note in the 3D shop is the enormous 3D printer capable of printing in 3-foot-by-3-foot (91.44 cm x 91.44 cm) cubic blocks, which can be used to print sculptures and even 3D landscapes. In Figure 2 the Jimmi large format 3D printer found in the Open Works 3D print shop is shown.

The electronics shop enables patrons to rapidly prototype electronics through tools such as soldering irons, regulated DC power supplies, and oscilloscopes. One wall boasts a number of workstations, allowing makers ample space for building and tinkering. Rounding out the upper floor is the textiles shop, which contains a number of machines, including 10 industrial sewing machines, two large cutting tables and mannequins for fitting as shown in Figure 3.

*Figure 1. 3D print farm*

*Figure 2. Jimmi large format printer*

*Figure 3. The sewing studio*

The heart of Open Works is the micro studio areas, which consist of roughly half of the first-floor space and half of the lower level as well. Each micro studio, as shown in Figure 4, is 7 by 7 feet (213.36 cm x 213.36 cm) and modular, enabling clients to combine them into larger studios if desired. Cohen described the studios this way:

*The walls are intentionally low so people actually get to know their neighbors. It's meant to be a shared open space, hence the name Open Works, is that we really want this to be a space of collaboration and working together ... Also creating open forums creates a community of trust. As we've been bringing members on, not even just the ones that have resident memberships but the day pass, not necessarily day passers, but month-long memberships, everyone goes. Develop this community, this culture ... So for members here, they're anything from people who have their businesses here like architects or craftspeople, to people who are hobbyists, we have fine artists here. We have a weaver who's here. It's been a real mixed bag. So, folks rent these month to month. They can use it as a postal address. Then with this studio rental they also have to get a baseline Maker membership so that they have co-working with a purpose.*

The micro studios are meant to encourage and support professional making whereby community members take ideas and develop functional products, services, and artifacts/exhibits beyond what is normally thought of as a prototype. It's here that the space is expected to develop an economic engine for the larger Baltimore community.

The lower level houses a digital fabrication shop, wood and metal shops, the micro studio area, and a space for the mobile makerspace van. The digital fabrication area contains 4-foot-by-8-foot (121.92 cm x 243.84 cm) CNC routers and laser cutters. The space has a well-thought-out air handling and ventilation system to vent dust and gasses from digital fabrication and the wood shop areas. The metal shop is quite extensive, with a number of tools including a CNC plasma cutter (as shown in Figure 5) and a paint booth. The wood shop, like the metal shop, contains a number of tools and machines to allow makers to design and create at almost any level. Everything is safe, clean, and incredibly well organized in all the shops. Cohen commented:

*There was a lot of consultation and love and time and research and development that was put into figuring it [the space] out. Now that it's been up and running for four months we're like, "Why was this decision made? What's this or*

*Figure 4. Micro studio space*

*this?" I think what's nice is Harrison who's not in there anymore, but he's an expert in digital fabrication. That's beautiful having him be a full staff member here. Hannah, she's a manager of the manual stuff, like wood shop, metal shop, textiles. She's an expert. That's amazing having that as part of our core staff. I'm the education person and then we have a membership person and then a general manager and then we have a parent company that does our marketing, finance and HR.*

## SETTING THE STAGE

The Open Studio maker business model can be described as a membership/subscription service in which members join the studio and usually pay on a recurrent monthly basis for access to the equipment and shops. There are also daily use fee options as well. Initial funding for the project was raised by the nonprofit BARCO and currently provides funding for the staff and operations. The space has six full-time employees (Membership Manager, Mobile Manager, Digital Operations Manager, Manual Operations Manager, Educational Manager, and Executive Director). In addition, there are 18 part-

*Figure 5. CNC plasma cutter*

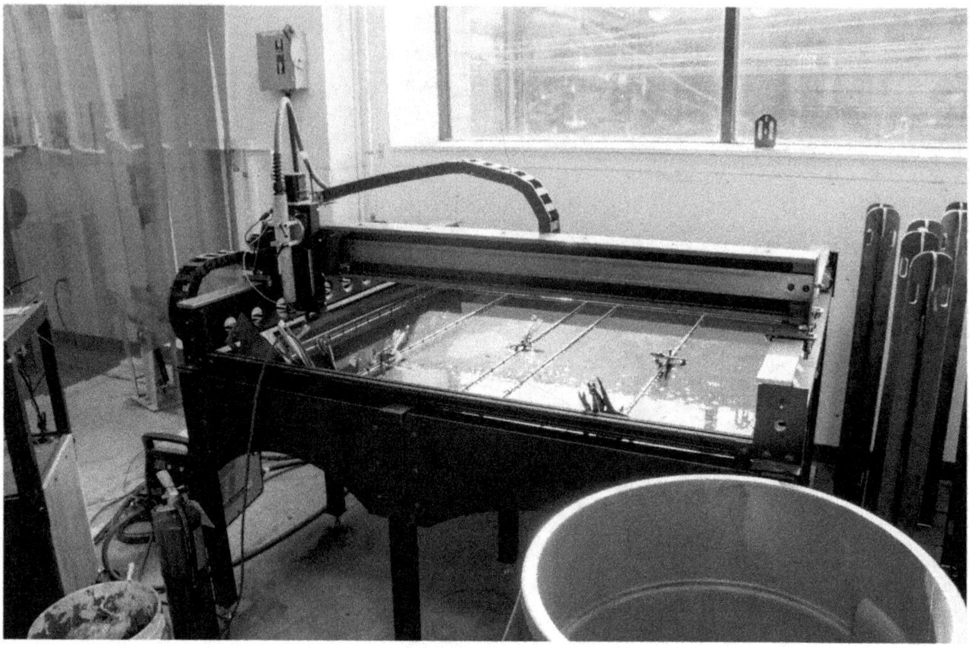

time techs, 5 part-time receptionists and two AmeriCorps Vista volunteers in the space that is open almost 80 hours per week. Operationally, the site relies on memberships and studio rental fees for a majority of its income. The site also offers services and room rentals. A major area of emphasis is serving the local population in the Station North area, which comprises all or part of three neighborhoods. A majority of the members in the space are male, as shown in Figure 6.

In addition, as shown in Figure 7. A majority (60 to 79%) of members are white, with less than 20% described as black or African-American, Native American and Asian.

Conceptually, Open Works is a platform for grassroots economic development in a disadvantaged neighborhood. In addition, the space is designed to bring together artists, makers, and entrepreneurs and provide them with the tools and space in an equitable way. Cohen describes the ideals behind the space as follows:

*I think that's something that's really beautiful about this place, which is why I was interested in working here. Was because of the focus on people first and community, and really having the space be a resource for folks, whether*

*Figure 6. Gender of members*

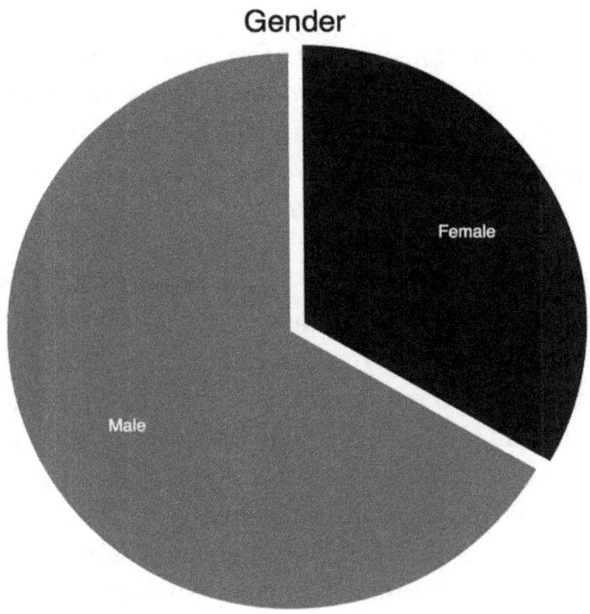


*Figure 7. Ethnicity of members*

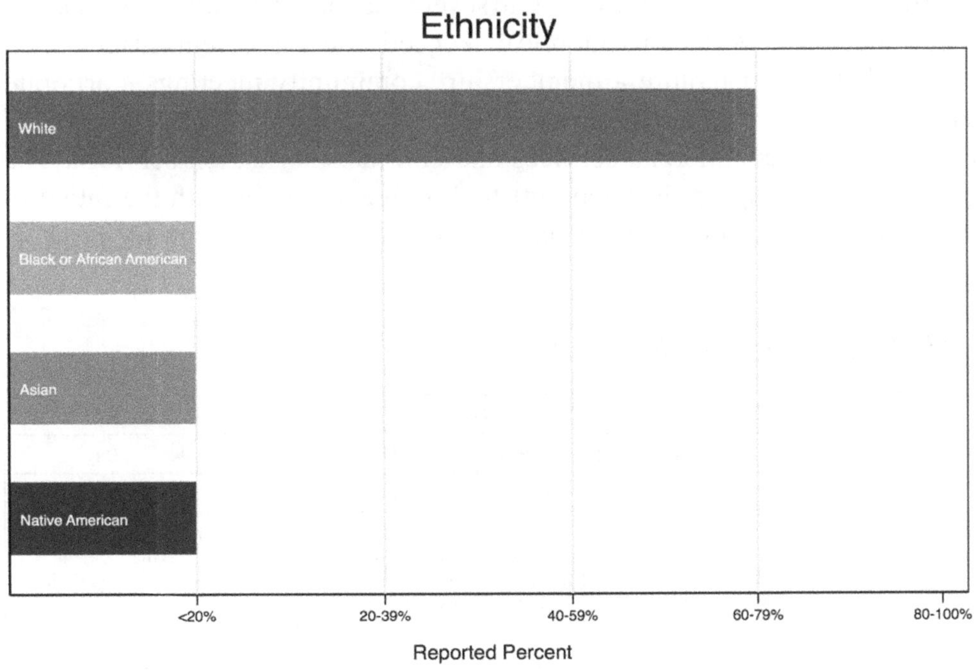

*you're a five-year-old from down the block or you're a 65-year-old retiree, or you're a student who just graduated. If you're black or you're white or you're whatever. If you're male, if you're female. Whatever your skill level and background, we want there to be a space for you here. Which is also really challenging, because how do you create an environment which is conducive to that, and that programming that matches that, and then also create a space that is authentically welcoming in that way.*

To join Open Works, potential members sign up for a tour with a staff member followed by an orientation that includes information about how to access and use the building. Then they have the option of signing a membership contract. Members are also required to pay for materials like PLA filament and wood. The different membership plans and pricing are outlined in Table 2.

In addition to the general membership, Open Works has a membership structure for the micro studios with the intent of providing start-ups an avenue to develop their products in an inclusive open environment. Open Works is located in a special economic area called a Historically Underutilized Business Zone (HUBZone). The US Small Business Administration (SBA) offers tax incentives to businesses starting up, permitting members to take advantage of the special tax incentives in the micro studios. Table 2 lists the studio membership structure.

Educational programming comes in several flavors, including adult classes, youth and family workshops, mobile maker activities, and events in the public spaces that do not require a membership, community meetings, corporate events and farmer's markets. The site also provides school programs, youth camps/classes, commercial services and contract fabrication services. The mobile maker program is a van outfitted with equipment with the intent to bring making activities to other spaces in the community. A mobile projects

*Table 2. Open Works membership structure*

| | Plan Name | | | |
|---|---|---|---|---|
| | **Maker** | **Builder** | **Pro** | **Day** |
| Price | $70/Month | $90/Month | $125/Month | $25/Day |
| Access | Computer Lab, Textiles, Digital Media, 3D Printing Studio | Computer Lab, Digital Fabrication, Metal Shop, Wood Shop | Computer Lab, Textiles, Digital Media, 3D Printing Studio, Digital Fabrication, Metal Shop, Wood Shop | Computer Lab, Textiles, Digital Media, 3D Printing Studio, Digital Fabrication, Metal Shop, Wood Shop |

*Table 3. Open Works studio membership structure*

| | Plan Name | | | |
|---|---|---|---|---|
| | **Upstairs Workshops** | **Downstairs Workshops** | **Full Studio** | **Day** |
| Price | $195/Month | $215/Month | $250/Month | $25/Day |
| Includes | 7'7 Cubicle Storage Locker, Workbench, Free WiFi, Access to Conference Rooms | 7'7 Cubicle, Storage Locker, Workbench, Free WiFi, Access to Conference Rooms | 7'7 Cubicle, Storage Locker, Workbench, Free WiFi, Access to Conference Rooms | 7'7 Cubicle, Storage Locker, Workbench, Free WiFi, Access to Conference Rooms |
| Access | Computer Lab, Textiles, Digital Media, 3D Printing Studio | Computer Lab, Digital Fabrication, Metal Shop, Wood Shop | Computer Lab, Textiles, Digital Media, 3D Printing Studio, Digital Fabrication, Metal Shop, Wood Shop | Computer Lab, Textiles, Digital Media, 3D Printing Studio, Digital Fabrication, Metal Shop, Wood Shop |

manager oversees the programming. The youth and family workshops are intended as multigenerational learning opportunities around different skills like sewing, 3D printing, and laser cutting. A freewill donation is asked for the courses, which are usually offered on Saturday afternoons. While the staff would like to expand its family of offerings, currently there is not capacity to do that from an educational perspective. Cohen and the staff support families learning in the space.

She described its importance as follows:

*As far as youth and family programming, our family programming has been, as far as like shared learning, has been awesome, because it's adult child pairings, whether it's like an actual parent or guardian or friend or whatever. In children, they're making projects together. For me, I have a lot of history with that, because you see such beautiful things happen in relationship building when people make together. There's physical time spent together when they actually make something together and worked together. It's a beautiful resemblance of how you can do that in other areas of your life. For me, I'm just like, "It's magical." That happens automatically with multigenerational programming …Yeah, right now most of our youth and family offerings are through scheduled programming because that's what we have capacity for currently. We dream stuff, we'll grow. We're just so new, because we're only in February. The beginning of the fifth month of being here.*

Adult classes are more formalized and are broken down into several categories (Safety and Certification, Crash Courses, and Master Level Courses). Adult classes are open to members and nonmembers aged 16 and older. Courses are taught by facilitators from partner organizations like Sew Lab USA and the Community College of Baltimore, as well as other organizations. Within Baltimore, Open Works is affiliated with two networks: the Industrial Arts Collective (IAC) and the Women's Maker Collective. Open Works uses these networks to connect makers but also to ensure that they are filling educational gaps in the maker ecosystem, instead of duplicating and competing with other spaces in the city.

Safety and certification courses prepare members to use certain machines and shops. Other courses are short, introductory, crash courses that are usually 40 minutes with hands-on learning to demystify certain aspects of machines or software. Master courses are meant for intermediate and advanced level makers and take a deep dive into various manufacturing processes and machinery. All courses carry an additional cost over the membership dues, and members must be certified in certain areas before they can use equipment in the shops, as outlined in Table 4.

## STARTING A NEW SPACE

Open Works has a membership business model and is transitioning from being run as part of BARCO to becoming a self-sustaining entity through its membership fees and services. Unlike many spaces, Open Works sought a location that met a certain set of criteria, including a suitable building, public transportation access, and a place where it could be established to serve a local community. This may be seen as the "build it, and they will come" model, making the assumption that the local community has buy-in and trust with the project. The choice of location, in a predominantly African-American neighborhood, was intentional but not without its challenges. It's not surprising that trust was identified as an issue and that new or high-dollar renovations of buildings don't build trust. Several issues are at play in Baltimore, according to Cohen:

*Being this newly renovated big building, people don't trust us. Because there's a lot of new construction that happens in Baltimore, and it's typically in neighborhoods that are disenfranchised in some way. They're typically for communities that are not for that community. There's been a lot of*

*Table 4. Course required for machine and/or shop access*

| Course Title | Dosage | Cost | Description |
|---|---|---|---|
| Sewing Basics and Certification | 6 hours | $85 | Course needed prior to using sewing machines. |
| Sewing Safety and Certification | 3 hours | $65 | Needed for access to textiles shop. |
| CNC Embroidery Safety and Certification | 3 hours | $65 | Course needed for access to the CNC embroidery machine. |
| Wood Shop Basics Safety and Certification | 3 hours | $65 | Course needed to use table saw, miter saw, band saw, drill press, stationary sanders. |
| Advanced Wood Shop Safety and Certification | 3 hours | $65 | Course need to use jointer, planer, and router table. |
| CNC Router Safety and Certification | 1 hour | $65 | Required prior to using the CNC machines in the digital fabrication shop. |
| Laser Cutting Safety and Certification | 3 hours | $65 | Required to use laser cutters in the digital fabrication shop. |
| Advanced Wood Shop Safety and Certification | 3 hours | $65 | Course need to use jointer, planer, and router table. |
| Metal Shop Safety and Certification | | $65 | Required for access to the metal shop; covers drill press, angle grinder, and other machines. |
| CNC Plasma Cutter Safety and Certification | 6 hours | $85 | Required for access to the CNC plasma cutter in the metal shop. |

*gentrification happening, and a lot of mistrust of government, and a lot of mistrust of money. That's a really big challenge that I've seen everywhere. Every neighborhood is so different in Baltimore that even if you've done this a thousand times, if you moved down the block it's a whole new game.*

*Watching the roll of gentrification wash through in this "L" that goes across this southeastern side of town (Baltimore), and then up through this central corridor. Seeing that there's these deserts of opportunity. Places that are in the mobile program, that's another way of thinking of work. Baltimore is a very black and white city. The "L" I think is the white L. In the area in Baltimore that's shaped like an L, where a lot of the white folks live and work and do their thing. That's expanding, it's surrounded by black communities. Much like other areas of the country, it was founded, created that way on purpose to keep people separate. So, I think we're still 100 or so years later really dealing with that on a very real basis ... People assume that [Open Works] is not for them. That's been historically what's happened. There's a lot of mistrust for institutions, especially ... higher education institutions because there's been a lot of manipulation and evil that's happened over the years here. Especially with medical research and stuff. Anyway, so it's a whole different thing.*

Open Works has undertaken numerous efforts and strategies to build trust within the community. For example, an AmeriCorps Vista member is assigned to community organizing. This member lives in the community and is working to establish a neighborhood community center by moving about the community, talking to people, building relationships, and inviting them into the space. As Open Works strives for equitable making, the staff is thinking about serving underrepresented populations, including females who traditionally have not participated in the maker movement in great numbers. Their hiring practices are designed to mimic the population that they serve, including hiring women and people of color. According to Cohen:

*They want to see that it's for them. For women in particular, it's really helpful that one of our core staff members who manages the wood shop and metal shop and textile shop is a woman and professional maker and amazing. That is really important. That sends a really strong message. It's really motivating. Yeah, and the same goes for other core stuff too. It's extremely important that as we're developing educational programming, in particular for youth and families and schools that are primarily around here, that are primarily young children of color that it's not like always white ladies like me going in. That's super important. We need to have black men and women, because these little kids need to see themselves in these leaders. That's really important. We're being very intentional with that whenever we can be. With that said too, I ask questions a lot because I'm a white woman and I have a certain perspective and so I don't always see things. I think being vulnerable and asking questions is really important and it's been one of the biggest challenges here, but I think that's the most important challenge for us in creating a space for people, feel like this is for them.*

Again, an enormous challenge for the space is building those relationships with the local community. Strategies to engage the local community include hosting monthly community meetings for the different neighborhoods, hosting workshops, sending out the mobile maker van into the neighborhoods, and reaching out through social media, print ads, and radio spots. Another example of how Open Works has thought about equity is the understanding that not all their potential community members have internet access to sign up for class. Therefore, they put only 50% of the youth and family programming tickets online to ensure that community members can walk in and join the classes. While the practice may be an administrative nightmare they can always ensure they have a spot for community members in the course offerings.

## LEARNING COMMUNITIES

Being a new makerspace, Open Works is still striving to establish its organization's culture around collaboration and sharing in the learning environment. The mantra for the space that new members hear during their orientation is:

*We're a community here. If you need questions or if you have questions, ask them or if you need help or if you see someone or ask someone what they're working on. If you don't know them, get to know them. Who's your neighbor? Who are you in the shop with?*

This mantra is the first introduction for members to the idea of learning communities and a shared learning environment. Technicians are also encouraged to build community within the space by asking probing questions and encouraging communication between members. Their role is to say:

*"Hey, what are you working on? Do you have any questions?" Then that happens with people who are working the shop together. They'll be, "Hey man, what's your name?" We're like, "Hey lady, what's going on? What are you doing? What are you working on?" Then it's like, "Cool, well I wonder if there's problem solving together that can happen." We've already seen it happen a little bit with numbers.*

It falls on Open Works staff to connect makers and build the learning communities. It's important for staff to be in the shops on a regular basis to encourage those connections. Some community building also happens organically between makers without staff involvement. Cohen has seen this especially in the wood and metal shops. There is a lot of crossover between the two since familiarity with wood is a suitable pathway into metalworking and vice versa. Another interesting crossover is digital fabrication to wood.

The mandatory safety and certification courses have been popular and another way to build community in the space, although members are mainly sticking with their own shops so there is not a lot of cross-pollination. One observation about the different shops is that they have doors and walls which may, in fact, make it more difficult for members to cross between learning communities. Unless there is a specific reason to visit another shop, woodworkers would not be likely to have a reason to interact with those in the electronics or digital media shops. One strategy Open Works has embraced is the use of Slack, an online meeting tool, to help members connect. The effectiveness of Slack is not really known because of the newness of the space.

Open Works offers programs in the public spaces for youth and family. In an attempt to draw families into the space and to gauge interest from the community, they have rotated themes on various topics. Cohen explains the offerings as this:

*We tried out a bunch of different things, including Future Maker programming, which was very well attended, people loved it of course. We also brought in different maker technologies and crafts. We brought in clay, we brought in papier-mâché and woodworking. Coding and all sorts of stuff. We did a pretty significant evaluation to kind of see how things were received, and then also for us to think about being a little more mindful of how we want to use the space. Now we're doing every month we have a different theme, and the themes are reflective of the different shops we have here. January was woodworking month, and so all the family programming focusing on building things with wood. Understanding wood. February is sewing month, so we're having it in curriculum and stuff going on.*

The educational team at Open Works consists of one full-time staff member and three fellows. Two of the fellows are members of the AmeriCorps Vista program; one is a fellow of Baltimore Corps, which is a local leadership job placement program. This fellow works full time on the mobile program. The two AmeriCorps members work part or full time developing the teen program that has not been launched yet and work as community organizers, creating indirect partnerships. Again, the courses offered to members providing them with a learning pathway starting with the safety and certification courses. These courses are very popular and usually hands-on with instructors covering basics of the machines, best practices and of course general safety. The course offerings are usually led by partner organizations in the community, mainly because the six core staff aren't able to both teach and manage the space. For example, wood and metal shop courses are taught by the Station North Tool Library that is just around the corner from Open Works. Sewing is facilitated by SewLab USA and the digital fabrication classes are taught by faculty from a local community college. The partnerships are important, according to Cohen:

*Well that does a couple things. One, working in partnership is amazing because you bring people who are expert and do what they do well and just do it here. They can grow too because they're growing their experience and their reach. Also, for us, it helps us have consistency with programming, because they're doing it. With teachers, though they develop relationships with people, they are here teaching all the time, and they're doing all that stuff ... As you hone in on more and more classes, we have a bunch of offerings to more elective project base stuff. Make your own robot, or skirt, or shirt, or CNC lantern, or coasters, or that kind of thing. That's more project-based, result-based stuff, rather than skill based. As we are able to push adult education offerings further, we'll be able to push that shared learning component more. I think as more and more people come into this space and use this space, there's just going to be more of that happening because we're so social teachers for the most part. We want to learn and we would much rather have somebody show us than read about it, generally.*

Courses are usually taught in teams to reinforce learning and also work to build communities. In addition, the class sizes are kept very small, between six and ten people with an average size of eight in a class. According to Cohen the small class size provides learners with an intimate experience, allowing them to be more comfortable and establish trust, and even take some risks, because, according to Cohen, it's vulnerable and scary when you don't know how to do something. Open Works also has another AmeriCorps Vista member who is working as an artist in residence, helping to develop and implement curriculum in the short-term.

## YOUTH IN THE SPACE

Open Works does not offer memberships for youth but does allow those 16 and older to attend training with a guardian. Youth in the space has been something Open Works has struggled with because the space is not geared towards serving youth on a full-time basis. There are concerns with safety and liability, with youth using the machines and being in the shops. Cohen also admits the space is struggling with how multigenerations of nonrelated makers can inhabit the facility. Cohen commented:

*It's like how can a professional maker and a 16-year-old co-inhabit a shop. These are the questions. How can a 13-year-old and a 60-year-old be learning at the same time? No. We're not there yet. We have people in the space at the same time, but they're here for programming. We have some youth programming that youth come for. With that said, the fiber shop's going to be open soon and people are going to be rolling in. We got to figure that out. It's a hard thing, because I think it takes staff, and it takes management, and it takes not doing things on purpose. I don't know that we're being essential about it, but I'm not sure that we're there yet.*

Much of the youth programming in the public spaces is accomplished with partner organizations. Open Works is working with the Future Makers program for youth-based workshops and after-school and weekend programs. Other partners like Woodworking on Wheels, another local organization, facilitates woodworking activities, and Sew Fabulous facilitates sewing activities.

Open Works has an additional teen program through the development of the mobile maker van that travels out into the community and schools to provide experiences, especially in the area of Science, Technology, Engineering and Mathematics (STEM). The mobile space utilizes an established STEM curriculum called SABES, which stands for STEM Achievement in Baltimore Elementary Schools, developed through Johns Hopkins University and the Baltimore City Public Schools. Open Works has selected and redeveloped some of the SABES curriculum to be used with the mobile makerspace. At the time of the visit the mobile makerspace had not yet been launched and the process of curriculum development and relationship building with schools was ongoing.

## THE MAKER MINDSET

When asked about how they approach the maker mindset and how it is instilled in members and the community, Cohen indicated it was something that was not at the forefront of the curriculum because of their staff capacity at the moment. One way they have approached teaching the maker mindset in adults is to develop capacity within the educators to teach them how to demonstrate skills like creative problem solving, grit, and perseverance. Cohen described it in this way:

*Then within that pedagogy, really thinking about creative problem solving, give students room to mess up, give them space to try out different things. Give them like, "Well how does this relate to my life? How does this or whatever," build on that. For our teen programming, that's been in the works. Again, we haven't piloted that yet. That's still in the development stage as far as curriculum is concerned. Yeah. It's there, but it's the thing where like every week I want to get further and further and every session further and further, but that capacity for me is the thing that prevents me from being like, "Alright, I'm going to take a month and dive in." I'm like, "No, because I have to keep the ship floating."*

Modeling failure and providing room for learning from failure is found in most of the adult program offerings. Instructors give members the opportunity to test a solution, and if it does not work, they are to keep going or try another iteration. However, this is not so easy when youth are involved. According to Cohen:

*It's like when the kids try something and they'll give up, they'll just be like, "This is stupid. I don't like this." Then they'll just try to leave. We're like, "No, try it one more time. This is a part of it. Do you know how many times I had to do this?"*

According to Cohen one strategy, when working with youth, is to model failure and ask those probing questions. For example, in the classroom Cohen would ask "What do I do now?" She would then somehow sabotage the build and ask for help from the youth to solve the problem.

## DEFINING A MAKERSPACE

When asked to define a makerspace and the core components of a makerspace, Cohen responded:

*That's fun. I mean it being a place is important. For me, a physical destination is important. I know that there are online platforms and virtual spaces too, but for me a physical space where people can physically get together and exchange ideas and skills and work on stuff and experiment and try out material and where we have shops and tools and equipment that people can use. Yeah. That's a big space, big part of it. A place where people make stuff. I would say physical objects are important in that. I think some people will disagree with that. Like hackerspace, it's like, "It's a place where you can exchange ideas," and I think that can definitely be part of it, but I think resulting in some physical object is important for skill development. I think for me it's important that makerspaces revolve around making objects and making community and establishing a sense of belonging and social engagement is super important. That makes for a better city and a better life.*

## CURRENT CHALLENGES

Open Works has tremendous potential to transform the lives and the economic success in the Station North Community. Being such a new space it's hard to evaluate how quickly it will be able to show sizeable impact on the community. The space has around 225 members, with a long-term goal of 400 to 500 members and a sustainability plan that calls for membership fees to replace funding from the BARCO parent company in the next couple of years. The need to grow membership with the mission of serving the community coupled with a small staff, seems to be pulling the space in many different directions.

One challenge facing the space is how to provide programming for youth. Cohen mentioned that Open Works is designated as a Safe Space. They have youth from the community visit public areas every day but do not have the capacity to provide continuous programming. A core group of young people from the neighborhood visit the space each day because they have nowhere else to go nor do they have food to eat. In the public space, there are games for youth to play and, when possible, the staff work with the youth but that is not always possible. Many times, youth come in their guardians are not able to pick them up until 8:00 PM. Cohen stated:

*I'll drive them home or walk them home, or I'll take them into my office and I'll have them help me by punching holes in stuff. Yeah. We should be making stuff with them, we should be churning out curriculum. I just can't. It's really frustrating, because I would want to do that, but I think the fall, I keep talking about capacity, but the fall, I was working six days a week, 12 hours a day because I wanted to like some of these kids and other people too. I was like, "I just can't do that." I was burning out working. I was like, no. I can't!"*

Cohen went on to explain:

*Also, we don't have things like guardian consent for them to be here and it's a little nerve racking and they're like eight years old. They're just playing. They're out biking around and doing whatever and then they come here and I just have food for them. There's that that happens. There's an instance where a young person came here because their grandma didn't pick them up from school and they didn't know where else to go, so they came here because they knew this was a safe space and they had been here for a program like two months before, like once, but they knew that we were a safe space. They were open and warm, so there's that, which maybe wasn't what we expected but that's the role we've been playing. That's this hub and this community in the center of this neighborhood. It's like a donut. There's everything around it and then nothing in it.*

Again, Open Works is being pulled in different directions because it needs to create memberships to keep the space running, but those in the local community with the greatest need cannot afford a membership, don't think the space is for them, or are too young to join. In the fall, Open Works provided programming once a week and the youth from the community would come on a Saturday and stay the whole day. Again, that created problems with the lack of offerings for youth when they spend weekdays and weekends in the space. Chess, checkers, and puzzles are available for the youth and sometimes Open Works staff will help the youth with their homework. Cohen went on to say:

*That's where we're at. We don't have capacity, but we're trying to build capacity as quickly as we can, but that requires resources. We just don't ... which is weird, because this is like big beautiful building, but we're just not there yet. That's very hard. It's really hard for me.*

Open Works is working with one of the AmeriCorps Vista members to open a community center down the road and create complementary programming so that youth can attend the community center after-school, do their homework and have a snack there. Then they would be walked down to Open Works for programming. With the space being public and the addition of a coffee shop, Cohen stated she was very concerned about having unaccompanied minors in the space.

Another less serious challenge is trying to figure out how to please the membership in the makerspace model. Course fees are charged on top of monthly dues in order to pay for partner organizations to come in and facilitate the courses. In this model, fees will continue to be a challenge and Cohen explained it like this:

*Also, realize that people are people and they all have their things and so do I and whatever. Making sure and being mindful about like, say, "Hey, this class is too expensive." I'm like, "Okay, well what's your perspective here?" Some people are like, "Well I don't understand why your XYZ class is this much. It seems ridiculous." Some people are like, "I went to school for three years for that, I spent thousands of dollars and apprenticed for a year and you can't learn everything you need in one class, you just need to come do it. It's just a perspective. Also, like on income, there are some folks that are like, "I couldn't spend $65 on a class let alone like at all."*

One strategy that Open Works has tested is providing a 75% discount on classes, with a limit of three participants per year. The space is also working on a program to give discounts on memberships through a work exchange program. Members have the option to assist in shops or with administrative tasks for a discount on their membership. The program also has the added benefit of encouraging members to become leaders in their areas of interests and expertise.

## REFERENCES

Greenmount West Community Association. (n.d.). *History*. Retrieved April 11, 2018, from http://www.greenmountwest.org/history/

Maryland State Arts Council. (n.d.). *Arts & entertainment districts*. Retrieved April 11, 2018, from https://www.msac.org/programs/arts-entertainment-districts

## KEY TERMS AND DEFINITIONS

**AmeriCorps Vista:** The domestic counterpart to the Peace Corps (Volunteers in Service to America).

**Baltimore Arts Realty Corporation:** BARCO is a nonprofit organization started in 2012 to create working spaces for artists, performers, makers, and artisans in Baltimore.

**Baltimore Arts and Entertainment Districts:** State-designated arts and entertainment districts are designed to foster economic development by offering property and sales tax incentives to arts-related businesses.

**Gentrification:** The process of renewal and influx of affluent people that displaces poorer residents.

**Greenmount West Neighborhood:** A neighborhood of Baltimore, it is in the southeast corner of the Station North Arts and Entertainment district.

**Historically Underutilized Business Zone:** Special economic areas established by the US Small Business Administration (SBA), which offers tax incentives to businesses starting up.

**Jimmi Printer:** A large format 3D printer.

**Micro-Studio:** Seven-foot by seven-foot spaces for makers business incubator spaces.

**Mobile Makerspace:** A makerspace that does not have a permanent physical location.

**Open Works:** A makerspace in the Greenmount Neighborhood of Baltimore, Maryland.

**STEM:** Science, technology, engineering, and mathematics.

# Chapter 11
# Station North Tool Library

## ABSTRACT

*Station North Tool Library is first and foremost a space that provides low-cost access to tools and information to residents in the Station North Arts and Entertainment District of Baltimore, Maryland. Unique in the fact that the tool library has a maker-type workshop space and offers classes and open times for members to make and create. With a staff of four full-time employees and a total square footage of 2,000 $ft^2$ (186 $m^2$), the space is not large but has a strong presence in the community and a membership that numbers around 2,300 individuals. Membership is based on a sliding scale at $1 per $1000 of income. Learning communities are supported in the space through inclusivity of all members and a management flat-structure where everyone is treated with respect and dignity. This chapter explores the Station North Tool Library.*

DOI: 10.4018/978-1-5225-8310-3.ch011

*Every day, somebody comes in and says, "Thank you. I wouldn't have been able to do this project on my house if it wasn't for you guys." - John Shea*

## ORGANIZATION BACKGROUND

Station North Tool Library (SNTL) or "Station North" is just around the corner from the state-of-the-art Open Works Fabrication and Makerspace building, in the Station North Arts and Entertainment District. Philosophically however, the two are worlds apart in their structure and operations. Open Works Baltimore and SNTL started with funding from the same foundation (Baltimore Arts Realty Corporation: BARCO) but as John Shea, co-founder of SNTL, noted their space is more modest, with around 2,000 $ft^2$ (186 $m^2$) of space and four full-time employees and that was done on purpose: to stay nimble and sustain the space. Station North has a relaxed and fun attitude, evidenced by the demeanor of Shea and the fact that not one but two dogs, *Super Dave* the shop dog and *Marty* (the Labrador Retriever), are featured as staff members on the SNTL site's web page. While dogs in the space are fun John finds they also put people at ease. Shea said it in this way:

*We're dog-friendly, too. And I think that's really important. We try to build a really relaxed environment, and there's three dogs here right now. There's usually like up to five or six. But you know, some places, it's really serious. And I think that that kind of translates into the space. Our most important rule here is be cool and be respectful, but that's kind of wrapped up in just like be cool. We trust people to not take advantage of things and just to [give] respect.*

The lending tool library movement started in the mid-1970s with sites in Columbus, Ohio and Berkeley, California as a way to provide local communities with access to tools and information on how to properly use these tools (Berkeley Library Online, n.d.). True to the original mission of the tool lending movement, Station North's purpose is to empower and serve the local community through access to tools and low-cost training and membership. While access to tools is their main emphasis of operation, Station North also acts as a makerspace by having classes and open times for their workshops. Physically, Station North Tool Library (SNTL) is situated amongst row houses and across the street there is a set of brightly colored, newly built houses which shows off the arts ambiance of the neighborhood. The outside of the Station North Tool Library is shown in Figure 1.

However, it's evident that there are still struggles in the neighborhood, and not all houses have been renovated and are in need of help. John described the recent past of the neighborhood:

*It is a really strong African-American neighborhood. It was a really amazing and then went through all different housing crisis stuff, and when we came in five years ago and started building our project, this entire neighborhood was like almost, I would say, 75% vacant. The entire block across the street from us was vacant, vacant homes. The buildings across the street didn't exist. The Baltimore Design School right up the street was an abandoned factory. There was really not a lot happening in this area.*

*This neighborhood, like I was saying, is a pretty interesting place because the train station is a couple blocks away. There's people in this neighborhood that are buying houses for $350,000 when a year ago, you could have bought one from the city for $2,000, that had no roof, completely destroyed, on the*

*Figure 1. The Station North Tool Library Space looking down East Oliver Street*

*same block. It was pretty wild. So, a lot of folks in this neighborhood have their homes through they're the third generation in a house that's been passed down to them. And they're living, in poverty, surrounded by wealth and rehab, so access to tools to keep up with the things happening around them is pretty important for us.*

Inside Station North there are obviously tools everywhere, with 500 square feet of space in the front reception area which is separated by a set of doors that lead to the workshop. The reception area is full of shelves from floor to ceiling with hand tools and power tools all marked and inventoried, ready to be loaned out to members. While small, the reception area does not seem claustrophobic and the number and variety of tools (over 2,700) will keep visitors gazing about for a long period of time. Tools range from very old hand-tools to modern portable tools. Many of the tools were donated or purchased second-hand from Craigslist and other places. Figure 2 provides a peek into the reception area.

Generally, tools are broken down into 10 categories including:

*Figure 2. The Station North reception area*

- **Automotive** (air compressors, pneumatic tools, grinders, engine hoist)
- **Bike** (bike repair stand, wrenches, bike helmet, hex wrenches, bike tire leveler)
- **Carpentry and woodworking** (hammer drills, chisels, levels, squares, joiners, saws)
- **Electrical and soldering** (conduit bender, voltage detector, multimeter, Dremel tool, fish tape)
- **Home maintenance** (putty knives, saws, drills, ladders, wrenches)
- **Metalworking** (grinders, tube cutters, MIG welder, plasma cutter)
- **Plumbing** (pipe wrenches, drain snakes, wrenches, reciprocating saw, caulk guns)
- **Remodeling** (flooring tools, stapler/nailer, dolly, paint brushes, sanders)
- **Sustainable living** (awl, electric chainsaw, buckets, chisels, compass, axe)
- **Yard and garden** (rake, pitchfork, sledgehammer, hedge trimmer, push mower).

There are also more the 200 books and reference items for members to checkout and help with tool usage and for project ideas. Members must agree to the borrowing policy which has stipulations such as:

- Members must be 18 years or older.
- Members must sign a waiver and indemnification form and have an ID.
- When they borrow a tool, members are certifying that they are capable of using the tool safely.
- Only members can use the borrowed tool.
- Tools must be returned of the due date or pay a late fee.
- If tools are out longer than 60 days members must pay the purchase cost or lose their membership.

What sets the Station North Tool Lending Library apart from many other tool lending libraries is their incorporation of workshop classes and open times for members. The workshop is roughly 1,500 $ft^2$ (139 $m^2$) and contains the following: miter saw, panel saw, band saw, drill press, scroll saw, sanders, table saw, planer, and jointer. Membership allows the use of the workshop tools; however, members must take a safety class (Shop Safety I) prior to using the miter saw, panel saw, band saw, drill press, scroll saw, and sanders. To use the table saw, planer and jointer members are required to take Shop Safety II or Woodworking I. In the workshop, the equipment is spaced throughout the floor area and there is wood stacked and stored in the nooks and crannies. While organized, it is a loud and dusty working environment. Figure 3 depicts the inside of the workshop at Station North. The space started out specifically as a tool lending library and then the founders of SNTL went back to the funders and asked for additional space for the workshop. As Shea noted:

*We had the support from the foundation in the first couple years, and whenever we were like, "Well, you know, it'd be really nice if we had a shop," and they were like, "Cool," and they funded another salary for the director of that space, and we stole him from a university teaching job to run that space, and then we got a grant for the equipment, and it was all pieced off of Craigslist and everything.*

*Figure 3. The Station North Tool Library workshop*

## SETTING THE STAGE

Station North Tool Lending Library combines tool access with making through a monthly fee-based sliding scale membership model based on income. The cost for members is as little as $15.00 a month, with a fee structure of $1.00 for every $1,000 of income for access to the tool lending library. This basic membership level provides members with access to eight tools per month, a free shop safety course, and access to the workshop during open shop hours. Membership levels are included in Table 1.

One of the goals of Station North is to be as small as possible while still effectively serving the community. In the past, the space had taken on service for hire projects. For example, they worked with the city of Baltimore on a workforce development program and had to expand their staff to support the program. Ultimately, Shea noted that the service-for-hire model did not meet the needs of the community nor their vision for the space. Shea stated:

*You know, I told you we lost the workforce development program that we were doing, because we kept like, "Oh, we need to expand to make money. We need to expand to do this." But we figured, the thing that we provide with access to tools, access to a space, and creatively selling classes to pay for it, and memberships to pay for it, you can kind of get money from people that have it to support everybody else. But if it's small, you can stay nimble. Like I said, at the end of this year, I think we will be almost ... We'll never probably be completely self-sustaining, but we'll be really close after this year, which is ... really important.*

*Table 1. Station North Tool Lending Library membership levels*

| | Plan Name | | | | |
|---|---|---|---|---|---|
| | **Sliding Scale** | **Class Pass 1** | **Class Pass 2** | **Class Pass 3** | **Class Pass 4** |
| Price | $1 for every $1000 in income | $9/month | $19/month | $29/month | $39/month |
| Access | Shop Safety Class 1<br>Borrow 8 tools/ week<br>Open Shop access | Shop Safety Class 1<br>10% off classes<br>Borrow 8 tools/ week<br>Free open shop hours | Choice of one class for the year<br>10% off classes<br>Borrow 8 tools/ week<br>Free open shop hours | Choice of two class for the year<br>10% off classes<br>Borrow 8 tools/ week<br>Free open shop hours | Choice of three class for the year<br>20% off classes<br>Borrow 8 tools/ week<br>Free open shop hours |

The process to join Station North is straight forward and well laid out on the website, with links to the various documents needed to join as well as a posting inside the space as shown in Figure 4. Members first read the tool borrowing policy document, select a membership level and then complete the membership application. SNTL does not verify income and it is up to the members to calculate their payment. Again, the relaxed attitude of the space is reflected on the membership application with the first membership option of a sliding scale that states:

*Sliding Scale $15 minimum — I would like to pay: $____________ Payment Method____________*

Other options listed on the form include:

*$9 x12 Month Auto Debit — so stoked about my FREE Shop Safety I Class!*

*$19 x12 Month Auto Debit — so stoked about my* **ONE** *class pass!*

*$29 x12 Month Auto Debit — so stoked about my* **TWO** *class passes!*

*$39 x12 Month Auto Debit — so stoked about my* **THREE** *class passes!*

Station North offers a wide array of courses but members who want to utilize the open workshop and take woodworking classes are required to take the Shop Safety I course. This certification course lasts 2.5 hours and costs $25. From an educational standpoint, Shop Safety starts at ground zero for learners, and instructors assume class participants have very little background knowledge. Fundamentals of woodworking and basic safety in a workshop are covered in the basic course. Another required class to use additional tools is the Woodworking I (Dimensioning Lumber) that introduces members to advanced equipment like the table saw, jointer, planer, and miter saw. The class is 3.5 hours in duration and costs $105 to attend. Aside from the two required courses, Station North offers a wide variety of classes divided between skill-based and product-based activities. Shea described these skill-based courses as follows:

*Skill-based … like router table class, joinery class … if you have no experience in woodworking and you want to get proficient, we do Safety I and then Woodworking I, Woodworking II, Woodworking III. So, Woodworking I is*

*Figure 4. SNTL fees*

*how to take rough sawn material and make dimensional pieces, basically in a nutshell. There's a little bit of a lecture on different types of wood, different types of materials that can be used in the shop in this equipment. And then Woodworking II is how do you take dimensional pieces and put them together. So, there's all different types of stuff. It doesn't really go super deep into advanced joinery, but there is how to use a kreg jig, how to do really simple joints, basically just how do you put those things together. Woodworking III is a finishing class, like common finishes, safe finishes, and stains or polyurethanes or water-based materials, like spraying, painting, rolling, waxing, and oiling sort of stuff.*

Product-based courses are those courses where participants build an actual product like a chef's knife, coffee table, or a set of Bluetooth-enabled concrete cast speakers. Courses generally cost $25 and will last 2.5 hours. Again, theoretically the space tries to provide learning opportunities for members to develop skills through the skill-based classes but also through specific projects that allow them to apply skills in the creation of a project. Once members are trained the staff becomes hands-off and doesn't try to direct projects as much as they try to provide members with access to everything they need. In addition, Shea indicated the priority and learning emphasis is in the process of learning and making, and not focused on the final product. He stated:

*We don't celebrate end goals as much as we celebrate learning and people getting better. Yeah, we celebrate learning. We celebrate people getting better, whether it's from their first time using a drill, which is like a huge thing that we conquer a lot in this space. But that's, in a way, much more important than just, you know, somebody masterfully exercising their craft. You know what I mean? We celebrate learning more than product, I think. Or like the conversations that you have in that object or in the construction of the object, or conquering new fears of using tools, and things like that. Yeah, right from the beginning, we talk about that, building healthy community and learning and how much fun that is in a space.*

On average, the SNTL program will serve 250 to 1,000 members per month. As shown in Figure 5. 40 to 59% of visitors are female, 40 to 59% are male.

*Figure 5. Gender balance of visitors*

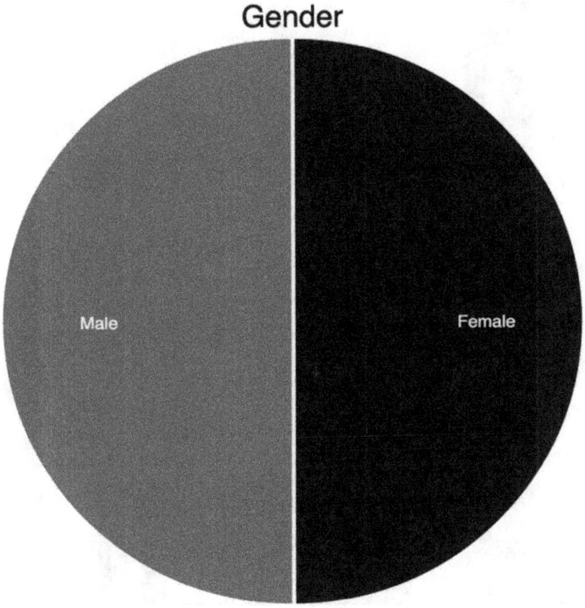

The types of users that visited the space are shown in Figure 6. Eighty to one hundred percent of users are considered hobbyists, 20 to 39% were college age students (18 to 24) and less than 20% were visitors or observers, startups, youth under 13 years of age, youth 13 to 18 and teachers.

The purpose of visits to the space are shown in Figure 7. 80 to 100% of users were there as an introduction to making, 60 to 79% were there to receive training, instruction or learn and skill, 40 to 59% to make one-off pieces, 20 to 39% were there to socialize and less than 20% were there for small batch production and to network.

## LEARNING COMMUNITIES

Learning communities in the space happen in part because of the attitude of the space, and that is to be *cool and respectful*. Everyone, even the dogs, when at ease can learn from each other in a fun and low-cost way. The tool lending library focuses to provide low-cost access to tools and, according to

*Figure 6. Types of visitors per month*

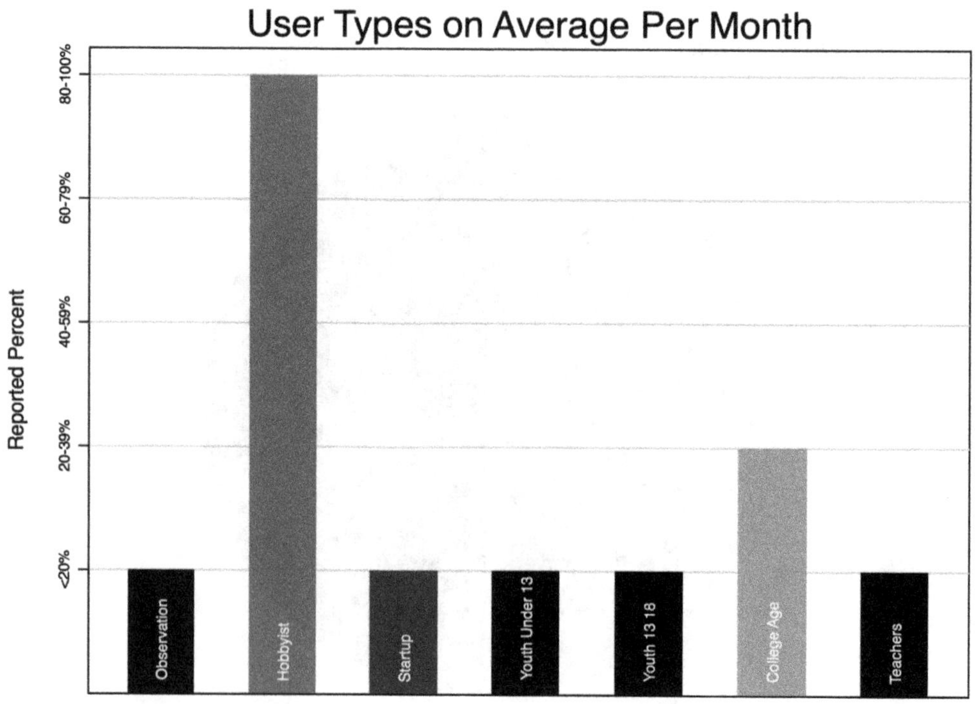

*Figure 7. Purpose of visits per month*

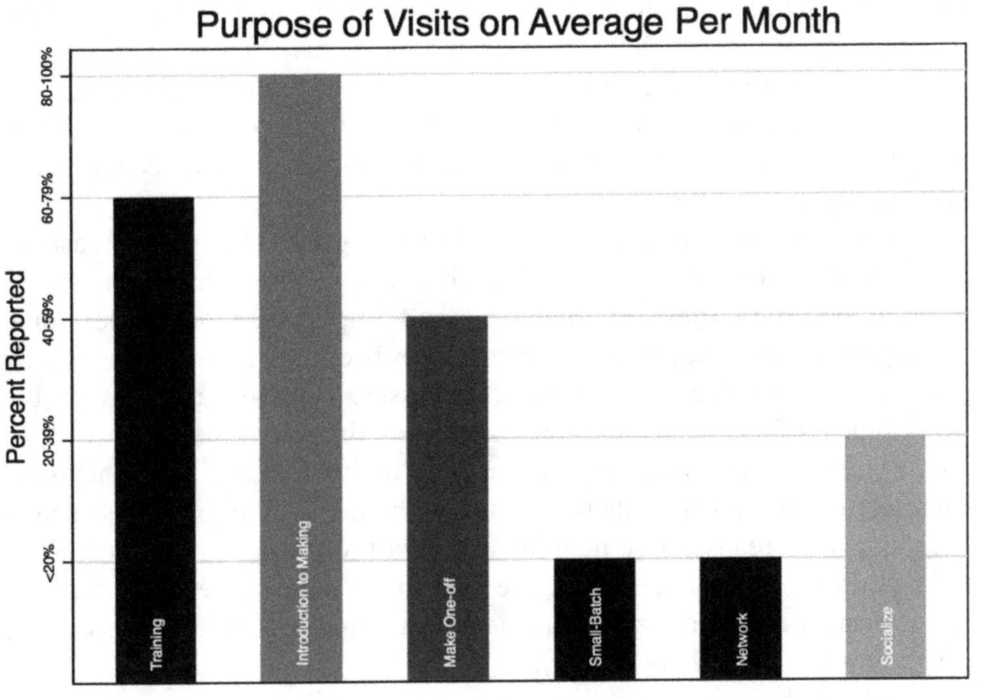


Shea, is one way that they establish learning communities. The tools bring together people that are interested in making and learning to make using their hands. It's about having shared access and shared information to build the learning communities. Staff and class facilitators are also important in creating learning communities within the space. Members are introduced in the classes to the ethos of the space:

*The way we build our Safety Class, like the first introductory class to the shop, we talk about building healthy community, working together, and not building a traditional, macho environment where there's one master and everybody feels, underneath of that person.*

The space carefully selects courses that are appealing and of interest to most members. In addition, to build healthy communities the space ensures that it is all-inclusive to everyone. Historically, spaces like a woodshop are "macho-driven" according to Shea, and Station North has recognized this and works very hard to make women feel like they belong in the space. While they did consider providing women's classes when they first started the space they soon realized that might send a message that women aren't welcome at other times in the space. As volunteers and staff are trained to teach and facilitate classes, they are taught how to build inclusive environments. In classes, learners, especially women, should be comfortable and not feel singled out. Ensuring this inclusive environment is of the utmost importance in the space and when volunteers have violated this in the past they have been asked to leave, according to Shea.

Teachers and mentors are developed from the ground up in many cases in the space. Most of the staff, including Shea, come from formal educational environments and they see the need and importance for professional development and mentoring of members as they become experts and eventually give back to the space through teaching classes. There is a pathway for the development of teachers in the space and many times members start with no prior knowledge and begin their journey by taking classes. Next, they start volunteering in the space, then assisting with classes with other instructors and then, when ready, these members will start teaching in the space. Time and repetition, according to Shea, are vital in the development of makers as experts and the teachers are instrumental in helping people figure out the language and a shared vocabulary.

Members also have the ability to propose and pilot courses in the space. Shea gave the example of the 'crazy French scientist' that was interested in developing a course on building cast concrete speakers for members. Because the scientist had a perceived lack of teaching experience, he was paired with staff members and they collaboratively developed and delivered the course. In general, most courses are taught through a mixture of direct instruction and hands-on practice, with a bit of inquiry built in. The courses are usually chunked in a way to reduce cognitive overload, that is, a small bit of lecture immediately followed by a hands-on activity. In addition, courses have a social learning context where learners are learning with and from each other as they progress through the course. Shea gave an example of this in the Workshop Safety I class:

*Our Safety I [covers] half the equipment in the shop, so we'll go through a series of the machines explaining safety and everything on those tools, and then everybody partners up and works together to use all those tools and kind of team-teach each other. So we kind of don't do the this is the talking head in front of everybody. We love for people to work together and learn together, so when you just give information ... if you give it to three people, those three people ... somebody got a little bit of this, little bit of that, little bit of that, and they share it.*

Another program in the space is the use of expert members to help others with specific projects through the *Hire an Expert* program. The program works much like a tutoring program where novice members, with a lack of background knowledge, can hire expert members to help them over the hump as they work through their projects. The service is $50 an hour and members can sign up online.

Lastly, Station North is set up as a way to allow people an alternative to the traditional education system. In a way, they can test vocational tracks without paying tuition fees at a university or trade school. To Shea this is very important:

*I have a background in teaching in higher education. So does the director here of the public workshop. We started off in university systems, and so we have history in teaching, could develop curriculum for classes, and then when we came here, it was to provide affordable access, not kids paying tuition for a university to learn how to work with their hands. I think it's kind of a gnarly thing. So, we're like an alternative education site. We have brought in people who have experience teaching in university systems, woodshops, different things like that, that come in and it was really easy for them to come in, recognize that we don't ever want to make somebody feel bad if they're not as good as somebody else. That's very deep in our ethos.*

When asked, Shea talked about the concrete speakers as one of the typical product-based artifacts that are built in the space. As mentioned earlier, the course was proposed by a French scientist and was developed in conjunction with staff from the Station North. The speaker project at first glance seems pretty simple but as you peel the layers off there is a lot of knowledge and skills that are learned in creating the project. For example, the base of the speaker cones are made with concrete using a mold. In addition, it has dimensional wood that needs to be cut and fitted together, and learners need to understand some electronics as they create the circuit to power the device and microcontroller. Class participants mix pour and properly cure the concrete for the project. Next, using a table saw and miter saw they make the necessary cuts for the project. A drill press is also used to make holes and a router is used for the edges. The wood is also properly sanded and finished. Incorporating some electronics, class participants wire and solder the electronic speaker components securing it to the wood structure. It takes about seven hours to complete the project. When asked how the skills transfer to other areas for the learners Shea responded:

*You know after you've gone through this class, you know how to cast concrete. You could make countertops, you could do things like that. Yeah, and then the woodworking, it's like once you know how to use a table saw and a miter saw, you can pretty much just rock and roll. And then sand and seal.*

## YOUTH IN THE SPACE

The Station North Tool Library is not set up to support youth due to the nature of the equipment and the general hands-off discovery-type learning approach to making. Meaning that once members are trained to safely use a tool, they are on their own to choose and guide their own learning. Knowledge has to be sought out through the others in the space or through their own internal design processes. While youth are quite capable of learning in this manner, they do require supervision and care in an open workshop environment. With the adult programs the space does not have the capacity to provide experiences for youth. In the past, the space has partnered with other organizations in the Baltimore area to come in and provide activities. While young people under 18 cannot be members, younger learners are able to take courses with their parents or guardians. Youth aged from 15 to 18 must have their parents sign off for them to take a class in the space. There are instances of even younger people taking courses. Shea told the story of one thirteen-year-old who took the chef's knife-making course with his father.

*In the chef's knife-making class right now, there's a kid that's taking the class. I think he's 13 years old. His dad's there just kind of making sure the kid gets everything, but the kid's already made a bunch on his own and he's coming in just to have access to nice equipment to do the same thing. So, the kid is pretty sharp. I think because we're not advertising it as a kids' environment, that it's usually like the kids come in kind of knowing that they're getting an adult experience... it's not like a kids' free-for-all. It's pretty serious for kids to come in and work in here. They're treated like adults.*

One child, eight years of age, comes in with his father and they work on simple woodworking projects in the space, but that is rare. The pair have a passion for woodworking and so they come in and work together on projects. The father is very encouraging, to enable the child's interest in the craft and making.

## IMPACT ON THE COMMUNITY

Station North Tool Library is an important anchor in the Greenmount West Neighborhood. The community is in transition with some redevelopment. Families in the community face challenges with higher property values and lack of income to maintain the properties they have had in their families for generations. The impact of the space is that these families have access to tools and knowledge to improve their properties and lives without the need to buy tools or take expensive classes to learn how to increase the value of their homes and their lives. The tool library also brings together a community of people, so they can learn and share with everyone else. SNTL is striving to "redefine the nature of people working with tools and working with a community." Residents will come to realize that they don't need to own these things and that they have this wonderful learning community to help. Another impact the SNTL has had on the community is that they have the ability to recycle and fix the tools that break. Shea commented:

*I have a background in that [fixing tools], so I love fixing and repairing things. I think people seeing that is really healthy, also. Providing access to tools for people to have a positive impact on their environment ... We have helped tons of artists do community art projects. We've helped a ton of community gardens get access to earth-working equipment. You know? Yeah, that's a pretty awesome impact. Just being a part of this culture in this area and people being like, "Oh yeah, that's where I go to get tools. I don't need to own this stuff." I think that's one of my favorite things.*

Station North has also had some entrepreneurs emerge from the space. The space has been instrumental in helping small businesses get started by providing them with both the access to tools and the open space. SNTL has helped jumpstart relationships within the community to connect members and needs together, leading to an improvement in the lives of the people living in the area. Without the space, those that need help the most in the community would face yet another challenge of keeping up with the wealth and rehab that is coming into the neighborhood. Shea said it like this:

*But for us, it's like every day, somebody comes in and says, "Thank you. I wouldn't have been able to do this project on my house if it wasn't for you guys."*

Shea believes one of the greatest impacts on learners is that they get to experiment with education and making without having to put in a big investment. Reflecting on his own experience going through graduate school and always wanting to make things, Shea found little opportunity in a formal graduate program. Sometimes he even questioned why he went down that route. So, he encourages people like himself to use the space to find for themselves their passions and work with their hands before making the choice in the formal educational system.

## DEFINING A MAKERSPACE

When asked to define a makerspace and the core components of a makerspace Shea responded:

*Everybody has their ideas of what a ... You know, some are like, "I want it to be like a gym, where like 3,000 people pay $90 a month and two people show up a month to use the space." I think a makerspace should be a creative art project that is like a bomb going off in a neighborhood, where instead of artwork that has an impact in a gallery, these projects should be like bombs going off in areas where the visual representation of that project is just having a positive impact in communities and changing the appearance of, you know, like a bad neighborhood ...*

*It's a healthy community center for people to learn how to work with their hands.*

## CURRENT CHALLENGES

The Station North Tool Library is well entrenched in the Station North neighborhood of Baltimore. The journey has not been easy. It took the library a long time to get established in the community. When they started the library five years ago, the neighborhood was about 75% vacant and there was not a lot happening in the area. The neighborhood was full of abandoned houses and factories, then SNTL moved in and they immediately began working with those in the housing and the arts community. It took time because when a space like the Tool Library moves in and offers something that seems impossible (for example, low cost access to tools), a lot of people questioned the motivation of the space. Trust had to be earned by staying in the community long-term, providing low cost access to tools and information, and helping to grow the intellectual capital of the community. The space is now recognized as a community anchor by most of the neighborhood and other partner spaces that request experts from the library in their own programs. Shea stated:

*So, I think it's an uphill battle that you always have to work at. And for us, it's just being here. People come in and they're like, "You mean, it's ..." our minimum is $15 for a year membership to the library. So, people can come in and say: "Really? $15 and I can check out eight tools a week for a year?" So just by being here over time, eventually, people will recognize it as a service to the community. But I mean, so down the street, it's still $90 a month for membership and then another hundred and something for space. So, you know, it's targeting a pretty different market.*

Station North Tool Library has to continually work at building those relationships with the community and it seems that there are always challenges, whether it is offering additional classes, acquiring new tools and equipment or even running the library and making sure access to tools continues. While Shea indicated the library is close to breaking even there seems to be a challenge to keep prices low and continue to run the space to meet demand with the current capacity. The library is running a campaign on its website to raise additional funds and is also asking for donations on the website. There was recent grant funding from a foundation to provide extended open hours for the workshop.

Another challenge seems to be a bias against women working/making in traditional male areas like woodworking. The Station North has worked very hard to alleviate bias against women. They have institutionalized the idea of being non-judgmental through their orientation practices for new members and professional development instruction for class facilitators. The library has even gone as far as asking members to leave for breaking this rule. It seems bias has roots in the space, even with these practices. There is a group of women in the community that have decided to start their own women-only woodworking shop just a few miles from SNTL. The equipment to start the space was donated through Station North to help get them started. When asked why a women's only space was needed Shea commented:

*I think it's completely necessary to create a space for ... where women feel like they don't have to worry about guys, telling them how to do things. And everything that's happened here ... You know, most of our class takers are women, serious project makers are women, they're organized, they'll have their lists. It's like a little bit ... yeah, different than a traditional guy's shop. Building something different ... Yeah, we take it pretty seriously. But them doing their thing, we think it's awesome. So, we try to support them as much as we can.*

## REFERENCES

Berkeley Public Library. (n.d.). *Tool lending library - a brief history.* Retrieved January 29, 2018, from https://www.berkeleypubliclibrary.org/locations/tool-lending-library/tool-lending-library-brief-history

Dunn, P. (2010). *How to start a tool library.* Retrieved October 16, 2016, from https://www.shareable.net/blog/how-to-start-a-tool-library

Swick, Z. (2014). *Community tool-lending libraries: What and where are they?* Retrieved January 29, 2018, from http://www.appfellows.org/appfellows-blog/2014/9/2/community-tool-lending-libraries-what-and-where-are-they

Tool Station North. (n.d.). *Annual membership options.* Retrieved January 29, 2018, from http://www.stationnorthtoollibrary.org/join-tool-library

## KEY TERMS AND DEFINITIONS

**Baltimore Arts Realty Corporation:** BARCO is a nonprofit organization started in 2012 to create working spaces for artists, performers, makers, and artisans in Baltimore.

**Cognitive Overload:** The situation where the capacity of learners for cognitive processing has exceeded their cognitive capacity.

**Greenmount West Neighborhood:** A neighborhood of Baltimore, it is in the southeast corner of the Station North Arts and Entertainment District.

**Hire an Expert Program:** The program works much like a tutoring program where novice members, with a lack of background knowledge, can hire expert members to help them over the hump as they work through their projects.

**Sliding Scale Membership:** Members pay only an amount based on their monthly income.

**Station North Tool Library:** A lending tool library and makerspace located in Baltimore, Maryland.

**Tool Lending Library:** A library that provides local communities with access to tools and information on how to properly use the tools.

# Chapter 12
# NOVA Labs


## ABSTRACT

*NOVA Labs, located in Northern Virginia, is a mature site with a stunning amount of sophisticated manufacturing equipment and tools for making. The space has a well-thoughtout membership structure, with different levels tied to access to the space and to the equipment. Key members, the highest level of membership, must be approved by the board of directors. Because it is an all-volunteer space, members are expected to give back to the community both in time and in their talents, by teaching classes and working in the space. The space hosts a cadre of professional makers and start-up businesses that utilize the collective expertise of the community to develop products and ideas. This chapter explores NOVA Labs.*


DOI: 10.4018/978-1-5225-8310-3.ch012

*You have to cultivate a culture where people are both getting something out of the community and interested in contributing back to it in some way. - Fred Briggs*

## ORGANIZATION BACKGROUND

Located in the somewhat crowded but very affluent northern Virginia community of Reston, sits the NOVA (northern Virginia) Labs' community-based makerspace. The main makerspace is housed in a commercial brick building amongst a number of different businesses. A secondary space is dedicated to youth and their NOVA Labs educational robotics initiative. NOVA Labs started in 2011 with 14 founding members and opened the first physical location in 2012. The current site, which opened in 2014, has 10,500 $ft^2$ (976 $m^2$) of space. At the time of the visit, an estimated 100 members were paying dues with 500 to 800 participants visiting per month. Approximately one-third of the space is used as an open work area and classroom space. The other portions of the space are studio areas and a few business incubator areas.

Once through the front doors, the space has a reception/check-in station where members can scan their RFID membership cards. Called the 'Orange Bay', the front space is open with tables and work areas as seen in Figure 1. Along the outside of the space are small project areas for project storage, crafter's guild, electronics station, kitchen area and a set of couches.

Farther into the space is a classroom area partitioned off by glass doors. The classroom can accommodate up to 50 people and has dividers, allowing for the creation of smaller spaces. Fred Briggs, a NOVA Labs member, small business owner, and instructor in the space, noted that much of the equipment and even architectural elements of the space were not purchased but donated. Briggs stated:

*Our woodshop came from a guy who had been divorced and basically didn't have a big house anymore or basement, so everything was sitting in a container, and he's like, 'Hey, how about I just co-locate everything there?'*

*So it's all a hodgepodge, secondhand. And then to move in here, we actually got $50,000 from Google, raised money to be able to refurbish this place. Those front doors, those beautiful glass doors right there, were from a building*

*Figure 1. The workroom area of NOVA Labs*

*that was being renovated in Georgetown, and we knew the contractor, and we said 'Hey, could we have those doors?'*

Just in front of the classroom space is a small dedicated 3D print area that was made by members of the space, as shown in Figure 2.

A long hallway leads deeper into the area, past incubator spaces and workshops. The space is purposefully closed off from visitors and the classroom as a way to ensure safety and enforce that members are trained prior to entering the workshops.

The incubator spaces are available to rent for Key members when available. As explained by Marybeth Haneline, the current president of NOVA Labs, the incubators are small businesses that Nova Labs is helping to get started. Small Batch Assembly is one such space, which is operated by Bob Coggeshall. According to Haneline, he's called SudoBob and he's a bit of a legend, because he co-developed the Unix SUDO program. Coggeshall runs Small Batch Assembly, which creates custom circuit boards.

Specific workshops include the digital fabrication lab, woodshop, and metal shop. The digital fabrication shop is a restricted access area, and members must be trained on the equipment to enter the room. It contains a

*Figure 2. The 3D print area*

100 watt laser cutter along with an interesting piece of equipment called a thermoformer. Haneline commented that one of the more popular projects is creating products using molds. Members make molds using either the 3D printer, laser cutter, or CNC router (Computer Numerical Control) to create the molds. As shown in Figure 3, the thermoformer heats plastic to a temperature that allows material to easily be formed into a specific shape by being placed in a mold.

Past the digital fabrication studio is a large area that contains the woodshop, the metal shop, and a small storage area. Storage is an important consideration as Haneline noted: "This is northern Virginia, so space is a concern." The woodshop is clean and neat, with machines around the space. Larger machines include a drill press, band saws, table saws, wood lathe, CNC routers, and a CNC desktop mill. Separated from the woodshop is the metal shop, which contains a MIG welder, milling machines, and a metal band saw. The entire equipment list is provided in Table 1.

*Figure 3. The thermoformer*

NOVA Labs supports youth through the FIRST (For Inspiration and Recognition of Science and Technology) educational robotics program by providing a dedicated space in an adjacent building and mentors for the robotics teams. The robotics program aptly named NOVA Labs Robotics is run as a separate program and supports youth of all ages to come together and learn about Science, Technology, Engineering, and Mathematics (STEM) through robotics and programming.

*Table 1. NOVA Labs equipment*

| | | |
|---|---|---|
| **General workshop equipment** | Couch and table(s)<br>Chairs<br>Folding tables<br>Lamps<br>Boards<br>Sturdy workbenches<br>Sturdy wooden "kitchen" table<br>Lockers<br>Shelves<br>Storage bins<br>File cabinets<br>Freestanding shelves<br>Extension ladder<br>Ladder | Vise<br>Power strips<br>Extension cords<br>Mini fridge<br>Coffee/tea maker<br>George Foreman® grill<br>Weber® propane grill<br>Clothes iron<br>Pots, pans, etc.<br>Shop vac<br>Hand tools<br>Label maker<br>Letter stamps<br>Duct tape<br>Painter's blue tape |
| **General Hand tools (powered)** | Various tools | |
| **Metalwork** | Safety glasses<br>Welding helmet, goggles, gloves, and aprons<br>Machine oil<br>Cutting oil / coolant<br>Cutters<br>Countersinks<br>Clecos (1/8") (3.175mm)<br>Rivet gun rivet sets<br>Pop/Blind rivet guns (pull rivets)<br>Ball-peen hammers<br>Shot bags<br>Rubber mallets (various sizes)<br>Welding magnets<br>Electric shears<br>(handheld)<br>Sliding mitre saw with ferrous and non-ferrous blades (7")(17.78 cm)<br>English wheel with various wheels for shaping aluminum<br>Welding rig (OA) with tanks<br>Welding rig (TIG) with tank | Large metal snips (Sears)<br>Medium snips (Wiss®)<br>Rivet squeezers (different throat sizes)<br>Dimple die sets for countersinking<br>Cleco pliers<br>Left, right, and straight aircraft snips<br>Air compressor capable of sustained 90 psi with a reservoir tank<br>48" bending brake (also a 36" (91.44 cm) manual brake/ bender/roller)<br>Throatless shear<br>10" (25.4 cm) table saw with 7" (17.78 cm) non-ferrous blade<br>Angle grinders with metal grinding wheels<br>Press<br>Milling machine with X-Y table<br>Metal (or metal capable) lathe |
| **Fabrics** | Sewing machines | |
| **Woodworking** | Table saw<br>Drill press<br>Drills<br>Drill bit sets<br>Circular saw<br>Chop saw | Band saw<br>Router<br>Compound miter saw<br>Reciprocating saw<br>Orbital sander<br>Detail sander<br>Vise table |
| **Computing** | Servers<br>Workstations<br>keyboards/mice<br>Monitors<br>Projector<br>Server rack<br>Laser printer<br>Network print server<br>Ink-jet printer | Wi-Fi<br>Relay rack<br>Patch panels<br>Cable management<br>switches<br>Cat5 cable<br>Keystone wall plates<br>Keystone cat5 jacks<br>Keystone blanks |

*continued on following page*

*Table 1. Continued*

| | | |
|---|---|---|
| **Digital fabrication** | Rep-Raps<br>Makerbot<br>Laser cutter | Small mantis<br>Shopbot<br>Vinyl cutter |
| **Electronics** | Soldering stations<br>Solder<br>Heat gun<br>Hot air rework station<br>Digital multi-meters<br>Oscilloscopes<br>Power meter/monitor | Logic probes/analyzer<br>USB sniffer<br>Reflow oven/skillet<br>Components<br>Microcontroller programmers<br>Solderless bread boards<br>Power supplies |

NOVA Labs (n.d.)

## SETTING THE STAGE

It is clear that NOVA Labs, entering its 7th year, has a sense of maturity about how a community-based makerspace should be run. The space has a detailed and well-laid-out membership policy, an official code of conduct manual, and an extensive 25-page safety and program manual. The space is all volunteer driven and relies on membership dues for most of its funding. Haneline indicated that there are other streams of income, including:

*We have the rent that we get from incubators, we have the revenue we get from classes, and we have corporate sponsors and donors, which is critical but not developed to the extent that I would like to see. We also have a couple events that we do every year.*

Membership and safety are tightly integrated, and access to different areas of the spaces is dependent on the membership level and training. Within the space are three safety levels, green, yellow, and red, each decidedly more restrictive as members progress through the safety levels, which are listed in Table 2.

The green level is a general safety and orientation level. It is achieved by attending an orientation and signing a liability waiver and safety acknowledgment form. Once the green level is obtained, members can use bench tools and attend classes.

The yellow level consists mainly of safety orientation courses for specific tools that are generally less hazardous than those found in the red safety area. Once courses are completed for the yellow and red areas, members receive a certification and are able to use the specific tools. Example tools that fall under the yellow certification include the floor-stand drill press, bench-top band saw, metal grinder, metal drill press, horizontal band saw, CNC crafting machines, and the CNC vinyl cutter.

Red certification provides access to the tools that are the most complex and have higher repair or replacement costs. Examples of machines that require red certification include laser cutters, thermoformer, table saws, CNC router, 3D printers, and MIG welders. All machines in the space are color banded (green, yellow, or red) to signify the safety level.

The membership policy for NOVA Labs is comprehensive and well thought out. Overall, there are five membership levels (guest, attendee, day pass attendee, associate member, key member). Each level of membership is built on the previous level, and there is a clear hierarchy of membership levels, roles, and benefits. As shown in Table 3, membership levels move from free for visitors, with little access to equipment, to associate members, who pay dues and can visit the space when others are in the space, to the Keyholder members, who pay $100 a month in dues and have unfettered access to the space.

Most members start as guests of the space and will start with the green orientation. Briggs described the guest level of access:

*First is just Joe off the streets, they want to come in and they're not really a member, and they're really only welcomed to use the space anytime there's a prescheduled event happening. That type of person is not paying ... They're paying just for the class they're in. They're showing up to one of the free events that we offer.*

Moving up the membership level is the Attendee membership, that is still meant as an introduction to the space. Attendees are required to take the orientation (green) course and then they are free to begin certification on

*Table 2. Safety levels*

| Level Code | Process to Obtain | Equipment Usage |
|---|---|---|
| Green | Complete orientation | Handheld bench tools, shop classes |
| Yellow | Attend class and receive certification from instructor | Specific shop tools that are less dangerous and less expensive to repair/replace than red |
| Red | Attend classes and receive certification from instructor | Highest level of danger and costs to repair/replace |

*Table 3. Membership levels*

| Level | Requirements | Benefits | Restrictions |
|---|---|---|---|
| Guest | None | Meet members of the space<br>Attend a scheduled event<br>Attend tour | Can only attend scheduled events<br>Must sign liability waiver for shop access<br>Not eligible to use tools or equipment independently<br>Cannot attend tool sign-off classes<br>No access to yellow or red tools |
| Attendee and Attendee (day pass) | Complete green orientation | Attend scheduled events<br>Attend tool certification courses<br>Day pass available for limited shop access<br>Limited shop usage: Use tools as part of a class<br>Use tools if certified independently with a day pass<br>Attend open office hours in shop areas and use noncertified tools for supervised practice<br>Attendees may attend open office shop events in any area of the lab | A day pass is required for independent use of any area or tool<br>Can attend only supervised events unless a day pass is purchased<br>Day passes grant attendees limited access to the shops |
| Associate | Attendee status Age 16+ $50/ month | Access during open hours or when a Key member has opened the space<br>Eligible to teach classes during open hours<br>Use of the following tools: ShopSabre CNC, HP banner printer<br>May invite visitors into space to accompany them<br>May attend member meetings<br>May serve on committees<br>May serve as tool and area stewards | Limited access to NOVA Labs<br>Some tool restrictions<br>Cannot serve on board of directors or occupy incubator office space |
| Key Member | Attendee or Associate Age 18+ Contribute $100/month | All associate benefits<br>24/7 front door and shop door access<br>Can sponsor Family Key Members: 1st family Key member free, additional family memberships are $10 per person, per month<br>Lockable storage tote in locked Key member storage area<br>Reserve conference rooms and classrooms for private business and planning meetings for free. Ability to occupy incubator office space<br>Ability to rent one or more storage cabinets<br>Use of Matsuura CNC<br>Ability to ship materials to NOVA Labs | Perform at least five hours of volunteer service<br>Sponsored by a current Key member<br>Approved by Board of Directors |

NOVA Labs (2017)

specific tools. Due to the fact Attendee members do not pay dues, they pay a daily fee to use tools for which they have certification. There are numerous additional restrictions at this level of membership. One of the responsibilities of the Key and Associate members is to protect novices in the space by making sure they are comfortable with the tools and following the safety program.

Associate members pay dues and have access to the space anytime a full member is present, which, according to Briggs, is almost always. At this level of membership, participants can start working on their own projects in their own time. Associate members can also serve as stewards for a shop. Haneline defined the steward role as:

*We have what's called 'stewards,' who are responsible for the different areas. They are responsible for the instruction. They're volunteers. We also have an events committee, which works with the stewards to ... the events committee are the people that interface with the public. If somebody wants to teach a class or take a class or find out information, they make the connection to help get classes going. I mean, the stewards end up teaching, but they're not the only ones. They have the responsibility for them [tools] being used properly.*

Key members are what make the space thrive. It is their responsibility to greet and make guests feel welcome in the space. Many times, key members act as stewards for the shops, and serve on committees and on the board of directors. Key members have access to the space 24/7. Briggs described the role of Key members:

*You then have an RFID to the front door. If you have the burning urge to laser cut at 2:00 A.M. on Sunday, you can do that. At that point, full members tend to be the managers of the space to some degree. They tend to be the ones who are here more often, giving tours, making sure people are following the rules and using equipment safely, and teaching a lot of the classes and that type of thing.*

Unique to NOVA Labs is the institutionalized expectation that members give back to the community through teaching, volunteering their time in the space by overseeing shops or working the front desk, and by greeting visitors and providing tours to guests. According to Briggs, in a volunteer-driven space, there is a need to create a culture where volunteers receive benefits yet also give back to the community:

*In order to transition to that full member level benefit, the board is looking that they've [the member] contributed back to the community in some way. They've taught classes or helped man the front desk, or volunteered in some capacity, because it is an all-volunteer organization. If people are coming in and they just say, 'Okay, I'm going to pay my $100 and that's it. I'm going to come in. I'm going to use the laser cutter when I want, leave when I'm done. That's it.' If I'm just going to consume the service, it doesn't work. If you have a whole bunch of people with that mentality, the place falls apart pretty quickly. You have to cultivate a culture where people are both getting something out of the community and interested in contributing back to it in some way.*

Instructors in the space are recruited from the membership base. As previously mentioned, one of the expectations for members is that they give back to the space, and leading classes is part of that expectation. Other instructors can be brought in to lead classes if they are sponsored by a member. Haneline also noted:

*We do have an incentive program, where a portion of the income from the classes goes back to the instructor. Not all instructors take that incentive, but many of them do. There is a charge for most of the classes and certainly the classes with the certification for tools.*

## LEARNING COMMUNITIES

Adult communities of learning in NOVA Labs mainly form around interest areas, according to Haneline. There are a number of interest areas from woodworking, metalworking, and electronics to 3D printing and the arts circle. Learners get together in the space, usually at predetermined times, to share and make. Interest group meetups tend to be free and are opportunities for people to visit the space and see what it is about; "dip their toes in the water." These interest group meetings are very informal gatherings for people of like interests to discuss and create. Other times, there are build groups where people will bring in their projects, for example, the 3D printer build group. During these build groups, members will walk through all the steps of purchasing kits and assembling them over an extended period of time. Haneline gave the following example:

*Another one [learning community] that has a model that's fairly easy to follow is the 3D printing. That actually is a good way to connect novices and experts. People who enjoy 3D printing come here on Monday nights, and they'll bring in their printers. They'll bring in their projects, but they also host these build groups. A novice would purchase a kit, and the kit is prepared by the volunteers in the build group. Some of the parts they purchase, some of the hardware, others we fabricate here. There's a plan and every build group improves the plan a little bit. If you bring it here and you build it, then the idea is, there are experts to help you, that kind of thing. There are those sort of structured, regularly scheduled interest groups that create one opportunity.*

NOVA Labs informs members and visitors of the current interest areas and meeting times through an online meetup and calendar system, as shown in Table 4. These meetups cover a variety of interests from arts to Arduino (open-source electronics platform for building electronics projects). Many times organizers are working to recruit new members. Meeting times are also available from the meetup.com website, and members and visitors are encouraged to check the site to confirm meeting dates and times. While each group is run differently, new members would find it easy to navigate the space and move in and out of learning communities.

Classes are another way to build communities of learners in the space. In addition to the meetups, a myriad of classes are offered for both novices and more experienced makers. Classes range from an introduction to 3D printers

*Table 4. Example interest area meetings*

| Project Area | Meeting times |
|---|---|
| Woodshop | Meets for woodshop office hours on Sundays, Wednesdays, and Thursdays. All levels of skills welcome. |
| Metal shop | Meets on 2nd and 4th Mondays for Metal Shop Mondays — all levels of skills. |
| Makers circle & art lab (MC&AL) | Arts and Crafts meetup meets regularly every other Friday night |
| Woodshop ShopSabre CNC | Open office hours each Thursday at 7 P.M. |
| Arduino Meetup | Meets the 3rd Tuesday of every month |
| Raspberry PI Meetup | Meets 4th Tuesday of every month |
| Field-Programmable Gate Arrays (FPGA) | Meets every other Wednesday night |
| Robotics Meetup | Meets the 3rd Saturday of every month |
| DIYBio Meetup | Biotechnology DIY, meets 2nd and 3rd Sundays of each month |

NOVA Labs (n.d.)

*Table 5. NOVA Labs courses*

| Course Title | Description | Prereq. | Duration | Sign-off | Cost |
|---|---|---|---|---|---|
| **3d printing 101** | Training on using 3D printers in the space. Class consists of a background lesson in a conference room, then attendees will fire off a quick print. Printer use is limited to Key and Associate Members only. | Green | 2 hr | Yes | $26 |
| **CS: Mold Making and Plastic Casting 101** | Training on box molds using silicone rubber and how to cast plastic parts in that mold. | | 3 hr | No | $40 |
| **BL: Intro to Blacksmithing Jewelry Cloak/Hair/ Hat Pins and Buckles** | Course covers different blacksmithing techniques; making small items. | Green | 2 hr | No | $30 |
| **MW:MIG Welding 101** | Certification course on safety practices and techniques for using the Millermatic 211 welder. | Yellow | 2 hrs 15 minutes | Yes | $40 |
| **GO: Green Orientation** | Mandatory prerequisite covers code of conduct, safety policy, culture, and procedures. | | 2 hrs | Yes | $15 |
| **MW: Metal Shop Orientation - Yellow Tools Safety Training** | Training on safely using the following tools:<br>Horizontal band saw<br>Abrasive cutoff saw<br>4-1/2" angle grinder<br>6" bench grinder<br>1"x30" Belt sander<br>Drill press<br>Media blaster | Green | 3 hrs | Yes | $65 |
| **BL: Blacksmithing 101 Introduction** | Covers hammer control, tapering, bending, and twisting of metal, and safety. | Green | 2 hrs | Yes | $40 |
| **MW: Metal Lathe 101** | Training on the Enco 12x36 metal lathe. | Yellow | 3 hrs | Yes | $65 |
| **AR: Arduino 101 for Beginners** | Introduction to the Arduino micro-controller. | | 2 hrs | Yes | $25 |
| **CD: Intro to 3d CAD with Fusion 360** | An introduction to computer-aided design (CAD) for novices. | | 2.5 hrs | No | $25 |
| **LT: Laser Cutter 101 Red Safety Training** | Training on the use of the laser cutters. | Green | 2 hrs | Yes | $40 |
| **Tech Toast: Technical speaking and presentation skills** | Course on communication skills for makers. | | 1 hr | | |

Meetup (n.d.)

to mold making, blacksmithing, and woodworking. In addition, certification classes are offered to achieve the associated safety level (yellow or red). These courses are an ideal way to learn skills and test the waters of making, but in addition, they are an introduction to a community of learners who have similar interests. Table 5 provides a partial list of classes offered in the space.

With two main catalysts, interest groups and formalized classes, learning communities form in an organic fashion. It all starts with new members expressing interest in a certain type of learning. The community is pretty open. According to Briggs:

*If we don't have something on our schedule, it's generally not an indication that we aren't interested in having that. It's just we didn't find the right person to lead that type of group yet. What we offer and how we offer it is constantly evolving because of the people that are coming in and teaching it or expressing interest. They like drones but maybe they like to see a different aspect of it taught so they take it in another direction.*

Interest groups are usually the first step in a new person becoming a learning community member. These informal meetups don't involve curriculum or formal learning, it's just a bunch of people hanging out and talking on that subject, according to Briggs. Members of the groups run the gauntlet from complete novices all the way to experts on the subject. Briggs gave an example of the drone interest group:

*You'll see everyone in the group, from someone who has no idea what a drone is, they saw it at the Super Bowl, thought it was cool and want to get involved, all the way to experts. Then, the next step is we have more formal classes, intro to drones 101 or this class I'm teaching, which is actually a 15-week, three-credit college course. The university said it was fine if we let NOVA Labs members just audit the course for free. They don't get any credit or anything. It's a free college course on drones, robotics, and sensory integration.*

This is the typical progression to join a community of learners and get involved in some way. And, according to Briggs, once involved members join a lot of the communities, they tend to want to keep going and give back, and so then they'll teach a class on their interest area. Again, this willingness to give back to the community is one of the traits the NOVA Labs membership committee is looking for in potential members.

The incubator spaces are another important catalyst in the development of learning communities for the NOVA Labs. Many of the proprietors in the incubator spaces work at NOVA Labs during regular business hours. This is an important asset in an all-volunteer-led space because they open the doors and oversee the space on a day-to-day basis. In addition, these small start-up owners in the incubator spaces greet people as they enter the space and make connections as part of their responsibilities. Briggs provided the following example:

*Someone comes in, they're like, 'Hey, I'm really interested in hydroponics, who could I talk to?' That's how the community builds and grows, and it's a tremendous benefit not only to the community but for the incubator. They're building their network and community as well, so it works out really well for everyone.*

These incubator space individuals also serve on the events committees and membership committees, and many times complete the day-to-day chores needed in the space. They tend to be the stewards of the studios because, as Briggs stated:

*If someone screws with the equipment, they're the first ones that are gonna be on them, right? Cause you're messing with their business, you can mess it up. There's a tremendous advantage to having those people kind of sitting here all day.*

## YOUTH IN THE SPACE

It's interesting that there is a separate space for youth to prepare and compete in the FIRST robotic competitions. According to Briggs, the space tries to keep the costs for youth to join the robotics team as low as possible.

Youth in the robotics program meet for three to four months during the robotics season. During that time youth meet three to four times per week, for hours on end every time.

Haneline noted that many different levels of robotics programs are formed in the space. Youth can join regardless of experience with robotics, and many teams are entirely made of rookie (1st year) members. When asked if there was a lot of crossover between the robotics team members and the adult members working in the makerspace, Haneline indicated that it was part of their vision.

But younger robotics teams typically do not utilize shops in the makerspace. Older teams and students of high school age have worked in the makerspace to fabricate parts and consulted with adult members on robotic builds.

In general, youth cannot become members of NOVA Labs until age 18. However, some programs are designed for youth, and other courses are open to youth under certain conditions. One example of youth programming in the space is the 'ikids Robotics', a robotics and programming meetup for youth ages 8 to 14 to learn robotics and Scratch programming.

Youth under 12 years of age are required to have a guardian in the lab during the program. There is no fee for youth to attend. They are encouraged to bring a laptop and a robot kit (GoBox, GoPiGo). A similar program, Technical Literacy for Kids, which takes place in the woodshop, is a meetup that enables youth ages 9 through teens to become comfortable with hand tools. Like the adult meetup, it is an informal meeting of youth and mentors centered on using tools to fix things. Youth also have the opportunity to attend some of the other course offerings in the space as well. Courses open to youth have different minimum age limits and requirements for guardians to remain in the space with the youth. An example is the Intro to Stained Glass course, which, as it sounds, is a course that covers the basics of cutting glass, soldering, and creating a panel. The course is open to children 12 years or older. On the other hand, the Introduction to the Industrial Sewing Machines course has a requirement that youth must be 16 or older. Minors in the course (ages 16 to 17) must have a parent or guardian on the premises at all times in case of emergency. The adult does not have to take the class with the youth.

NOVA Labs is a traditional community-based makerspace and, like many such spaces, has some inequity in female membership. However, the space was purposeful in establishing the presence of females in leadership positions. For example, in the last round of recruitment for directors, there was a focus on recruitment of females who had the skills for the leadership team. Haneline noted:

*They brought me into the board probably two and a half years ago. There are now three women out of seven [board members]; two of the officers are female, and I'm the president ... Part of it was a commitment to trying to make the space friendlier to women ... This last round when we recruited for the directors, we did include that we had an interest in female leadership and other kinds of diversity, but we also had skills that we were looking for, and we placed a primary focus on skills that we were looking for. We were able to get both.*

Haneline believes that female leadership has made a difference, but they have not tracked this information.

When asked if they encourage the maker mindset and, in particular, the idea of perseverance, Haneline commented that the first thing that she thought of when the maker mindset was mentioned was: "The failure, the freedom to fail." When asked if they incorporate the freedom to fail or other maker mindset practices, she said that she didn't think they were explicitly taught in the courses. She commented that many courses are more about developing the skills and not as much about the process of making. Certification courses, for example, are largely skill based because of the need to provide the necessary skills and safety information in a compressed amount of time.

## FAMILIES IN THE SPACE

According to Haneline, not a lot of families visit the space. For many adults, they are working on their project or networking with others and don't consider the time especially useful for children. Parents will bring their children to the youth-based programs and stay if required, but they are not usually learning alongside their children. Haneline did provide some examples of members coming in with a child:

*For example, one of our members has an incubator here. He came here to an arts and crafts class. He brought his daughter, and they designed this Valentine gear on the spot, and they ended up selling it. He did it with her, but 90% of the time when I see him here, his daughter's not here. He does use the space with his daughter, but it's not his primary means.*

When it comes to the robotics programming, however, there is much more family involvement in that program. The robotics side offers opportunities for parents to mentor and coach teams. Haneline noted: "Some of the coaches don't have kids in the program, but most of them, many of them, do."

## IMPACT ON THE COMMUNITY

NOVA Labs has an impressive array of equipment, but what truly makes the space stand out is the fact that it is run entirely by volunteers who willingly give their time and talents for the betterment of the membership. One visible influence on the community can be seen in their work with the FIRST Robotics teams and other community events. The NOVA Labs Community Maker Faire is attended by over 4,000 people a day and provides a showcase for members' work. Another project the space has been a part of is the Tikkun Olam Makers (TOM) DC global makathon to help disadvantaged communities. According to Briggs:

*The event was a three-day makathon designed to develop solutions for people with disabilities. Those got quite a bit of exposure and was directly giving back to the community, specifically the disabled community.*

The other impact on the community has been around developing and connecting entrepreneurs and small businesses in the area. The space provides important tools and expertise that permits small scale prototyping and fabrication. Briggs touched on the idea of professional makers, defined as makers who are generating businesses and jobs. A number of professional makers have emerged from NOVA Labs, with businesses starting to mature and generate more work and jobs in the community. Briggs described his own experience as a professional maker:

*I've hired a few people. Composites is another incubator office here. He's probably hired four or five different people. He's doing similar stuff as me: prototype development. He has a niche. I'm more on the prototype side. His business tends to take prototypes and then move them from prototype into small volume manufacturing. They're filling a gap between large scale manufacturing in the prototype phase there. Small Batch Assembly, they do PC board assembly work. He's hired at least one person that I know of.*

Briggs noted that there are several reasons why he chose to locate his business at NOVA Labs. Primarily, the type of work that he does often can differ from project to project and therefore, he needs a diverse talent pool to choose from to complete the work. In addition, the projects are usually prototypes that people want done quickly so they can move on to manufacturing. NOVA Labs provides access to the equipment and the community to accomplish these types of projects. He noted:

*I'm meeting people constantly. It's just an amazing place to network. When I need talent for a project, it's really easy for me to reach out and put together a team really quickly. I know who's got what skills, who's looking for work and this type of thing.*

These small businesses and professional makers also work together and share resources at the space as the projects they work on crossover. According to Briggs:

*A lot of the incubator companies work together. If I need PC board assembly work, I take it over to Small Batch Assembly. If I need mechanical stuff, I can go over to Theta Composites. We're all passing work around based on what our schedules are like, what our needs for the project are.*

Without NOVA Labs, Briggs indicated that it would be very hard to build these projects. In addition, tapping into the community is another important aspect of his work since it is difficult to develop the types of contacts and build the relationships to utilize the expertise needed. Briggs noted:

*I can spin up a project really, really fast because I can find and put together a team quickly. Anywhere you go, any kind of project you're talking about, one of the challenges they face is 'Jeez, where do I find the really talented people? How do I get them in here and how do I get them tasked?' That's not a hard thing to do at NOVA Labs. That's something that's unique.*

Another interesting topic is the idea of how urban areas compare with rural areas in terms of making. For example, makerspaces are difficult to establish in rural communities because of small populations and geographic distances. Haneline described her husband's upbringing in rural Kentucky:

*It's so interesting because my husband grew up on a farm in West Kentucky, and one of the things that he was sad about was not being able to spend time with his dad like he did when he was a kid. They would fix a combine in the field, the time that he had with his dad is special to him, and he was sad that he couldn't pass that on to his own children. I think there's still a certain sadness about it, but one of the reasons I'm committed to this space is that I feel it gives us the opportunity, in a way, to pass on to our kids some of those connections and skills that he had with his dad. In a way, this fills a need in the city that you already have in the rural areas because here you can't, there's no space for the tools that you want. And also, even connecting up with that community of people. I almost think it's more important in the city than it is in a rural area.*

Haneline believes that rural communities are already makers by necessity. When a piece of equipment breaks, it has to be fixed, and being geographically isolated sometimes requires that individuals develop the necessary skills and obtain or build tools. In a sense, NOVA Labs is bringing what the rural community has to the city.

## DEFINING A MAKERSPACE

When asked to define a makerspace and the core components of a makerspace, Haneline responded:

*I do this so it should be a little easier for me. I think that right now a makerspace is a movement, and it's kind of a new idea so it's still being defined and there's a lot of opportunity to make it what you want it to be. I think that, at least for this makerspace, the themes around the learning and teaching are critical to it. I think that makerspaces tend to attract people who are empathetic, and they're good people. They also attract people who are a little different, a little on the edge; they'll tell you what they think. They may be, I don't want to use the word misfit because it has a negative connotation, sort of like the island of misfit toys.*

*We find a place to belong. Certainly, from a leadership perspective, it's a fun, challenging group to work with. There are so many people who are so dedicated to it, and they all have strong personalities, and figuring out how to make that work together is a challenge but it's also rewarding if you can.*

*On a personal note, when my kids were born I was an engineer, and then I stepped back from that and I wanted to be more involved in the community, and one of the things I did was I got involved in a giving circle. The giving circle is also, I think, sort of new, people say 'Well, what is a giving circle?' I say 'Well, you form around it and you form a nonprofit and you decide how you want to give back to the community but it can be different.' Ours, we wanted, the giving circle I became involved in, wanted to help low income, really help nonprofits that were grassroots and work with them.*

*Another giving circle could help dogs, they…have different charters, and they connect around their passion so I feel like the makerspace has a lot in common with that. And I'm not sure how much you can transfer from one, there are certainly things you can transfer but you still, there is what makes it unique. The makerspace defines its own charter and its own passion with still having room to grow. That's part of what we've done here, we've said 'Well, there's what the original founder envisioned for this space, and then it's what we're growing into, and what kind of change do we want to embrace? Some of that change is good.*

Briggs defined a makerspace in the following way:

*I would define a makerspace as a community. That's probably the biggest thing. It's a community that focuses around technology and generally making physical things. At least for us, the biggest part of that is the community aspect. That's what really makes NOVA Labs work. That's what keeps people interested. We always talk about, well, you're paying membership dues to get access to the laser cutter and then the woodshop and the metal shop and whatever. That's not really what keeps people coming back. Very few people really have a burning need to have 24/7 access to a woodshop. They just don't. If they really had that strong need, they'd just go plunk down five grand, build themselves a woodshop in the basement, and that's that.*

*For most people, it's the community, the friends, and the projects: the collaboration. There are a lot of times you'd just be hanging out here, and there'll be another group. You just get to talking and the next thing you know, someone says 'Wouldn't it be cool if …' There's the talent in the room to make that 'if' happen, and so the next thing you know, you're sucked into a project, and you're having a good time making whatever crazy, wild thing.*

One of NOVA's greatest endeavors is the Rhino Hawk project that members have worked on over the past few years. The project originated as a way to create low-cost drone technology to stop the poaching of rhinoceroses in South Africa. The prototype is shown in Figure 4.

A diverse team was formed in the space to work on the project, and it ranged from novices in drone technology to experts with 15 years of experience working in aerospace engineering. The team was broken down into different areas, from developing the physical airframe, logistics and sourcing of materials,

*Figure 4. Rhino Hawk prototype*

to software engineering with GPS route planning and machine vision. The team ended up creating custom PC boards for the project. Throughout the undertaking, the team project areas would meet independently to figure out tasks and timelines and would report back to the full group during weekly meetings. The project was entirely volunteer-based, with a flat reporting structure. Briggs commented on the outcomes:

*It built a pretty solid community of people here who got a great sense of accomplishment. They really enjoyed their time at the space and on the project so much that a lot of those people have gone on to be even greater contributors to the space, teaching additional classes. There are a lot of things that have to happen around here to make things work. There is the Tech Coms [Technology Communications] committee that makes sure the webpage stays online and emails function.*

*You need another wire poled for electrical. You got to have someone do that or the lightbulbs are out. There's a lot of little things that have to happen, so there are groups that manage all that. A lot of people who are on that team funnel into these various behind the scenes roles helping to just make the space work. Yeah. Everyone had a pretty strong connection to the space. It's that type of thing that keeps people coming and interested.*

## CURRENT CHALLENGES

In general, NOVA Labs is a mature space that has figured out a lot of the logistics for running an all-volunteer space. It has in-depth membership and visitors' procedures, as well as detailed training and certification processes. The space has an impressive array of equipment and, more importantly, a membership base that continually gives back to the community and the space.

It was interesting that the space really focuses on teaching skills and knowledge to use equipment but that the concepts around the process of making and the maker mindset are not covered, at least explicitly, in the course offerings. How do members of the space learn to become makers?

Haneline indicated that the shop stewards offer open nights to help people get started on projects. During an open night, members expect to find people in the shop who can help with the project. Some of the making process may happen in the learning communities. Haneline commented:

*It's actually on our list of topics for our member meeting this Thursday. It is one of our folks talking about how to get started in the community but maybe that's part of it, too. How do you get started with a project, and I don't know, I don't know if people come here and don't really have an idea of how to do a project, somehow you need a connection.*

NOVA Labs did not provide statistics on its membership so it was not clear what the gender mix or ethnic makeup of members consisted of. At some point, the NOVA Labs decided to make a commitment to make the space friendlier to women, indicating that they may indeed be lacking in female membership and participation. Haneline commented: "The directors told me that they wanted more women in the space and they needed female leadership." Which led, in part, to additional females being elected to the board of directors. It's not clear if other initiatives are under consideration to diversify membership.

Finally, the space has a wonderful youth robotics program with the FIRST series of LEGO robotics teams and a few youth-based courses offered in the space. However, there does not seem to be a lot of crossover from the robotics program into the makerspace. From the outside, the robotics initiative (NOVA Robotics) — with a separate website and building — seems entirely separated from the makerspace.

## REFERENCES

Meetup. (n.d.). *NOVA Makers*. Retrieved from https://www.meetup.com/NOVA-Makers/events/

NOVA Labs. (2017). *Membership Policy*. Retrieved from http://www.nova-labs.org/wiki/_media/policies/novalabs_membership_policy_v._8-17-17.pdf

NOVA Labs. (n.d.). *Equipment*. Retrieved from http://www.nova-labs.org/wiki/

## KEY TERMS AND DEFINITIONS

**Arduino:** A small microcontroller used for rapid prototyping.

**Bench Tools:** A collection of tools like a handsaw, belt sander, and drill press.

**Bob Coggeshal:** The inventor of the Unix Sudo command.

**FIRST:** For Inspiration and Recognition of Science and Technology runs the FIRST collection of robotic competitions.

**GoBox:** A robotics subscription service on the Raspberry Pi.

**GoPiGo:** A complete robot kit.

**NOVA Labs:** Community-based makerspace located in Northern Virginia.

**Open Nights:** Times that the shops are open and shop stewards are available for consultation by members.

**Reston, Virginia:** An affluent community located in Northern Virginia.

**RFID:** Radio-frequency identification.

**Thermoformer:** A machine used to heat plastic in order to shape it in a mold.

**Tikkun Olam Makers (TOM) DC:** Makeathon for assistive technology.

# Chapter 13
# Deep Green Machines


## ABSTRACT

*Deep Green Machines (DGM) was founded in the village of Rutledge, Missouri with a population of approximately 100 residents. Nearby, there are other larger specialized communities, which include the Anabaptist Mennonite community and three intentional communities with a focus on sustainable ecological living. DGM was established as a disruptor to break a continuing cycle of low wages and defunct microeconomic practices. In the end, it was the heterogeneousness of these communities that prevented DGM from making an impact, and ultimately led to it relocating. This chapter explores Deep Green Machines.*


DOI: 10.4018/978-1-5225-8310-3.ch013

*In my alternate reality, DGM would be a space that provided people and community with agency to become more abundant. It would only take a few repeating projects with steady predicable volume -- billed out at $75 to 120 per hour to make a difference in people's lives. — Frank Cicela*

## ORGANIZATION BACKGROUND

Experiments that end in failure tend to provide as much rich detail and understanding of a topic as exemplars. Frank Cicela, the founder of Deep Green Machines (DGM) in the small town of Ruthledge, Missouri, shared with the author his vision for establishing, running and ultimately shuttering of the DGM space. At the time of my visit Deep Green Machine in Rutledge was being moved to the larger community of Warsaw, Missouri. Cicela describes attributing the name, Deep Green Machine, as an acknowledgment to Derrick Jensen, the author of *Deep Green Resistance* (McBay, Keith, & Jensen, 2011). In the book, the authors examine environmental issues and propose societal action to bring change to current environmental trends. In a follow-up email, Cicela wrote Deep Green Machines (DGM) pays homage to the book's call for action. Establishing DGM was "My attempt to break free from paralysis and offer some sort of meaningful action." DGM was founded in May of 2013 by Cicela, after moving from Cedar Rapids, Iowa. Cicela describes the decade before making the move to Rutledge, where he held two corporate positions: one in Crawfordsville, Indiana and the other in Cedar Rapids, Iowa. In both instances, his job was eliminated, and he and his family had to relocate to find employment. It's important to understand how Cicela arrived in Missouri because it helped define his later actions to establish the DGM makerspace. While in Cedar Rapids the Cicela Family decided to move to Missouri, he noted:

*After finding myself unemployed for the second time in three years I asked, "Okay, what do we want to do now?" We were trying to find a way to lick our wounds and find a space to recover financially. In parallel, my family and I, have had a relationship with the Dancing Rabbit Eco-Village which is within walking distance of Rutledge. We've had the relationship going on seventeen, years. We made visiting the intentional communities a summer vacation destination; we'd come out to visit and volunteer.*

According to their website, Dancing Rabbit Ecovillage is a sustainability and social structure demonstration project located in Northeast Missouri on 280 acres of land (Dancing Rabbit, n.d.). The Ecovillage has permanent members and also has: internships, work exchange programs, and short-term stays. Likewise, but on a smaller scale (76 acres), Red Earth Farms (Red Earth Farms, n.d.) is dedicated to sustainability, and Sandhill Farm (Sandhill Farm, n.d.) (155 acres) grows 80% of their food and is an egalitarian community. Modern intentional communities like those found in northeast Missouri evolved from the hippie communes of the 1960s and 70s to their current form focused on ecological and environmental concerns (Mazella, 2010). An intentional community is a physical community of people with a political and economic direction, bounded by an intention or goal of living in a certain way as a community (Mazellam, 2010).

Cicela next found a corporate purchasing job that allowed him to telecommute, and made the move to Rutledge, Missouri. The decision to move to Rutledge was also influenced by economic factors, not the least of which was the cost of the property. Cicela was able to rent a home for less than his annual property tax bill in Cedar Rapids. The current site of DGM consists of multiple village lots in Rutledge, which included two medium-sized out-buildings and a house. The entire property was purchased for $10,000, as part of a bank foreclosure. Cicela put on a new roof, added 200-amp electrical service and poured a concrete floor in the primary shop building. There were plans to also convert the house into a small business incubator. In his words he stated:

*I wanted to set the house up as a sort of a small business incubator, the walk-in entrance would be joined to a reception and an office space, open meeting space and private meeting space. Additional areas would include a small library along with rooms dedicated to craft studio for fiber and digital arts, and commercial looking. There would also be a bathroom and laundry.*

Another factor that led Cicela to establish a makerspace was his experience and opportunities in high school vocational education, which included: woodshop, machine shop, welding, electronics. These high school experiences, combined with a traditional education in the college preparatory areas, enabled Cicela to pursue his interests in technology. Reflecting on the current vocational educational options schools offer, Cicela believes contemporary students are missing out on and therefore wanted to provide these educational opportunities for the surrounding communities.

Cicela's experiences, sometimes fortuitous, led him to establish DGM. For Cicela it was a combination of economic hardship, the desire to give back take action, his experiences with intentional communities, and his judgement that the current school's curriculum was not providing robust vocational opportunities for students. Cicela noted:

*I had more time than money. I kind of went into creating this makerspace with the notion that "If I build it, they'll come." DGM created and offered a Little Free Library about the size of an old-fashioned telephone booth. It held more than 300 books. Books varied and included topics such as: Community Building, Gardening, Green Building, Food and Health, Environment, Ecology, Conservation, Science, Slow Food, Simple Living, Sustainable Business, Fiction, Non-Fiction, and Inspirational. The collection also includes titles for children and young adults. The closest public library is Memphis, Missouri, which is about 15 miles away. A little free library operates on the honor system Patrons stop by and take whatever catches their interest, whenever they want. Patrons return and/or bring books to contribute. It is that simple. No business hours, no library cards, no due dates or fines. Simply take a book — leave a book."*

Deep Green Machines sits on a 1/2 block in the village of Rutledge, Missouri. Figure 1 shows the property adjacent to DGM.

*Figure 1. A property in Rutledge, MO*

Many properties in the village were dilapidated and in need of demolition or repair. According to the 2016 American Community Survey (ACS) conducted by the United States Census Bureau, the total population of Rutledge is 77, comprised of 50 females and 27 males (ACS, 2016). There are roughly 22 youth under the age of 19 living in the village as well. Seventy-three of the 77 residents are white, while four residents are two or more races. In Rutledge, 16 out of the 55 residents 16 years or older are reportedly in the workforce. About 30% of the workforce in Rutledge earn $10,000 to $15,000 per year while the mean household income is $22,903, and about 13% of residents receive food stamp benefits. The per capita income for residents of Rutledge is $10,236. Three of the residents hold a bachelor's degree.

The American Census Survey (ACS, 2016) data does not include the members of intentional communities. Cicela points out, significant portions of the intentional community populations are transient and do not stay in the community long-term. He also noted that there are people in the region that are not food secure:

*Some neighbors here earn less than $10,000 (US) a year. Some are not food secure. I've tried hard to, redirect the surplus that I have and push it out into the community. Whether it's through making the tools and space available, or whether it's through supporting workshops on permaculture, growing mushrooms. My wife and daughter are a master-gardeners. We shared eggs and meat from chickens and rabbits we raised.*

DGM is more like a campus spread across four main buildings. The business incubator space is located in the house, which at the time of the author's visit was in the middle of being renovated. Adjacent to the house was the primary shop space, which was 24 feet long by 32 feet wide (7.3 meters by 9.8 meters) converted metal pole building that had a cement floor added. Figure 2 provides a view from the outside of the space.

With a large overhead garage door, the main makerspace has room for vehicle repair. Just inside the main garage doors is a large computer numerical controlled (CNC) plasma cutter that takes up a considerable amount of floor space. The plasma cutter is shown in Figure 3.

While specific areas are not segregated in the space, there are an impressive number of tools and pieces of machinery available to makers. Figure 4 shows the welding station and Craftsman tool box in the middle of the space with a

*Figure 2. Deep Green Machine main building*

*Figure 3. The CNC plasma cutter*

full complement of mechanics hand tools. Other items in the space include a MIG welder, SMAW welder, OAW welder, hand-held plasma cutter, CNC router, CNC milling machine, manual lathe, sand blast cabinet, wood lathe, belt sander, brake roller, small metal shear, hydraulic press, and air compressors. Cicela commented:

*The shop has been a lifetime of accumulation. While growing up, making things brought me a lot fun and happiness. I wanted to relive that happiness and share it with others. And I figure well, why not find a way to share it because, like I said, a lot of joy and fun that I had growing up was having outlets that, again, I don't see unless you want to go to community college. But then it's like why pay for something, in my mind's eye should have already been a birthright.*

While not small, the space in some areas is crowded. In the far corner near the rear exit are additional storage shelves and additional machinery, as shown in Figure 5.

The woodworking area and aquaponics are in a separate building 24-foot-long by 24-foot-wide, just a fraction smaller than the main building, as shown in Figure 6.

One of the visions for the wood-working space was to establish an aquaponics set-up in ½ of the space. While not complete, Cicela wanted to rework the roof to allow sunlight in the building as shown in Figure 7, he acquired a number of intermediate bulk containers (IBC) to use for the aquaponics system. Eventually, half of the space was to be used for the aquaponics and the other for the wood shop.

The equipment and machinery used in the space was acquired by Cicela. He noted:

*Figure 4. Welding station*

*Figure 5. DGM storage area*

*Figure 6. The outside view of the DGM woodworking and hydroponics*

*I try hard to not purchase anything new. I strive to buy things at auction, flea markets or items that are in need of repair. I shop a lot of eBay or Craigslist. I have [a] full complement of hand and woodshop tools, drills, circular saws, routers, hammers, pry bars, framing squares, speed squares, anything required for basic and intermediate carpentry*

*Figure 7. IBC aquaponics space behind the woodworking tools*

DGM also boasts a tool lending library, as shown in Figure 8. The library was designed for community members of Rutledge to complete improvements in and around their properties. The library had an extensive range of tools from: gardening, drywall, painting, automotive and general carpentry tools. The tool lending library also contained a chicken plucker for butchering chickens, a unique offering not often found in makerspaces or tool lending libraries.

*The biggest case that can be made for this kind of a space in an impoverished rural community is that sharing can ease the burden of making a living. A tool-lending library compliments this movement. If someone decides to paint their kitchen it may cost up to $25 per gallon for paint. A tool lending library will save them from having to spend another $20 on paint trays, brushes, drop clothes and other items to get the job done – a 50% savings.*

The induction process to become a member of DGM was to communicate with Cicela about potential projects. He described the process as follows:

*DGM doesn't have the foot traffic of a storefront in an urban area and therefore doesn't have regularly scheduled office hours. People that need to use DGM resources telephone or email me and set up an appointment that meets the needs of the project.*

*Figure 8. DGM tool library*

DGM does not have a membership fee but established a sliding needs-based scale. In this model members pay what they can or, in some cases, he asked members to donate something to the space to show that the experience was worth it to the individual learner. Cicela noted members are also free to make and sell products from the space:

*DGM was born out of surplus. The goal is to have the idea behind the space grow by paying things forward. A saying I have heard before, goes something like, "Thousands of candles can be lit from a single candle, and the life of the candle will not be shortened." I think that is a fair comparison of what DGM is trying to accomplish.*

Cicela believed that the space would not have legitimacy if he were to extract a fee for usage from the community. He noted:

*It goes back to trust. My needs are met by pulling a "Big City Paycheck" into a rural community. DGM won't have legitimacy or trust if it is taking from people that are just getting by.*

The representative list of equipment for Deep Green Machines is provided in Table 1.

*Table 1. DGM equipment*

| | | |
|---|---|---|
| General Workshop Equipment | Workbenches<br>Shop vacuum<br>Vises | Parts washer<br>Sand blaster<br>Brooms |
| **General Hand Tools** | Complete automotive hand tool set<br>Aircraft hand tool set<br>Drywall lift<br>PVC and Copper plumbing tools | Complete carpentry hand tools<br>Drywall hand tools<br>Electrician tool set<br>Conduit bender<br>Fish tape |
| **Metalwork** | SMAW welding equipment<br>MIG welding equipment<br>TIG welding equipment<br>OAW welding equipment<br>Hand-held plasma cutter<br>Metal Lathe | Brake<br>Roller<br>Calipers<br>Micrometers<br>Height gages<br>Shear |
| **Textiles** | Loom<br>Sewing machine | Drop spindle |
| **Woodworking** | Table Saw<br>Band saw<br>Planer<br>Jointer | Dust collection Table mounter<br>4' x 4' CNC router<br>Compound miter saw<br>Wood lathe |
| **Computing** | (3) Desktop computers for CNC machines | Laptop computer |
| **Science** | Meade 12" LightBridge truss tube Dobsonian telescope balances | Nikon 7X-45X zoom magnification Stereo microscope |
| **Digital Fabrication** | CNC plasma table<br>CNC milling machine<br>CNC router CAD/CAM | Software:<br>BobCAD/CAM<br>Draftsight<br>OnShape<br>Vectric 2D |
| **Electronics** | 2/24VDC power supplies<br>Multi-meters<br>Continuity Tester | Soldering irons<br>OBDII automotive scan tools<br>Voltage tester |
| **Digital and Graphic Arts** | Digital arts studio computer | Cintiq tablet<br>DSLR camera |

## SETTING THE STAGE

Cicela set up DGM as a US Internal Revenue Service 501(c)(3) designated not-for-profit organization. The original vision for the space was to offer people in the surrounding communities a place to create, repair their property, vehicles and other equipment. Additionally, the space was also meant to be an incubator for small businesses to get established. The vision was to allow for experimentation with alternative business-social models in which community and the environment were valued and profit was made ethically. DGM was meant as a way to reduce the barriers in starting a business, especially start-up capital by making support available through the space. The space was started and operated by Cicela, although he had hopes that others in the community would eventually offer their support. Cicela thought if he built the space the community would rally around it. Geographically the community is isolated. By way of example, the nearest public library is 15 miles away and the closest tool rental business is a 45-minute round trip drive. The vision of the space was to help the community be more abundant. With training and access to equipment, Cicela felt that community members could have agency to improve their lives through making. Cicela noted:

*When I was a young kid, I just wanted to spend time making sawdust and metal chips. I wanted to learn by doing. I figured kids hadn't really changed. My desire was to open the doors and make a place like that available for youth. By extension, if a person was entrepreneurial and had an idea for a business, that person could use DGM as a ladder to pull themselves and their idea up by. DGM would limit risk and hopefully catapult the idea forward.*

The tools and machines were all purchased by Cicela allowing him to pursue his passion of making and tinkering. The accumulation of equipment provided a surplus allowing him to share with others. In part, from his experiences with the intentional communities he says it was his desire to share with the community the equipment that had brought him pleasure through making.

Cicela does not have a list of members but estimated that he had 0 to 10 visits per month in 2016. His members were almost exclusively white. Other information on the membership was not shared.

## LEARNING COMMUNITIES

Again, in practice the space did not advance a model of learning communities per se and there was not quite a plan but more of a vision of what learning in a community could have looked like in the space. First, there was a hope that there would be a multi-generational bridge whereby members would share skills. Cicela noted:

*My hope was that the space would become a "barbershop" of sorts, whereby retired folks might hang out. A lifetime of acquired skills and knowledge might then be shared and passed onto youth. What I had really hoped to do was find a retired expert that was either a tractor mechanic when he grew up or when he made his living. Or he's a cabinet maker or something like that and then it would give him a place to practice his skills and teach others. And whatever whipper snappers came in and walked in the front door, "Here, let me show you how we used to do things back in my day." That kind of thing.*

At a philosophical level Cicela believes that even in the corporate environment the ability to actually make things is diminishing. He gives the example of an engineer designing a project in CAD but does not understand how to physically move a project from the digital realm into the real world. He noted:

*There are some pretty neat technologies that can do some pretty amazing things. In the end there is the need to be practical. How does a block of raw material get physically transformed into a finished widget? The next iteration might then take into consideration how to optimize the design for maintenance or repair.*

In the current iteration of DGM, Cicela is the only full-time member of the space and worked with others to create the community of learners. He noted that many of the community members had experience with woodshop tools and did not need much help or support in using those tools. Computer based manufacturing, however, did require training and work within a community for projects. Cicela provided an example of how community worked in DGM, he stated:

*For example, a person resurfaced reclaimed barn siding to use as paneling in their house. After showing off their remodeling to friends and neighbors people began to ask where the tools were obtained to do the work. Before long people began to organically learn about the resources that DGM had to offer and started to make use of the space.*

Learning communities were not strong in the space because there were so few people using it. Community members did take advantage of using the equipment with Cicela's help. For example, he hired a resident of Rutledge to help remodel a house. Cicela explained the arrangement:

*I hired an individual who had a cabinet making background. But he didn't have indoor shop space or a whole host of tools. He's like, "I'd love to do the work for you if you can provide me with the tools." So, I'm like, "Well, let's work that out." He redid all the window casings, installed a hardwood floor and built (8) bookcases for me. So again, it's one of those things where kind of how I shared with you of being a poor community. Where's the capital equipment come from? To be able to kind of bootstrap yourself.*

In another example, Cicela mentored a member of the Dancing Rabbit Ecovillage using a hands-on, problem-based approached. In the process, he worked with the member, drafting the initial designs on paper, then digitalizing the plans with a computer assisted drawing (CAD) program to finally co-creating on the CNC plasma cutter. Cicela noted:

*A person was building a shipping container house and needed custom rafter ties made that could then be welded to the container and then used to tie the wood roof rafters to the containers. I offered a CNC plasma cutting 101 [course]. He sketched up what he wanted on a piece of paper. I demonstrated how to take that sketch drawing, drew it up in CAD, then from CAD made a CNC program. The CNC program is then run on the plasma table. It was a one-on-one needs-based approach. DGM supported a project by taking a person from A to Z.*

Certification on equipment depended on Cicela's judgement. If he thought a member needed training he would provide it, otherwise if the member had experience they were welcome to use the equipment. He stated:

*I would have conversations with people and make a judgement based on understanding of their life experiences. Did a person go to trade school? Did a person have experience from an employer? Did a person take vocational classes in school? Were they taught by an elder from a family business? In the end it came down to me judging if the person had the experience and knowledge to work safely in the space.*

The CNC plasma cutter, for instance, was used by one member that had extensive experience working professionally in a machine shop and only needed a brief introduction to the CAD software. Many members used the wood tools, for finishing reclaimed lumber, which is dangerous if there are nails or screws in the used wood. To help members and to protect the equipment, Cicela set up a metal detector to identify the metal and remove it before processing the lumber. To help educate others Cicela worked for three years with the Dancing Rabbit Eco Village to bring in university student interns during the summers. The interns would spend 50% of their time at DGM performing shop work and 50% at the Eco Village, performing hands-on sustainability work. In DGM the interns would work on project-based learning processes with community members. Cicela, worked with the interns to create learning communities. As Cicela describes the process, they trained members in very specific project skills.

*People brought in mowers, manure spreaders, Brush Hogs, tractors, automobiles in need of repair. Together we built an ad hoc plan to learn the skills needed to make the individual repairs. For example, a person brought in a car needing an oil change. By the time the person left, not only did the car have fresh oil and a new filter, but the person learned the skill of safely and responsibly changing the oil and filter on their car.*

Training in the space consisted mostly of safety training on the equipment. There was not a curriculum for the machines and not a clear pathway to become an expert on the machines. DGM did have safety manuals for each machine, which generally consisted of typical safe usage of the equipment. Any project-based or creative instruction was led by interns or Cicela himself.

Within the village of Rutledge there may have been some confusion about the purpose of the space. For example, Cicela recounts people coming in for a specific purpose, which was usually to repair something, and while there were members that wanted to learn skills many others wanted a service done for little money. Cicela gave the following example:

*After repairing a neighbor's mower, another person had a bale spear that didn't fit the tractor that he had. He requested if something could be done so that the bale spear would fit the tractor. So, "Can you do something to make this, so I can use this bale spear on my tractor?" He was more like, "Just do it." He just wanted to pay some money to make the problem go away and wasn't invested in learning to solve the problem. "I don't really care about it, I'll give you some money, make it happen. Make my problem go away."*

Other times people would express interest in a topic as he was making repairs for example they would say; "I've always wanted to learn how to weld." DGM was never able to create the inertia to draw community members back in after their repair or project was complete. DGM was viewed as a job shop more than a community makerspace, despite the best efforts of Cicela who worked with local newspapers and radio stations to market the space.

DGM had a grand opening celebration for the Tool Lending Library, inviting local newspapers and radio stations which ran stories on the space. Cicela recalls DGM had about 20 people at the grand opening with snacks and fruit punch as part of the celebration. Cicela also attempted to partner with the University of Missouri Extension office in Memphis, Missouri and noted that he traveled to their office on a couple of occasions to meet with staff about DGM. His disappointment concerning extension was:

*DGM, a community makerspace, exists right here in rural Scotland County. This is something that would normally only exist in a much larger urban area. I was really disappointed because my judgement is that the Extension service mission and vision complemented the DGM's and that they would be keen on offering support and promoting the space.*

Ultimately these efforts failed to engage the community of Rutledge as well as the extension office in Memphis. In another attempt to market DGM, Cicela visited the Baptist church in town. The church was supportive of the space and the work being done, especially after he created a name plate for the new pastor. He recalled:

*The Baptist church in town had a sign out front that advertised church services and Sunday school. When the church hired a new pastor, they put a piece of duct tape over the old pastors' name and wrote the new pastors name on the tape. I didn't think that this was appropriate for a church. I headed over to DGM, fired up the CNC Router, made and then installed an attractive wooden placard that had the new Pastors name and telephone number on it. While the elderly church community was appreciative of DGM, there wasn't a tangible way for them to plug into DGM and support the space.*

When asked about the maker mindset and teaching failure as a part of making Cicela noted that he taught others through his own actions and iterative process for making. He gave the following example:

*I guess using that one bracket [Dancing Rabbit Eco Village house project] as an example. I had to make 30 brackets. I made the first one based on a hand drawn sketch and I said, "Go try it out before I go cut another 29 of them." After he [a member of Dancing Rabbit Eco Village] brought it back he said, "Oh yeah, change the diameter of this hole a little bit more so it gives more clearance on the bolt." So, I guess it's kind of an implied lesson in terms of do your first article versus making 30 of them that are wrong. A minor design change was made to provide extra bolt clearance and then the remaining 29 brackets were cut out of steel.*

## FAMILIES IN THE SPACE

DGM did not cater to families in the space. The only family function was the opening celebration of the Tool Lending Library that was attended by a few of the families in town. Likewise, there were not many young people that utilized the space. Cicela's daughters were frequent visitors to the site but most visitors were over 18 years of age. Many of the youth in the village are Mennonite and, according to Cicela, would not engage with DGM. In brief, Mennonites, named after Milo Simons, are part of the Anabaptist movement based on the belief that baptism should be made by adults not infants (Dyck & Schroeder, 2005). It is Cicela's judgement that the Mennonites are an insular group and therefore did not participate in DGM.

## IMPACT ON THE COMMUNITY

In light of DGM closing in Rutledge the impact on the community is hard to determine as are the lasting impacts it may have had on the community. In the short term, there were people who utilized the space to better their situation and their properties. The community did not rally around the space and it's clear that trust was a part of the problem. Cicela was not and never had been part of the community. In addition, unbidden he came to the town and purchased an entire city block and setup DGM. Residents of Rutledge had to trust that coming to the space and learning new skills could indeed change their lives.

When asked if DGM had an impact on individual participants Cicela noted:

*For the most part, the biggest thing that I got was genuine gratitude of, " I wouldn't have been able to do this without the generosity that you showed, by having DGM available." the biggest return was the gratitude that I felt from people having been able to take advantage of the space.*

Continuing, he noted that he was never going to win over the Mennonite community and he was never going to break through the Rutledge community as an outsider not born and raised in Scotland County, Missouri. Cicela believes that if he could have found a partner, an insider from the village, who was willing and able to garner trust, it could have made a difference in the success of the space.

## DEFINING A MAKERSPACE

When asked to define a makerspace and the core components of a makerspace, Cicela responded:

*As far as my definition of a makerspace, I look at it as a repository of knowledge, equipment and materials. I see the ideal space as being glued together with sharing individuals that have wisdom and experience that are willing to help collaborate and problem solve. Where there's this exchange of energy and ideas and bodies to bounce stuff off of.*

## CURRENT CHALLENGES

Obviously, Cicela closing down the space is a challenge both for the community and for Cicela, but it's worth examining the root causes for the failure of the space. He believes that there were four primary contributors, these included in no certain order: a family member moved away, the lack of assimilation to the local community, inability to recruit passionate people to the space, and a transient population.

The Cicela family has a desire to stay together. When his eldest daughter married and relocated he decided to relocate closer to the daughter. As Cicela noted:

*My eldest daughter got married and moved to Warsaw, Missouri. I still had a corporate job that allowed me to work as a remote employee. As long as I had an internet connection and cell phone, it wasn't important where I lived. We didn't want to be four hours apart so that was a contributing factor of leaving Rutledge.*

Another impetus for shutting down DGM was the lack of assimilation of Cicela into the Rutledge community. There was a great deal of conflict between Cicela and certain members of the community. It's not clear if there was a tipping point that led to the hostilities or if it was indeed just some members of the community that could not accept an outsider. Cicela described living in Rutledge:

*I really underestimated this ... I have lived all over the country. I lived up and down Illinois, Indiana, upstate New York, Iowa. I have travelled extensively domestically and internationally. I've moved around. In coming to a small rural Missouri town, I overestimated the capacity for locals to embrace people from the outside. It has been really, really hard living in Rutledge for the last six years. Constant property vandalism. I lost count of how many flat tires I've had. Every time something happened I'd call the sheriff's department. The sheriff has priorities other than petty nastiness that happens out in the middle of nowhere. [It] was just constant low-level warfare.*

Cicela noted he had supported the intentional communities (Dancing Rabbit Eco Village, Red Earth Farms, and Sandhill Farm) that surround Rutledge over the past 17 years. In his experience, these communities struggle in maintaining a viable economy as compared to the Mennonites. He believed that the Mennonites are able to provide goods and services that are sold into the dominant economy to support their unique culture. On the other hand, as Cicela noted, the intentional communities are agrarian focused, DGM would have allowed a viable way to create and sell products to support their community, emulating the Mennonite economic model. Cicela noted:

*My judgement is that out of the three intentional community groups, they don't have a viable sustainable economy. There's only so many carrots that you can sell to your neighbor. And so many onions that they can sell back to you I saw the DGM space as sort of a disruptor in terms being able to extract resources from the dominant culture in order to support an alternative culture.*

Cicela mentioned earlier that he had trouble finding community members that were passionate about making. A makerspace without members is just a shop or lab. In the case of DGM the vision was to be open to everyone and eventually expertise would rise up and help lead and manage the space. That did not come to fruition in part because of Cicela not being native to Rutledge but also because the other communities, Mennonites and the intentional communities, were not open to using the space, and in the case of the intentional communities, the members were highly transient. Cicela noted:

*The communities are transient. People come and stay for six months, eight months, a year and then pull the eject handle and leave. I'm no exception, I've been here six years and now I'm pulling the eject handle, it was tough to get to a tipping point of inertia, where the place stood up and thrived on its own without a lot of my life energy.*

It was Cicela's sentiment that the Mennonite community is an insular culture; not open to outsiders. Evidently, they are willing to take from the dominant culture but unwilling to reciprocate.

Cicela noted:

*My experience is that Mennonites don't share with those outside of their Church Community. It's really ironic, because I would support them, their businesses as well as being a helping neighbor. I would see a need and step in to help them. One time I was in desperate need of a trailer. Two different Mennonite neighbors had trailers that would have served my needs. Neither of them would allow me to rent or borrow their equipment.*

Cicela has plans to relocate DGM to a new space in Benton County, Missouri, which has a larger population base and is nearer to Kansas City, a large urban center. He is cognizant of the mistakes outlined above and is working to avoid those as he starts on his next journey. Unlike the Rutledge initiative, in the new space he has canvased the community including: The Chamber of Commerce, Homeschool Groups, Public Library, Public Schools, Boys and Girls Club and Other Businesses, looking for support and buy-in before establishing the new space. He noted that perhaps the biggest struggle will be finding a location for the space. He stated:

*I'm really trying to take the lessons learned from Rutledge. I hope to make a whole new set of mistakes rather than repeat the same mistakes. Property in Benton County is 5 to 7 times more expensive than rural Rutledge. It is a calculus problem that I will have to figure out how to solve in terms of getting into a suitable and affordable place.*

In the end Cicela does not regret his ambitions and work in Rutledge, and will use these lessons to establish a new space. He noted:

*Life isn't neat. It can be pretty sloppy, messy, random and unorganized, and that's sort of how I've gotten to where I am right now. All in all, I don't regret having put the energy into the DGM space. There's lots of good things that have come out of this space in the time that it was in operation.*

## REFERENCES

American Census Survey (ACS). (2016). *2012-2016 American Community Survey 5-Year Estimates*. Retrieved from https://factfinder.census.gov/faces/nav/jsf/pages/index.xhtml

Dancing Rabbit Ecovillage. (n.d.). *About*. Retrieved from https://www.dancingrabbit.org/about-dancing-rabbit-ecovillage-2/

Dyck, B., & Schroeder, D. (2005). Management, Theology and Moral Points of View: Towards an Alternative to the Conventional Materialist-Individualist Ideal-Type of Management. *Journal of Management Studies*, *42*(4), 705–735. doi:10.1111/j.1467-6486.2005.00516.x

Manzella, J. (2010). *Common Purse, Uncommon Future: The Long, Strange Trip of Communes and Other Intentional Communities*. Praeger. Retrieved from http://www.myilibrary.com?ID=272855

McBay, A., Keith, L., & Jenson, D. (2011). *Deep Green Resistance*. New York: Seven Stories Press.

Red Earth Farms. (n.d.). *About*. Retrieved from http://redearthfarms.org/about.html

## KEY TERMS AND DEFINITIONS

**Aquaponics:** The combining of aquaculture with hydroponics in a symbiotic environment.

**Deep Green Machines:** A former makerspace started by Frank Cicela in Rutledge, Missouri.

***Deep Green Resistance*: *Strategy to Save the Planet*:** A book McBay, Keith, and Jenson (2011), calls for the downfall of industrial civilization to save the planet.

**Little Free Library:** Free structures that hold books in communities where books are scarce.

**Mennonites:** Named after Milo Simons, are part of the Anabaptist movement based on the belief that baptism should be made by adults not infants.

**Rutledge Town, Missouri:** A small town in the Scotland County, Missouri.

# Chapter 14
# Columbia Gadget Works


## ABSTRACT

*Columbia Gadget Works is a small, community-based makerspace located in the town of Columbia, Missouri. Gadget Works began, and is still working under, a club model with a flat management structure and around 15 paying members. The space is located in one of the few industrial zoned areas of Columbia, and the building that houses the makerspace is owned by one of the members. Columbia Gadget works has been around since 2009 in various forms and met at members' houses and rented a space before settling into their current building. The onus of learning and forming communities is on members. However, in an attempt to develop a sense of community, the space offers open nights for members and non-members and has undertaken larger projects that require a substantial participation from members. The space struggles and at the same time is accepting of its slow growth and lack of equipment, for now. This chapter explores Columbia Gadget Works.*


DOI: 10.4018/978-1-5225-8310-3.ch014

*We have 15 members paying. I'd like to have 30 members paying. I personally don't ever see having 100 members paying. Even 30 is a lot. It's a whole other management idea when you have 30 people. Again, other people feel differently. They're like, "Let's get a bunch of members." Not everybody wants to do what you want to do, so would you rather have 15 people that have something in common that want to do something or 300 people with a core of 15 people that want to be makers and a bunch of other people that come that are customers. — Daniel Goldstein*

## ORGANIZATION BACKGROUND

Columbia Gadget Works, a community-based makerspace, is located in Columbia Missouri, home of the University of Missouri (MU). Founded in 1839, MU is an important economic anchor for Columbia, with more than 33,000 students and 13,000 employees (MU, n.d.). According to the US census the estimated population was 120,000 in 2016 (ACS, 2016). Daniel Goldstein, a member of the space, provided the author with a tour and spoke to the author about the Columbia Gadget Works. Operating in various forms the space has been around since 2009 and in the beginning, was tied to a university club then transformed into a Linux club that morphed into a maker club around 2010, when Goldstein joined. Goldstein is, what he refers to as, a recovering academic with a Ph.D. in engineering and now pursues his interests of sculpture and art. Goldstein's initial training in all things mechanical was derived from his time in a machine shop at Purdue University.

Prior to having a permanent space, Columbia Gadget Works rotated meeting locations amongst the different dwellings of members. Goldstein recalled:

*For a while ... We went through a period of meeting at different people's houses and that was both interesting and challenging. People get tired of ... It's like 25 people in your living room. It's hard to do anything when your location switches constantly and you're in people's living rooms. You just can't do anything. We had fun one night at Zack and Ryan's doing non-Newtonian fluids and blowing up speakers. You don't have a dedicated workspace though. You can do a lot of stuff but it's just limited.*

Around 2012, with about 15 permanent members, the group began their search for a location outside of members' houses. Initially the plan was to purchase a building with a few of the members pooling funds and renting the space out to other businesses. However, that plan quickly fell apart because, as Goldstein recalls, it was very difficult to organize, so members of Gadget Works decided to look for a space to rent. As members of Gadget Works were looking for a permanent location they soon realized that they would have to figure a vision for the space. Goldstein noted:

*When we were looking for, not this, but the space before, a group of us started going to look at buildings for rent, not a whole building, spaces … When we looked at the more expensive places, they were really excited. They really wanted to do it and they were enthusiastic. At one point, we were at one of the spaces that was really beautiful, that would've been great to get, and they said, "Okay, this is $600 a month base." Everyone was like, "We could teach classes and it'll work out. We can teach classes." We happened to have a really good turnout of the people at that ... We all went together to see it. I said, "Okay, who's going to teach a class? I know there are people here who are qualified." There's a couple college professors. There's people who used to work for Outreach.*

During this debate between lower cost space and a higher cost space Goldstein recalls asking the members who would dedicate their time and energy to teach and give the proceeds back to the space. He stated:

*I looked at them and I said, "Who is specifically going [to] teach a class and announce it the next month?" Pretty quickly people admitted that that's what they did in the daytime. They didn't really want to organize classes to bring in money and then start running it, where basically we can't pay the rent unless we either get much bigger very quickly or we start working for free and running classes and bringing people in and charging them, and nobody had a stomach for it. In a rare moment of maturity, because I've often been the one that ... These things come up and then I'm like, "Okay, I'll do it." I was like, "I don't want to teach classes right now. I've got other things in my life. I [am] busy.*

Gadget Works ended up renting a small garage located on the outer edge of town. It was the first time that the membership had a dedicated location. As members settled into their new location they began working together to build it out with shelves and storage areas, and at this time members were able to bring equipment to use in the space. While the space worked it soon became apparent members were outgrowing the location, and with no heat or air conditioning, it was uncomfortable to work in much of the time. After two-and-a-half years Gadget Works moved to their current location.

Interestingly, the current location of Columbia Gadget Works is owned by Goldstein, who purchased the building in November of 2016. Once the idea of a shared ownership model dissolved Goldstein began a search for a building that would provide space for his art and sculpture projects, and also provide a more suitable location for the makerspace. According to Goldstein he had a set of requirements that had to be met for the building, he noted:

*It took six months looking for this place, largely because of cost concerns, but I wanted to be [located] in town enough that younger people who don't drive out of town can get here. It's not right in the center of town but it's close. The highway is a divider and it's within that. There's very little industrial property … I was a little bit reticent to get into a situation where I buy a property and then try to go through a zoning battle to try to bring in a makerspace. I didn't want to be that above the radar. I just wanted some place where I could move in and be pretty-well covered so I was looking for commercial (C3), so more open commercial or here it's called manufacturing. There's very little of this in Columbia. I found this place and that's what led to this place.*

In addition to Columbia Gadget Works, six other entities rent space in the building. Some businesses are owned by members, including Purple School Games (well known for making wooden games, including the popular Mancala board game). Another entity in the space makes custom furniture, while another area is used by a contractor who does cabinetry and other art-based projects. Goldstein also has a space dedicated to his art and sculpture projects. Overall, the space is very busy with lots of equipment, tools and partially complete projects strewn about. The makerspace consists of an electronics room and space in the open garage area. There is room enough for expansion as the membership grows for Gadget Works. As the landlord, Goldstein worked with the space to ensure that they could build up the space and membership in a sustainable way by providing a reduced rent. Goldstein recalled the beginning agreement as:

*"Okay, let's give it a year and make sure that we can break even." They're breaking even now. We're trying to get a couple more memberships and as you*

*get a little bigger, you have to do a little more organization and accounting. We're working on that.*

At the time of the author's visit the space was in the process of attaining their US Internal Revenue Service (IRS) status as a non-profit 501(c)(3) business. Goldstein noted that they became a club first then began to seek additional members and slow growth. At the opposite end of the spectrum are those spaces that, according to Goldstein, start as a business while others start with a large community grant or government funding. He stated:

*I look at members as part of it, not as clients or customers, and we've had somewhat of people show up. It's like, "Can you do this for us?" We've had a loose policy of, if somebody shows up and says, "Hey, can you do some work on the laser cutter?" It's up to a member, either you take it on, you're the member, you're doing it. You can do a job for someone and charge them a little bit. We don't have any process for therefore then you pay this much to the maker space. It's up to you. Can you donate some of what you make? I tend to go the other direction. I had a friend that wanted to use the laser cutter for a really quick, neat, cloth sculpture project for a film festival. She'd go in for two months and set her up and she came in and used it. We got her going with membership and she got to use the machine, so there's different ways to try to make it work.*

The space is a mix of new and old equipment, although it appears that most equipment has been donated or acquired by individual members brought into the space for use. Goldstein recalls how two members visited spaces in Detroit Michigan and noted how they are "bootstrapping" the space by bringing in personal equipment. These same two members of the space proceeded to bring into the space a 40-watt laser cutter for members to use. The first 3D printer is also owned by one of the members and used by the space. Goldstein elaborated on bootstrapping the space with equipment:

*People have just been bringing in stuff. I brought in one of my band saws ... They also call me the safety czar and I've gotta do more because it scares me to death that people are gonna hurt themselves in here. I don't know how makerspaces deal with insurance. Both as a building owner and as a dad, and as someone that used to work in a machine shop years ago, I've worked in shops and I've seen bad things happen. It always scares me. Early on a couple moves ago, before we even had a space, a guy who was a member for ... I don't know. I think he came a couple times but someone else knew him and he's working out of a little company that was a California company working local and they bought him some shop equipment to fabricate some stuff. He was moving back to California. He was like, "My company said they don't want me to move this stuff but I can make a donation. They don't want to screw around selling it." We were like okay. I swung by with my trailer and we ended up with a little mill, a lathe, an old metal cut-off saw, a band saw. We've slowly acquired stuff, and, like I said, the band saw is my long-term loan. We just are slowly leapfrogging.*

Goldstein also noted the space has a philosophy of growing from the ground up. In this philosophy, members present voices and points of view but combined they have decided that the space will grow slowly and methodically. He noted:

*As far as equipment, some makerspaces are really equipment oriented. They come in. They take a big loan. There have been a number of groups locally here that had these grand plans. A group of students and they know people with money and they're gonna borrow a half million dollars and they're gonna buy tools. I always shake my head. Not that I don't think it's a good idea, just because I don't think it works in this market. I could be entirely wrong. It hasn't worked so far, but the next person could come along and make it work.*

Coming together as a space to purchase equipment in general has been elusive for members as they have a hard time agreeing on what should be purchased. As Goldstein noted, members were pushing to purchase equipment:

*We've had a hard time getting people to come together to buy stuff and it's been a little like pulling teeth because one person says we need a welder, we need this. Another person is like, that's not what I want to buy. So, we haven't really organized to the point that we're buying a lot of equipment. One of the things that I really want to do is to start putting a little money aside, so we can ... I love the laser cutter and those tubes don't last forever, so I want to have money aside so when it dies, we can get it back going right away. We've had people come by and join for a couple months just to use that which has been new, that people actually want to join for a piece of equipment.*

*Figure 1. Inside of Columbia Gadget Works*

*Figure 2. Tools*

Figure 1 is an image of the open making space inside Columbia Gadget Works. This open bay is available to members for creating larger projects and for storage.

In Figure 2 many of the tools and workbench is shown, as well as the entrance to the main work area.

Moving deeper into the walled-off section of CGW is the heart of the space that contains the laser cutter attached to the air handling system.

Also, as shown in Figure 4 the middle section of the space has some work areas and equipment storage on the outside walls.

On the outside walls, as shown in Figure 5, are clearly marked machines, computers and other supplies.

Organizationally, the space follows a flat management system where all members have a say in the direction of the organization. Goldstein defines the consensus building in the space as "chaotic." He also noted that they had not had a management meeting in months as many of the members are "scared of meetings" based on their previous experiences with organizations and their overbearing management structure. Goldstein does not have an

*Figure 3. Laser cutter*

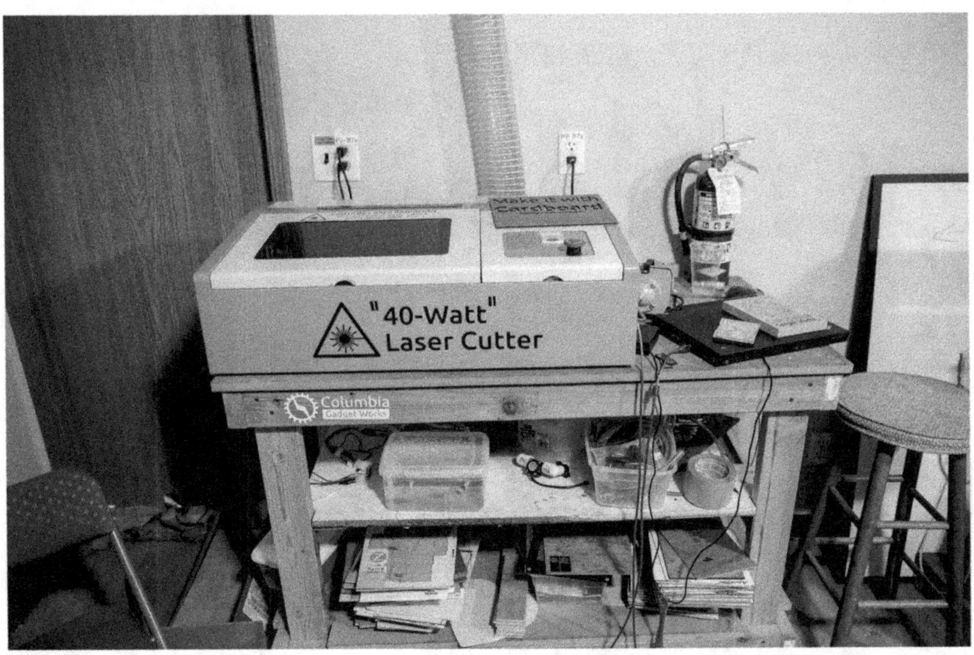

*Figure 4. Work area*

*Figure 5. CGW work areas*

official officer role in the space but does encourage members to organize to ensure the space is running smoothly. As he opined, he has learned a lot about how to organize the space from the younger members and somehow the space manages to function. Goldstein consciously decided not to take on a leadership role in the space for many reasons, he noted:

*The other aspect is this thing about things get done if one person takes it on. I didn't want to be that person in the makerspace. I've been that person in a lot of other things, where I have a bad habit of walking into things as an outsider and then pretty soon I realize I'm in the middle of running it. That's not a good thing. It's not like I have some great management skills. It's just that people like somebody who will say they'll do it. In the makerspace there was a point where they were looking for people to be officers. I remember having a discussion with my wife because I was getting off some of the city boards and commissions, and I was like, "I don't want another thing where I go from being somewhat involved to being chair to being the one running everything. I don't want to do that right now." I'm really happy I made that decision because I tend to be overbearing in that position because I organize everything. We are less organized but I think we're a much better organization because instead of having an organization that focuses around one person, we have an organization that really focuses around a group of people. There really is [sic.] four or five people who are actively involved in making it work. It's loose. It's disorganized.*

When asked about gaining the trust of the community Goldstein noted that the space does not have much contact with the community. Being in an industrial area of Columbia, Missouri there is very little housing in the area, reducing the chance that neighbors are annoyed or concerned with noise or activities within the space. With fewer than 20 members the space does not have a large footprint in the community. Open houses and other outreach events are conducted to bring in new members, but rarely within the specific neighborhood of the space. Goldstein went on to talk about trust through the story of Tom and Ray Magliozzi, the hosts of the Car Talk radio program that ran from 1987 to 2012 in the US. He stated:

*Back in the late 60s, 70s, they [Magliozzi brothers] had a community garage, where their idea was other people could come in and work on their cars and they had tools and they pay a little bit. They'd hang out and help people. It's interesting to hear them talk about it because they said that that worked for a while, but people really only wanted to a learn a little bit and then they wanted somebody else to do it. They'd be like, "Ray, I can't remember but can I just pay you to do this?" He'd do a brake job. Pretty soon they realized that the number of people who actually wanted to work on their own cars was pretty small. People basically wanted them to work on the car at a place that they trusted, so they turned from a co-op, essentially what we call a makerspace, an auto makerspace, to a service shop where they worked on people's cars because they found that's what people wanted. Some of the people that talk about everything is gonna be a makerspace and everyone is gonna be in a makerspace, missed the point that not everybody wants to be a maker.*

It's clear Columbia Gadget Works does not want to become a service center, but a space that allows members to grow in their skills and knowledge by pursuing their own personally meaningful projects. In fact, Goldstein recounts times when they have become annoyed with people dropping in to get advice and consultation on projects without becoming members. To be makerspace members you need to give back and contribute to the space. Goldstein recalled his experience with some visitors:

*It hasn't happened in a while but I got grumpy because basically, there were people who were like, "Hey, if I came in Thursday night, can I chat with someone for a couple hours and get free consulting?" I had a number of people who lighted on either me or a couple other people that have experience with certain areas and they're basically just looking for free consulting. So, I got to a point where I was like, "Okay, join for a month or two. Be part of the organization. Everyone wants to help but don't just come through for free consulting and leave." We actually had a number of people do that.*

The overall equipment list is provided in Table 1.

## SETTING THE STAGE

Columbia Gadget Works membership dues are generally $30 per month and had roughly 18 members at the time of the author's visit. Costs are extra for families and some members pay $50 a month, but it was not clear why they were paying the extra dues. To receive a key to the space, members need to be have been a paying member for two consecutive months. Goldstein noted that he implemented that rule as the landlord because he did not want to

*Table 1. Columbia Gadget Works Makerspace equipment*

| | | |
|---|---|---|
| **General workshop equipment** | Workbenches<br>Shop vacuum | Dust collection |
| **General Hand tools** | Corded drills<br>Oscillating saw | Cordless drills |
| **Woodworking** | Band saw | Miter saw |
| **Metalworking** | Welder<br>Bench Lathe | Bench mill<br>Band saw |
| **Fabrics** | Sewing machine | |
| **Plastics** | Vinyl cutters | |
| **Science** | Microscope | Vacuum oven |
| **Computing** | Linux/Windows computers | |
| **Digital fabrication** | 3D printer<br>CNC mill | CNC Lathe |
| **Electronics** | Soldering iron<br>De-soldering iron<br>Oscilloscope<br>Function generator | Multi-meter<br>Frequency counter<br>Variable power supply |

give out keys to someone who joins one night and then never comes back. The process "scares me every day," he noted, but has worked so far for the space. Membership provides access to the space 24 hours a day, seven days a week, access to tools and equipment, and the power to vote on issues brought forward. Google groups and Meetup are the two main programs used for communication between members. A Wiki page provides general information and other channels are used for communication, including an IRC and Trello. However, Trello and IRC had few entries and did not appear to be used by members.

To recruit new members, each Thursday is hack night which is open to the public and members are encouraged to bring visitors into the space. Usually the space will have up to four visitors experiencing the space during hack nights. Goldstein noted that they are looking to grow by a few members to help pay for the space. To join the space, recruits show up a few times to the Thursday Hack Nights and a member will ask if they are interested in joining. Next, they are encouraged to sign up using PayPal or an automatic bank withdrawal because, as Goldstein noted, it is hard to keep track of payments. He described the process to join:

*Show up a couple times until somebody says, "Hey, do you want to join?" Get them to sign up on PayPal or pay for a month. [We] try to get people to sign up on PayPal or bank deposit because otherwise people pay once or twice and they forget about it and it's hard to support an organization like that if revenue doesn't keep coming in every month. I take care of the access, so if somebody hasn't paid for a while I disable their card. We're pretty unorganized. It's kind of scary when I described it.*

There are no official classes listed on the Columbia Gadget Works website but Goldstein stated that they had been teaching a few classes around the three pieces of machinery that require training. These include the laser cutter, wood lathe and wood mill. Goldstein noted that he learned machining in a machine shop and the learning was very different from how Gadget Works members are taught. He recalled:

*After being pushed for two years, I finally did a class on the machine tools and I'll do more of those because it's just ... I joke that I have a hard time teaching machining because I learned in a machine shop. It was a university job shop over at Purdue. The teaching methodology was - there was an old guy would yell at you until you figured it out. Then if you did something wrong, they'd yell at you some more. Sometimes they just yell because it felt good.*

*Figure 6. Gender balance of visitors*

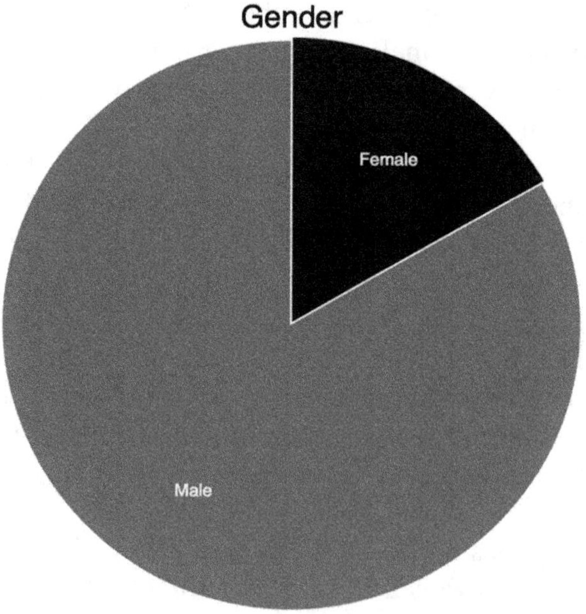

*You learn to take it. I haven't yelled at people when I've taught them. I had a lot of fun a couple weeks ago. I had four people in and we went through the basics of building and machining and I intend to do that regularly now.*

On average, Columbia Gadget Works will see 10 to 50 total visits per month. As shown in Figure 6, less than 20% of visitors are female.

The ethnicity of visitors is shown in Figure 7. About 80 to 100% are white, less than 20% are black or African-American, Asian, Native American, Alaska Natives, Native Hawaiians and other Pacific Islanders, and two or more races that may be included in the other ethnicities.

The types of users that visited the space are shown in Figure 8. Less than 20% are visitors or observers, 80 to 100% are hobbyists and less than 20% are youth under the age of 13.

*Figure 7. Ethnicity of membership*

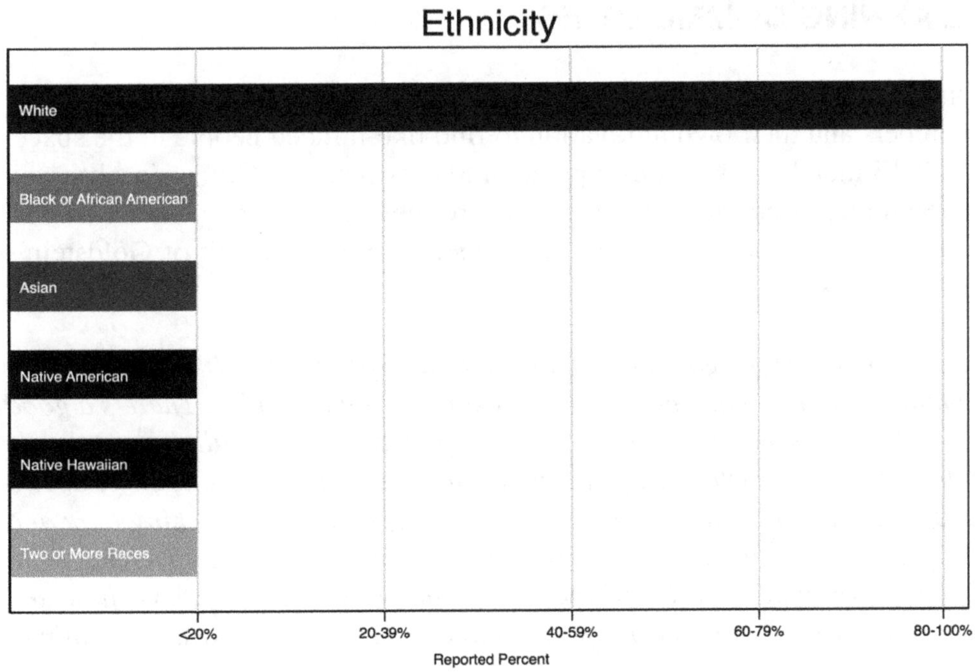

*Figure 8. Types of visitors per month*

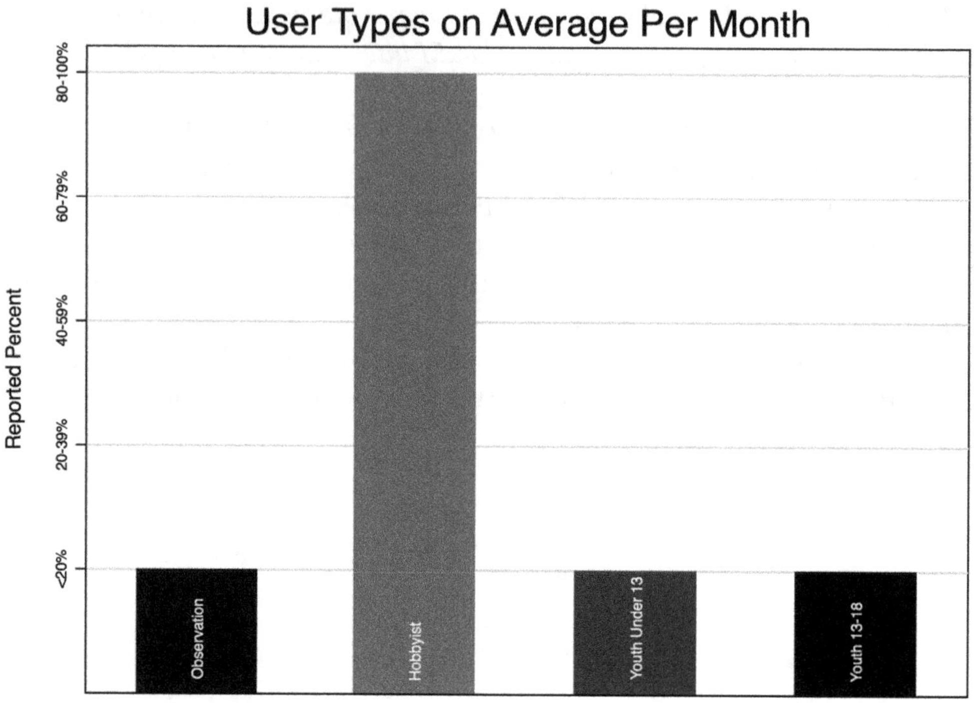


## LEARNING COMMUNITIES

Until three years ago the development of learning communities was up to members and their own motivation to find like-minded people in the space. With 15 members, small groups naturally formed, but Goldstein observed communities were not growing nor were they crossing content areas. The Open Thursday hack night was developed as a direct result of Goldstein's observations.

*About three years ago, starting in the other space, I felt like people were coming in, doing parallel play. I don't know if you have kids. There's a good age where kids get along great, they just play along in parallel, don't really interact. I noticed where I'd come in any night and there would be one or two people doing something here, one or two people doing something here and people didn't really ... There weren't that many of us but there wasn't a lot of cross pollination, so I instituted First Thursday of the month is show and tell ... It's what are you working on and do you need help with something?*

*Are you trying to look for something? Sometimes you have times where it really clicks. Someone is like, "I've been working on this" and someone else is like, "I bought some of those." Boom, you've got a little group of people working together.*

Goldstein noted that the First Thursday hack night program helped inform and connect members based on current interests and projects. Goldstein explained:

*Sometimes we all just talk about what we're doing and then we're like, okay. There's no real ... There's not a spark every month. But there have been some good collaborations because somebody talked about what they were doing on Thursday and other people were like, "I'm trying to do that too." We also encourage new people and non-members to come in on Thursdays, because it's a time that if someone is not a member, they can see what the membership is doing. If they're not a member and they're working on something, they can talk about it. That's a mixed thing because sometimes it works perfectly where someone is not a member. They come in, they're like, "Hey, I'm working on this," and someone else helps them and maybe they join or not.*

At the time of the author's visit, hack night were still open to non-members and members were encouraged to attend to learn more about what others were working on in the space. In this way learning communities are formed and reformed on a regular basis, based on members' projects and ideas presented during the Open Thursday nights. Goldstein explained:

*I always encourage people to be there for that because it's a time to introduce yourself and say what you're working on. Then beyond that, myself and other people have quietly, "Hey you should go talk to ..." Just putting people together. You should go talk to this person, they're doing similar stuff. But we haven't had anything as organized as explicit learning communities. There's some sub communities. There's a gaming sub community, where some of the guys are really into gaming and they show up on Saturday nights gaming or get a projector somewhere and watch a movie and that's a cool subgroup. I've tried to get some other groups going.*

Goldstein remarked that community is an essential part of the making experience. To learn, one must have a community with which to share and do things with community members. He related learning a language to learning a technical language. Goldstein then relates how difficult it is to learn a foreign language when you are not in a community and if there is no audience.

*I had a really hard time learning any language. My wife is French. I learned maybe half a dozen words in French before we went to France and ended up a two-week trip turned into a three and a half year stay, and I learned French the hard way, basically being there. You learn a language by having to community. I don't think it's any different with technical languages. You learn to do things if there's an audience and environment to do them.*

When asked what instruction looks like in the space, Goldstein stated that his philosophy is very much direct instruction. With a Ph.D. and a little teaching experience at the university level he believes that hands-on teaching is perhaps the best way to instruct members on the safe and proper use of the machines. In the certification courses members generally, all make the same item and receive a hands-on experience with the machine. Goldstein described the learning experience:

*Everyone touched the machine and ran the machine. To me, that's how you learn how to do something. I'm also really concerned about safety and sometimes I don't know how to tell everybody what they need to worry about, without watching them do it wrong. Somebody goes up to a machine and they've got their hoodie laces down, I'm like that's something. It's watching people do things and then just giving them feedback. I don't yell at people but it's similar to the old guys. I never did a machining class. I just started working there, running a forklift of a snag grinder and worked my way up to the job shop where I was machining stuff out of metal and plastic or whatever and just each job that I was willing to take, if I was willing to do it, someone would go, "You don't know how to do that." I'm like, "Well, teach me." If you were willing to say teach me, they teach you. Move to the next thing and keep your eyes open. That's how I learned, so that's how I teach. It seems to work. I've taught classroom, a little bit of fluid mechanics, a little bit of math. I don't have any real experience in that. I teach hands-on.*

In the space, certain machines are said to require training before members can use them, but as Goldstein mentioned the process of certification is very loose. Basically, there is an existing rule that requires members to ask another member if they do not know how to use a piece of equipment. Goldstein reflected on the certification process:

*It's been loose at this point, where the rule basically is if you don't know how to use it, ask. At first, that really worked because we didn't have that many people and people showing up and doing dumb stuff. It surprises me it's worked. We've had people, new members that have joined, and they're like, "Can I use the machine tools?" I'm like, "Well have you ever used them?" "Yeah, I used them in my dad's garage," and they tell me what they've done. Knock on wood, so far it's worked. But I see the limit to that. I see the need to ... Especially when you talk about a Bridgeport or bigger machines, to have some kind of threshold that somebody needs to show they can do something without hurting themselves.*

When asked if it was an expectation that members give back to the space Goldstein affirmed it was an implicit expectation. If a member knows how to run a machine then they are expected to instruct others. The mentoring system in the space has little structure and is informal. Members are working to make it more formalized with additional classes and teaching. In an interesting pivot Goldstein talked about how important community is to the younger members of the space and compared it to the self-focused in academia. He stated:

*We've got some 20-somethings that are, I think, just fantastic, as far as they're community focused. The idea of doing something for a community, as opposed to just themselves, which I think is really missing in this world. Academics were incredibly me, me, me. When I was around academia, everything was me, me, me. Coming from academia, I get around here and sometimes I'm just amazed that these young guys that aren't college educated, are incredibly smart, are hardworking and willing to share. They're willing to share their knowledge, willing to bring in a piece of equipment. I learned to be more laid back from them. I got away from academia. I was doing more research. I really wasn't teaching. I didn't teach and I always felt like something was missing in big classrooms. We've got a core of really good mid-20's guys; 20's, that are really the core of putting together a community. We have some older members. Of those 15 people, we've got a couple people that never show up but they're just quietly supportive. They see the long term. They keep paying their dues but they don't really show up.*

Like the training and certification process, the identification and promotion of members to experts in the space is not done in a systematic way. If a member asks for help, they will find it according to Goldstein. In other instances, when a member is messing about with equipment other members will watch and jump in to help when needed. The leadership team is looking at creating areas of responsibilities for experts in the space. One member, for example, oversees the electronics portion of the space and will help other members with projects and ensure that the work area is kept tidy. Goldstein stopped and said that as the interview progressed he felt that the space appears very unorganized. He ruminated that there are reasons for the slow growth and loose management practices in the space:

*I've been involved in groups, again not makerspaces so I don't know if it really applies, but I've been involved in groups that move too fast. A club years ago that always wanted to be bigger so we kept going to bigger spaces. Then eventually it imploded because people kept ... At that point, it was somebody didn't pay the taxes for three years. There's always a reason but if you move too fast, you don't have the organizational resources and you don't have a base. Then it really becomes a startup where you meet a small group of people that take responsibility. I visited a makerspace up in Vancouver. It's a guy that started a business. He hired four, maybe five, people that work for him and they've got a big building. Half of the space is really small makers and companies renting from him and then there's the makerspace area. He financed buying a bunch of equipment and they seem to be doing okay, but they're very much a management-customer model. When I was up there, they were shocked at the idea of running a makerspace as a club.*

As previously mentioned, the space has a number of communication channels—some more active than others. Goldstein revealed that communication between members has been a struggle in the space. They have tried various channels like Meetup and Trello; neither are used by the membership regularly. A list-serve was also started but soon Goldstein realized non-members could get the same information as members, thereby reducing their motivation to join. The space is now experimenting with Slack as a communication tool for members. Goldstein talked about the challenge of communication and switching platforms to reach members:

*Fragmented communications have been an issue. I've been involved in a lot of, not makerspace related groups, but different political groups and often I've ended up, because I do computer stuff, being the guy that makes a list serve or tries to put something together and as soon as you get one thing working, it's like clockwork. Somebody else is like, "Hey, I found something new." They want to open another channel of communication. I'm like, "We have a list-serve." That's so old school. This is so new. I'm like, "Wait a second. It took us three years to get a core of people on a list-serve and boom, you want to go to something new. Slack was like that but it's worked so far. Anymore, things get communicated either via the list serve or Slack. That's the chief challenge.*

When asked about the maker mindset and the idea of learning from and allowing failure in the space, Goldstein reflected that he has a strong personal philosophy in the area. In particular, there is an emphasis on learning by doing and that includes pure discovery-type learning by taking artifacts apart to learn subsystems and how they work. This learning philosophy can be frustrating to adults, especially when younger learners are taking things apart, but in the end, according to Goldstein, it is a powerful learning tool. He relates a story of an experience with his own children:

*Which can be somewhat frustrating with kids, but my kids always took stuff apart, to the point where they took stuff apart and I was like, "Okay. I wasn't expecting it to be apart," and I'm like, "That was good." I always tell the story, my youngest was in Montessori school for years. At a Montessori school, one of the things they do is cut things. You cut things apart, when they're young. One day we have friends over and we're all sitting around and I had this lace doily thing over a table, so it was all these crocheted lace pieces. They were all connected. There was a snowflake piece and there was this big piece. It was a beautiful piece and Luke comes in one day. He's got his scissors and he's got all the pieces stacked together and he puts them down on the table and I look at it and I go, "Didn't that use to be a big tablecloth?" He looked at me and he goes, "I cut it apart." The people who we were with were just beside themselves. They were waiting for this explosion and I just laughed and laughed. They were like, "What are you laughing at?" I'm like, "It makes perfect sense to him because in Montessori school, they cut stuff apart and here's these beautiful snowflakes and they're all together and he just cut them apart." It was so funny. He started looking uncomfortable when I was laughing. I was like, "No, no, no. It's really okay." It makes perfect sense.*

Taking stuff apart within a community offers interest as well, according to Goldstein. Deconstruction and learning is done in a social context as a way to share knowledge and the experience. Youth are particularly proficient in taking items apart and when they join a community, as did Goldstein's children, they begin to build and explore. Goldstein recalled another one of his children's experience:

*I guess that's what you'd call learning communities in a way, but he had a community where his experience in taking things apart or fixing things and building a quadcopter and flying all of a sudden was really valuable. He became part of that community. I realized how much he was really part of it when he left for college and the others really sad to see him go. He was part of their community. When he comes back, everyone is looking forward to him coming back.*

Eventually, according to Goldstein, the cycle of taking things apart comes around to the point where learners will begin to put things together and building new knowledge. Goldstein recounted that both his sons benefited from this learning process and are in engineering areas. In the space, members have hosted take-apart days and asked them not to worry about breaking things. The exercise is about tearing into equipment like old printers, to see how they work. According to Goldstein:

*You bring in a big old printer that you can get at auction for five bucks and there's a good power supply, good motors and there's good shafts and bearings. Just taking stuff apart, some of the young people just go nuts. They're like, "I get to take it apart?" It always leads to ... It's stepper motors and different kinds of stepper motors and power supplies. You show them that this is a good power supply and what are you going to do with it? Anything you need 24 volts for, we've got a power supply now. I've always encouraged people to do that. Again, you have that line where some people take things apart that are functioning and it's like, no, we don't have another drill, don't take it apart. One guy who's a real doofus, he always takes apart the wrong thing, and he's an adult, or should be. I love taking stuff apart. That's how you learn and that's how you learn how things work and you learn about gears and you learn about stuff.*

Failure is another area that Goldstein believes is important for learning. Failure is a tool and members of the space are coached not to impede or comment on the work of others in the space. To an extent, members are not allowed to make judgements regarding project failure. Likewise, members are asked to withhold judgement on the legitimacy of projects and do not ask why the project is being attempted. He stated:

*As far as failing, I try and everybody else tries to be supportive of, if you fry something, there's an unsaid rule: don't laugh at people. If somebody says, "I want to build this," I always try really hard to enforce the rule about don't ask why. You don't get to ask why, because people have projects and it's just for the fun of it, or it's just because they want to. A couple of people have built aluminum smelting ovens that are ... There's always a better way to do something but it's fun to build something just for the heck of building it. That's my philosophy. I think people pretty much follow ... Don't give other people a hard time for their projects.*

Gender balance is very much skewed towards males in the space and is an issue the membership has spent time contemplating. They have had a few female members off and on, but the space has not been able to keep them as members over the long-term. Starting off as a club with mainly male membership, the space may on outward appearances look like it is not welcoming towards women. One attempt to attract women to the space was the establishment of a sewing studio and talk of expanding that area. Goldstein noted that there is an important concept of making as a technical endeavor versus making as a form of art. He suggested that with more of an art focus woman would be more amiable to joining the space:

*Again, I wear all hats. I do techie stuff but I've been doing art since I was in high school. I took a little detour to get a PhD and do academia but now I'm back to doing sculpture and art, so I would like to get more people from the art bent and add a little bit of collaboration and more art-oriented people involved, and I think there are more women in those groups who would be willing and interested to be part of the group. I think a group has a different dynamic when it has women involved, in a positive way. That's always lacking in our group. We started as a group of guys. It just worked that way. I think that many of us would like that to evolve away from that. We're not quite there yet.*

The space has also encouraged women to teach classes to get more females involved. CGW offered a jewelry making class under the tutelage of a local artist. Unfortunately, the courses did not last because as Goldstein put it, "This isn't her crowd. She doesn't really have a reason to be here." Women are welcomed and encouraged to become members of the space but Goldstein believes there is no community within the space that draws them in.

*Figure 9. The cardboard boat project*

Few barriers exist between learning communities in the space but because of the small number of members, these communities remain fairly small and members are working on disparate projects. To get the entire membership to work together the space has engaged in larger projects that require the member base to work together. In 2013 the space entered the cardboard boat fundraiser as shown in Figure 9.

Goldstein recalled:

*The cardboard boat was one of the first projects that ... I have a hard time doing things simply so the other space, somebody talked about doing this cardboard boat race. It's a fundraiser that's local. They brought some boxes in and then I got involved and totally took over it, which I probably shouldn't have. That was a lot of fun. I focused that and different people came in and helped, so we put that together. That was a good group effort. That was fun, and we won the races. We did really well. It was nice.*

Goldstein reflected on a number of artifacts that have been developed in the space. These group-led projects are important in creating learning communities and developing comradery within the space. The cardboard boat project was the first community-wide project for the space and involved a number of members. As a local fund-raising project, the group was charged with building a boat, out of cardboard, that would float with a certain number of members on board. As the first all-member function, Goldstein cited a number of mistakes and organization improvements made from the experience. He noted:

*I learned a lot about organizational stuff and I know how things are supposed to work, and I've never seen them work that way. I've never seen a project here or other places that doesn't happen because one person, and maybe one person and a friend of theirs, really wants it to happen. I would like to say for the boat building we had a club and we had meetings. No - I did everything wrong. We had a couple people interested. They brought some boxes in that had simple ideas. I brought my canoe in as a plug mold and said, "No, let's do it this way," and started working. Some other people helped. Other people were sane enough to go on with their lives. I spent every day for about five weeks building that. Then other people would come in for a couple days and help.*

There came a point in the building process where members began to recognize the value and feasibility of the project and then chose to participate. At the onset of the project Goldstein may not have adequately shared his vision for the project, but as it was revealed to members they contributed their time and talents. He noted:

*As it got close to done, and people realized I wasn't crazy, that this thing actually was going to get done and float, then there was a burst of energy. The dragon heads were envisioned by a five-year-old. His dad and I were talking about what to put on it. Everyone had a different idea and I looked at him and I said, "What does the boat need?" He goes, "It needs dragons." Dragons it is! Everyone looked at me like, aren't we going to vote. No. He says it's gonna be dragons. We're gonna do dragons.*

Different members with unique skillsets collaborated to create and paint the Dragon figureheads perched at the front of the boat as shown in Figure 10.

*Figure 10. The cardboard boat figurehead*

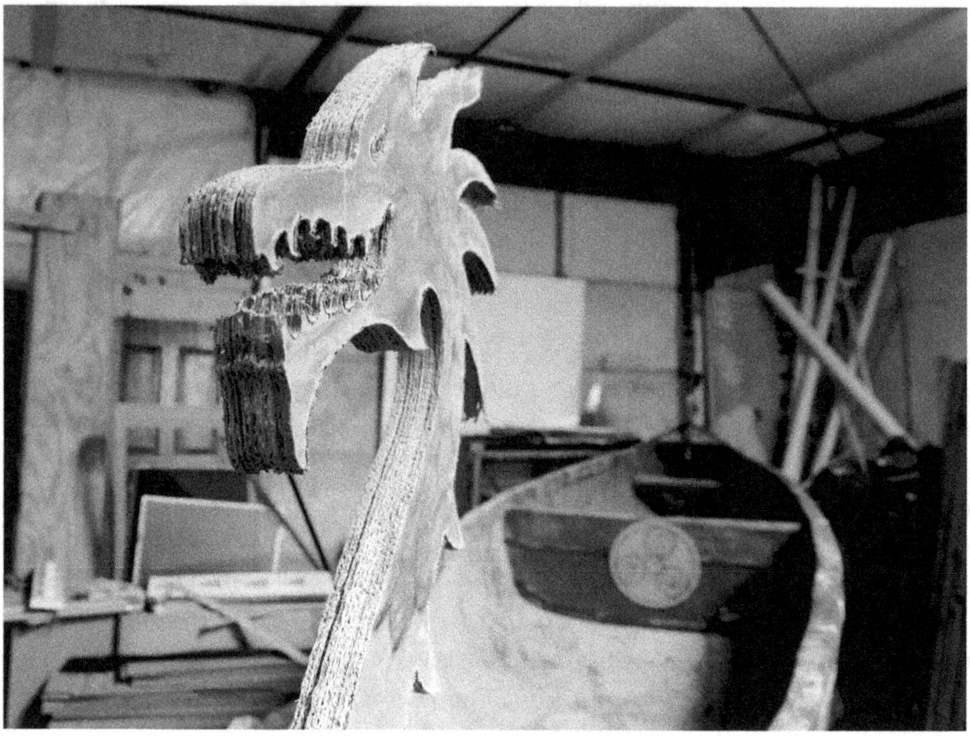

In another site-wide project members had toyed with the idea of releasing a high-altitude balloon filled with hydrogen gas. Like the boat project, the balloon project was slow to grow legitimacy in the space but once started it galvanized members. To begin the project a sub community was formed, and they contributed a small amount of money to order supplies to get started. These site-wide projects require a leader: someone to be in charge of the projects. According to Goldstein they have not figured out how to manage or at least start large projects by committee. Goldstein recounted the story of the high-altitude balloon.

*We did a high-altitude hydrogen balloon, which was a cool project. The guys actually wanted to do hydrogen, not helium, and it scared me. I said, "Okay, we can do hydrogen but I'm in charge of safety and filling." So, I did a bunch of research. The night before we did it, I talked to a friend that's a biologist and I said, "Have you ever worked with hydrogen?" He goes, "Yeah, it's not that bad." I said, "So what precautions did you take?" It's like, "Well, I've never actually gotten the experiment to complete because it always blows up." So, I've got this big cylinder of hydrogen. We had filler tanks and I had ground rods pounded in. I had copper wire going through all the filling tubes. I was scared to death and that part came flawlessly. (We) filled it, we got the electronics on it. We made some circuit boards. We had cameras on it. It went up and we had these two radios on it. It went up enough and we had visual sight. It was transmitting for about 28 minutes and then it went dark.*

*We looked for it. Literally, some of us spent days crisscrossing the countryside, trying to figure out where it might have come down. We had some vague hints that it pinged a couple times on the way down. I think it just broke up in the air and came down. Fully one year later we got a ping from the GPS locator. He had that (a spot GPS locator) up on it and it was supposed to keep transmitting. What basically happened is it went up, it got too cold. Everything shut down and what we didn't realize is when it started to come down, and at that point, I think the case had broken up, so it was in free fall. Those things didn't restart, so it was a learning experience. A year later, on the website, this guy gets an email that's like, your latest location ... He's like, "What?" A couple of them jump in and they drive out, like 30 miles away where they got this and they get some farmer's field. The [farmers] dog basically brings them out to it. He's sniffing around and it's got chew marks on it. So as far as they can tell, this thing free fell down because it never restarted. The dog picked it up, turned it on, by clicking the button and it had just enough battery to ping the satellite a couple times. They found the spot device, never found anything else. We had go pro camera, radios. Everything is gone. That was a fun group project.*

## YOUTH IN THE SPACE

Columbia Gadget Works permits youth in the space under the age of 13 when they are accompanied by an adult. The space however, during normal business hours, does not make allowances for youth. Youth are treated like adults and are expected to follow basic machine safety rules, while at the same time guide their own learning. Goldstein recalled, in the past, parents have wanted to drop youth off and the membership has been adamant in rejecting the presence of youth in the space without an adult. The un-school group organized by parents and a few members of the space did hold learning activities but have not met in the space for a considerable time. Goldstein described how youth get absorbed into learning communities:

*We have a lot of people who show up once or twice, with a parent that's obviously very non-technical and a young kid that has a general interest. The kid usually seems very happy because people are willing to show them everything they're doing but they [youth] tend not to really get involved because there's not really a path. I will admit that for a young kid to get involved in this group, they have to be independent and they have to have a certain amount of confidence to ask people and do things.*

Goldstein observed that youth in the space are more inclined to work with members that are not their parents. For the youth, it can be a creative outlet to explore areas that their caretaker might not be interested in or have the experience to teach. One member and his son bought a 3D printer and left it in the space and worked with community members to build the printer. The son was more interested in the printer and was able to work with Gadget Works members to build and gain insight on using the machine.

The space has not embraced youth as members and has considered ways to offer a learning pathway for youth. He acknowledged:

*We may get to the point where we're a little more organized in bringing kids in, but at this point, we've had a lot of people that come once or twice and don't come back. We feel a little bad about that, but then again, there's this model of, if you're looking for clients or customers, you worry if somebody doesn't come back. Some people worry about that. Again, it's not monolithic. I look at it as I'm already busy and I already wear enough hats that I don't really want clients or customers. I like collaborators and some of those collaborators can be 15 years old. That's fine. They're smart kids, but I do see us moving toward doing classes because I think that you can't really support a space just on a club of people. You need to bring in people who are willing to pay for the class. It's also a way to get more members as people learn, so we'll see what happens.*

## FAMILIES IN THE SPACE

When asked about families in the space Goldstein noted that they have had some families attend in the past. He recalls four families, including his own frequenting the space over the past few years. The space has not done a lot of family outreach events, so they don't have high expectations of family visits or membership. Goldstein's son attended the space but from the onset wanted to do his own thing and not solely work with his father. During their time in the space, his son was working with another community of learners or, as Goldstein describes it, was "telling me I was doing something wrong."

## IMPACT ON THE COMMUNITY

Columbia Gadget Works is meant as a place where creative people can come together, make, learn and be a part of a community, according to Goldstein. It's also about providing a space for people in the community who are willing to join and contribute to the maker movement. Overall, however, the space has not done a lot of outreach to the community and therefore does not have a large impact on the overall community within Columbia, Missouri. The space has not directly created any businesses but there are entrepreneur minded members that have established businesses in the same building that give support to other members of the space. There are a few members that are using the space for entrepreneur endeavors and are working towards starting businesses. The space has had a profound impact on Goldstein's life. He described the impact as:

*What I'm doing, I wouldn't have done if it was in the makerspace but it's art sculpture projects that I'm doing for art shows and it's not something I make that much money at. Probably the only real business example that's spun out is me buying this building and running that because I might have done it otherwise, but I was really motivated because I wanted the makerspace to end up in a nicer space. I was very motivated to make that happen. That gave me a reason. I decided it was worth running my money at the building and then I paid to build out this space for them. It's not totally altruistic. I'm renting to them, so I'm making some money but I'm not going get rich at it. It's been a good thing for me.*

While Goldstein could not speak about the impact on others in the space, he felt that the impact of the makerspace on him personally was dramatic. He started a company because of the space and was able to part from academia and spend time with his children and pursue his art and sculpture. In addition, the impact on his children and their participation in the Gadget Works community was a positive experience for them from technical and the social considerations. Goldstein related how the space impacted his son:

*I think he got a lot of confidence because when he was growing up, I always let them take stuff apart and I rarely bought them stuff. When he was 16, he saw little plastic quadcopters and he wanted a big one and he was looking at big expensive ones, so the agreement was, I said, "I'll buy you the parts." I bought him a pile of electronics and motors and wires and everything he needed, minus a frame and a working thing. He had to choose all the parts. He went from a pile of parts to a beautiful tri-copter that just flew better than anything I've ever seen.*

*They're really different than quadcopters because they have a tail motor that tilts, so it can rotate like a plane, like a plane tail. A quadcopter tends to be flat. A tri-copter, I've only seen a few people do this, but he flew it really aggressively. He was fearless with it because he can fix it. We built it out of bamboo flooring for the arms, which is a great material. It's really high-quality bamboo and a couple plywood plates for the body. He would fly that aggressively. The street in front of our house, totally tree lined. This is not a safe place to fly anything and this thing was big. He would fly it down the street and do high speed hammerheads where you'd go ... Flip it around. That was a great learning experience for him because he took a pile of parts and he made something that functioned. Everyone loved it and he was real proud of it. He did that while we were members here, so as he was putting stuff together, some of the other guys who had flown more and had a little more experience, he was able to talk to them. Then really quickly he realized at 16, that he was the expert. He was on par with the other people who had flown. When other people would come in, he would be like, "No, no, no." He was teaching other people and people would buy quadcopters or buy a pile of parts and they wouldn't get it to work and he would work on it with the other people. He wasn't the only expert but he quickly realized that he had expertise. I think that was a really big thing, and the same thing in a lot of areas.*

## DEFINING A MAKERSPACE

When asked to define a makerspace and the core components of a makerspace, Goldstein responded:

*I guess I would define a makerspace as a place that people can go and it helps them make things but I don't think beyond that, there's very different models. The model of the guy in Vancouver, that was a makerspace that was a business. There's makerspaces that are totally a business that you pay money and there's employees. It's like joining a gym. If you want to use the elliptical machine, they show you how to use the elliptical machine and they send you off. The same thing if you want to use the mill, you pay the mill class and they put you on the mill and you're a customer. That's totally legitimate. They all look different.*

*I would say what defines this makerspace is a community of somewhat like-minded people that you can get help from and sometimes that just being outside of your own world. I did projects with my kids for years. I built model airplanes. I built electronics, all sorts of stuff. I had a little crossover but we weren't really a model airplane club because I didn't really like what they were doing here. We did LEGO club and a couple things. But honestly, the business side of why I started here, as far as the building and renting, would not have happened if it wasn't for my connection with the makerspace, because I went from doing stuff with the kids, to vague ideas of doing stuff that I wanted to do, to having a community of people that when I wanted to do or machine control or things I hadn't done as much, other people had done so there was crossover.*

*More than that, in academia, you have a structure. Your grad students have to come to a meeting and say what they've done and they have to produce a document. They have to write that thesis at the end of three, four, five years. You have this focus but when you're a maker and you're making any project [you want]. If you don't have someone to show it to, and if you don't have someone to ask questions but even if you're capable of doing it yourself entirely, it's really lonely to just build stuff yourself. Especially for people who come out of academia, because when I worked in a machine shop and when I worked with blue collar people, there was more of a, you built that, cool. You go look at it, but in academia, I didn't see that and all of a sudden, I had a place. One of the reasons I started the Thursday night show and tells is because I had a deadline. I wanted to show something on Thursday night, so projects that kicked around, I had a motivation to finish it enough to show people.*

*I think that served the same purpose for other people. I say, it is a place that helps people making things and helping people make things can be a community to show it to: motivation. It can be a piece of equipment like the laser cutter, the 3D printer, the mill. It can be help technically. I want to do something but I haven't done it before. It can be, this is something that I want to do but I don't have time to do myself so a couple people might get together and do it, so helping people make things takes all sorts of different forms. I think within that definition of makerspace, there's a whole bunch of different models and they're all equally legitimate. There's completely different uses of the term, which have nothing to do with what I call makerspace.*

*Some makerspaces, there was a group locally that were the local entrepreneurs club. They all wanted to come together at a conference table and make a million dollars. That was the goal. That's fine. It doesn't interest me. They consider the term makerspace as they're going to make a company. That's not how I look at it. I look at it as you're going to make things. It might be software. It might not be physical things but you're going to make things and that might end up leading to a company. It's really about making things whether it be art or just for the fun of it or learning something.*

Goldstein went on to discuss how terminology is abused. The makerspace movement has enjoyed a great deal of momentum and popularity; that many activities have subscribed to the name and yet they really don't fit the makerspace model. He was incredulous that schools, especially the university, would have a makerspace. He stated:

*Schools have a makerspace. The university has a makerspace. It's like, you're a university, what do you mean you have a makerspace? This is a place where people can come in and learn. It's like, you're a university. The whole damn thing is supposed to be a place where people can come in and learn. If it uses a certain technology, they call it makerspace; 3D printers are a makerspace, but we've had a couple different groups that have been in town that have come to talk to us because they're starting a makerspace. There's been a couple of them that I call conference room makerspaces. They have a conference room and they have a space and a table, and they make a makerspace. One was related to journalism. One was related to small business. I don't know if we have any more right to the word than they do, but it has nothing to do with what I call a makerspace.*

According to Goldstein even public funding gravitated to the moniker of a makerspace. In his experience policymakers have little understanding about the maker movement. The city offered to fund the space but, as Goldstein noted, he was skeptical of the public funding. He stated:

*With the city [Columbia] at one point, the city economic development people, they got tired of breathlessly giving tax breaks and then somebody told them they needed a makerspace, so they breathlessly were like, "We need to make a makerspace right away. It's amazing."*

*I was like, so what do they want in return? Nothing, they're just giving us money. This is a city. It's like, if you become part of the city, you're a municipal space. Completely different from what we were doing, and they had no idea what a makerspace was. It was a checkbox in a grant application or a checkbox in a company. They were going to these conferences to go throw tax breaks at companies and the companies were like, "Okay, do you have a park? Do you have a bike route? Do you have a makerspace?" They wanted to check it off, so they wanted to have a makerspace. That worried me because I've seen organizations bubble and die when they get involved with people who just want a checkbox. Some people look at that as a missed opportunity, I look at it as we dodged the bullet getting involved with them.*

In another observation Goldstein talked about the desire of makerspaces to reinvent everything from scratch. He shared a story of building an arc lamp in the space and how they needed carbon rods. As a site-wide project they had plans to meet on a Saturday and purchase a number of D cell batteries and take them apart to get at the carbon rods. Then Goldstein said:

*Having worked at a shop, it just occurred to me, I'll bet this is something a welding shop has. Maybe it's expensive, so I go to a local welding shop and I'm like, "Yeah, we're going to make an arc lamp. Do you have carbon rods?" He's like, "How many do you want?" I said, "How much are they?" I'm thinking like $25 a piece. He's like, "$1.90 each. How many do you want?"*

*The maker movement wants to reinvent everything, like a lot of movements and there's a lot of good to that because you reimagine things and you rethink things. It just annoys me sometimes when people want to reinvent something from scratch. It's just like, read outside a little bit of your little thing. There are people who do this for a living. Some of what makerspaces are trying to do, there are already businesses that do those things. You might be able to do it better but don't be naïve and pretend there's nothing or no one else that does that.*

## CURRENT CHALLENGES

The juxtaposition of needing to grow and wanting to stay small is a challenge for Columbia Gadget Works. On the one hand members and Goldstein do not want to dedicate time and resources for running a large organization, yet on the other they want to be able to pay for the space and eventually expand and garner additional machinery. They are makers in the truest form and want to make and create and deal less with organizational details. The flat structure requires members to volunteer to take care of certain areas. If this is not done, then the whole space suffers. Accounting and collection of monthly fees, for example, is vital to the space and yet takes considerable time and effort. Goldstein shared this experience:

*One of the real big problems in a small organization is details. Who takes care of the details? We're just a club. David [a member] took over the accounting and I started asking questions about how many people pay, this and that. He gave me numbers. I'm like, "That doesn't make sense. I know people have been paying for years." He's like, "No, they haven't been paying." I'm said, "Okay, if I know they've been paying, they told me they're paying, we're not getting the money." So, if you don't have anyone who's very proactive, people could be members and just their PayPal runs out and they don't pay. No one is doing anything wrong. You can't run an organization like that. That's one of the things we've been running into. We're trying to go through our books more regularly. How many people are paying? Who's paying? Who stopped paying? Did they want to stop paying?*

Moving beyond a small club-orientated space would require additional organization around learning, and possible the development of certification courses as more members filter into the space and use the equipment. There is also an issue of growth and tools. How can the space attract new members without a large inventory of tools and machines? And how can the space purchase new tools and expand without new members?

## REFERENCES

American Census Survey (ACS). (2016). *2012-2016 American Community Survey 5-Year Estimates*. Retrieved from https://www.census.gov/quickfacts/fact/table/columbiacitymissouri/BZA010215#viewtop

MU. (n.d.). *About.* Retrieved from http://missouri.edu/about/

## KEY TERMS AND DEFINITIONS

**Bootstrapping:** To get out of a condition using existing resources.

**Car Talk:** A popular US National Public Radio (NPR) radio program.

**Columbia, Missouri:** City located in central Missouri home of the University of Missouri – Columbia.

**Columbia Gadget Works:** Makerspace located in Columbia, Missouri.

**Direct Instruction:** A teaching method whereby the instructor provides content to students, usually in a lecture format.

**Figurehead:** A carving or bust located at the front of a ship.

**Google Group:** Online Google program that allows you to create and participate in online forums and email-based groups with a rich experience for community conversations.

**Hack Night:** A night open to the public and a venue for members to share projects.

**Mancala:** A two-player board game played with stones or beans with holes in the board.

**Non-Newtonian Fluid:** A fluid that does not follow Newtonian physics.

# Appendix 1

## MAKERSPACE MULTIPLE CASE STUDY

Dear makerspace facilitator:

Purpose of the Research: The Makerspace Multiple Case Study project is looking at how learning is structured in makerspaces. The goal of this multiple case study is to provide a better understanding of how collaborative learning communities support a successful making experience. The data collected will help us document the different models of learning found in makerspaces. You are invited to participate because you are 19 years of age or older and implement a makerspace site. Procedures: You will be asked to complete one survey asking about your makerspace and how it is set up which will take approximately 15 minutes of your time. You will also be asked to participate in an interview that will take up to 2 hours of your time. By reading this notice and completing the form you are telling us you want to be included in the study. You are free not to participate in this study or withdraw from the study at any time without adversely affecting your relationship with the investigator, 4-H, or the University of Nebraska. Your decision will not result in any loss of benefit to which you are otherwise entitled. Sometimes participants have questions or concerns about their rights. In that case, please contact the UNL Institutional Review Board at 402-472- 6965 or irb@unl.edu. If you do not wish to participate in this study or have any questions about this survey, please contact the investigator of this study, Dr. Bradley Barker, at 402-472-9008 or bbarker@unl.edu. Thank you for your time and interest; it is greatly appreciated.

Original questions came from the Nesta (http://www.nesta.org.uk/blog/mapping-uk-makerspaces-building-useful-data- set) survey through the CC Attribution-ShareAlike 4.0 International (CC BY-SA 4.0). More details here:

## Part 1: About You

Description (optional)

1. First Name, Last Name *

Short answer text ________________________________

2. Your email address *

Short answer text ________________________________

3. Your relationship to the space you're going to tell us about, e.g., are you a member, manager, founder, etc.

Long answer text ________________________________
After part 1 Continue to next section

## Part 2: About Your Makerspace

### Basic Makerspace Information

1. Name of makerspace *

Short answer text ________________________________

2. Website/URL *

Short answer text ________________________________

3. Twitter

Short answer text ________________________________

4. Facebook

Short answer text ________________________________

5. Phone Number

Short answer text ______________________________

6. Address

Long answer text ______________________________
__________

7. Postcode

Short answer text ______________________________

8. Type of location *
    a. Permanent location (Library)
    b. Permanent location (Community-based)
    c. Permanent location (School-based)
    d. Temporary location
    e. Mobile makerspace
    f. Other…
9. Physical space, access, and facilities

Description (optional) ______________________________

10. What access do people have to the space?
    a. Member (or key holder) access any time
    b. Member (or key holder) access in set hours
    c. Bookable time
    d. Access by appointment only
    e. Public access any time
    f. Public access for special events only
    g. Public access for courses or training only
    h. Other …
11. Notes on access rules

Description (optional) ______________________________

12. Are there any special conditions about access (e.g., level of training required, or probation periods)?

Long answer text ______________________________

---

13. Please tell us about your membership fees (e.g., what rates do you charge, how are fees levels structured, what levels of access are offered at each?

Long answer text ______________________________

---

14. Amenities / facilities

    a. Long-term project storage
    b. Shared kitchen
    c. Bookable event space
    d. Social, nonworking area
    e. Reception desk or area
    f. Toilets
    g. Café on site
    h. Library
    i. Wi-Fi
    j. Offices or incubator space
    k. Other …

## Tools and Equipment

We'd like to get as comprehensive a list as possible of your tools and equipment. We've created some top-level categories that cover most kinds of making. If these make sense to you, please use them. If not, there's a box at the beginning where you can add all of your tools in one go.

What should you list? Anything down to the scale of hand tools. We don't need to know how many pencils you have, but even small tools like sewing needles, chisels, or soldering irons can give a good picture of the types of making people can do at your space.

Of course, if you've got a lathe or a forge, we want to know about that too!

If you've a list of your tools and equipment, feel free to copy and paste it here (instead of answering the following questions).

Long answer text ______________________________

---

1. General workshop equipment (e.g., Workbenches, sinks, vacuum cleaners, dust/fume extraction)

   Long answer text ______________________________________________

2. General Hand tools (powered) (e.g., Drill, circular saw, hand sander)

   Long answer text ______________________________________________

3. Woodwork (e.g., Band saw, table saw, router)

   Long answer text ______________________________________________

4. Metalwork (e.g., Welder, forge)

   Long answer text ______________________________________________

5. Fabrics (e.g., Knitting machine, loom, sewing machine)

   Long answer text ______________________________________________

6. Ceramics (e.g., Potters wheel, kiln)

   Long answer text ______________________________________________

7. Plastics (e.g., Vacuum former, vinyl cutter)

   Long answer text ______________________________________________

8. Glass (e.g., Shears, knives, moulds)

Long answer text ______________________________________

__________

9. Painting and graphic arts (e.g., Canvas stretchers, easels, lightbox)

Long answer text ______________________________________

__________

10. Science, Synthetic Bio, Chemistry (e.g., Centrifuge, microscope, pressure

Long answer text ______________________________________

__________

11. Computing (e.g., Computers, server, data backup, drawing tablet, kinect

Long answer text ______________________________________

__________

12. Digital fabrication (e.g., 3D scanner, 3D printer, laser cutter, CNC mill, robotic assembly

Long answer text ______________________________________

__________

13. Electronics (e.g., Soldering irons, oscilloscope)

Long answer text ______________________________________

__________

14. Audio and music (e.g., Mixing desk, recording booth, microphones, monitors, instruments)

Long answer text ______________________________________

__________

15. Construction and architecture (e.g., Large-scale building machinery and tools)

Long answer text ______________________________________________
__________

16. Are there any other areas of practice you support?

Long answer text ______________________________________________
__________

17. Does your space specialize in any tools or technologies?

Long answer text ______________________________________________
__________

18. Which tools can be operated only after training or orientation?

Long answer text ______________________________________________
__________

19. Which tools are operated only by staff?

Long answer text ______________________________________________
__________

20. Describe any other restrictions on access to tools (e.g., Do members provide some specific tools and control access to them?)

Long answer text ______________________________________________
__________

## Materials

Description (optional)

1. Do you have a materials shop?
   a. Yes
   b. No
2. Types of materials used in the space
   a. Metals
   b. Plastics

c. Fabrics, yarns
d. Wood and derivatives
e. Paper and card stock
f. Electronics
g. Biological or organic
h. Stone, clay, ceramics
i. Inks, paints
j. Chemicals
k. Other …
l. Add option

3. Does your space specialize in any materials?

Long answer text ________________________________________

## People

Description (optional)

1. Do you keep a list of members or regular users?
   a. Yes
   b. No
2. Current membership or user base

   Short answer text ____________________________________

3. Is your space open to youth under the age of 13? *
   a. Yes
   b. No
   c. Yes, with training
   d. Other …
4. At what age can youth use the equipment with or without training? *

   Short answer text ________________________________________

5. How do you recruit new members?

Long answer text ____________________________________________

__________

6. Gender balance of members or regular users

Can you tell us how your users are split along the categories shown in Box 1? An estimate is fine.

7. What ethnic groups are represented in your membership? (Box 2)
8. What percent is Hispanic or Latino? (Box 3)
9. On average how many total visits per month in 2016?
   a. 0-10
   b. 10-50
   c. 50-100

*Box 1.*

| | <20% | 20-39% | 40-59% | 60-79% | 80-100% | Don't Know |
|---|---|---|---|---|---|---|
| Female | | | | | | |
| Male | | | | | | |
| Other | | | | | | |
| Prefer not to say | | | | | | |

*Box 2.*

| | <20% | 20-39% | 40-59% | 60-79% | 80-100% | Don't Know |
|---|---|---|---|---|---|---|
| White | | | | | | |
| Black or African American | | | | | | |
| Asian | | | | | | |
| Native American and Alaska Natives | | | | | | |
| Native Hawaiians and Other Pacific Islanders | | | | | | |
| Two or more races | | | | | | |

*Box 3.*

| | <20% | 20-39% | 40-59% | 60-79% | 80-100% | Don't Know |
|---|---|---|---|---|---|---|
| Hispanic or Latino | | | | | | |
| Don't know | | | | | | |

   d. 100-250
   e. 250-1000
   f. 1000-5000
   g. 5000+
10. Staff and support
    a. Full-time technician(s)
    b. Part-time technician(s)
    c. No staff
    d. Volunteer staff
    e. Informal user support
    f. Business support (e.g., affiliated with accelerator, mentoring, or agency service provided)
    g. Other …
11. On average user types per month in 2016 (Box 4)
12. On average purpose of visits per month in 2016
    a. Receive training, instruction or learn a skill
    b. Introduction to making
    c. Make something specific
    d. Make one-off pieces
    e. Small batch production
    f. Network or find a maker/partner/designer, etc.
    g. Socialize
    h. Other (Details below)
13. Other reasons for visit (Is there something people do at your space that we missed? If so, please tell us here, and indicate a % if possible.)

    Long answer text ______________________________________

___________

## Programs

Description (optional)

*Box 4.*

| | <20% | 20-39% | 40-59% | 60-79% | 80-100% | Don't Know |
|---|---|---|---|---|---|---|
| Visitors or observers | | | | | | |
| Hobbyist | | | | | | |
| Startups | | | | | | |
| Youth under 13 | | | | | | |
| Youth ages 13-18 | | | | | | |
| College Age Students (18-24) | | | | | | |
| Teachers | | | | | | |
| Other/ don't know | | | | | | |

1. What training do you offer?
   a. Formal classes
   b. Technical support
   c. Informal help
   d. Specific training on tools and machines
   e. No training offered
   f. Online training
   g. Online user groups
   h. Other …
2. What events do you run?
   a. Public events
   b. Free events
   c. Member events
   d. Family events
   e. Corporate/business events
   f. Other…
3. Other programs
   a. School programs
   b. After-school programs
   c. Youth camps or classes
   d. Home school programs or classes
   e. Commercial services
   f. Other…

Description (optional) ______________________________

4. Floor space specific unites in sq ft or sq m

Short answer text ______________________________

5. Date your space opened

Month, day, year __________

6. Ambitions, challenges, successes

Description (optional) ______________________________

7. What are your ambitions for your makerspace?

Long answer text ______________________________

8. What problems or challenges has your makerspace encountered?

Long answer text ______________________________

9. Do you regularly collaborate or work with any other makerspaces in

Long answer text ______________________________

# Appendix 2

*Table 1. Codebook*

| Color, Parent Code, Code | Coded Segments of All Documents | % Coded Segments of All Documents | % Coded Segments of Activated Documents | Documents |
|---|---|---|---|---|
| gold star | 1 | 0.05 | 0.00 | 1 |
| laugh out loud | 5 | 0.23 | 0.00 | 3 |
| Lexicon Lab | 2 | 0.09 | 0.00 | 2 |
| Dun Laoghaire Library | 2 | 0.09 | 0.00 | 2 |
| introductory session | 1 | 0.05 | 0.00 | 1 |
| RQ3Sub1A: Principles of practice RQ3Sub1b: Background knowledge | 3 | 0.14 | 0.00 | 1 |
| Mission of the Makerspace Personal Demographics | 2 | 0.09 | 0.00 | 1 |
| RQ3Sub1: Learning pathways RQ3Sub2: Impact on community | 18 | 0.82 | 0.00 | 2 |
| RQ3Sub3: How do you evaluate learning RQ3Sub1A: Principles of practice | 0 | 0.00 | 0.00 | 0 |
| RQ2Sub2A: How are experts identified and recruited RQ2Sub2A: Expectation of members to give back | 8 | 0.36 | 0.00 | 3 |
| RQ2: Learning Communities RQ2Sub2: Training and Certificates | 5 | 0.23 | 0.00 | 2 |
| RQ2Sub1: Physical Space RQ2Sub1B: Equipment Use | 0 | 0.00 | 0.00 | 0 |
| RQ2: Learning Communities RQ2Sub2A: How are experts identified and recruited | 7 | 0.32 | 0.00 | 1 |
| Mission of the Makerspace People are afraid of free | 0 | 0.00 | 0.00 | 0 |
| CHALLENGES for the space | 0 | 0.00 | 0.00 | 0 |
| volunteer artists | 8 | 0.36 | 0.00 | 1 |
| observer role | 1 | 0.05 | 0.00 | 1 |
| Print Room Dundee | 1 | 0.05 | 0.00 | 1 |

*continued on following page*

*Appendix 2*

*Table 1. Continued*

| Color, Parent Code, Code | Coded Segments of All Documents | % Coded Segments of All Documents | % Coded Segments of Activated Documents | Documents |
|---|---|---|---|---|
| young creative scheme | 2 | 0.09 | 0.00 | 1 |
| Print City | 1 | 0.05 | 0.00 | 1 |
| Dundee Print Collective | 2 | 0.09 | 0.00 | 1 |
| eye tracker | 1 | 0.05 | 0.00 | 1 |
| Dundee Design Festival | 2 | 0.09 | 0.00 | 1 |
| small scale manufacturing | 1 | 0.05 | 0.00 | 1 |
| service side | 1 | 0.05 | 0.00 | 1 |
| your makers member demographics - history | 10 | 0.45 | 0.00 | 1 |
| summer camps | 1 | 0.05 | 0.00 | 1 |
| THAT | 27 | 1.23 | 0.00 | 1 |
| your makers | 10 | 0.45 | 0.00 | 2 |
| "Is this the best it can be?" | 1 | 0.05 | 0.00 | 1 |
| national funding body | 1 | 0.05 | 0.00 | 1 |
| select the student | 1 | 0.05 | 0.00 | 1 |
| Showcase | 1 | 0.05 | 0.00 | 1 |
| AmeriCorps members | 2 | 0.09 | 0.00 | 1 |
| groups | 1 | 0.05 | 0.00 | 1 |
| disenfranchised | 1 | 0.05 | 0.00 | 1 |
| people first and community | 1 | 0.05 | 0.00 | 1 |
| social currency | 1 | 0.05 | 0.00 | 1 |
| gentrification | 1 | 0.05 | 0.00 | 1 |
| Reservations | 1 | 0.05 | 0.00 | 1 |
| mezzo-tint | 1 | 0.05 | 0.00 | 1 |
| rural vs urban food secure | 1 | 0.05 | 0.00 | 1 |
| Some people started it then | 1 | 0.05 | 0.00 | 1 |
| rural vs urban why did the space fail | 7 | 0.32 | 0.00 | 1 |
| why did the space fail new space | 0 | 0.00 | 0.00 | 0 |
| marketing | 1 | 0.05 | 0.00 | 1 |
| rural vs urban | 4 | 0.18 | 0.00 | 1 |
| Mennonites | 2 | 0.09 | 0.00 | 1 |
| interns | 1 | 0.05 | 0.00 | 1 |
| Warsaw | 1 | 0.05 | 0.00 | 1 |
| transient | 1 | 0.05 | 0.00 | 1 |
| capital equipment | 1 | 0.05 | 0.00 | 1 |

*continued on following page*

*Table 1. Continued*

| Color, Parent Code, Code | Coded Segments of All Documents | % Coded Segments of All Documents | % Coded Segments of Activated Documents | Documents |
|---|---|---|---|---|
| small business incubator | 1 | 0.05 | 0.00 | 1 |
| do this again | 1 | 0.05 | 0.00 | 1 |
| service | 4 | 0.18 | 0.00 | 1 |
| mobile maker manager | 1 | 0.05 | 0.00 | 1 |
| studio rental | 6 | 0.27 | 0.00 | 2 |
| work exchange | 1 | 0.05 | 0.00 | 1 |
| scholarships | 1 | 0.05 | 0.00 | 1 |
| organizational culture | 1 | 0.05 | 0.00 | 1 |
| organizational culture partners | 1 | 0.05 | 0.00 | 1 |
| partner | 1 | 0.05 | 0.00 | 1 |
| woodshop | 2 | 0.09 | 0.00 | 1 |
| small town | 3 | 0.14 | 0.00 | 1 |
| Regenerative Organic Agriculture Program | 1 | 0.05 | 0.00 | 1 |
| color-coded card | 1 | 0.05 | 0.00 | 1 |
| University of Iowa | 1 | 0.05 | 0.00 | 1 |
| transcendental meditation | 2 | 0.09 | 0.00 | 1 |
| hours | 1 | 0.05 | 0.00 | 1 |
| Ru | 2 | 0.09 | 0.00 | 1 |
| Time | 2 | 0.09 | 0.00 | 1 |
| Sustainable Living Department | 1 | 0.05 | 0.00 | 1 |
| unique relationship with the town | 1 | 0.05 | 0.00 | 1 |
| donated | 4 | 0.18 | 0.00 | 1 |
| jewelry 3D | 1 | 0.05 | 0.00 | 1 |
| bike shop | 3 | 0.14 | 0.00 | 1 |
| tiny houses | 3 | 0.14 | 0.00 | 1 |
| farm building | 1 | 0.05 | 0.00 | 1 |
| micro-businesses | 1 | 0.05 | 0.00 | 1 |
| Facebook | 2 | 0.09 | 0.00 | 2 |
| tension | 1 | 0.05 | 0.00 | 1 |
| Thursday night hack nights | 1 | 0.05 | 0.00 | 1 |
| Four months in | 1 | 0.05 | 0.00 | 1 |
| un-school | 1 | 0.05 | 0.00 | 1 |
| growing from the ground up | 2 | 0.09 | 0.00 | 1 |
| free consulting | 1 | 0.05 | 0.00 | 1 |

*continued on following page*

**Appendix 2**

*Table 1. Continued*

| Color, Parent Code, Code | Coded Segments of All Documents | % Coded Segments of All Documents | % Coded Segments of Activated Documents | Documents |
|---|---|---|---|---|
| gaming nights | 1 | 0.05 | 0.00 | 1 |
| Bro Sew | 1 | 0.05 | 0.00 | 1 |
| gender | 1 | 0.05 | 0.00 | 1 |
| workshops | 1 | 0.05 | 0.00 | 1 |
| entrepreneurial | 6 | 0.27 | 0.00 | 2 |
| Transformation Tuesdays | 4 | 0.18 | 0.00 | 1 |
| micro businesses | 3 | 0.14 | 0.00 | 1 |
| strategic partners | 1 | 0.05 | 0.00 | 1 |
| Roadside | 1 | 0.05 | 0.00 | 1 |
| quilting group | 1 | 0.05 | 0.00 | 1 |
| people to make what they want to make | 1 | 0.05 | 0.00 | 1 |
| lottery | 1 | 0.05 | 0.00 | 1 |
| rules and policies | 1 | 0.05 | 0.00 | 1 |
| two classes | 1 | 0.05 | 0.00 | 1 |
| underperformance school | 1 | 0.05 | 0.00 | 1 |
| lending library | 1 | 0.05 | 0.00 | 1 |
| Maker elective classes | 1 | 0.05 | 0.00 | 1 |
| communication | 1 | 0.05 | 0.00 | 1 |
| teaching methodology | 3 | 0.14 | 0.00 | 1 |
| hydrogen balloon | 1 | 0.05 | 0.00 | 1 |
| cardboard boat race | 1 | 0.05 | 0.00 | 1 |
| Terminology | 1 | 0.05 | 0.00 | 1 |
| management customer model | 4 | 0.18 | 0.00 | 1 |
| being parented o | 1 | 0.05 | 0.00 | 1 |
| reinvent | 3 | 0.14 | 0.00 | 1 |
| two day workshop | 1 | 0.05 | 0.00 | 1 |
| robot petting zoo | 2 | 0.09 | 0.00 | 1 |
| Maker Vistas | 1 | 0.05 | 0.00 | 1 |
| Music Room | 1 | 0.05 | 0.00 | 1 |
| curriculum | 2 | 0.09 | 0.00 | 1 |
| step closer to the student led learning | 1 | 0.05 | 0.00 | 1 |
| wait list | 1 | 0.05 | 0.00 | 1 |
| Robotic Classroom | 1 | 0.05 | 0.00 | 1 |
| create a toy | 1 | 0.05 | 0.00 | 1 |

*continued on following page*

*Table 1. Continued*

| Color, Parent Code, Code | Coded Segments of All Documents | % Coded Segments of All Documents | % Coded Segments of Activated Documents | Documents |
|---|---|---|---|---|
| Kindergarten | 1 | 0.05 | 0.00 | 1 |
| expeditionary learning school | 4 | 0.18 | 0.00 | 2 |
| resident substitutes | 1 | 0.05 | 0.00 | 1 |
| lightboxes | 1 | 0.05 | 0.00 | 1 |
| cardboard city | 2 | 0.09 | 0.00 | 1 |
| history of the creativity lab | 1 | 0.05 | 0.00 | 1 |
| low-tech tool | 1 | 0.05 | 0.00 | 1 |
| skill builders | 1 | 0.05 | 0.00 | 1 |
| choice | 1 | 0.05 | 0.00 | 1 |
| inquiry group | 1 | 0.05 | 0.00 | 1 |
| sex pairs | 1 | 0.05 | 0.00 | 1 |
| fail to learn | 1 | 0.05 | 0.00 | 1 |
| teacher coaching role | 1 | 0.05 | 0.00 | 1 |
| prescriptive | 1 | 0.05 | 0.00 | 1 |
| varying my level of intervention | 1 | 0.05 | 0.00 | 1 |
| Think Tank | 1 | 0.05 | 0.00 | 1 |
| goal setting and social emotional development | 2 | 0.09 | 0.00 | 1 |
| creativity lab workshop | 1 | 0.05 | 0.00 | 1 |
| King of the Hill Competition | 1 | 0.05 | 0.00 | 1 |
| instructional stances | 1 | 0.05 | 0.00 | 1 |
| teachers | 2 | 0.09 | 0.00 | 1 |
| adult mentor | 1 | 0.05 | 0.00 | 1 |
| high school | 1 | 0.05 | 0.00 | 1 |
| musical bench | 1 | 0.05 | 0.00 | 1 |
| Explainers | 1 | 0.05 | 0.00 | 1 |
| workshop area | 1 | 0.05 | 0.00 | 1 |
| Tinkering Tiles | 1 | 0.05 | 0.00 | 1 |
| half-baked ideas | 1 | 0.05 | 0.00 | 1 |
| Light Play | 5 | 0.23 | 0.00 | 1 |
| scribbling machines | 1 | 0.05 | 0.00 | 1 |
| storytelling element | 1 | 0.05 | 0.00 | 1 |
| gasoline truck to an electric truck | 1 | 0.05 | 0.00 | 1 |
| Agency by Design Project | 1 | 0.05 | 0.00 | 1 |
| tinkering process | 1 | 0.05 | 0.00 | 1 |

*continued on following page*

## Appendix 2

*Table 1. Continued*

| Color, Parent Code, Code | Coded Segments of All Documents | % Coded Segments of All Documents | % Coded Segments of Activated Documents | Documents |
|---|---|---|---|---|
| Machine shop | 1 | 0.05 | 0.00 | 1 |
| automata | 1 | 0.05 | 0.00 | 1 |
| Tinkerer's Clock | 1 | 0.05 | 0.00 | 1 |
| marble machines | 1 | 0.05 | 0.00 | 1 |
| PIE | 1 | 0.05 | 0.00 | 1 |
| cross-setting learning framework | 1 | 0.05 | 0.00 | 1 |
| ethnographic study | 1 | 0.05 | 0.00 | 1 |
| we care about people loving learning | 1 | 0.05 | 0.00 | 1 |
| certificate program | 1 | 0.05 | 0.00 | 1 |
| expert and novice | 1 | 0.05 | 0.00 | 1 |
| STEM pipeline | 5 | 0.23 | 0.00 | 1 |
| low threshold, wide walls, high ceiling | 1 | 0.05 | 0.00 | 1 |
| "problem space" | 10 | 0.45 | 0.00 | 1 |
| animation stations | 2 | 0.09 | 0.00 | 1 |
| vending machine | 1 | 0.05 | 0.00 | 1 |
| staff workspace | 1 | 0.05 | 0.00 | 1 |
| Pin-ball | 1 | 0.05 | 0.00 | 1 |
| professional development | 1 | 0.05 | 0.00 | 1 |
| The Learning Studio | 1 | 0.05 | 0.00 | 1 |
| Learning Dimensions | 10 | 0.45 | 0.00 | 1 |
| Learning Dimensions Making vs tinkering | 3 | 0.14 | 0.00 | 1 |
| non commercial | 1 | 0.05 | 0.00 | 1 |
| advancement of science | 1 | 0.05 | 0.00 | 1 |
| ones weren't successful | 4 | 0.18 | 0.00 | 1 |
| service model | 2 | 0.09 | 0.00 | 1 |
| structure | 3 | 0.14 | 0.00 | 1 |
| Few classes | 1 | 0.05 | 0.00 | 1 |
| Dublin Maker | 1 | 0.05 | 0.00 | 1 |
| public engagement | 4 | 0.18 | 0.00 | 1 |
| computer science weeks | 1 | 0.05 | 0.00 | 1 |
| transition year | 1 | 0.05 | 0.00 | 1 |
| postgraduate certificate | 1 | 0.05 | 0.00 | 1 |
| change the education system | 1 | 0.05 | 0.00 | 1 |
| Educate Together | 1 | 0.05 | 0.00 | 1 |

*continued on following page*

*Table 1. Continued*

| Color, Parent Code, Code | Coded Segments of All Documents | % Coded Segments of All Documents | % Coded Segments of Activated Documents | Documents |
|---|---|---|---|---|
| design and deliver | 1 | 0.05 | 0.00 | 1 |
| activity model | 0 | 0.00 | 0.00 | 0 |
| our model into the schools and apply it | 2 | 0.09 | 0.00 | 1 |
| Bridge 21 | 1 | 0.05 | 0.00 | 1 |
| STEM camp | 1 | 0.05 | 0.00 | 1 |
| public sector got their salaries cut | 1 | 0.05 | 0.00 | 1 |
| computer science curriculum | 1 | 0.05 | 0.00 | 1 |
| identity | 1 | 0.05 | 0.00 | 1 |
| staff training | 3 | 0.14 | 0.00 | 1 |
| different trajectories | 1 | 0.05 | 0.00 | 1 |
| 18 to 35-year-old males | 1 | 0.05 | 0.00 | 1 |
| ducks | 1 | 0.05 | 0.00 | 1 |
| national weeks | 1 | 0.05 | 0.00 | 1 |
| standard box | 1 | 0.05 | 0.00 | 1 |
| brewery group | 1 | 0.05 | 0.00 | 1 |
| Potluck | 1 | 0.05 | 0.00 | 1 |
| Members paid for laser | 1 | 0.05 | 0.00 | 1 |
| social constructivist | 1 | 0.05 | 0.00 | 1 |
| curation of events | 1 | 0.05 | 0.00 | 1 |
| Personal Demographics | 10 | 0.45 | 0.00 | 7 |
| Personal Demographics People are afraid of free | 5 | 0.23 | 0.00 | 2 |
| History of the Space tool library | 7 | 0.32 | 0.00 | 3 |
| Mission of the Makerspace History of Museum | 5 | 0.23 | 0.00 | 2 |
| History of the Space metal shop | 2 | 0.09 | 0.00 | 1 |
| History of the Space aquaponics | 2 | 0.09 | 0.00 | 1 |
| Vision for the space new space | 2 | 0.09 | 0.00 | 2 |
| Mission of the Makerspace History of the Space | 193 | 8.76 | 0.00 | 25 |
| Meetup.com | 1 | 0.05 | 0.00 | 1 |
| ecosystems | 1 | 0.05 | 0.00 | 1 |
| maker drop in evenings | 1 | 0.05 | 0.00 | 1 |
| bizarre people | 1 | 0.05 | 0.00 | 1 |
| free events | 1 | 0.05 | 0.00 | 1 |
| maker meet-ups | 1 | 0.05 | 0.00 | 1 |
| Lexicon | 1 | 0.05 | 0.00 | 1 |

*continued on following page*

### Appendix 2

*Table 1. Continued*

| Color, Parent Code, Code | Coded Segments of All Documents | % Coded Segments of All Documents | % Coded Segments of Activated Documents | Documents |
|---|---|---|---|---|
| didactic | 1 | 0.05 | 0.00 | 1 |
| RQ3: Learning and Maker mindset Failure | 16 | 0.73 | 0.00 | 6 |
| Failure Think THEN Do | 1 | 0.05 | 0.00 | 1 |
| RQ3: Learning and Maker mindset RQ3Sub3: How do you evaluate learning | 26 | 1.18 | 0.00 | 9 |
| RQ3: Learning and Maker mindset RQ3Sub3: Impact on learners | 84 | 3.81 | 0.00 | 24 |
| RQ3: Learning and Maker mindset RQ3Sub2: Impact on community | 41 | 1.86 | 0.00 | 19 |
| RQ3: Learning and Maker mindset RQ3Sub1: keychain syndrome | 5 | 0.23 | 0.00 | 4 |
| RQ3Sub1: Learning pathways RQ3Sub1A: Divergent outcomes | 1 | 0.05 | 0.00 | 1 |
| RQ3Sub1: Learning pathways RQ3Sub1b: Background knowledge | 29 | 1.32 | 0.00 | 11 |
| Mission of the Makerspace | 2 | 0.09 | 0.00 | 1 |
| Mission of the Makerspace Vision for the space | 48 | 2.18 | 0.00 | 14 |
| RQ6: Definition of a Makerspace | 63 | 2.86 | 0.00 | 23 |
| RQ6: Definition of a Makerspace RQ7: Other | 7 | 0.32 | 0.00 | 6 |
| RQ4: Artifact Learning that took place | 17 | 0.77 | 0.00 | 8 |
| RQ5: Sustainability | 12 | 0.54 | 0.00 | 5 |
| RQ4: Artifact | 62 | 2.81 | 0.00 | 19 |
| RQ4: Artifact Role of community | 13 | 0.59 | 0.00 | 7 |
| RQ3: Learning and Maker mindset RQ3Sub1: Constructivism | 2 | 0.09 | 0.00 | 1 |
| RQ3: Learning and Maker mindset RQ3Sub1: Leveling up | 3 | 0.14 | 0.00 | 3 |
| RQ2: Learning Communities RQ2Sub1A: peer-to-peer interaction | 3 | 0.14 | 0.00 | 2 |
| RQ3: Learning and Maker mindset | 100 | 4.54 | 0.00 | 17 |
| RQ2: Learning Communities RQ2Sub4A: Gender discussion | 12 | 0.54 | 0.00 | 7 |
| RQ2: Learning Communities RQ2Sub3: parent involvement | 1 | 0.05 | 0.00 | 1 |
| Staff Preparation What we call the staff | 3 | 0.14 | 0.00 | 3 |
| RQ2: Learning Communities Direct Teaching | 11 | 0.50 | 0.00 | 5 |
| RQ3Sub1: Learning pathways RQ3: Sub1A: Free choice learning | 14 | 0.64 | 0.00 | 7 |

*continued on following page*

*Table 1. Continued*

| Color, Parent Code, Code | Coded Segments of All Documents | % Coded Segments of All Documents | % Coded Segments of Activated Documents | Documents |
|---|---|---|---|---|
| RQ3Sub1: Learning pathways RQ3Sub1A: Principles of practice | 2 | 0.09 | 0.00 | 2 |
| Inquiry learning Authentic learning | 5 | 0.23 | 0.00 | 3 |
| RQ3Sub1: Learning pathways RQ3Sub1: Leaning structure | 30 | 1.36 | 0.00 | 10 |
| RQ3Sub1: Learning pathways Inquiry learning | 3 | 0.14 | 0.00 | 3 |
| Inquiry learning Mass Customization | 1 | 0.05 | 0.00 | 1 |
| RQ3: Learning and Maker mindset RQ3Sub1: Learning pathways | 92 | 4.18 | 0.00 | 25 |
| RQ3Sub1: Learning pathways Reflective Practice | 3 | 0.14 | 0.00 | 3 |
| RQ2Sub2: Training and Certificates RQ2Sub2A: How are experts identified and recruited | 59 | 2.68 | 0.00 | 17 |
| RQ2Sub2A: How are experts identified and recruited RQ2Sub2A: Expectation of members to give back | 27 | 1.23 | 0.00 | 9 |
| RQ2: Learning Communities RQ2Sub3: Meet outside of space | 12 | 0.54 | 0.00 | 9 |
| RQ2Sub3: Meet outside of space RQ2Sub2: Training and Certificates | 91 | 4.13 | 0.00 | 20 |
| RQ2Sub1: Physical Space New vs old technology | 13 | 0.59 | 0.00 | 2 |
| RQ2Sub1: Physical Space RQ2Sub1:3D Printer | 7 | 0.32 | 0.00 | 5 |
| Membership levels RQ2Sub1B:Equipment Use | 20 | 0.91 | 0.00 | 9 |
| RQ2Sub1: Physical Space RQ2Sub1B:Process to join | 34 | 1.54 | 0.00 | 14 |
| RQ2: Learning Communities Staff interacting with members | 1 | 0.05 | 0.00 | 1 |
| RQ2: Learning Communities Staff Preparation | 40 | 1.82 | 0.00 | 10 |
| RQ2Sub5: Families in the space Youth Adult Relationships | 6 | 0.27 | 0.00 | 4 |
| RQ2Sub5: Families in the space Youth in the space? | 45 | 2.04 | 0.00 | 16 |
| RQ2Sub4: Underrepresented populations Serve Underrepresented | 8 | 0.36 | 0.00 | 3 |
| RQ2: Learning Communities RQ2Sub5: Families in the space | 55 | 2.50 | 0.00 | 19 |
| RQ2: Learning Communities RQ2Sub4: Underrepresented populations | 12 | 0.54 | 0.00 | 7 |
| RQ2Sub4: Underrepresented populations females in the space | 63 | 2.86 | 0.00 | 12 |
| Funding and sustainability | 17 | 0.77 | 0.00 | 8 |
| Use for quote | 13 | 0.59 | 0.00 | 11 |
| RQ2Sub1: Physical Space Sewing Studio | 3 | 0.14 | 0.00 | 1 |

*continued on following page*

*Appendix 2*

*Table 1. Continued*

| Color, Parent Code, Code | Coded Segments of All Documents | % Coded Segments of All Documents | % Coded Segments of Activated Documents | Documents |
|---|---|---|---|---|
| RQ2Sub1: Physical Space Membership levels | 23 | 1.04 | 0.00 | 12 |
| RQ2: Learning Communities | 149 | 6.76 | 0.00 | 27 |
| RQ2: Learning Communities RQ2Sub1: Physical Space | 98 | 4.45 | 0.00 | 20 |
| RQ1: Trust | 63 | 2.86 | 0.00 | 19 |

# About the Author

**Bradley Barker** is a Professor and Youth Development Specialist with 4-H Extension. Dr. Barker is spent eight years with Nebraska Educational Telecommunications where he was an Interactive Media Producer. Dr. Barker has directed media productions for the CLASS project, the Nebraska Law Enforcement Training Center, and the Nebraska National Guard. Dr. Barker has been the Principal Investigator on several National Science Foundation including the Nebraska 4-H Robotics and GPS/GIS project, the *Nebraska 4-H Wearable's Technologies* (WearTec) Wearable Technologies Grant, and most recently the Nebraska Innovative Maker Co-Laboratory (NiMC). Dr. Barker's research interests include the development and evaluation of educational technology systems for STEM education in non-formal learning environments. Dr. Barker has authored a number of peer-reviewed journal publications. He is the co-editor of the chapter book *Robots in K-12 Education: A New Technology for Learning* (2012) and co-authored a book chapter titled *Developing an Elementary Engineering Education Program through Problem-Based Wearable Technologies Activities* (2015) in the chapter book *Handbook of Research on Wearable and Mobile Technologies in Education*. Recently (2018) he has written two books: the *American Perspectives on Learning Communities and Opportunities in the Maker Movement* and *European Perspectives on Learning Communities and Opportunities in the Maker Movement.* Dr. Barker received his Ph.D. in Administration, Curriculum and Instruction in the area of Instructional Technology in 2002 from the University of Nebraska-Lincoln and is an Army veteran having served in Operation Desert Storm in 1991.

# Index

## E



## F



## G



## H



## I



## J



## K



## L



## M

## U



## V

50% Off**
Encyclopedia of
Information Science and Technology
Fourth Edition

www.ingramcontent.com/pod-product-compliance
Lightning Source LLC
LaVergne TN
LVHW080347011026
849161LV00009B/2216